# NETWORKING ESSENTIALS MCSE STUDY GUIDE

# NETWORKING ESSENTIALS MCSE STUDY GUIDE

**Jason Nash**

IDG Books Worldwide, Inc.

An International Data Group Company

Foster City, CA ● Chicago, IL ● Indianapolis, IN ● Southlake, TX

Networking Essentials MCSE Study Guide

Published by
**IDG Books Worldwide, Inc.**
An International Data Group Company
919 E. Hillsdale Blvd., Suite 400
Foster City, CA 94404
`http://www.idgbooks.com` (IDG Books World Wide Web site)

Library of Congress Catalog Card No.: 97-77805
ISBN: 0-7645-3177-8
Printed in the United States of America
10 9 8 7 6 5 4 3 2 1
1DD/RX/QS/ZY/FC
Distributed in the United States by IDG Books Worldwide, Inc.

Distributed by Macmillan Canada for Canada; by Contemporanea de Ediciones for Venezuela; by Distribuidora Cuspide for Argentina; by CITEC for Brazil; by Ediciones ZETA S.C.R. Ltda. for Peru; by Editorial Limusa SA for Mexico; by Transworld Publishers Limited in the United Kingdom and Europe; by Academic Bookshop for Egypt; by Levant Distributors S.A.R.L. for Lebanon; by Al Jassim for Saudi Arabia; by Simron Pty. Ltd. for South Africa; by Pustak Mahal for India; by The Computer Bookshop for India; by Toppan Company Ltd. for Japan; by Addison Wesley Publishing Company for Korea; by Longman Singapore Publishers Ltd. for Singapore, Malaysia, Thailand, and Indonesia; by Unalis Corporation for Taiwan; by WS Computer Publishing Company, Inc. for the Philippines; by WoodsLane Pty. Ltd. for Australia; by WoodsLane Enterprises Ltd. for New Zealand. Authorized Sales Agent: Anthony Rudkin Associates for the Middle East and North Africa.

For general information on IDG Books Worldwide's books in the U.S., please call our Consumer Customer Service department at 800-762-2974. For reseller information, including discounts and premium sales, please call our Reseller Customer Service department at 800-434-3422.

For information on where to purchase IDG Books Worldwide's books outside the U.S., please contact our International Sales department at 650-655-3172 or fax 650-655-3295.

For information on foreign language translations, please contact our Foreign & Subsidiary Rights department at 650-655-3021 or fax 650-655-3281.

For sales inquiries and special prices for bulk quantities, please contact our Sales department at 650-655-3200 or write to the address above.

For information on using IDG Books Worldwide's books in the classroom or for ordering examination copies, please contact our Educational Sales department at 800-434-2086 or fax 817-251-8174.

For press review copies, author interviews, or other publicity information, please contact our Public Relations department at 650-655-3000 or fax 650-655-3299.

For authorization to photocopy items for corporate, personal, or educational use, please contact Copyright Clearance Center, 222 Rosewood Drive, Danvers, MA 01923, or fax 978-750-4470.

John Kilcullen, *CEO, IDG Books Worldwide, Inc.*
Brenda McLaughlin, *Senior Vice President & Group Publisher, IDG Books Worldwide, Inc.*
The IDG Books Worldwide logo is a trademark under exclusive license to IDG Books Worldwide, Inc., from International Data Group, Inc.

# ABOUT IDG BOOKS WORLDWIDE

Welcome to the world of IDG Books Worldwide.

IDG Books Worldwide, Inc., is a subsidiary of International Data Group, the world's largest publisher of computer-related information and the leading global provider of information services on information technology. IDG was founded more than 25 years ago and now employs more than 8,500 people worldwide. IDG publishes more than 275 computer publications in over 75 countries (see listing below). More than 60 million people read one or more IDG publications each month.

Launched in 1990, IDG Books Worldwide is today the #1 publisher of best-selling computer books in the United States. We are proud to have received eight awards from the Computer Press Association in recognition of editorial excellence and three from *Computer Currents'* First Annual Readers' Choice Awards. Our best-selling *...For Dummies®* series has more than 30 million copies in print with translations in 30 languages. IDG Books Worldwide, through a joint venture with IDG's Hi-Tech Beijing, became the first U.S. publisher to publish a computer book in the People's Republic of China. In record time, IDG Books Worldwide has become the first choice for millions of readers around the world who want to learn how to better manage their businesses.

Our mission is simple: Every one of our books is designed to bring extra value and skill-building instructions to the reader. Our books are written by experts who understand and care about our readers. The knowledge base of our editorial staff comes from years of experience in publishing, education, and journalism — experience we use to produce books for the '90s. In short, we care about books, so we attract the best people. We devote special attention to details such as audience, interior design, use of icons, and illustrations. And because we use an efficient process of authoring, editing, and desktop publishing our books electronically, we can spend more time ensuring superior content and spend less time on the technicalities of making books.

You can count on our commitment to deliver high-quality books at competitive prices on topics you want to read about. At IDG Books Worldwide, we continue in the IDG tradition of delivering quality for more than 25 years. You'll find no better book on a subject than one from IDG Books Worldwide.

John Kilcullen
CEO
IDG Books Worldwide, Inc.

Steven Berkowitz
President and Publisher
IDG Books Worldwide, Inc.

*Eighth Annual
Computer Press
Awards ≥1992*

*Ninth Annual
Computer Press
Awards ≥1993*

*Tenth Annual
Computer Press
Awards ≥1994*

*Eleventh Annual
Computer Press
Awards ≥1995*

IDG Books Worldwide, Inc., is a subsidiary of International Data Group, the world's largest publisher of computer-related information and the leading global provider of information services on information technology. International Data Group publishes over 275 computer publications in over 75 countries. Sixty million people read one or more International Data Group publications each month. International Data Group's publications include: **ARGENTINA:** Buyer's Guide, Computerworld Argentina, PC World Argentina; **AUSTRALIA:** Australian Macworld, Australian PC World, Australian Reseller News, Computerworld, IT Casebook, Network World, Publish, Webmaster; **AUSTRIA:** Computerwelt Osterreich, Networks Austria, PC Tip Austria; **BANGLADESH:** PC World Bangladesh; **BELARUS:** PC World Belarus; **BELGIUM:** Data News; **BRAZIL:** Annuario de Informatica, Computerworld, Connections, Macworld, PC Player, PC World, Publish, Reseller News, Supergamepower; **BULGARIA:** Computerworld Bulgaria, Network World Bulgaria, PC & MacWorld Bulgaria; **CANADA:** CIO Canada, Client/Server World, ComputerWorld Canada, InfoWorld Canada, NetworkWorld Canada, WebWorld; **CHILE:** Computerworld Chile, PC World Chile; **COLOMBIA:** Computerworld Colombia, PC World Colombia; **COSTA RICA:** PC World Centro America; **THE CZECH AND SLOVAK REPUBLICS:** Computerworld Czechoslovakia, Macworld Czech Republic, PC World Czechoslovakia; **DENMARK:** Communications World Danmark, Computerworld Danmark, Macworld Danmark, PC World Danmark, Techworld Denmark; **DOMINICAN REPUBLIC:** PC World Republica Dominicana; **ECUADOR:** PC World Ecuador; **EGYPT:** Computerworld Middle East, PC World Middle East; **EL SALVADOR:** PC World Centro America; **FINLAND:** MikroPC, Tietoverkko, Tietoviikko; **FRANCE:** Distributique, Hebdo, Info PC, Le Monde Informatique, Macworld, Reseaux & Telecoms, WebMaster France; **GERMANY:** Computer Partner, Computerwoche, Computerwoche Extra, Computerwoche FOCUS, Global Online, Macwelt, PC Welt; **GREECE:** Amiga Computing, GamePro Greece, Multimedia World; **GUATEMALA:** PC World Centro America; **HONDURAS:** PC World Centro America; **HONG KONG:** Computerworld Hong Kong, PC World Hong Kong, Publish in Asia; **HUNGARY:** ABCD CD-ROM, Computerworld Szamitastechnika, Internetto online Magazine, PC World Hungary, PC-X Magazin Hungary; **ICELAND:** Tolvuheimur PC World Island; **INDIA:** Information Communications World, Information Systems Computerworld, PC World India, Publish in Asia; **INDONESIA:** InfoKomputer PC World, Komputek Computerworld, Publish in Asia; **IRELAND:** ComputerScope, PC Live!; **ISRAEL:** Macworld Israel, People & Computers/Computerworld; **ITALY:** Computerworld Italia, Macworld Italia, Networking Italia, PC World Italia; **JAPAN:** DTP World, Macworld Japan, Nikkei Personal Computing, OS/2 World Japan, SunWorld Japan, Windows NT World, Windows World Japan; **KENYA:** PC World East African; **KOREA:** Hi-Tech Information, Macworld Korea, PC World Korea; **MACEDONIA:** PC World Macedonia; **MALAYSIA:** Computerworld Malaysia, PC World Malaysia, Publish in Asia; **MALTA:** PC World Malta; **MEXICO:** Computerworld Mexico, PC World Mexico; **MYANMAR:** PC World Myanmar; **NETHERLANDS:** Computer! Totaal, LAN Internetworking Magazine, LAN World Buyers Guide, Macworld Netherlands, Net, WebWereld; **NEW ZEALAND:** Absolute Beginners Guide and Plain & Simple Series, Computer Buyer, Computer Industry Directory, Computerworld New Zealand, MTB, Network World, PC World New Zealand; **NICARAGUA:** PC World Centro America; **NORWAY:** Computerworld Norge, CW Rapport, Datamagasinet, Financial Rapport, Kursguide Norge, Macworld Norge, Multimediaworld Norge, PC World Ekspress Norge, PC World Nettverk, PC World Norge, PC World ProduktGuide Norge; **PAKISTAN:** Computerworld Pakistan; **PANAMA:** PC World Centro America; **PEOPLE'S REPUBLIC OF CHINA:** China Computer Users, China Computerworld, China InfoWorld, China Telecom World Weekly, Computer & Communication, Electronic Design China, Electronics Today, Electronics Weekly, Game Software, PC World China, Popular Computer Week, Software Weekly, Software World, Telecom World; **PERU:** Computerworld Peru, PC World Profesional Peru, PC World SoHo Peru; **PHILIPPINES:** Click!, Computerworld Philippines, PC World Philippines, Publish in Asia; **POLAND:** Computerworld Poland, Computerworld Special Report Poland, Cyber, Macworld Poland, Networld Poland, PC World Komputer; **PORTUGAL:** Cerebro/PC World, Computerworld/Correio Informatico, Dealer World Portugal, Mac*In/PC*In Portugal, Multimedia World; **PUERTO RICO:** PC World Puerto Rico; **ROMANIA:** Computerworld Romania, PC World Romania, Telecom Romania; **RUSSIA:** Computerworld Russia, Mir PK, Publish, Seti; **SINGAPORE:** Computerworld Singapore, PC World Singapore, Publish in Asia; **SLOVENIA:** Monitor; **SOUTH AFRICA:** Computing SA, Network World SA, Software World SA; **SPAIN:** Communicaciones World Espana, Computerworld Espana, Dealer World Espana, Macworld Espana, PC World Espana; **SRI LANKA:** Infolink PC World; **SWEDEN:** CAP&Design, Computer Sweden, Corporate Computing Sweden, Internetworld Sweden, it.branschen, Macworld Sweden, MaxiData Sweden, MikroDatorn, Natverk & Kommunikation, PC World Sweden; **SWITZERLAND:** Computerworld Schweiz, Macworld Schweiz, PCtip; **TAIWAN:** Computerworld Taiwan, Macworld Taiwan, NEW ViSiON/Publish, PC World Taiwan, Windows World Taiwan; **THAILAND:** Publish in Asia, Thai Computerworld; **TURKEY:** Computerworld Turkiye, Macworld Turkiye, Network World Turkiye, PC World Turkiye; **UKRAINE:** Computerworld Kiev, Multimedia World Ukraine, PC World Ukraine; **UNITED KINGDOM:** Acorn User UK, Amiga Action UK, Amiga Computing UK, Apple Talk UK, Computing, Macworld, Parents and Computers UK, PC Advisor, PC Home, PSX Pro, The WEB; **UNITED STATES:** Cable in the Classroom, CIO Magazine, Computerworld, DOS World, Federal Computer Week, GamePro Magazine, InfoWorld, I-Way, Macworld, Network World, PC Games, PC World, Publish, Video Event, THE WEB Magazine, and WebMaster; online webzines: JavaWorld, NetscapeWorld, and SunWorld Online; **URUGUAY:** InfoWorld Uruguay; **VENEZUELA:** Computerworld Venezuela, PC World Venezuela; and **VIETNAM:** PC World Vietnam. 3/24/97

# THE VALUE OF MICROSOFT CERTIFICATION

As a computer professional, your opportunities have never been greater. Yet you know better than anyone that today's complex computing environment has never been more challenging.

Microsoft certification keeps computer professionals on top of evolving information technologies. Training and certification let you maximize the potential of Microsoft Windows desktop operating systems; server technologies, such as the Internet Information Server, Microsoft Windows NT, and Microsoft BackOffice; and Microsoft development tools. In short, Microsoft training and certification provide you with the knowledge and skills necessary to become an expert on Microsoft products and technologies — and to provide the key competitive advantage that every business is seeking.

Microsoft offers you the most comprehensive program for assessing and maintaining your skills with our products. When you become a Microsoft Certified Professional (MCP), you are recognized as an expert and are sought by employers industry-wide. Technical managers recognize the MCP designation as a mark of quality — one that ensures that an employee or consultant has proven experience with Microsoft products and meets the high technical proficiency standards of Microsoft products.

As an MCP, you receive many benefits, such as direct access to technical information from Microsoft; the official MCP logo and other materials to identify your status to colleagues and clients; invitations to Microsoft conferences, technical training sessions, and special events; and exclusive publications with news about the MCP program.

Research shows that organizations employing MCPs also receive many benefits:

o A standard method of determining training needs and measuring results — an excellent return on training and certification investments

o Increased customer satisfaction and decreased support costs through improved service, increased productivity, and greater technical self-sufficiency

o A reliable benchmark for hiring, promoting, and career planning

o Recognition and rewards for productive employees by validating their expertise

- Retraining options for existing employees, so they can work effectively with new technologies
- Assurance of quality when outsourcing computer services

Through your study, experience, and achievement of Microsoft certification, you will enjoy these same benefits, too, as you meet the industry's challenges.

Nancy Lewis
General Manager
Microsoft Training and Certification

# FOREWORD TO THE MCSE SERIES

Certifications are an effective way of "selling your skills" to prospective employers, since they represent a consistent measurement of knowledge about specific software or hardware products. Because of their expansive product line and tremendous marketing efforts, Microsoft certifications have become the gold standard in the exploding certification industry. As a Microsoft Certified Professional (MCP), you are recognized as a "Subject Matter Expert" as defined by objective standards. As a training organization, we recognize the value of offering certification-level training. In fact, approximately 55 percent of students in our Microsoft classes are working toward certification, and I expect that number to continue to rise.

Studies have been conducted that show increased productivity among Microsoft Certified Solutions Developers(MCSDs) versus noncertified programmers. Additionally, compensation for Microsoft Certified Systems Engineers (MCSEs) and MCSDs averages higher than for those without certification. For individuals looking for a career in these areas, there is no better metric of legitimacy that can be placed on a resume than Microsoft certification credentials.

Information Systems/Information Technology (IS/IT) decision-makers for ExecuTrain clients worldwide increasingly require certifications for their IS employees. Often, individuals are required to be certified or find that certification was their competitive edge in landing the job. Conventional wisdom and every study you read indicates these trends will continue as technologies become more a part of daily business in corporations.

Microsoft recently certified the 100,000th MCP. I expect this number to balloon as corporations make certification part of IS staff job descriptions. I predict certified candidates can expect better-paying jobs and positions with more technical responsibility to match their hard-won certification. Although the number of MCPs rises daily, that population is eclipsed by the more than 200,000 open IT positions reported today. Microsoft tracks these open positions and would like to fill each of them with MCPs. My bet is that if anyone can make the math work, they can.

Congratulations on continuing your path towards certification. In addition to training, hands-on experience, and in-depth product knowledge, the IDG Study Guides are an excellent resource for review, study, and practice. These comprehensive books can help you track down the details and find answers to very specific questions quickly. Of particular importance are the Instant Assessment questions, review activities, and hands-on lab exercises. After all, practice makes perfect. You can't be too well-prepared. Good luck, and study hard! It will make a difference.

Kevin Brice
Vice President/General Manager
Technical Training
ExecuTrain Corporation

# CREDITS

**ACQUISITIONS EDITOR**
Anne Hamilton

**DEVELOPMENT EDITORS**
Jennifer Rowe
Tracy Thomsic

**TECHNICAL EDITOR**
Johnetta Scales, M. Ed., MCT, MCSE

**COPY EDITORS**
Timothy Borek
Ami Knox

**PRODUCTION COORDINATOR**
Katy German

**BOOK DESIGNER**
Kurt Krames

**GRAPHICS AND PRODUCTION SPECIALIST**
Jude Levinson

**ILLUSTRATOR**
Donna Reynolds

**PROOFREADER**
David Wise

**INDEXER**
James Minkin

# ABOUT THE AUTHOR

Jason Nash currently lives in Raleigh, North Carolina, with his wife Angie (another CNE and MCSE!) and works for Advanced Paradigms, Inc. (http://www.paradigms.com). Advanced Paradigms is one of the top Microsoft Solution Providers in the country. His certifications include MCSE, MCT, Novell CNE, and CNP (Certified Network Professional). He is currently finishing his MCSD and working on a B.A. in computer science. He welcomes comments from readers; his e-mail address is jnash@intrex.net, and his home page is at www.intrex.net/nash.

*To the memory of Grady Hamby. May his strength inspire those adjusting to life without him.*

# PREFACE

Welcome to the MCSE Certification Series! This book is designed to help you acquire the knowledge you need to pass Microsoft Exam 070-058 Networking Essentials. This book will also give you a solid understanding of current network technology, even if you do not plan to become Microsoft certified.

This book will not turn you into a networking wizard, but is intended to be a single reference with everything you may need to pass the Networking Essentials exam.

# HOW THIS BOOK IS ORGANIZED

This book is organized into four main parts, followed by a Resources section that contains the appendixes, supplemental material, and a description of the CD-ROM's content. Each chapter starts with an overview of the topics covered in the chapter, followed by the material to be presented. A Key Point Summary follows the chapter material and serves as a quick reference guide to the important facts contained in that chapter. At the end of each chapter is a group of Instant Assessment questions. Most chapters also contain Critical Thinking labs to further test your knowledge and understanding of the material presented.

Critical Thinking labs challenge you to apply your understanding of the material to solve a hypothetical problem. The questions are scenario based, requiring you to decide "why" or "how" and write a written response. The questions can also prompt you to devise a solution to a problem. You need to be at a computer to work through some of these labs; for others, the goal is to make you analyze a problem and explain why a particular solution will or will not work and/or describe how best to solve the problem.

## Part I: The Theoretical Network

I begin the book with a discussion about the theoretical network standards — including the OSI model and the 802 standards — to give you a solid understanding of the underlying architecture on which networks and protocols are built.

## Part II: Network Media and Topology

The second part begins by covering the many types of network media found in today's networks. The different types of media are compared to give you the understanding necessary to make confident choices when planning and designing a network. The second chapter in this part covers the physical topologies and network types currently being deployed — Ethernet, Token Ring, FDDI, and more.

## Part III: Connectivity

This part covers the different popular network protocols. Various protocols are contrasted to show strengths, weaknesses, and characteristics that make them unique. The second chapter in this part talks about the means of connecting networks together, and takes you through the different hardware devices and wide area network (WAN) protocols that can be deployed to grow networks and connect them to form large, wide area networks.

## Part IV: Administration and Troubleshooting

The final part in the book is also one of the most important. Microsoft is known for the number of administration and troubleshooting questions it puts on exams, and this part prepares you for those questions. The first chapter, on administration, covers the different choices and options network administrators may have when managing their network. The second chapter in this part goes over the processes and tools you may use when troubleshooting. The final chapter is an optional one to help you add services to your network.

## Part V: Resources

The supplemental materials at the back of the book contain a wealth of information. In addition to a detailed glossary and thorough index, you'll find the following information in the appendixes: exam preparation tips, a guide to building your own network, answers to Instant Assessment questions and Critical Thinking labs, and a Mini-Lab Manual that includes all of the Critical Thinking Labs from the book. Appendix A contains the exam objectives for the Networking Essentials exam and also includes a detailed quick-reference chart for study purposes.

## CD-ROM

The CD-ROM included with this book contains the following materials: an electronic version of this book in Abobe's Acrobat format; excerpts from *MCSE Career Microsoft®!* (IDG Books Worldwide, 1997); excerpts from *Windows NT® 4.0 MCSE Study Guide* (IDG Books Worldwide, 1997); Adobe's Acrobat Reader; Microsoft Internet Explorer version 4.0; MeasureUp test assessment software and sample Networking Essentials practice questions; Microsoft Training and Certification Offline CD-ROM; and *Micro House Technical Library* (evaluation copy).

# HOW TO USE THIS BOOK

This book can be used either by individuals working independently or by groups in a formal classroom setting.

To get the most from the information provided in the book, I suggest using the following method. First, read the chapter and Key Point Summary section at the end. Be sure you fully understand everything presented in the Key Point Summary. If you are not sure of yourself on some points, go back over the appropriate section(s). Once you are confident you understand the material, proceed to the Instant Assessment questions, and then complete the Critical Thinking labs. Be sure to answer *all* of the Instant Assessment questions and Critical Thinking labs.

note ▼ **When you do the Critical Thinking labs that require you to be at the computer and are asked to type something, the text you are instructed to type will be printed in bold, like this: 172.25.16.21. Important words and concepts appear in italics, and all file names, directories, Uniform Resource Locators (URLs), and code appear as monospaced font.**

The chapters in the book should be read in order because the information presented in the later chapters builds on the initial chapters. As with networks and protocols, this book employs a layered approach. Use the exam objectives quick-reference chart in Appendix A to make sure you cover all the necessary material for the exam.

## Prerequisites

Although this book is a comprehensive study and exam preparation guide, it does not start at ground zero. I do assume you have the following knowledge and skills at the outset:

1. Basic terminology and basic skills to use a Microsoft Windows product. (This could be Windows 95, Windows for Workgroups, or a Windows NT product.)
2. Basic mouse skills: being able to left-click, right-click, use the pointer, and so on.

If you meet these prerequisites, you're ready to begin this book. If you don't have the basic Windows experience or mouse skills, I recommend you either take a one-day Windows application course or work through a self-study book, such as *Windows 95 Bible* (IDG Books Worldwide, 1997) or *Windows 95 FOR Dummies* (IDG Books Worldwide, 1995) to acquire these skills *before* you begin this book.

# HARDWARE AND SOFTWARE YOU'LL NEED

You will need access to various hardware and software to be able to do some of the Critical Thinking labs in this book. It is extremely important that you do these labs to acquire the skills tested by the Microsoft Certified Professional exams. There are only a few labs requiring the hardware and software listed below.

**Minimum hardware requirements:**

- Intel-based computer with 486/33 processor, 16MB RAM, and 500MB–1GB available hard disk space
- CD-ROM drive
- Mouse
- VGA monitor and graphics card

**Optional additional hardware:**

- Additional computer (with the same minimum specifications as the first one)
- Network adapter and cabling (if you have the additional computer listed above)

Software requirements:

o Microsoft Windows NT Workstation 4.0

o Microsoft Windows 95

# ICONS USED IN THIS BOOK

Several icons used throughout this book draw your attention to matters that deserve a closer look:

 **This icon points you to another place in this book (or to another resource) for more coverage on a given topic. It may point you back to a previous chapter where important material has already been covered, or it may point you ahead to let you know that a concept will be covered in more detail later on.**

 **Be careful here! This icon points out information that can save you a lot of grief. It's often easier to prevent tragedy than to fix it afterwards.**

 **This icon identifies important advice for those studying to pass the Microsoft Certified Professional exams on Networking Essentials.**

 **I know this will be hard for you to believe, but sometimes things work differently in the real world than books — or software documentation — say they do. This icon draws your attention to the author's real-world experiences, which will hopefully help you on the job, if not on the Microsoft Certified Professional exams.**

 **This icon points out an interesting or helpful fact, or some other comment that deserves emphasis.**

 **This icon indicates an online resource that you can access to obtain products, utilities, and other worthwhile information.**

 **Here's a little piece of friendly advice, or a shortcut, or a bit of personal experience that might be of use to you.**

That should be all the information you need to start reading! You can now start learning about the world of networking! Enjoy.

# ACKNOWLEDGMENTS

I know all acknowledgments start this way, but it is true. You don't realize how many people and how much effort it takes to write a book until you do it yourself. The first group I'd like to thank are those at IDG Books. It all began with my acquisitions editor, Anne Hamilton. She is the one who gave me this great opportunity. Next is Tracy Thomsic, my lead development editor. Tracy kept me on my toes and did her best to make me stick to my deadlines. If it weren't for Jennifer Rowe, my development editor, this book would be a loose collection of Word documents filled with grammatical errors. Last but not least, thanks to the rest of IDG Books, including copy editors Timothy Borek and Ami Knox, and the production staff.

The most important on my list to thank is my wife, Angie. She should be credited as a coauthor because of all of her ideas and help. She is the most important thing in my life, and everything I do, I do for her.

Next is my family. Without the help and support of my mother and stepfather, Peggy and Timmy Franks, and my grandmother, Marie Ward, there is no way I would be where I am today. Special thanks is also due to others in my family, including my sister, Jeanie, my father, Bill Nash, and my grandparents, Homer and Frances.

The final people in my list to thank are those that made it hard to finish my book. They are the ones that did their best to pry me away and do things when I should have been writing. First, the guys at work: Todd Shanaberger, Johnathan Harris, Blain Lefort, Dave Gerisch, Tim Whitesides, Chuck Lebaron, John Dwyier, and Jim Taylor. Next are the guys in #doom on IRC. Special thanks to Derek and Jeff Stutsman, Andy Scherrer, Cliff Sheldon, Joakim and Johan Erdfelt, and Yossarian Holmburg. Finally, thanks to two very good friends: Jacob Hall and Robert Mowlds.

# CONTENTS AT A GLANCE

# TABLE OF CONTENTS

# The Theoretical Network

**W**elcome to the exciting and always changing world of networking!

To begin your adventure in the world of networking, I first cover the high-level ideas and fundamentals of networking. From this, you will be able to move on to more technical and detailed concepts.

Chapter 1 starts with a discussion of different network types, their functions, and what services they can provide. Important exam topics such as the difference between peer-to-peer networks and client/server networks are covered, as well as network services.

Chapter 2 covers the sometimes scary, but always important, OSI model. This model is the precursor to the technical chapters about network protocols and how they interact with each other. While sometimes confusing, the OSI model is an important fundamental to understand, and it is something you can use long after you finish this book and the Networking Essentials exam.

# Basics of Networking

# About Chapter 1

**W**elcome to the first chapter of the Networking Essentials MCSE Study Guide.

In this chapter I discuss the basic components of networks. You will learn about different types of networks, including the three network models: centralized, collaborative, and distributed. You will learn the differences between these models, including the benefits and drawbacks of each. I also explore the two types of networks: peer-to-peer and server based. By the end of this chapter, you will know the requirements for each network type, as well as when each type should be used. You will learn the different services provided on the network and their purposes. At the end of the chapter, I cover the differences between local area networks (LANs), metropolitan area networks (MANs), and wide area networks (WANs). There are review questions along the way and at the end of the chapter to reinforce what you read.

# WHAT IS NETWORKING?

Computers are powerful tools that enable users to store and process large amounts of data quickly. Practically every business, no matter how small, uses computers to handle bookkeeping, track inventory, and store documents. As businesses grow, they often need several people to input and process data simultaneously. For this to be beneficial, those people must be able to share the data each person enters. Networking computers becomes beneficial in this situation. *Networks* are simply a group of computers connected by cable or other media so they can share information. Networks made sharing data much easier and more efficient for users. Before networking, Sneakernets, in which data is copied to a floppy disk and carried to another computer, were the only option for sharing data. When the systems are networked, users are not only more productive because several people can enter data at the same time, but they can also evaluate and process the shared data. So, one person can handle accounts payable, another can handle accounts receivable, and someone else processes the profit-and-loss statements. When companies combine specialized software with a computer network, they can track and utilize information to help make the business run smoothly.

Users need to share resources other than files, as well, a common example being printers. Printers are utilized only a small percentage of the time; therefore, companies don't want to invest in a printer for each computer. Switch boxes can be used to help a couple of computers share printers but are impractical for most business situations. Many offices have several types of printers that need to be shared by many users. Networks can be used in this situation to allow all the users to have access to any of the available printers. Devices other than printers can also be shared. In large companies, networks can become complex as more devices are shared, but they still serve the same purpose as the small network. Networked computers can share many things, including:

o Printers

o Fax devices

o Electronic messages

o Files and/or documents

o Modems

o Data

o Messages

Figure 1-1 shows computers set up to share one print device.

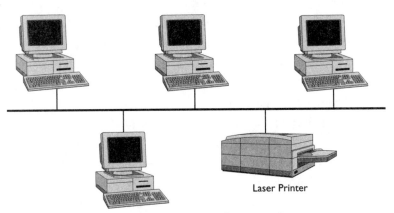

**FIGURE 1-1    Sharing a print device across the network**

While connecting computers sounds simple and basic, doing so allows users to do much more than was originally thought possible. Users no longer are limited to sharing information with their officemate. They can share information throughout the building, the city, the country, and the world. This is possible due to the wide variety of options for connecting networks. Some of these options include satellites, lasers, and telephone lines. This is most evident in the Internet. With the increased popularity of the Internet, users not only gather and share information with other users in their company but also with their clients throughout the world.

note **The first two chapters in the Theoretical Network part contain many theories and high-level ideas. These theories and ideas are important as a starting point to understanding more complex networking technologies.**

## Network Considerations

There are several things to consider when networking computers. First, *sharing files* is useful only if everyone is working with the same version of the file. For example, a construction company may be working on an invoice for a customer. Over time, more items are added, and adjustments are made in the costs of each item. As changes are made to the invoice, it's important that the most recent version of the invoice is being updated. If the file is stored in multiple locations, there is a chance that the user will not be working with the most recent version, and the invoice will not be accurate.

Another consideration is *fault tolerance*. There needs to be an effective system of backing up data. If a hard drive crashes or files become corrupt, there needs to be a recent backup of those files available, or all the work will be lost. You also need to consider *administration*. Someone needs to be in charge of sharing resources and managing security. Whether the network has *centralized* or *distributed* administration is determined by the type of network.

## Network Components

Before you can learn the types of networks and their services, you need to be familiar with the different parts of a network. The following list explains some of these parts:

o **Server:** Powerful computer that provides services to the other computers on the network.

o **Client:** Computer that uses the services that a server provides. The client is usually less powerful than the server.

o **Peer:** A computer that acts as both a client and a server.

o **Media:** Physical connection between the devices on a network.

o **Resources:** Anything available to a client on a network is considered a resource. Printers, data, fax devices, and other networked devices and information are resources.

o **User:** Any person that uses a client to access resources on the network.

o **Protocol:** Protocols are written rules used for communications. They are the languages that computers use to talk to each other over a network.

Figure 1-2 shows the common components on a network.

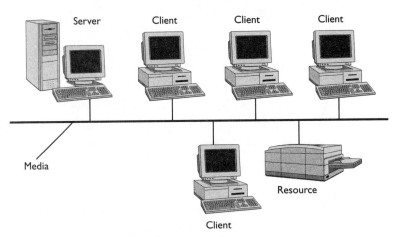

**FIGURE 1-2   Common network components**

These components can be set up so the network operates in different ways, depending on what you need to provide for your users and how they access it. There are a few different networking models that define the various setups for sharing and accessing data on a network.

# NETWORKING MODELS

*Network models* describe how information is processed by the computers on the network. Data can be processed by clients, by a central server, or by everyone. The best server model for your needs is generally determined by the applications you need to run.

This section explains the different network models, as well as which services they offer. You will learn when and why the different models are used.

There are three basic models of networks:

- Centralized
- Collaborated
- Distributed

## Centralized Computing

The first computers were large mainframes. They were too large and expensive for everyone to own. They were also not networked as most computers are today. Tasks were sent to them for processing, and the results were printed out. Later, terminals that let users enter data and see results quicker were added, but they were just input/output stations. Terminals did no processing of their own; everything was done on the mainframe. These early centralized networks gave users the ability to access the mainframe from a remote location.

*Centralized networks* are used today for a variety of reasons. This type of computing keeps all the data in one location, assuring that everyone is working with the same information. It is also easy to back up data, since it is all stored on the server; the servers are the only systems that need to be backed up. This also means that the servers are also the only systems that need to be secured, because the terminals have no data. And because everything is done on the server, terminals do not require a floppy drive — so the chances of the network being infected with a virus are low. This type of network also costs less overall because, although the servers need to be powerful systems with a lot of storage space, the terminals are inexpensive because they require no real processing or storage capability of their own.

**note** You may not realize it, but you use a centralized network all the time. Bank ATMs run over a centralized network. They are the clients, and the large computers at the banks are the central server. These ATMs use many common networking standards and protocols to operate, as well.

This type of network has disadvantages, as well. Because the computing is done by the server, this type of network can be somewhat slow. In addition, if the users have a variety of needs, meeting these needs in a centralized computing network can be difficult because each user's applications and resources have to be set up separately, and it's no longer efficient to have them operate from the same centralized server. Also, connectivity can become a large problem on centralized networks, since all users must connect to one central site. Due to these limitations, most networks today are based on either the distributed or collaborative network computing model (discussed later in this chapter).

 **exam preparation pointer** To do well on the Networking Essentials exam, you should know the advantages and disadvantages of the centralized computing model. They are listed here to help you quickly review them.

**Advantages of centralized computing:**

- Ease of backup
- Security
- Low cost

**Disadvantages of centralized computing:**

- Slow network access
- Fewer options

# Distributed Computing

The popularity of personal computers enabled processing power to be distributed to all computers on a network. Unlike centralized computing, where all work is done on the server, data storage and processing is done on the local workstation in a *distributed network*. This allows for faster access to data. Because each computer can store and process data, the servers do not need to be as powerful and expensive. This type of network accommodates users with a variety of needs, yet it allows them to share data, resources, and services. The computers used in distributed computing are capable of working as standalone systems but are networked together for increased functionality.

This type of system has many benefits, but it also has some drawbacks. A distributed network is more susceptible to viruses, because any user could introduce an infected file and spread a virus throughout the network. Also, developing an effective backup plan is more difficult if users store data on their individual systems instead of keeping it all on a central system. This can also cause users to work with different versions of the same file.

Distributed computing is the opposite of centralized computing; the advantages of distributed computing solve the disadvantages of centralized computing. However, the advantages of centralized computing are often lacking in distributed networks. Distributed computing is the preferred choice as many companies move from mainframes to intelligent desktops.

 exam preparation pointer

**For the exam, you should know the advantages and disadvantages of the distributed computing model so you can compare them to the other models. They are listed here so you can review them quickly.**

**Advantages of distributed computing:**

o **Quick access**

o **Multiple uses**

**Disadvantages of distributed computing:**

o **Virus susceptibility**

o **Backup difficulty**

o **File synchronization**

# Collaborative Computing

*Collaborative computing* allows computers to share processing power across a network. Applications can be written to use the processing on other computers to complete jobs. This type of network can be faster because users are not limited to the processing power of one system to complete tasks. Aside from the ability to process tasks on multiple systems, this type of network is similar to distributed computing in its ability to share resources and data.

This likeness introduces many of the same advantages as distributed computing networks. A variety of users can be accommodated on a collaborative network. This type of network also has many of the same drawbacks as distributed networks. For example, viruses can be quickly spread throughout the network. Because data can be stored throughout the network, backing up all important data can be difficult. File synchronization is also an issue, with several copies of a file stored throughout the network.

web links

**If you would like to try out the power of collaborative computing, a couple of interesting projects are currently going on over the Internet. The first is an effort to show the inadequacies of today's encryption. The largest site for this project is home to the Bovine group at** `http://rc5.distributed.net`.

**The other interesting project that should start some time in early- to mid-1998 is** `SETI@HOME`. **This is a project to help the Search for Exraterrestrial Intelligence (SETI) organization search for intelligent life in the universe. Information can be found at** `http://www. bigscience.com/setiathome.html`.

exam preparation pointer

**For the exam, you should know the advantages and disadvantages of the collaborative computing model so you can compare them to the other models. They are listed here so you can review them quickly.**

Advantages of collaborative computing:

- Extremely fast
- Multiple uses

Disadvantages of collaborative computing:

- Susceptible to viruses
- Difficult to back up
- Difficult file synchronization

# DIFFERENT NETWORK TYPES

Computer networks can consist of two different types: *server-based* and *peer-to-peer*. A server-based network is the type that typically comes to mind when one mentions networks. These networks consist of clients that make requests to a server. The other type of network is peer-to-peer. In this type of network, each machine can act as both a client and a server, requesting and providing resources. In fact, most networks consist of a combination of the two types.

## Peer-to-Peer Networking

The simplest form of networking is peer-to-peer. In a *peer-to-peer network*, each workstation acts as both a client and a server. There is no central repository for information and no central server to maintain. Data and resources are distributed throughout the network, and each user is responsible for sharing data and resources connected to their system. Figure 1-3 shows a peer-to-peer network with shared resources.

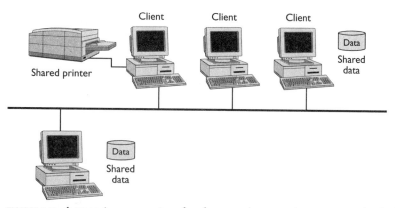

**FIGURE 1-3**  A peer-to-peer network, where each computer serves as both the client and the server and there is no central server

concept link    **If you would like to set up a small network at home, you can read Appendix E for instructions. Appendix E covers the installation of a small peer-to-peer network.**

## *Advantages of peer-to-peer networking*

While peer-to-peer networks may not always be the best choice, they do have their place and advantages. Small, inexpensive networks can easily be set up using peer-to-peer systems.

The peer-to-peer network model works well for small office networks. Once your network has reached about ten clients, it can become too hard to maintain. This type of network is common in home networks and is typically the type of network most businesses use when they make the decision to share resources and connect their individual systems.

Since the peer-to-peer model does not need a powerful dedicated server, it is usually the cheapest type of network to install. All that is needed to connect several individual systems and create a peer-to-peer network are network adapters, cable or other transmission media, and the operating system.

## *Disadvantages of peer-to-peer networking*

The general rule is to stop using peer-to-peer networking once your total number of clients reaches about ten. Consider the problem of having twenty-five users on a peer-to-peer network sharing and updating documents. Before long, you would have people with different revisions of the documents on different client computers. Also, think of the issues you would run into when setting up the twenty-sixth client on the network if you had to get information from the other clients. You would be connecting that client to one client for your printer, another for documents, a third for the fax device, and so on. If the network had a central server, you would only need to get information from one source.

Training is also difficult when you have a large number of clients. If you use peer-to-peer networking, your users need to be trained on how to share resources. Each user is responsible for acting as administrator of their systems. This can be a confusing task for many users, who have other responsibilities, as well.

Security in a peer-to-peer network becomes difficult to maintain. Users need to know how to secure their own resources. Because there is no central administration, it is the users' responsibility to ensure that only authorized users can access their data. The users themselves handle sharing out the data as well as setting any permissions that may be needed. Most peer-to-peer security consists of a single password for each resource; this is known as *share-level security*. Share-level security requires a user to know the password for a resource before it can be accessed. Users usually need access to a variety of resources, and they often must remember a different password for each resource. If an unauthorized person gains possession of the resource password, you must change it and then tell all the authorized users the new password.

exam preparation pointer **On the Networking Essentials exam, you will get questions concerning when to use peer-to-peer networking. The two keys to answering those questions usually have to do with the current or projected network size, and security.**

**If the question states there are fewer than ten computers on the network, then peer-to-peer is a good choice. Be sure to keep in mind the projected growth if that information is given to you. If a network in an exam question needs share-level security, then peer-to-peer should be used.**

### Which operating systems can you use?

A number of operating systems support peer-to-peer networking. Some operating systems have this capability built-in, while others can have the capability added.

The following operating systems have peer-to-peer networking built-in:

- Windows 95
- Windows for Workgroups
- Windows NT Workstation
- OS/2

For most operating systems without this capability, such as Windows and MS-DOS, you can add software such as NetWare Lite or LANtastic.

### Summary of peer-to-peer networks

Peer networks can be an excellent choice for a small office network where users keep their data on their own local workstations. This allows them to handle their own security and bypass the need for a large and expensive server. The absence of an expensive server, as well as the built-in peer-to-peer networking capabilities of most current operating systems, keeps the total cost low, greatly helping a small office network that is just starting.

The ability for users to manage their own security is also one of peer-to-peer networking's biggest disadvantages. Since the network data is spread among all the workstations, it can sometimes be hard to track down. This hinders backups, as well as keeping a single current copy of the data. Users can become confused without a central data repository.

 exam preparation pointer **For the Networking Essentials exam, you should know the advantages and disadvantages of peer-to-peer networks. This list should help you quickly review each of them.**

**Advantages of peer-to-peer networks:**

o **Inexpensive**

o **Easy setup**

o **Easy maintenance**

**Disadvantages of peer-to-peer networks:**

o **No central administration**

o **Scattered data**

o **Evasive resources**

o **Weak security**

o **Dependent on user training**

## Server-Based Networks

When a network comes to mind, most people think of the *server-based network*. In a server-based network, you have one computer — usually larger than the clients — which is dedicated to handing out files and/or information to clients. Figure 1-4 illustrates the configuration of a server-based network. The server controls the data, as well as printers and other resources the clients need to access. The server is not only a faster computer with a better processor, but it also requires much more storage space to contain all the data that needs to be shared to the clients. Having these tasks handled by the server allows the clients to be less powerful because they only request resources.

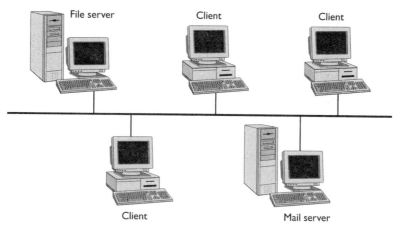

**FIGURE 1-4**   A server-based network with a few clients and two main servers

Since the server is dedicated to handing out files and/or information, it cannot be used as a workstation. Its purpose is strictly to provide services to other computers, not to request services. Servers are optimized to hand out information as fast as possible.

## Having multiple servers

As your network grows, you will probably come to need more than just a single server to handle all the requests from clients. You may also need to have different servers to handle different tasks.

The two main types of dedicated servers are the *file and print server* and the *application server*. *Specialized servers* are also used.

### File and print servers

These servers are optimized to hand out files to clients and to handle printing requests. They are mainly used to store data and applications. When a client runs an application from a file and print server, it copies the needed files down locally and runs the application (all in the background). No application processing is done on the server; everything is done locally on the client. One example of a file server is a server with the installation code for all the applications the users need. The users can access the installation files stored on the file server, but the running of these files and the installation of the applications occurs on the users' computers. This way, an administrator only needs to update the files on the server to upgrade an application.

### Application servers

Application servers are almost opposite of file and print servers. The application the client runs is stored on the client. Requests are then sent to the server to be processed, and the processed information is sent back to the client. This way, little information is processed by the client, and everything is done by the server.

A good example of this is a database application with a front-end on the client. A *front-end* is a small application that runs on a client and sends and receives information to and from the server. The front-end acts mainly as an interface to the database stored on the server. When a user at the client needs information from the database, an instruction is sent from the client to the server telling it to search for that information. The server then sorts through the database, locates the information that was requested, and sends the answer back to the client. Little was done by the client, and almost all the processing was done by the server.

### Specialized servers

You may also have servers that have a single specialized purpose. Some examples of this are:

- Mail servers: These are servers specifically set up to handle clients' e-mail needs. Some e-mail systems are capable of running from a standard file server, but as they increasingly support groupware and other applications, they need more hardware. The easiest solution is to place the e-mail server applications on their own file server.

- Communications servers: Communications servers are set up to handle remote users dialing into your network. The communications server applications are normally put on a separate server for security. It is much easier to secure a server that only does one thing than try to secure a server that internal users also access.

## Advantages of server-based networks

If your network has more than ten to fifteen clients, you should really consider a server-based network. With a network of this size, a peer-to-peer network would be almost impossible to manage over time.

With a server-based network, you only need to have your clients connect to one or a few servers to get the resources they need. This helps maintain a synchronized file set that everyone works from instead of each user working with the copy that is stored on their local computer.

Security is also much easier to manage in a server-based network. Since you only need to create and maintain accounts on the server instead of every workstation, you can assign rights to resources easily. Access to resources can be granted to user accounts. This is much more secure than peer-to-peer, in which a single password is used by everyone who accesses the resource. Specific users can be granted access to resources using their account on the server. This type of security is known as *user-level security*. Since the server on the network acts as the central repository for almost all your information, you only need to perform backups to the server. You can also replicate this information to other servers on your network easily in case one server should go down. Using replication tools on the server is an effective way to synchronize files. These tools copy the most current version to other servers so those users are working from the same version and not many different versions of the same file.

This type of network can also be quite cost efficient. With the server storing almost all of the information on your network, you do not need large hard drives on the client computers. You also do not need extra RAM and processing power on your clients to provide server functions. This can help offset the price of the server because each client computer can be a less powerful, less expensive system.

exam
preparation
pointer

**The exam questions on server-based networks go along with the ones on peer-to-peer networks. Usually it is an either/or type of question.**

**The keys to knowing if the answer has to do with server-based networking are the opposite of peer-to-peer. If the network requires user-level security, or has more than ten clients, it should be a server-based network.**

**Another clue might be if the proposed network does or does not have a central server. Remember that server-based networks must have a large central server with a server operating system of Windows NT or Novell's NetWare. If every computer on the network only has Windows 95, the only option is peer-to-peer.**

### Summary of server-based networks

Server-based networks are the most popular network type today, due to the ease of accessing and backing up data. While they are more expensive than peer-to-peer networks, their administration can be greatly reduced since the data is not spread across their entire network. Security is easily maintained since a user normally has an account on the central server to which their access is tied. This way, an administrator can grant or deny access to one single account per user instead of having to give each user an account on everyone's workstation, as in a peer-to-peer network.

There are few disadvantages to a server-based network. The two main disadvantages are the requirement of a server and a dedicated administrator. Servers can be expensive when compared to a normal workstation, but they also usually have features to help it handle client requests better. Since users no longer maintain their own data and security, an administrator must be involved to maintain the network.

exam
preparation
pointer

For the Networking Essentials exam, you should know the advantages and disadvantages of server-based networks. This list should help you quickly review each of them.

Advantages of server-based networks:

o Centralized security

o Dedicated servers

o Easy accessibility

o Easy backup

o Synchronized files

Disadvantages of server-based networks:

o Dependent on an administrator

o Expensive server

# NETWORK SERVICES

What good would a network be if it did not provide services to the user? Networks are meant to make us more productive by providing services to make us more efficient. Some common services are:

- File services
- Print services
- Message services
- Directory services
- Application services

## File Services

The primary reason for networking computers is for the file services that a network can provide. Instead of having to copy files to a floppy disk, users can now easily and seamlessly share files.

The following jobs use file services:

- File transfer
- File storage and migration
- File update synchronization
- Archiving

### File transfer

Transferring files electronically is the simplest and most common service on the network. The ability to share files and information across a network allows users to share any information they need and make them more productive than ever. This service becomes even more important over great distances. There are other ways to share files, such as copying files to a removable storage device such as a floppy or a Zip drive, but these methods are only possible when all the users are located in the same office. When users are spread throughout the country and the world, this is not an option. Reliable file transfer across the network then becomes a more noticeably important network service.

The need for security also becomes evident with this service. It is important that only authorized users access files. Methods such as access rights, passwords, and encryption are used to keep unauthorized people from accessing information.

### File storage and migration

Data can be stored on many different media, such as hard disks, CD-ROMs, and magnetic tape. Data is said to be stored *online*, *offline*, or *near-line*, depending upon the media on which it's stored.

*Online* data is stored information that's readily available on a server. Central data storage on a server is one of the primary uses of a network. Users can access this data at any time instantly. The devices most commonly used for online storage are hard drives. Hard drives provide quick access to data allowing it to be accessed almost instantly. The main limitation of hard drives is their cost. Although drives are continuously being developed in larger sizes and price continues to drop, the cost of hard drives is still greater than other types of storage media.

Since you may not want to keep all your data online at all times due to cost, you can migrate it *offline*. Hard disks are fast but can get expensive if you plan to keep many files that are rarely accessed. A common way to migrate data offline is to put it on magnetic tape so that it can be loaded back if needed. Offline storage devices provide a low-cost solution to storing data. Unfortunately, this data storage method does not provide easy access. Offline storage is used primarily to archive and back up data.

Suppose you need to keep a large amount of data available to users, but cannot afford to buy the necessary amount of space on hard disks. *Near-line* storage is a way to keep data migrated off expensive hard disks but close enough to let users access it. This may be done by using such things as jukeboxes with large numbers of tapes or optical disks. They can automatically put the needed data back online fairly quickly. Near-line storage is more convenient because it requires little intervention from the administrator.

Data is *migrated* when it is moved from one form of storage to another. Most network operating systems have at least a simple backup program included. However, most companies prefer a third-party product that has more features and capabilities. The administrator can choose the criteria for migration.

### File update synchronization

This network service keeps track of different versions of the same file. If two clients open a file at the same time and then try to save the changes that each have made, one file will overwrite the other. *File update synchronization* tries to coordinate these changes. This can be a difficult task, which requires the software to know which changes are most current and complete. Several third-party applications try to accomplish this task. At this time, however, users are merely alerted to most problems because the software is not capable of determining which file is correct.

### *Archiving*

*Archiving* is the processes of backing up data in case of a hard disk failure. This important task must not be overlooked. Without a well-designed backup plan, there is the potential of losing important data that can be difficult to reproduce. Many types of hardware and software simplify this task for the administrator. Several machines, both clients and servers, can be backed up using the same hardware and software from one location. Using this software and hardware, the administrator can schedule all computers on the network to be backed up from one location at scheduled intervals.

## Print Services

Another major service that networks provide is the ability to share print devices. Before networks, users had to have their own printer attached to their workstation. This was costly, especially if a user needed to print multiple types of forms or paper, since they would need a different printer for each. With network print services, companies need only buy small numbers of printers and share them among all their users.

Other features of print services are *queue-based printing* and *fax services*. Queue-based printing allows a client's application to spool the print job off to a network server so the application thinks the job has printed and lets the user continue to work. While the user continues to work, the network server handles sending the print job to the print device. Print queues can be given different priorities. This enables users to print more-important documents quickly while lower priority jobs wait.

## Message Services

*Message services* allow for e-mails with attachment files. Many people have come to rely on e-mail attachments as a way of transferring information, so message services have become a necessity on most networks. E-mail is no longer just sending text messages back and forth over a network. You can now send video, sound, documents, and almost any other type of data. Groupware applications that use e-mail as their connection backbone are also becoming popular. These enable users to share calendars and scheduling information as well.

# Directory Services

One of the newest services on the networking scene is *directory services*. Directory services let you maintain information about all of the *objects* in your network. An object is anything you can store information about, such as users, printers, shared resources, servers, and so on.

Before directory services were popular, you had to keep separate configuration information about users on each file server. If a user wanted to connect to resources on multiple servers, they needed an account on each one. With directory services, you only create one user account object for that user. Each of the servers see that object, and you can then assign resource rights to that user account.

The actual directory information is stored in files on the server, which are usually hidden. The network operating systems that support directory services have predefined methods to share and update this information.

# Application Services

As you remember, we discussed client/server networks earlier in the chapter. *Application services* are basically a client/server process. The server is providing the application service.

Normally with application services, a small application is loaded on the client computers, and the main application and data is loaded on the server. The small application on the client is usually just a front-end to give the user an interface. It does no processing of its own. The client application sends queries to the server and lets it do the processing. The server then returns the requested information.

in the
real world

**The application that the customer support staff at my company employs uses application services. We load a small front-end application on our workstations that we use to query the main database server. When we need information about a support ticket, we enter the ticket number into the front-end, which in turn sends it to the database server. The database server looks up the ticket and returns the information about it. No processing is done on the local workstation.**

## Database Services

One major consideration of a networked database is the coordination of multiple changes. All or part of the databases may also be replicated to other servers on a network to distribute the load. It can be more efficient to have portions of the database in the same regional location as the users who access it. When using distributed data, the database appears to be a single database to the users. Replicating the database to other servers can also serve as a form of backup. The database is not dependent on one particular server. Database services are responsible for updating replicated databases and keeping them current.

# DIFFERENCES BETWEEN LANs, MANs, AND WANs

A network is no longer just a group of computers in one office or even one large building. Networks are constantly being connected to each other to form larger *internets* (not to be confused with the popular Internet). An internet is a large network made up of connected smaller networks.

The sizes of networks are generally categorized into three different groups: local area networks (LANs), metropolitan area networks (MANs), and wide area networks (WANs).

## Local Area Networks

The smallest network size is a *local area network*, or LAN. LANs are normally contained in a building or small group of buildings. Some characteristics of a LAN are high speed, small error counts, and inexpensive price. Figure 1-5 shows computers set up on a LAN.

Since LANs are contained in small areas, high-speed cable can be used. Also, since the installed media is usually high quality, few to no errors are generated on the network. Prices of LAN equipment are fairly cheap. Network cards for individual computers can be found for as little as $30 each.

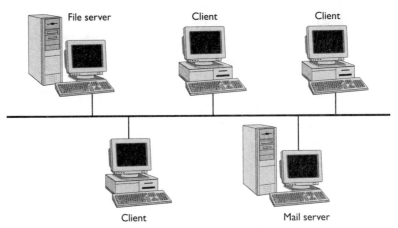

**FIGURE 1-5**    A small, one-office local area network

## Metropolitan Area Networks

*A metropolitan area network*, or MAN, is a group of LANs located in a city. For example, if a college had campuses with networks at each spread over the majority of a city, they could be connected to create a MAN. Figure 1-6 illustrates networks set up as a MAN. MANs are slower than LANs but usually have few errors on the network. Since special equipment is needed to connect the different LANs together, they have a high price.

## Wide Area Networks

The largest network size is a *wide area network*, or WAN. WANs can interconnect any number of LANs and WANs. They can connect networks across cities, states, countries, or even the world. Figure 1-7 illustrates a WAN. The term *Enterprise WAN* refers to a network that connects all the LANs and WANs within an entire organization.

WANs normally use connections that travel all over the country or world. For this reason they are usually slower than MANs and LANs, and more prone to errors. They also require a lot of specialized equipment, so their price is high.

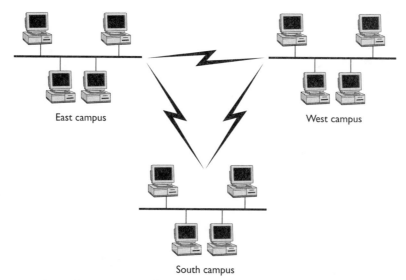

East campus

West campus

South campus

**FIGURE 1-6**   Campus networks connected through a metropolitan area network

exam preparation pointer

On the Networking Essentials exam, you will probably not see the term MAN. You should, however, be familiar with the differences between a LAN and WAN. The characteristics of LANs, MANs, and WANs are listed here to help you review.

LAN characteristics:

o Small areas, usually in one office or building

o High speed

o Most inexpensive equipment

o Low error rates

MAN characteristics:

o Larger area than a LAN — usually a large campus or organization spread over a city-size area

o Slower than a LAN, but faster than a WAN

o Expensive equipment

o Moderate error rates

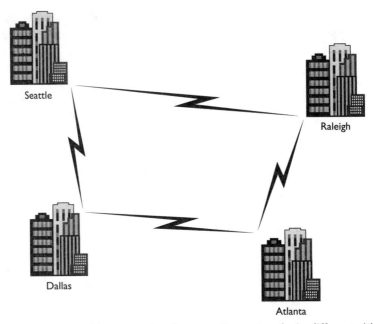

**FIGURE 1-7**  A wide area network connecting networks in different cities

WAN characteristics:

- Can be as large as worldwide
- Usually much slower than LAN speed
- Highest possible error rate of all three types
- Expensive equipment

# KEY POINT SUMMARY

In this chapter I discussed the basics of networking. I discussed the basic components of a network and the types of resources networks can share. You learned the three computing models: centralized, collaborative, and distributed. You were introduced to peer-to-peer and server-based networks. You learned there are several network services which provide different functions on the network. Those include file services, print services, message services, directory services, application services, and database services. I finished the chapter by discussing the characteristics of LANs, MANs, and WANs. You now have learned some of the basics, which will be used throughout this book and your career.

- *Networks* are a group of computers connected together by some type of media to allow them to share information.

- *Servers* are large, powerful computers that provide services to clients.

- *Clients* are smaller desktop computers that users use to access network services.

- *Peer* computers act as both clients and servers.

- *Media* is the physical connection between the computers on a network.

- Anything that clients access is a *resource*. Printers and hard disks on a server are two examples.

- People who use clients and resources are *users*.

- The written rules for communication between devices on a network are *protocols*.

- *Centralized computing* has a large central system with terminals as clients. All processing is done by the large system, and the terminals are for input and output.

- When clients have their own separate processing power, this is a *distributed computing* model. Unlike centralized computing, each client does its own processing and may only use the central server for storage.

- *Collaborative computing* allows each of the client computers to cooperate and process the same information. This way, tasks are completed faster than if they ran on only one client computer.

- *Peer-to-peer* networking is a simple form of networking. Clients on the network may also act as servers, and a large central server is not needed. Since security is hard to maintain in this type of network, the number of users must be kept low.

- The opposite of a peer-to-peer network is a *server-based* network. In this system, clients do not act as servers. They use a larger, central network server for their storage and/or processing. Security is easier to maintain, so server-based networks can grow large.

o *File services* allow users to transfer files over a network. Part of file services is *file update synchronization*, which coordinates changes between two versions of the same file.

o *Print services* allow the sharing of print devices over a network. Print services can be enhanced to allow for queue-based printing and fax services.

o E-mail is provided by using the *message services* of a network.

o *Directory services* allow you to maintain information about every object in your network. This allows users to only have one account on the entire network and connect to any resources that support those directory services.

o Clients can let the central network servers process data for them by using *application services*. An example of this would be the querying of a large database that is stored on a central database server. The server, not the client, would actually search the database.

o *Database services* coordinate multiple changes to large network databases and replicate them if necessary.

o *Local area networks* are small networks usually contained in one office or building. They have high speed, low error rates, and their equipment is fairly inexpensive.

o *Metropolitan area networks* usually cover a large campus-type environment, or an organization spread over a city. Their stats fall in between LANs and WANs, in that they are relatively fast, have moderate error rates, and their equipment prices fall between LANs and WANs.

o *Wide area networks* can cover an entire organization's enterprise network. WANs can cover a few states or the entire globe. Since this is the largest network, it is the most expensive. It is also usually low speed when compared with the other network size models.

# APPLYING WHAT YOU'VE LEARNED

It is now time to review the material covered in this chapter. The following Instant Assessement questions will reinforce what you have just learned about network models, types, and components.

## Instant Assessment

1. You are asked to consult on a project for a small law firm. They have four lawyers in the office, and three assistants. They need to keep a central repository for their document templates to which everyone has access. They also need a place to store their individual case documents that only the lawyer on the case should be able to see. One assistant in the office has some network administration knowledge, but everyone else does not. Would you implement peer-to-peer networking? Why or why not?

2. Computers in a peer-to-peer network act as a _____ and a _____.

3. Why is security a consideration when deciding the type of network is used?

4. Which service allows users to share word-processor documents?

5. Which computer in a network is usually the most powerful?

6. What are the rules that govern the communication between devices on a network called?

7. _____ are computers that use resources on the network.

8. Which networking model has a central mainframe?

9. The _____ _____ model has clients that can process information for themselves.

10. Which network model would you use if you had a room with fifty client computers and needed to solve a complex mathematical problem?

11. Terminals are used in which networking model?

12. Which network type is best when you have thirty client computers?

13. A company has just started operations. They currently only have five computers in their office but plan to expand to about thirty in six months. Which network type would you choose?

**14.** Would Windows 95 be a good choice for operating system in a peer-to-peer network?

**15.** What network service allows users to only log in to the network once, and access any server or resource on it?

**T/F**

**16.** Clients do most of the processing in a server-based network with a file server.    ⎯⎯⎯

**17.** Users need more training in a peer-to-peer network.    ⎯⎯⎯

**18.** By far, the cheapest network to install is a server-based network.    ⎯⎯⎯

**19.** There are no special considerations to keep you from putting the communications server software on the departmental file server.    ⎯⎯⎯

**20.** Networks can help companies save money by allowing users to share hardware and software.    ⎯⎯⎯

**21.** Applications must be written to utilize collaborative computing.    ⎯⎯⎯

**22.** Peer-to-peer networks are the easiest to back up.    ⎯⎯⎯

**23.** Mainframes and terminals are used in distributed computing.    ⎯⎯⎯

**24.** WANs require specialized, expensive equipment to connect LANs.    ⎯⎯⎯

**25.** E-mail is one of the most basic file services used on the network.    ⎯⎯⎯

**26.** Your company is planning to roll out clients, which have no drives for storage. These systems boot and load all files and applications, including the operating system, from the server. Which computing model does this network follow?

　**a.** Server-based

　**b.** Centralized

　**c.** Collaborative

　**d.** Distributed

**27.** Molly's Home Furnishings currently has twelve computers on their network and are expecting to add five more this year. Security is not a major consideration for their network. It is important that they have all data backed up regularly. Which network type is best for their network?

　**a.** Server-based

　**b.** Peer-to-peer

**c.** LAN

**d.** MAN

28. Which of the following is an advantage of peer-to-peer networks?

    **a.** Ease of backup

    **b.** Data spread across the network

    **c.** Easy setup

    **d.** Utilizes powerful servers

29. Server-based networks provide which of the following?

    **a.** Fault tolerance

    **b.** Security

    **c.** Small clients

    **d.** All of the above

30. Which network service allows you to maintain information about objects on your network?

    **a.** File services

    **b.** Message services

    **c.** Directory services

    **d.** Database services

31. A college has a network that spans many buildings on campus, as well as a few buildings across town which house the continuing education center. Which category does this network represent?

    **a.** LAN

    **b.** MAN

    **c.** WAN

    **d.** TAN

32. Which of the following is a component of file services?

    **a.** Archiving

    **b.** Print queue management

    **c.** E-mail

    **d.** Object management

**33.** What is a function of message services?

    **a.** E-mail

    **b.** Groupware

    **c.** Sending video

    **d.** All of the above

**34.** Which of the following does not describe collaborative computing?

    **a.** Quick access

    **b.** Allows for a variety of desktop setups and functions

    **c.** Utilizes processing power across the network

    **d.** Provides a high level of security

**35.** Your company has just added a new server. This server processes requests sent from the client; the processed data is then returned to the client. This type of server is known as a/an:

    **a.** File server

    **b.** Print server

    **c.** Application server

    **d.** Communications server

concept link **For answers to the Instant Assessment questions, see Appendix C.**

# The OSI Model

# About Chapter 2

In this chapter you learn about the Open System Interconnect (OSI) model. The OSI model provides the guidelines for the topics covered throughout the remainder of the book. I cover the different layers of the OSI model — what each layer does and how the layers work together.

By the end of the chapter, you will be able to name all parts of the OSI model, describe what happens at each layer, and decide which layer a protocol operates at given the description of that protocol. The OSI model is an important part of networking. It can help you better understand protocols, how they interact, and why the suites of protocols fit together the way they do.

This chapter is the basis for many of the concepts and items you will learn throughout the book. Make sure you are comfortable with this material before moving on.

# WHAT IS A PROTOCOL?

Before I can discuss the Open Systems Interconnection (OSI) model in detail, I first need to talk about protocols. For computers to be able to communicate, a language must be defined among them that they understand. This language is a *protocol*. A protocol defines almost every aspect of the language that is used for computers to communicate. Some common protocols discussed later are *Internetwork Packet Exchange* (IPX), *Transmission Control Protocol/Internet Protocol* (TCP/IP), and *NetBIOS Extended User Interface* (NetBEUI).

Protocols can either be mandated by one company or organization, or created, used, and maintained by the entire networking industry. A *de jure* standard, Latin for "according to law," indicates a protocol designed by one company or organization. Normally this organization maintains control of the protocol and is responsible for any additions or changes. A *de facto* standard, Latin for "existing in fact," indicates a protocol controlled by the entire industry, and is thus also known as an "industry standard." Anyone can use a de facto standard free of charge. Changes to these standards are sometimes very hard to make, as you must convince the rest of the industry that the changes are needed.

When a company does not publish specifications for a protocol, it's considered a closed standard. If the specifications are published, then it's an open standard. De jure standards can be either open or closed standards. Most de jure standards are now open, and by definition, all de facto standards are open. TCP/IP and IPX are both open protocols. *DECnet* and IBM's *Systems Network Architecture* (SNA) were once closed protocols but are now more open.

# PROTOCOL STACKS

Computers use protocols to talk to each other, and when information travels between computers, it moves from device to device, or layer to layer as defined by the OSI model. Each layer of the model has different protocols that define how information travels. The layered functionality of the different protocols in the OSI model is called a *protocol stack*.

I cover the layers of the OSI model in more detail later, but basically the protocol stack works by moving data through the various layers. When data is sent from a source device down the OSI model, each layer attaches its own header to that information. As you can see in Figure 2-1, the process starts when the user's application sends the "Hello World!" data to the *Application layer*. The Application layer adds its information to the data and passes it down to the next layer. When the *Presentation layer* receives the information, it does not distinguish the original data from the Application layer's header. Everything that it receives is considered just data. The Presentation layer then adds its own header to that "data" and forwards it to the *Session layer*. This process continues all the way down the OSI model until it gets to the *Physical layer*, where it is converted to 1's and 0's.

After the data, in the form of frames, is sent across the media to the destination device, this process works in reverse. At each layer, the appropriate header is stripped and the data is passed up to the next layer. Each layer only removes its corresponding header.

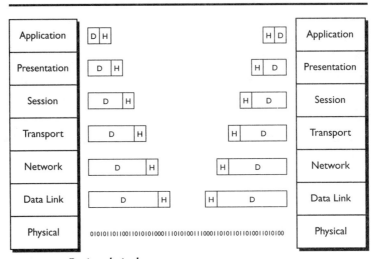

**FIGURE 2-1**   Protocol stack

# WHAT IS THE OSI MODEL?

In 1984 the International Standards Organization (ISO) released a model to be used as a guide for future network protocols. This model is called the *Open Systems Interconnection* model.

## THE INTERNATIONAL STANDARDS ORGANIZATION

The International Standards Organization is a voluntary, nontreaty organization that produces international standards. It was founded in 1946. The members of ISO are actually other organizations from eighty-nine member countries. The United States representative in ISO is the American National Standards Institute (ANSI). ISO standards are sometimes coordinated with International Telecommunications Union, Telecommunication Standards Sector (ITU-T) recommendations to avoid two incompatible international standards.

ITU-T, headquartered in Geneva, Switzerland, is an international organization within which governments and the private sector coordinate global telecommunications networks and services. ITU-T activities include the coordination, development, regulation, and standardization of telecommunications. (ITU-T was formerly known as the Consultative Committee for International Telegraphy and Telephony.)

The ISO issues standards on a large number of subjects, ranging from data communications protocols to telephone pole coatings. The ISO has almost 200 technical committees, each dealing with a specific subject. Each committee has subcommittees that are themselves divided into working groups.

Working groups are where most of the real work is done. Over 100,000 volunteers are part of the working groups. These volunteers are usually assigned to work on ISO matters by companies whose products are affected by the standards being created.

The OSI model depicts the stream of information down the seven layers of the model on the source device, across intermediate devices, and up through the seven layers on the destination device. These devices can be any type of network equipment. Networked computers, printers, and faxes, as well as internetworking devices such as routers and switches, are all examples of these devices. The model is a theoretical object, most often followed loosely and not to the letter, that breaks down the functions of a network into seven layers. Most protocol standards can be placed into one of the seven layers. If you know the layer or layers that a protocol fits into in the model, you have some idea of its purpose and function. The layers are shown from bottom to top in Figure 2-2.

 tip

For the exam, you'll need to know the layers of the OSI model. Here are a couple of ways to easily remember them:

**All People Seem To Need Data Processing**

**Please Do Not Throw Sausage Pizza Away**

The second line is preferable, as it follows the correct order of the layers.

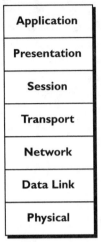

**FIGURE 2-2**   OSI model

Table 2-1 shows an overview of the OSI layers and their functions. Each layer is discussed in detail later in the chapter.

| TABLE 2-1 OSI MODEL AT A GLANCE | |
| --- | --- |
| *OSI LAYER* | *FUNCTION* |
| Application | Interface between the user's application and the network |
| Presentation | Negotiates data exchange formats |
| Session | Allows users to establish connections using easily remembered names |
| Transport | Provides end-to-end, reliable connections |
| Network | Routes data through a large internetwork |
| Data Link | Determines access to the network media |
| Physical | Transforms data into bits that are sent across the physical media |

As data moves through the various layers of the ISO model, it is referred to by different names. Table 2-2 shows what data is called at each OSI layer.

| TABLE 2-2 DATA NAMES AT DIFFERENT OSI MODEL LAYERS | |
|---|---|
| *OSI LAYER* | *DATA NAME* |
| Application | Messages |
| Presentation | Packets |
| Session | Packets |
| Transport | Datagrams and segments |
| Network | Datagrams |
| Data Link | Frames |
| Physical | Bits |

Sometimes the term *packets* is used as a generic term for describing data at any layer.

# PHYSICAL LAYER

The first layer of the OSI model is the *Physical layer*. The function of this layer is the transmission of bits over the network media. It provides a physical connection for the transmission of data among the network devices. The Physical layer is responsible for making sure that data is read the same way on the destination device as it was sent from the source device. Figure 2-3 shows Physical layer transmission.

The Physical layer specifies the mechanical, electrical, and functional means to establish and maintain physical connections. For example, the Physical layer specifications on a network include the amount of voltage on a cable, how a signal changed to signify a 1 or 0 being sent, and in what order a signal was sent.

exam
preparation
pointer

**For the exam, you should know what each layer of the OSI model handles. The Physical layer**

- o **Transmits bits**
- o **Specifies requirements for how transmission occurs**
- o **Ensures compatible data transmission with other devices**

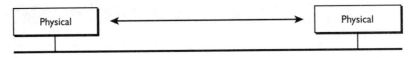

01010110110011010101000111010100111000110101101101001101010100

**FIGURE 2-3**   Physical layer transmission

# DATA LINK LAYER

The second layer of the OSI model is the *Data Link layer*. The main purpose of this layer is to provide a reliable method of transmitting data across the physical media. A Data Link layer transmission is shown in Figure 2-4. This layer breaks the input data into frames, transmits the frames sequentially, and processes the acknowledged frames sent back by the receiver. It adds a header and trailer to the frames it creates. These allow the destination device to see when a frame begins or ends on the physical media.

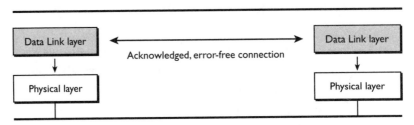

01010110110011010101000111010100111000110101101101001101010100

**FIGURE 2-4**   Data Link layer transmission

The Data Link layer is divided into two sublayers, as shown in Figure 2-5: the *Media Access Control (MAC) sublayer* and the *Logical Link Control (LLC) sublayer*.

exam
preparation
pointer  **For the exam, you should know the characteristics of the Data Link layer:**

- **Packages data into frames**
- **Transmits data sequentially**
- **Processes acknowledged frames sent from the receiver**

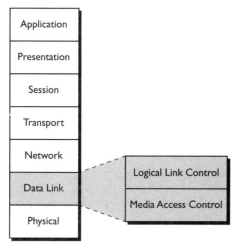

**FIGURE 2-5**   MAC and LLC sublayers

# Media Access Control

The *Media Access Control sublayer* of the Data Link layer is responsible for physical addressing and access to the network media. Only one device at a time may transmit on any type of media. If multiple devices attempt to transmit, they will scramble each other's signal.

The three ways to control access to media are as follows:

o Addressing

o Contention

o Deterministic

## Addressing

The Data Link layer is responsible for the physical addresses of devices on the network. Every device on a network has a hard-coded address attached to it. An example of this address for an Ethernet card would be 00-AA-00-59-65-71. From here I refer to this address as the *MAC address*.

## Contention

In a *contention-based* network, any device can transmit whenever it needs to. The advantages of this system are that it allows equal access to the network media, but at the expense of possible collisions. Collisions occur when two devices try to transmit at the same time and disrupt each other's signaling.

On modern contention-based networks, devices listen for other signals on the media before transmitting. Collisions are not totally eliminated, but they are kept down to manageable levels. This is known as *Carrier Sense Multiple Access*, or CSMA.

The two types of CSMA are CSMA/CD and CSMA/CA. CSMA/CD stands for *Carrier Sense Multiple Access/Collision Detection*. The transmission sequence on a CSMA/CD network goes as follows:

1. The device "listens" to the media for any other transmissions.

2. If the network media is quiet, then the device proceeds to start transmitting its data.

3. After the device transmits its data, it listens to the network media to detect any collisions.

4. If the device detects a collision, it will send out a signal for all other devices to receive. This signal tells the other devices to keep from sending data for a small period to clear all signals from the media.

5. The transmitting stations will then wait a random amount of time before sending their data.

6. If a second collision occurs with the same devices, they repeat the above steps, but double the random time-out before they transmit again. Once the devices have transmitted successfully, other devices are allowed to transmit again.

The idea behind CSMA/CD is that most collisions can be avoided by simply checking the media to see if it is free before transmitting. Collisions can still occur by devices transmitting at the exact same time, or transmitting before another device's signal reaches the other end of the physical media.

Ethernet uses the CSMA/CD method.

*Carrier Sense Multiple Access/Collision Avoidance* networks use a different method of avoiding collisions. The sequences of events in CSMA/CA are as follows:

1. The device wanting to send checks the media for any active transmissions.

2. If the media is clear, the device sends a Request to Send message.

3. If it is okay to transmit, the network server responds with a Clear to Send signal.

4. When the device receives the Clear to Send signal, it transmits its data.

5. After the transmission is completed, the device sends out an abort sequence to signal that it is finished.

CSMA/CA is most often used by Apple's LocalTalk network.

 **For the Network Essentials exam, you may also need to know the advantages and disadvantages of controlling media in a contention-based network.**

**Advantages of contention-based systems:**

o **Low overhead**

o **High speed on networks with less than roughly 40 percent utilization**

**Disadvantages of contention-based networks:**

o **Degradation of performance due to collisions under moderate-to-high network loads**

o **Inability to assign  priorities to special devices**

o **Channel access not always predictable**

## Deterministic

Unlike a contention-based network, where devices are free to transmit whenever they want, a *deterministic* network has a system that determines transmitting order. The two types of deterministic networks are *token passing* and *polling*.

### Token passing

In a *token-passing* system, a small data frame is passed from device to device across the network in a predetermined order. The device that has control of the token frame has the ability to transmit data across the network. Even on large networks where contention would start to break down due to increased levels of collisions, token passing maintains an orderly network.

exam
preparation
pointer
**For the exam, you should know the advantages and disadvantages of using token passing to determine data transmitting order.**

Advantages of token passing:

o Special devices can have higher priorities than normal devices.

o Token passing is much more efficient under high network loads than contention-based networks.

o Network access is predictable due to the predetermined transmitting order.

Disadvantages of token passing:

o Contention-based systems on networks with low utilization are faster.

o Network devices and interface cards are more expensive due to their increased intelligence.

### Polling systems

In a *polling system* a master device checks the other secondary devices on the network to see if they need to transmit. The order of the devices polled and their priority can be set by the administrator.

Most networks that use this configuration operate in a multipoint configuration, where each secondary device is directly connected to the primary.

exam
preparation
pointer
**For the exam, you should know the advantages and disadvantages of using polling to determine data transmitting order.**

Advantages of polling:

o The priority and amount of data allowed to be transmitted at a time can be predetermined.

o Little bandwidth is lost when the network reaches high utilization.

Disadvantages of polling:

o The process of polling each secondary device uses more bandwidth than the other methods.

o Transmissions can be delayed from secondary devices while they wait to be polled by the primary device.

# Logical Link Control

The *Logical Link Control (LLC) sublayer* of the Data Link layer establishes and maintains data link connections between network devices. It is responsible for any flow control and error correction found in this layer.

The following are connection services the LLC sublayer supplies:

o  Unacknowledged connectionless service: The fastest means to transfer data at the LLC layer. It is also the most unreliable. Although it is the most unreliable, it is commonly used because the upper layer protocols handle their own error checking.

o  Connection-oriented service: The opposite of unacknowledged connectionless service is *connection-oriented service*, which uses a sliding-window flow control and acknowledgments for error checking.

Not all network devices run at the same speed. For this reason, there needs to be a method to control the amount of data sent to another device so the device will be able to handle it. The LLC sublayer supports flow control, as do other layers of the OSI model. The LLC sublayer implements flow control in the following ways:

o  Sliding window: Allows the two communicating devices to negotiate the number of allowable outstanding frames. Using this method, the receiving device does not need to acknowledge each frame it receives and then wait for the next; it can send one acknowledgment for a group of frames.

o  Stop and wait: Simply a green-light way of handling flow control. When the receiving device has no memory left to store incoming data, it suspends transmission. When memory is free again, it sends a signal to the transmitting device to resume.

Error control is implemented using *cyclic redundancy checks* (CRCs) and *checksums*. A CRC is a method of detecting errors in the transmission of data. Before data is sent, a CRC number is calculated by running the data through an algorithm and producing a unique number. At the receiving end of the transmission, the data is run through the same algorithm again to produce the number. If the numbers match, the data was sent error free. The unique value generated from the algorithm is called a *checksum*.

# NETWORK LAYER

The third layer of the OSI model is the *Network layer*. This layer is responsible for routing information from one network device to another. The Network layer decides what path data will take if the destination device is located on another network. Data passes through the network by devices called *intermediate devices*. The source and destination devices are *end systems*. Figure 2-6 shows data being sent between the Network layer of two devices.

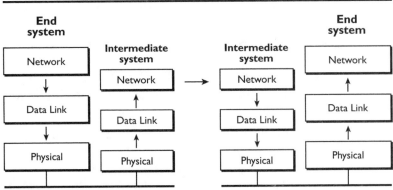

**FIGURE 2-6    Network layer transmission**

The Network layer accepts messages from the source host, converts them to packets, and makes sure that the packets are directed toward the destination. The Network layer is also responsible for deciding on the best route the packet should take through the network. It does this by checking to see if the destination device is on another network. If it is, then the Network layer must decide where to send the packet to so it will reach the final destination. In addition, if too many packets are present in the network at the same time, they will get in each other's way, forming bottlenecks. The Network layer controls such congestion.

Connections between devices at the Network layer are thought of as *connectionless:* no connection setup and maintenance goes on at this layer. Any data sent is considered a best effort attempt. If it does not arrive or is corrupt, then it is the destination device's job to request a retransmit.

Be sure to know the responsibilities of the Network layer for the exam.

- o Routes information from sender to receiver
- o Converts data into packets
- o Uses connectionless transmissions

Data being sent between the Network layers of two devices can be sent a few different ways. Some data is sent directly to the device; some may be sent through many intermediate devices and stored there for a length of time. These types of data transfer are referred to as *datagram switching*.

The job of the Network layer is to get data through the network in the best possible way. By using the processes of switching, routing, and addressing, it finds the most efficient route through the network.

## Switching

Datagram switching describes how data is forwarded across an internetwork. The type of datagram switching that a service or application may use depends on how fast the data needs to be delivered. For example, e-mail does not need to be delivered in real time, so it does not have to go directly to the destination device. There are three main methods:

- o Circuit switching: In circuit switching, a dedicated connection is made between the two communicating devices. Two advantages of this method are no congestion (because the link is dedicated) and almost no channel-access delay. The disadvantages are inefficient use of the media and a possible long wait to establish a connection. Figure 2-7 shows circuit switching on a network.

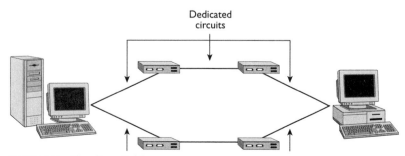

**FIGURE 2-7**   Circuit switching

o **Message switching:** With message switching the data is sent from device to device in whole across the network. This is also known as *store and forward*. Devices must store all the information as it is sent in whole. The media is used more efficiently with this method, and congestion can be controlled. Priories on information can be set so important data arrives first. This method will not work with real-time applications such as voice or video. Figure 2-8 shows message switching.

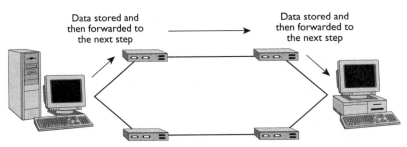

**FIGURE 2-8**    Message switching

o **Packet switching:** A combination of circuit switching and message switching. With packet switching, data is broken into small pieces and routed from device to device. Devices that forward the data only need to keep the information in memory instead of in physical storage, because the data was split. There are two methods of packet switching, which are:

o **Datagram:** *Datagram packet switching* is a connectionless method. Each piece of information is tagged with the destination address so no dedicated connection is needed. Every piece of data is routed individually through the network to its destination. At the destination device, the data is pieced back together by using a *Packet Assembler/Dissambler* (PAD). Figure 2-9 shows datagram switching.

o **Virtual circuit:** Similar to dedicated circuit switching, except the connections are virtual. This way, more than one communication can go over the physical media. This is considered *connection oriented*. Figure 2-10 shows virtual circuit switching.

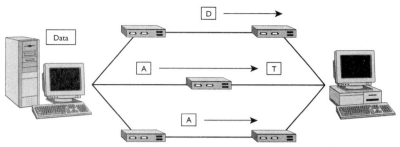

**FIGURE 2-9**   Datagram switching

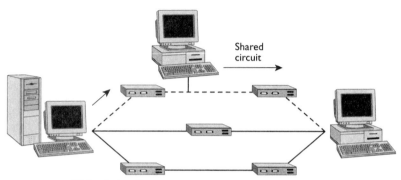

**FIGURE 2-10**   Virtual circuit

# Routing

The Network layer is responsible for routing packets across a network. For packets to be correctly routed, there needs to be a table set up to show the shortest routes between two networks. These tables can either be dynamic or static.

*Static* routing tables are set up manually by administrators. *Dynamic* routing protocols use one of two methods to define the shortest route. With the following two dynamic routing methods, network administrators are not required to enter any information. All configuration settings can be detected by the network routers. They are:

o Distance vector: The simplest method to use. It simply calculates the shortest number of hops between two points. Distance vector can take a considerable amount of time to configure and change on a large network.

o Link state: Link state routing protocols are newer and more complex than distance vector. Link state takes more into account than just hop count — it usually considers link speed, latency, and congestion.

## Addressing

Since the Network layer is concerned with getting data from one computer to another, even if they are on a different network, it uses network addresses. A device on a network has not only a device address but also a network address that tells other computers where to locate that device. By using this address the sending device can tell whether the destination device is on the same network segment (local) or on another network segment (remote). The fact that a device is local or remote may dictate certain sending parameters such as protocol and time-out values.

# TRANSPORT LAYER

The *Transport layer* is the fourth layer of the OSI model. It provides a transport service between the Session layer and the Network layer. This service takes information from the Session layer and splits it up if necessary. It then passes this information to the Network layer and checks to make sure the information arrived at the destination device successfully. Figure 2-11 shows Transport layer communications.

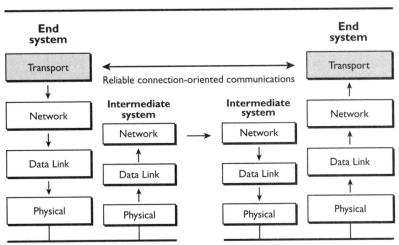

**FIGURE 2-11**   **Communication between the Transport layers on two devices**

The Transport layer is a true source-to-destination layer. This means that a program on the source device carries on a dialogue with another program on the destination device by using message headers and control messages. These message headers and control messages are used for error detection, sequencing, and flow control.

Unlike the Network layer, the connections at the Transport layer are considered connection oriented. Data passed through this layer will be acknowledged by the destination device. If an acknowledgment is not received in a specified time-out period, the data is re-sent.

exam
preparation
pointer

**You should know the responsibilities of the Transport layer for the exam.**

- **Breaks up and restores data**
- **Provides end-to-end reliability**
- **Uses connection-oriented transmission of data**

The Transport layer provides a few connection services. They are as follows:

- Segment sequencing: When a large amount of data is sent across the network, it sometimes must be split into smaller pieces. Because of the way the Network layer routes packets, they may arrive at the destination out of order. The Transport layer resequences information before passing it to the Session layer.

- Error control: The Transport layer can check for errors in data by using methods such as checksums. It will also request retransmissions of data should it not receive a piece of information. It does this by keeping track of packet sequence numbers.

- Flow control: Flow control is managed by the use of acknowledgments. The sending device will not transmit the next piece of information if it has not received an acknowledgment that the destination device has received the previous packet.

# SESSION LAYER

The fifth layer of the OSI model is the *Session layer*. This layer lets users establish a connection — called a *session* — between devices. Once the connection has been established, the Session layer can manage the dialogue. Figure 2-12 shows Session layer communication.

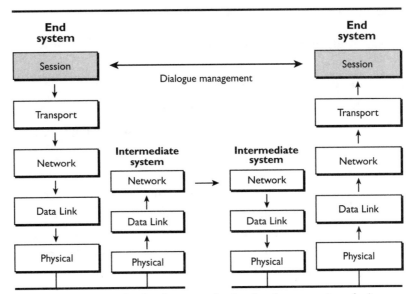

**FIGURE 2-12** **Communication between the Session layers on two devices**

Sessions can be set up so that they are:

o **Half-duplex:** A two-way alternate method of communication (only one way at a time). This is like talking on a CB radio. While one device talks, the other must listen.

o **Simplex:** Simple, one-way communications. No two-way communications are allowed. Some examples include a speaker, television, or radio.

o **Full-duplex:** Allows for a full, two-way, simultaneous connection. Either device can transmit and receive at will. A modern telephone uses full-duplex communications.

exam
preparation
pointer

The characteristics of the different Session layer communication methods is a very good exam question topic.

Advantages of half-duplex:

o Costs less than full-duplex

o Enables for two-way communications

Disadvantages of half-duplex:

o Costs more than simplex

o Only one device can transmit at a time

Advantage of simplex:

o Cheapest communications method

Disadvantage of simplex:

o Only allows for communications in one direction

Advantage of full-duplex:

o Enables two-way communications simultaneously

Disadvantage of full-duplex:

o The most expensive method in terms of equipment because two bandwidth channels are needed

To establish a session, the user must provide the remote address to which they want to connect. These addresses are not like MAC or network addresses; they are intended for users and are easier to remember. Examples are DNS names (www.microsoft.com) or computer names (SERVER41).

exam
preparation
pointer

For the exam, you should also know the characteristics of the Session layer.

o Allows users to establish connections between devices

o Manages dialogue

o Uses remote address to establish connections

# PRESENTATION LAYER

The sixth layer of the OSI model, the *Presentation layer*, negotiates and establishes the format in which data is exchanged. This layer is responsible for any character set or numeric translations needed between devices. It is also responsible for data compression to reduce the amount of data transmitted, as well as encryption. Figure 2-13 shows Presentation layer communication.

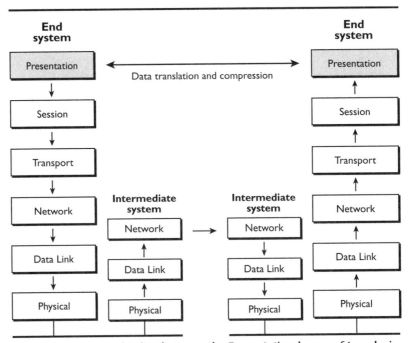

**FIGURE 2-13**    Communication between the Presentation layers of two devices

Saying the Presentation layer does "translation" is very vague. There are a number of ways it translates information between different types of network devices. Some devices read bits and bytes in different directions. Three such translation services are bit order, byte order, and character codes translation.

Do computers read the strings of 1's and 0's from left to right, or from right to left? This varies between the different manufacturers. The Presentation layer takes care of the job of sending the bits in the correct order. Should the destination device receive the information out of order, the data would be extremely garbled.

As with bit order, different computers read the order of bytes in different ways. Some computers designate the least significant byte first, and are said to use the little endian method. Computers based on Intel processes use this method. Other computers do just the opposite and use the big endian method.

Within the internals of computers, there are no such things as letters and punctuation marks — computers use numbers to represent everything. Since they can only use numbers, they need some way to correspond letters to some sort of numeric convention. Computers use character codes to represent the numbers and letters that users see. The codes are normally binary numbers that directly relate to a physical character. For example, on an IBM compatible the letter *A* is decimal number 65, which relates to binary 01000001.

Two main character codes exist:

o **EBCDIC**: Stands for *Extended Binary Coded Decimal Interchange Code*. Originally designed by IBM and used in their mainframes, it uses eight bits to represent up to 256 different characters.

o **ASCII**: Stands for *American Standard Code for Information Interchange*. It was designed by the American National Standards Institute, or ANSI. The normal ASCII character set uses seven bits to allow for up to 128 characters. The eighth bit is normally used for parity checking. *Parity* is a way to check for small errors in data. An example of a parity error check would be to count the total number of 1's in the binary data. If the number was even, the eighth bit would be set to 1. If the total number was odd, the eighth bit would be set to 0. Using this method only allows for one bit of information in the data to be changed in transmission; if two get changed the error checking may not work. Extended ASCII permits the eighth bit to be used for data. This allows for up to 256 different characters.

exam preparation pointer **For the exam, you should know the responsibilities of the Presentation layer.**

o **Establishes format for data exchange**

o **Handles character set and numeric translations**

o **Performs data compression**

# APPLICATION LAYER

The top layer of the OSI model is the *Application layer*. This layer is the interface between the user's application and the network. It allows the application that the user sees to transfer files, send e-mail, and do anything else it needs to on the network. This should not be confused with the actual application that the user is running. Figure 2-14 shows Application layer communication.

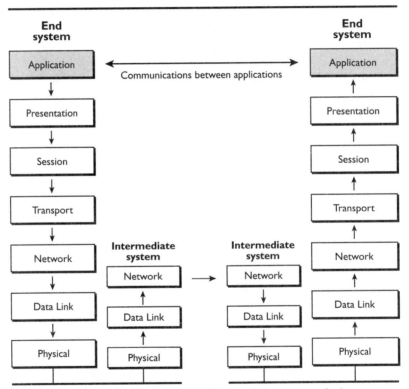

FIGURE 2-14    Application layer communication between two devices

 An exam question might concern characteristics of the application layer, so be sure to review them.

- Serves as the interface between user applications and the network
- Enables user applications to interact with the network

# EXAMPLE OF A CONNECTION

Now that you know the seven layers of the OSI model, you can go through a sample connection between two devices. Assume that a user is running some sort of chat application on their computer that enables them to connect to another person's computer and talk to that person over a network. Figure 2-15 shows a protocol stack that I will use in this example.

The user types the message "Good morning" into the chat application. The Application layer passes the data from the user's application to the Presentation layer. At the Presentation layer the data is translated and encrypted. The data is then passed to the Session layer, where the dialogue is set for full-duplex communication. The Transport layer packages the data as segments. The recipient's name is resolved to the corresponding IP address. Checksums are added for error checking.

Next, the Network layer packages the data as datagrams. After examining the IP address, the destination device is discovered to be on a remote network. The IP address for the intermediate device is then added as the next destination. Data is sent to the Data Link layer, where it is packaged as frames. The physical address of the device is resolved. This is the address belonging to the intermediate device, which will forward the data on to its destination. The access type for the network is determined to be Ethernet.

The data is then passed on to the Physical layer, where it is packaged as bits and sent from the network adapter across the transmission media. The intermediate device reads the bits off the network media at the Physical layer. The Data Link layer packages the data as frames. The physical address of the destination device is resolved to its IP address. The Network layer packages the data as datagrams. After examining the IP address of the destination device, the location of this device on the network is determined. The data is passed back to the Data Link layer, where it is again packaged as frames. The IP address is resolved to the MAC address. The access type for the network is determined to be Ethernet.

The data is then sent to the Physical layer, packaged as bits, and sent across the network media. The destination device reads the bits off the network media at the Physical layer. The Data Link layer packages the data as frames. The physical address of the destination device is resolved to its IP address. The Network layer packages the data as datagrams. It is determined that the device has reached its final destination, where it is reordered into the proper sequence.

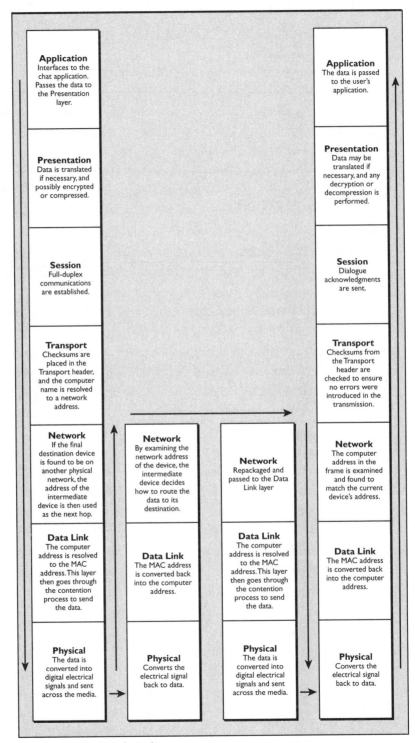

**FIGURE 2-15**    Protocol stack

It is then passed on to the Transport layer. Data is compiled into segments, and error checking is performed. Checksums are compared to determine that the data is error free. The Session layer acknowledges that the data has been received. At the Presentation layer the data is translated and unencrypted. The Application layer then passes the data from the Presentation layer on to the user's chat application. The message "Good morning" then appears on the recipient user's screen.

Now that you understand the flow of information through the OSI model, I can now discuss the IEEE 802 standards. Unlike the theoretical OSI model, the 802 standards are documented, real-world standards that define different technologies, such as Ethernet.

# THE IEEE 802 STANDARDS

The Institute of Electrical and Electronic Engineers (IEEE) started a project called Project 802. The 802 comes from the date the project began, February 1980 (*80* for the year, *2* for the second month). The goal of this project is to create device standards for different LAN needs.

The twelve different 802 standards are as follows:

802.1     The 802.1 standard created what is now known as the *spanning tree algorithm*. The spanning tree algorithm is used by transparent bridges (you will learn about those in Chapter 6). They use this algorithm to detect other bridges on the network, remove loops, and to detect when another bridge fails.

802.2     Remember that the Data Link layer of the OSI model is made up of two parts. The two parts are the LLC sublayer and the MAC sublayer. 802.2 defines the standards for the LLC sublayer of the Data Link layer.

802.3     CSMA/CD, for example, Ethernet, is defined by the 802.3 standard.

802.4     Token-passing bus network systems are defined in 802.4. Almost all modern token-passing networks are rings, not bus types. This standard never really took off, and you will very rarely see it used.

802.5     The 802.5 standard is based on IBM's Token Ring network standard. This standard uses a logical ring topology running at 4 or 16 megabits.

802.6     802.6 defines standards for MANs. The main purpose of this standard is to define *Distributed Queue Dual Bus* (DQDB), a network with two physical channels.

| 802.7 | The 802.7 standard simply defines the Broadband Technology Advisory Group. |
| 802.8 | The 802.8 standard is the Fiber Optic Technical Advisory. |
| 802.9 | The 802.9 standard is the Integrated Data and Voice Networks. |
| 802.10 | Network security issues are defined in 802.10. |
| 802.11 | As users start to roam more, the idea of wireless networks is beginning to unfold. The 802.11 standard committee is currently working on the problems associated with this type of network. |
| 802.12 | Hewlett-Packard has developed its own 100-megabit standard for the next generation of networks. This new network type is called *100VG-AnyLAN*. 802.12 defines the standards for this new technology. |

Table 2-3 shows 802 standards and their purposes so that you can easily review.

**TABLE 2-3  802 STANDARDS AT A GLANCE**

| *802 STANDARD* | *PURPOSE* |
| --- | --- |
| 802.1 | Spanning tree algorithm |
| 802.2 | LLC portion of the Data Link layer |
| 802.3 | Ethernet |
| 802.4 | Token Bus |
| 802.5 | Token Ring |
| 802.6 | DQDB (Distributed Queue Dual Bus) |
| 802.7 | Broadband technology |
| 802.8 | Fiber optic technology |
| 802.9 | Integrated data and voice |
| 802.10 | Network security |
| 802.11 | Wireless networks |
| 802.12 | 100VG-AnyLAN |

 tip **For the Networking Essentials exam, the two main 802 standards you should know are 802.3 and 802.5.**

# KEY POINT SUMMARY

In this chapter you learned the seven layers of the *OSI model*. *Protocol suites* are the real-world implementation of the OSI model. The OSI model has seven layers, each of which outlines tasks that allow different devices on the network to communicate.

- The *Physical layer* specifies transmission of bits across the network media.

- The *Data Link layer* packages data into frames and provides for reliable transmission of data. The Data Link layer contains the Media Access Control and Logical Link Control sublayers.

  - The *Media Access Control sublayer* is responsible for access to the network media. Access can be provided using a contention or deterministic system. In a *contention-based* system, any device can transmit when it needs to. *Deterministic* systems require that a device first possess the right to transmit. Ethernet is a contention system, while Token Ring is deterministic.

  - The *Logical Link Control sublayer* establishes and maintains network connections and performs flow control and error checking.

- The *Network layer* is responsible for routing data across the network. Data is converted to *datagrams* at this layer, which are sent using *connectionless* transmission to a specific network address.

- The *Transport layer* provides end-to-end reliability using *connection-oriented* transmissions. Data at the Transport layer is packaged in segments and sent using connection-oriented transmissions, in which an acknowledgment is sent after data is received. If the sender receives no acknowledgment, the data is then re-sent.

- The *Session layer* allows users to establish communications between devices using easily remembered computer names. Dialogue between devices is managed at this layer. At the Session layer, data is packaged as *packets*.

- The *Presentation layer* negotiates and establishes the format for data exchange. Data compression and translation are handled at this layer.

- The *Application layer* is the final layer of the OSI model. At this layer all of the interaction between the user's application and the network is handled.

o You also learned about the 802 standards.

o *802.3* is the standard that describes CSMA/CD, used in Ethernet.

o *802.5* defines the logical ring topology used in Token Ring.

# APPLYING WHAT YOU'VE LEARNED

It is now time to review the material covered in this chapter. The following Instant Assessment questions will reinforce what you have just learned about the OSI model.

## Instant Assessment

1. The method of error control in which data is run through an algorithm before and after transmission is known as:

   **a.** Stop and wait

   **b.** Cyclic redundancy check

   **c.** Segment sequencing

   **d.** Flow control

2. Data that passes through the Transport layer will be acknowledged by the destination device. This type of connection is:

   **a.** Half-duplex

   **b.** Segment sequencing

   **c.** Connectionless

   **d.** Connection oriented

3. A system in which a master device will check the secondary devices on the network to see if they need to transmit is known as:

   **a.** Polling

   **b.** Token passing

   **c.** CSMA/CD

   **d.** CSMA/CA

**4.** The switching method in which a dedicated connection is made between the two communications devices is:

**a.** Message switching

**b.** Virtual circuit

**c.** Circuit switching

**d.** Packet switching

**5.** Connections that allow two-way simultaneous dialogue are known as:

**a.** Half-duplex

**b.** Full-duplex

**c.** Simplex

**d.** Datagram

**6.** Languages that allow the computers to communicate are known as:

**a.** Protocols

**b.** Addressing

**c.** Polling

**d.** Dialogue

**7.** Which type of system works best for large networks?

**a.** Contention

**b.** Deterministic

**c.** Simplex

**d.** Full-duplex

**8.** Which OSI layer packages data into frames?

**a.** Transport layer

**b.** Physical layer

**c.** Session layer

**d.** Application layer

**9.** Which OSI layer is responsible for routing data across the network?

**a.** Physical layer

**b.** Network layer

      **c.** Session layer

      **d.** Application layer

**10.** Which layer of the OSI model implements error checking using checksums?

      **a.** Logical Link Control

      **b.** Media Access Control

      **c.** Application layer

      **d.** Session layer

 

                                                    **T/F**

**11.** The Physical layer of the OSI model is responsible for access to the network media.       _____

**12.** A de jure standard is controlled by the organization that designed it.     _____

**13.** Polling systems have little loss of bandwidth at high utilization.     _____

**14.** Unacknowledged connectionless service is fast but unreliable.     _____

**15.** CSMA/CD prevents any data collisions from occurring on the network.     _____

**16.** Link state routing considers link speed and other factors when routing packets.     _____

**17.** At the Physical layer, data is packaged in bits.

**18.** The Application layer handles data compression, which can reduce the amount of data being transmitted.     _____

**19.** In a token-passing system, the device that wants to transmit data must request the token before sending.     _____

**20.** The Data Link layer is divided into the Media Access Control and the Logical Link Control sublayers.     _____

**21.** In circuit switching, data is sent using the store and forward method.     _____

**22.** By definition all de facto standards are open.     _____

concept link    **For answers to these Instant Assessment questions, see Appendix C.**

# Network Media and Topology

**N**ow that you have the fundamentals and theory out of the way, it is time to get to the real-world technical information! I start this part with a discussion about the types of network adapters, such as PCI and EISA, that you may encounter in the field and on the test. After that, you get an in-depth discussion about the different kinds of network media and when and why to use each.

Part II also covers the important topic of network design. You begin by learning about the different network topologies. I cover important aspects such as maximum network size, ease of installation, and troubleshooting. Then I compare the different network models, including Token Ring and Ethernet.

# Network Media

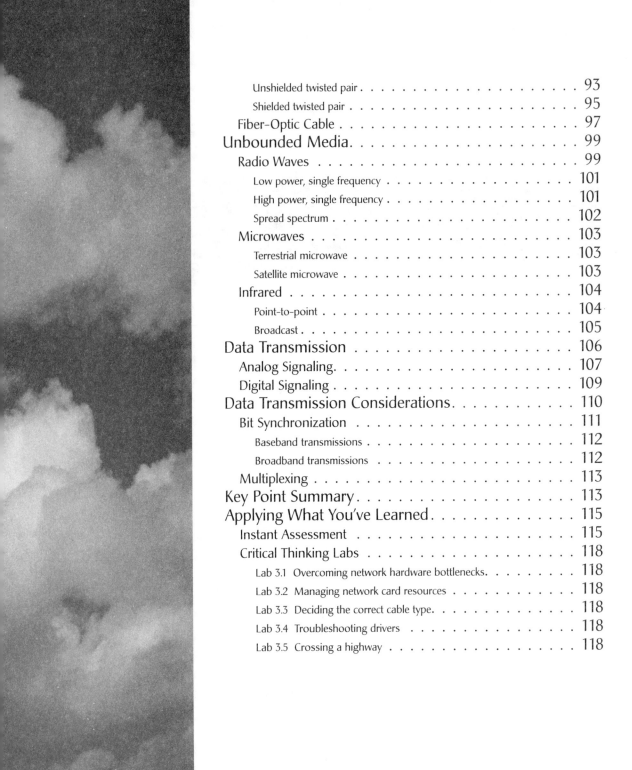

# About Chapter 3

**N**ow that I have discussed the OSI model, look at some implementations of the model.

This chapter covers implementations of the Physical layer. The discussion begins with network adapters and moves on to transmission media and transmission types. By the end of this chapter, you will understand how the different components work together to provide data transmissions. This chapter provides real-world information that must be considered when implementing a network.

Upon completion of this chapter, you will also be able to choose transmission media based on your network's needs. You will also understand the differences between digital and analog transmissions. Then, I'll introduce broadband and baseband transmissions. The implementations covered in this chapter are being utilized all around you. Your objective in this chapter is to gain an understanding of the purpose and function of this technology.

# UNDERSTANDING NETWORK ADAPTERS

The *network adapters*, commonly known as *network interface cards* (NICs) or simply network cards, are responsible for moving data from the computer to the transmission media. The network adapter transforms data into signals that are carried across the transmission media to its destination. Once the signals reach the destination device, the NICs translate the signals back into information the computer can process. Exactly how the adapter functions can vary according to the type of adapter being used. To understand this better, you will discover the different types of network adapters later in this chapter.

 **note** **Network adapters work at the Data Link layer of the OSI model. Because of this, they provide the MAC and LLC sublayer functions of that layer.**

Network adapters basically convert computer data into a signal that can be transmitted over media. When a network adapter transmits data, it first receives the data from the computer. It attaches its own header containing a checksum and the network card's address. The data is then converted to signals that are passed over the network media. During the conversion, the data may be changed to 5-volt (V) electric current signals transmitted over coaxial cable or to pulses of light when sent over fiber-optic cable.

The circuitry on the card that does the conversion of the signal is known as a *transceiver*. Ethernet can run over a few different cable types, but the main circuitry on all the Ethernet cards should be the same; only the transceiver should be different. Most Ethernet cards have built-in transceivers. Figure 3-1 shows the transceiver on a network adapter.

If you plug the cable directly into the card, you can be sure the transceiver is built-in, or *on-board*. Some Ethernet cards have what is known as an *AUI port* which allows you to use an external transceiver. With an external transceiver, you could use your network card to run over fiber optic, although there isn't a fiber-optic connector on the card.

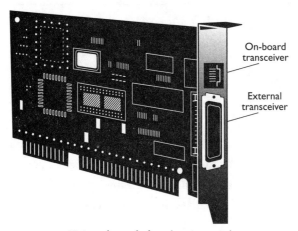

On-board transceiver

External transceiver

**FIGURE 3-1**   Network card showing transceivers

# INSTALLING AND CONFIGURING NETWORK ADAPTERS

The key to making a network adapter work correctly is to make sure it is correctly installed and configured. While this may seem simple, it is easy to unknowingly configure a network adapter incorrectly. Sometimes this mistake shows up right away, and the card will not function at all; other times, performance can be more sporadic.

## Adapter Settings

One of the hardest parts about network cards is configuring them. Like most adapter cards installed in a computer, such as sound and video cards, they are configured by setting some parameters. These parameters can have systemwide implications if they are not properly set. You must be sure to set their addresses so they do not conflict with any other cards in the computer. Most network cards require you to set some combination of the following parameters:

- IRQ
- I/O address
- Shared memory address
- DMA

Before you can properly adjust these settings to configure the adapter, you need to understand what each one controls.

### *IRQ*

An *IRQ*, or interrupt request, value is an assigned value that a device sends to the computer's processor to interrupt its processing when it needs to send information. For example, when a modem has finished sending data, it may interrupt the processor so the CPU can give it something else to send.

An essential thing to remember about IRQs is that each device in the computer must have a unique one. You must also remember that some IRQs are already in use by devices built into the main board of the computer. Table 3-1 shows the standard, or common, IRQ usage in computers. Please remember that IRQs can be changed, therefore this table may not always be accurate.

| **TABLE 3-1** STANDARD IRQ USAGE | |
| --- | --- |
| **IRQ NUMBER** | **USED BY** |
| 0 | System timer |
| 1 | Keyboard |
| 2 | Cascade IRQ controller or video adapter |
| 3 | COM2 & COM4 |
| 4 | COM1 & COM3 |
| 5 | LPT2 (second printer port) and sometimes sound card |
| 6 | Floppy disk controller |
| 7 | LPT1 (first printer port) |
| 8 | Real-time clock |
| 9 | Cascade from IRQ2 |
| 10 | Unassigned (sometimes used by SCSI controllers) |
| 11 | Unassigned |
| 12 | PS/2 mouse |
| 13 | Math coprocessor |
| 14 | Primary hard drive controller (usually IDE) |
| 15 | Secondary hard drive controller, if it exists |

IRQ 2, cascade, was implemented to allow for IRQs higher than 8. On the original ISA design, only 8 IRQs were allowed, but this number proved to be inadequate. By doing some slight of hand with IRQ 2, they allowed computers to have up to IRQ 15. Be aware that while some computers allow you to use IRQ 2 or 9, some will not, and some only enable you to use one of the two. Usually the only way to find out if they are available is to try them and see if your new device functions properly.

exam
preparation
pointer

Be sure to memorize the IRQs in Table 3-1. On the exam, you will be asked to make a decision as to which IRQ should be used for a network card. A list of the hardware inside the example computer will be given so you know which IRQs are free and which are in use.

## I/O address

After a network card has interrupted the CPU with an IRQ, it needs a way to communicate with the main board. Most cards use an *input/output*, or *I/O*, *address* to do this. You give the card a set number that the software driver also knows, and they use this to communicate. Think of an I/O address like a postal mail address. Any information sent to that address in the computer is picked up by the network card.

I/O addresses are given as *hexadecimal numbers*. You will see them written as starting with "0x" or with a trailing "h", as in "300h". Some common I/O addresses are 0x280, 0x300, and 0x330. Table 3-2 shows the common I/O address usage. Again, these addresses can change, so it may not be correct on all computers.

**You should know the information in Table 3-2, because even though it may not be correct on all computers, it will be correct for the Networking Essentials exam.**

**TABLE 3-2** I/O Address Uses

| Port Number | Device |
| --- | --- |
| 0x200 | Game port |
| 0x230 | Bus mouse |
| 0x270 | LPT3 |
| 0x2F8 | COM2 |
| 0x370 | LPT2 |
| 0x2B0 | LPT1 |
| 0x3F8 | COM1 |

**0x300 is usually a good choice for a network card I/O address. It is usually free and almost all cards support it.**

## DMA

*Direct memory access*, or DMA, enables your adapter cards to work directly with the computer's memory. Normally the CPU must be involved any time an adapter needs to move data into or out of memory. If your adapter uses a DMA channel, it can handle communications directly with memory without the help of the CPU.

Other devices built into the computer use DMA channels, so you will need to pick a free one. If your network card supports DMA transfers, you should enable it, as this could bring about a significant performance increase.

### Shared memory address

An option to I/O address transfer is *shared memory addresses*. Using this method, the network card and software driver use a shared RAM address in the high memory range to communicate.

The shared memory address is slower than the I/O address method, and it can be more trouble. You must be sure to block out the assigned range from any memory management software so it does not try to use that area at the same time.

 **Shared memory ranges will normally appear as D8000, C8000, CFFFF, and so on. Occasionally you will see manufacturers abbreviate this by dropping the last number, such as C800.**

## Hardware Configuration

After you have decided which settings you need to adjust to configure your network card, how do you make these adjustments? The answer depends on the network card in question, as well as the bus type of the card. You normally use either *jumpers*, *DIP switches*, or software to actually configure the network card.

### Jumpers

*Jumpers* are small metal pairs of pins that stick out of the card. You change their configuration by putting small plastic covers with metal internal connectors over them. By doing this, you are actually completing the circuit between the two pins. A jumper with the plastic cover on it is considered "closed," and one without is considered "open." Figure 3-2 shows a set of jumpers.

### DIP switches

*Dual In-line Package* (DIP) switches are small banks of switches on the adapter card. They can be toggled to be either open or closed, on or off, or 0 or 1. Depending on how the manufacturer phrased the settings, you could have one of those three pairs of settings. Figure 3-3 shows DIP switches.

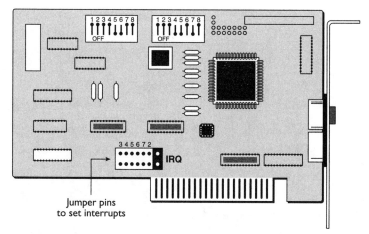

**FIGURE 3-2   Jumpers**

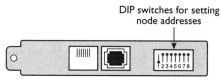

**FIGURE 3-3   DIP switches**

## *Software configuration*

The easiest way to configure a network card is by software. Network adapters using the *Extended Industry Standard Architecture* (EISA) and *MicroChannel Architecture* (MCA) bus type are almost always configured via software. The software configuration for them is stored in the computer's CMOS. PCMCIA cards are also automatically configured via the computer's BIOS. Some also come with utilities that let you manually configure the card if necessary.

Now *Industry Standard Architecture* (ISA), *Video Electronic Standards Association* (VESA), and *Peripheral Component Interface* (PCI) cards are commonly configured using software. Some of the newer cards also support Plug and Play, which enables automatic configuration.

Figure 3-4 shows an example of a software configuration utility used to configure a network adapter.

**FIGURE 3-4**    Software configuration utility

 Today's network cards are almost always software configurable. This is the best type because you can easily change any setting during troubleshooting without the use of a screwdriver.

# INTERFACING THE ADAPTER

There is a lot more to installing and configuring network adapters than just setting up the hardware. You also have to interface the adapter with your computer.

## Adapter Drivers

After making sure the card is configured correctly and working in the computer, you then need to install a *driver* for it into the operating system. The two standards of drivers that you are most likely to see on the exam are *Network Device Interface Specification* (NDIS) and *Open Datalink Interface* (ODI).

The main purpose of these driver standards is to allow network card manufacturers to write one driver and have it support multiple operating systems. Another important feature of the ODI and NDIS standards is the ability to use more than one protocol on each network card. Before these standards existed, you could only load one driver per protocol, but with these you can load one driver and any number of protocols.

 exam preparation pointer **The key point to remember for the Networking Essentials exam is the purpose of ODI and NDIS network card drivers. They allow third-party vendors to easily write drivers that work with the Microsoft and Novell operating systems. They also allow you to use multiple network protocols and NICs at the same time.**

**Also remember that where functionality and purpose are concerned, NDIS is to Microsoft as ODI is to Novell.**

## NDIS

*Network Device Interface Specification*, or NDIS, was created by Microsoft and 3Com. It is used by most companies in the PC networking community. There are two current versions of the NDIS protocols being used.

Version 2.0 is the older 16-bit implementation. Mainly used by DOS and Windows 3.1 clients, it can also be used under Windows 95 if a more recent driver cannot be found.

Version 3.0 is the newer 32-bit implementation. This is the preferred version when using Windows 95 and is required under Windows NT (Windows NT 4.0 supports the current NDIS 4.0 standard). Some smaller revisions of the v3.0 specification has been released that allow Windows 95 and Windows NT to use the same exact driver, but it has not become popular yet.

Operating systems that use NDIS:

o MS-DOS

o Windows for Workgroups

o Windows 95

o Windows NT Workstation

o Windows NT Server

o Artisoft LANtastic

The following shows an NDIS driver loading:

```
SMC Ethernet Adapter DOS NDIS Driver v4.01 (941223)
Copyright(c) 1994 Standard Microsystems Corporation. All
 rights Reserved.
 Adapter - 8216C
 I/O Base Address - 280
 IRQ - 10
 RAM Base Address - D0000


The command was completed successfully.
```

## ODI

*Open Datalink Interface* (ODI), is Novell's answer to the driver specification question. It has many of the same features as NDIS and serves much the same purpose.

Like NDIS, there are 16-bit and 32-bit implementations of ODI. The 16-bit version is used primarily on MS-DOS and Windows 3.1 workstations to connect to a Novell NetWare server. The 32-bit implementation is a newer driver used under Windows 95. This driver can completely replace the NDIS driver normally used in Windows 95. With this driver, users can connect to any type of server, not just NetWare.

The following shows an ODI driver loading:

```
SMC Ethernet Adapter DOS ODI Driver v4.04 (940314)
(C) Copyright 1992-94 Standard Microsystems Corp. All Rights
 Reserved.

Adapter 8216C, Int 10, Port 280, Mem D0000, Node Address
 C0682EBB L
Max Frame 1514 bytes, Line Speed 10 Mbps
Board 1, Frame ETHERNET_802.3, LSB Mode
Board 2, Frame ETHERNET_II, LSB Mode
Board 3, Frame ETHERNET_802.2, LSB Mode
Board 4, Frame ETHERNET_SNAP, LSB Mode
```

tip    Always be sure to check the version of the ODI drivers you are using. Sometimes the easiest solution to a network driver issue is an updated driver.

# Bus Architecture

The first things you must learn before diving into adapters are the different bus types. The term *bus* refers to the connection that your adapter cards have to the rest of your computer. Any adapter card you have, such as a modem, sound card, or a printer port card connects to the rest of your computer over this bus. There are more than a few different types of buses in computers. Some are better than others, and some cards only support one bus type. I will discuss the standard bus types, as well as the most common proprietary types.

exam preparation pointer    The exam will cover the different bus types used by network cards. You should be familiar with the different speeds and bus widths of each.

## ISA

The *Industry Standard Architecture,* or ISA, bus was designed by IBM and used in the IBM PC. An ISA card is shown in Figure 3-5. Due to the need for compatible devices, IBM decided to make ISA an open standard, allowing third-party manufacturers to produce hardware without paying IBM for the use of the standard. This bus was originally designed to transfer 8 *megabits per second* (Mbps). This was done using 8-bit paths, which worked well in the 8086 and 8088 CPUs which could only handle 8 bits at once. When the 80286 was released, there became a need for 16-bit cards. At that time, ISA was modified to allow 8- or 16-bit adapters. The addition of the 16-bit adapter didn't pose a problem for people who owned the 8-bit adapters because they fit in the 16-bit slots.

As processors have become faster, there have been several new bus systems introduced. However, ISA is still a popular system for devices that don't require higher than 16-bit transmissions. Printers, sound cards, and modems are all examples of equipment that still tend to use an ISA bus. Many workstations still use ISA bus NICs, however, while servers benefit from a faster bus.

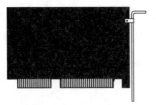

**FIGURE 3-5**    ISA network card

## *MCA*

When the 32-bit 80386 processor was introduced, there was a need for a faster bus type to end the bottleneck caused by 16-bit ISA adapters. IBM introduced *MicroChannel Architecture* (MCA) to solve this problem. In an attempt to reclaim sales lost due to the openness of the ISA standard, they decided to patent MCA. If other manufacturers wanted to use the MCA bus, they were required to pay IBM. Figure 3-6 shows a MicroChannel card. They are generally full-length cards and use small, compact connectors.

**FIGURE 3-6**    MicroChannel network card

MCA operates at 16Mbps or 32Mbps and uses software to configure the resource settings. MCA was not designed to be backward compatible with ISA, requiring people to buy new MCA adapters. Because IBM was the standard that all other PCs were judged by, many companies paid to use this better technology. Other manufacturers preferred to use open standards that didn't require them to pay IBM.

MicroChannel cards require what is known as a "Reference Disk" to be configured. This disk contains special software to help configure the card. Few MCA cards have jumpers or DIP switches to manually set configuration settings.

## *EISA*

Many companies did not agree with IBM's idea of having to license the MCA architecture. As people started buying the 386 family of computers, they started to run into the ISA bus bottleneck. While their processing power was growing, their I/O speed was not. The answer to this problem was the *Extended Industry Standard Architecture* (EISA) bus. This bus was developed by a group of industry leaders and released as an open standard. You can see the longer contacts of the EISA card in Figure 3-7 as compared to the ISA card in Figure 3-5.

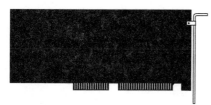

**FIGURE 3-7**   EISA network card

The EISA bus runs at 8MHz and can transmit 32 bits at a time. Although this is slightly slower than MicroChannel's speed of 10MHz, the 8MHz speed maintains compatibility with the ISA standard. EISA slots look much like ISA slots but are deeper. ISA cards can fit into them and function perfectly but do not go all the way into the slot. EISA cards have longer contacts that let them go all the way into the slot. This way, any EISA slot on a computer's main board can also be used by an ISA card.

The EISA bus also introduced another important feature, *Bus Mastering*. Bus Mastering allows a card in a computer to operate without the main CPU being involved. For example, a disk controller can read and write to a hard disk by itself without involving the CPU. Normally the CPU itself handles the transaction while putting other processes on hold. Bus Mastering greatly helps multitasking operating systems.

EISA cards are configured using software. The manufacturer of the card usually provides a small configuration utility and a disk. All settings can be made from that utility.

## VESA

A new bus was needed to enhance the existing ISA bus. Windows 3.1 was popular by then, and it was becoming apparent that the ISA bus was not fast enough for the graphics it needed, and EISA was too expensive.

The answer to this problem was the *Video Electronic Standards Association* (VESA) bus. Originally designed for video cards, it was later used for hard drive controllers and network cards. The *VESA Local Bus*, or VLB, could transfer 32 bits of information at a time, and ran at speeds of up to 40MHz, depending on the system's CPU speed. Figure 3-8 shows a VESA card. Due to the physical configuration of the card, they are all fairly long.

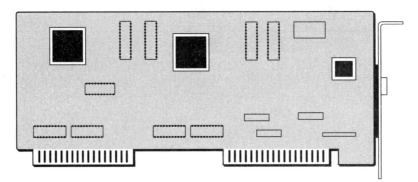

**FIGURE 3-8**  VESA network card

A limiting factor of VLB was that it had a limit of three slots on the motherboard. Another problem was that the standard was interpreted differently by different hardware vendors. It was not uncommon, especially when VESA was first introduced, to have certain adapter cards that would not work in certain computers. VLB had problems with bus speeds in excess of 40MHz. Although some motherboards claimed to support it, it was not officially supported.

## PCI

*Peripheral Component Interface*, or PCI, is a relatively new bus type. A PCI card is shown in Figure 3-9. They are usually small cards, but occasionally a full-length card can be seen.

PCI runs at up to 33MHz and can transfer 32 bits at a time. PCI was originally developed to help speed up graphics on newer computers. Most new PCI cards are software configurable and usually support the new Plug and Play standard to automatically configure the card.

PCI slots are not backward compatible with any other type. They use a small, condensed connector on the main board of the computer. One great feature of PCI is that it is not tied to any one type of computer. Computers based on the Intel line of processors, Digital Alphas, and Apple Macintosh computers all support and use PCI cards.

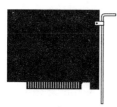

**FIGURE 3-9**   **PCI network card**

## PCMCIA

*PCMCIA*, which is an association name, not a standard name, is a new type of bus mainly for notebook and laptop computers. It stands for *Personal Computer Memory Card International Association*.

The PCMCIA v1.0 standard defines specifications for memory cards. Later, when other types of devices were needed, v2.0 of the standard was established. This allowed other devices, such as modems, disk drives, and network cards, to be used. Figure 3-10 shows the small credit card shaped PCMCIA card.

PCMCIA cards come in three different types:

o  Type I: 3.3 mm thick. Type I slots on notebooks can only use Type I cards.

o  Type II: 5 mm thick. Type II slots can use Type I and Type II cards.

o  Type III: 10.5 mm thick. This allows you to use any of the three card types. The Type III slot is basically two stacked Type II slots. With this you can either use either two Type II cards or one Type III.

**FIGURE 3-10**   PCMCIA network card

All three PCMCIA card types use the same 68-pin connector. Another great feature is that with the PCMCIA software you can insert and remove cards on-the-fly without rebooting the computer.

## Network Adapter Ports

Now you get to see how the adapter card connects to the network media. The type of connector you can use may depend on the brand of network adapter you chose or the type of network to which it is connecting.

I'll discuss the four most common connectors:

o **BNC Connector:** No one is sure what BNC stands for. A lot of the people you ask will say "British Naval Connector," but that may not be correct. BNC connectors are used in Attached Resource Computer Network (ARCNET) and in thin Ethernet (10Base-2). The connector is a small, round cylinder with two small prongs on the outside that allows a connector to attach to it. A small hole for a copper wire to go into is inside the connector. Figure 3-11 shows a *T connector*, which has three BNC connectors on it. The T connector is used to connect the network adapter to the two pieces of coaxial cable.

**FIGURE 3-11**   A T connector showing three
BNC connectors

- **RJ-45 Connector:** The RJ-45 connector looks much like a normal telephone cable connector, but larger. It uses *twisted-pair cabling* with four pairs of wires. A normal telephone jack uses an *RJ-11 connector*, which is a twisted pair with two pairs of wires.

- **DIX Connector:** These connectors are not often used anymore but were widely used when thick Ethernet was popular. DIX is a 15-pin connector with two rows of pins. A cable was attached to the NIC through this port and was attached to the thick Ethernet cable by use of a "vampire tap". The tap had to be drilled into the cable and tightened down. DIX stands for the three companies that invented it: Digital, Intel, and Xerox.

- **AUI Connector:** *Attachment Unit Interface* or AUI, is actually a renamed DIX connector. When Xerox had to release its patents and trademarks to the public domain after turning over Ethernet to the 802.3 committee, DIX was renamed. Other rival companies did not like the connector named after three rival companies.

The main use today of AUI connectors today is for external transceivers.

A network card with a couple of these connectors is shown in Figure 3-12.

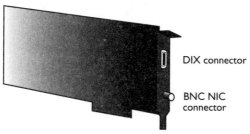

DIX connector

BNC NIC
connector

**FIGURE 3-12**  **Network card showing DIX and BNC connectors**

# BOUNDED MEDIA

Once you have the network cards installed and interfaced in your computer, you need a way to connect them to each other. The network media you use to do this can be a wire, or it can be wireless. The first network media types I discuss are wires, or *network cables*. They are referred to as *bounded media* because the signal travels through a physical media shielded on the outside (bounded) by some material. After these I will describe wireless media, or *unbounded media*.

The type of cable you use depends on different things. Does your building have existing cable? How many devices do you want to network? What speed network do you need? Which network topology (such as Ethernet, Token Ring, and so on) do you plan to use? You must consider each of these when choosing the cable type for your network. Most network protocols will run on many different cable types, unlike the older networking days when the protocol usually defined the cable.

Bounded media are made up of a central conductor (usually copper) surrounded by a jacket material. Bounded media are great for LANs because they offer high speed, good security, and low cost. However, sometimes they cannot be used due to distance limitations.

Cables differ by their properties. Depending on your needs, you may opt for one cable type over another because it has some characteristics that are more important to you. For example, coaxial cable is fairly resistant to outside interference but cannot be used for some high-speed LANs. Some of the characteristics you will look at for each cable type include the following:

- **Cost:** Cost can be an important consideration when deciding on a network cable. Only a few years ago, fiber-optic cable was extremely expensive, and almost no one could justify the cost to use it.

- **Installation:** Using the example above, one reason fiber-optic cable was so expensive was due to the installation. Only highly skilled technicians were capable of installing this cable correctly. Obviously the best situation is having someone on staff that can install the cable. If you need to get an outside contractor, the installation cost may outweigh the actual cable cost.

- **Capacity:** So you are past the cost and installation issues, and now the question is, "How fast will it go?" Normally, cable speed is referred to as *bandwidth* and is an important characteristic of a media type. Bandwidth is usually measured in *bits per second*. For example, standard Ethernet cable is usually up to 10Mbps, which is 10 *megabits per second* (notice the small *b* for bits, not *B* for Bytes).

- **Attenuation (Maximum Distance):** Depending on what you need to network together, the maximum cable distance may also be another consideration. Attenuation will be discussed more deeply in the next section.

o **Immunity to Interference:** The last property is how well the cable holds up against interference, normally *electromagnetic interference,* or EMI. EMI could play a big part in which cable type you use, depending on the location. Suppose you needed to run a network into a manufacturing facility with a lot of heavy machinery that used electrical motors. An unshielded type of cable may not be the best choice in that situation.

Three common types of bounded media are used out in the world and covered on the exam. They are:

o Coaxial

o Twisted pair

o Fiber optic

Before I discuss the cable types, you can take a quick lesson in electricity and some of its properties.

## Electrical Properties

Installing network cable can be tricky because of the way it can react to different electrical properties. The maximum speed and distance a cable can be run is also affected by these properties. To fully understand cabling, you need to know the following electrical properties:

o **Resistance:** When electricity moves through a media it meets resistance. Resistance only affects the transmission of *direct current* (DC), and it is measured in *ohms*. When more resistance is met, more electricity is lost during transmission. The resistance causes the energy to be converted to heat. Cables with small diameters have more resistance than cables with large diameters.

o **Impedance:** The loss of energy from an *alternating current* (AC) is impedance. Like resistance, it is measured in *ohms*. DC travels through the core of the wire while AC travels on the surface.

o **Noise:** Noise is a serious problem for cabling and is sometimes hard to pinpoint. Noise can be caused by *radio interference* (RFI) or *electromagnetic interference* (EMI). Many things can cause noise in a cable. Some common causes are fluorescent lights, transformers, the power company on a bad day, and nearly anything else that creates an electrical field.

o Noise can be easy to avoid if you plan your cable installation well. Route new cable away from lights and other EMI sources, try to use shielded cabling if you can, and ground all equipment.

o Attenuation: Attenuation is the fading of the electrical signal over a distance. The above properties all affect the rate of attenuation in a cable. Eventually, devices at the other end of a cable are unable to distinguish between the real signal and induced noise after a certain distance.

o Cross Talk: Cross talk is when the signal from one cable is leaked to another by an electrical field. An electrical field is created whenever an electrical signal is sent through a wire. If two wires are close enough and do not have enough EMI protection, the signal may leak from one wire and cause noise on the other.

Now you can look at the types of cable that allow you to connect your networks.

## Coaxial Cable

Most people are familiar with some type of *coaxial cable* (*coax* for short). For example, cable TV wire is usually coaxial. Coax cable gets its name because it contains two conductors that are *parallel* to each other, or on the same axis. The center conductor in the cable is usually copper. The copper can be either a solid wire or a stranded material. Outside this central conductor is a nonconductive material. It is usually a white, plasticlike material, used to separate the inner conductor from the outer conductor. The outer conductor is a fine mesh made from copper. It is used to help shield the cable from electromagnetic interference (EMI). Outside the copper mesh is the final protective cover. Figure 3-13 shows the different layers in coaxial cable.

 tip **Coaxial cable is a good idea for a home network because it is easy to install and no hub is needed.**

The actual network data travels through the center conductor in the cable. EMI interference is caught by the outer copper mesh. Coax cable should be grounded at one end to dissipate this electrical interference. Do not ground it to a computer on the network, but to something like a wall outlet ground.

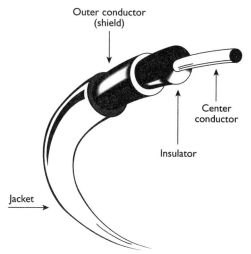

Outer conductor
(shield)

Center
conductor

Insulator

Jacket

**FIGURE 3-13** Coaxial cable

Not all types of coax cable are equal. With network coax cable being inexpensive, there is no need to skimp on this important piece of equipment. The best coax cable will use a stranded central conductor with a tight mesh outer conductor. You can easily check the cable by cutting open a small piece and investigating for yourself.

The importance of stranded wire is the ability to bend the cable. Take a piece of solid wire and bend it back and forth a few times, and what happens? It breaks. Stranded wires also do not kink as badly as a solid cable. Stranded wire does not affect the performance of the media at all.

Tightly meshed EMI protection should be obvious. The better the cover around the internal conductor, the less EMI interference it will let in.

When you go to the store to buy some coax cable, you'll see many different kinds. Which one do you buy? That depends on which type of network you plan to use. The different types of coax cable vary by *gauge* and *impedance*.

Gauge is the measure of the cable's thickness. It is measured by the *Radio-Grade measurement*, or *RG number*. The higher the RG number, the thinner the central conductor core; the lower the number, the thicker the core. So, 18-gauge wire is thicker than 24-gauge wire. How do you tell what gauge cable you have? Usually it is printed on the side of the cable, somewhere on the outer material. Look at the upcoming list to see which type of network needs which gauge of cable. For example, thin Ethernet uses RG-58. So the measurement for that on the Radio-Grade standard is 58.

The measure of resistance in the cable is called impedance. Just like the RG number, each different type of network uses a different resistance. The essential point to remember about the impedance is that each piece of equipment attaching to the cable must use the same impedance. This means all NICs, terminators, and cable segments must be the same. It is common to see the wrong type terminator on a cable. Again, refer to the following list to see which network type uses which impedance.

Here are the most common coaxial standards:

o **50-ohm RG-7 or RG-11:** Used with thick Ethernet

o **50-ohm RG-58:** Used with thin Ethernet

o **75-ohm RG-59:** Used with cable television

o **93-ohm RG-62:** Used with ARCNET

Coaxial cable is an inexpensive media to buy. It is also one of the easiest types of cable to install. It is easy to test using a multimeter, and the connector installation can be simple. Expanding a coaxial network is also easy since you can just add a new segment of cable (as long as you have not reached the maximum distance). One of the best advantages of coaxial cable is its level of protecton from EMI interference. In some circumstances, such as in a factory, most other types of cables will experience too much interference to operate properly.

The main reason that coaxial cable is not used anymore is the possibility of taking the entire segment down because of one small problem. Should one piece of coaxial cable break, the entire segment will stop working. Connectors may fail, since they are more complicated than others, also causing the network to go down.

exam preparation pointer

**For the exam, be sure to know the characteristics of coaxial cable and also the advantages and disadvantages of using coaxial cable.**

**Characteristics:**

o **Low cost**

o **Easy to install**

o **Up to 10Mbps capacity**

o **Medium attenuation**

o **Medium immunity from EMI**

Advantages of coaxial cable:

o Inexpensive

o Easy to wire

o Easy to expand

o Moderate level of EMI immunity

Disadvantage of coaxial cable:

o Single cable failure can take down an entire network

# Twisted-Pair Cabling

The most popular network cabling right now is *twisted pair*. It is lightweight, easy to install, inexpensive, and supports many different types of networks. It also supports speeds of up to 100Mbps.

Twisted-pair cabling is made up of pairs of solid or stranded copper twisted around each other. The twists are done to reduce the vulnerability to EMI and cross talk. The number of pairs in the cable depends on the type. The copper core of the cable is usually 22-AWG or 24-AWG, as measured on the *American Wire Gauge standard*.

There are two varieties of twisted-pair cabling:

o Unshielded twisted pair

o Shielded twisted pair

### *Unshielded twisted pair*

*Unshielded twisted pair* (UTP) is the more common of the two types. It can be either voice grade or data grade, depending on the application. UTP cable normally has an impedance of 100 ohms. UTP costs less than *shielded twisted pair* (STP) and is readily available due to its many uses. There are five levels of data grade cabling:

o Category 1: This category is intended for use in telephone lines and low-speed data cable.

o Category 2: Category 2 includes cabling for lower-speed networks. These can support up to 4Mbps implementations.

- **Category 3:** This is a popular category for standard Ethernet networks. These cables support up to 16Mbps but are most often used in 10Mbps Ethernet situations.
- **Category 4:** Category 4 cable is used for longer distance and higher speeds than Category 3 cable. It can support up to 20Mbps.
- **Category 5:** This cable is intended for high-performance data communications. This is the highest rating for UTP cable and can support up to 100Mbps. Any new installation of UTP should be using this cable rating for later upgrades.

UTP data cable consists of two or four pairs of twisted cables. Cable with two pairs use RJ-11 connectors, and four-pair cables use RJ-45 connectors.

UTP cable for networks is installed in much the same way as a telephone cabling project. A small cable known as a *patch cable* is used to connect the user's workstation to an RJ-45 network jack in their office. The cable from the wall jack runs to a *punchdown block* in a wiring closet. These are similar to the punchdown blocks used by telephone systems you see in your telco closet. From the punch-down block the cables run to a *patch panel*. A patch panel is a set of jacks that allow the administrator to connect the individual wall jack cables to a network device such as a hub or router. Because of the similarity to telephone wiring, many cable installers can now do both at once, which saves some trouble.

UTP has a good capacity. It can currently support up to 100Mbps using Category 5 cable. The most common type used is 10Mbps, usually with Category 3 cable. Should you install new cable, be sure to use Category 5 in case you ever plan to upgrade to 100Mbps. While the idea of having 100Mbps to the desktop may sound extreme today, it won't in a few years.

With its ease of installation and its high speed, why would you not use UTP? First, its distance is limited to a relatively short distance due to attenuation. Also, remember that it is unshielded, so EMI interference could be a large problem. Under normal office LAN implementations, these disadvantages are usually not problems.

Unshielded twisted pair is the most common type of network cable seen today for many reasons. Since it has a similar installation routine as normal telephone cable, finding someone to wire your network is easy and inexpensive. The promise of higher speeds is also another factor that makes people want to use UTP. Category 5 UTP enables transmission rates as fast as 100Mbps. This gives your current 10Mbps network a real boost when it is needed later. Probably the best characteristic of a UTP network is the fact that a single media failure only brings down one workstation. Since UTP networks are normally configured in a star topology, only the "leg" of the star is affected by the failure.

UTP cable, since it is unshielded, is susceptible to electromagnetic interference. This may limit its use in environments with a lot of machinery. The maximum distance that UTP can run is also shorter than other cable types.

exam
preparation
pointer

**For the exam, be sure to know the characteristics of UTP and also the advantages and disadvantages of using UTP.**

**Characteristics of UTP:**

o  **Low cost (but slightly higher than coaxial).**

o  **Easy to install**

o  **High speed capacity**

o  **High attenuation**

o  **Susceptible to EMI**

o  **100 meter limit**

**Advantages of UTP:**

o  **Easy installation**

o  **Capable of high speeds for LANs**

o  **Low cost**

**Disadvantage of UTP:**

o  **Short distances due to attenuation**

## Shielded twisted pair

*Shielded twisted pair* (STP) is mainly used in *Token Ring*, which is covered in Chapter 4. It is similar to UTP but has a mesh shielding that protects it from EMI, which allows for higher transmission rates and longer distances without errors.

IBM has defined different levels for STP cable similar to the categories of UTP cable.

o  Type 1: Type I STP features two pairs of 22-AWG, with each pair foil wrapped inside another foil sheath that has a wire braid ground.

o  Type 2: This type includes Type 1 with four telephone pairs sheathed to the outside to allow one cable to an office for both voice and data.

- **Type 6:** This type features two pairs of stranded, shielded 26-AWG to be used for patch cables.
- **Type 7:** This type of STP consists of one pair of stranded, 26-AWG wire.
- **Type 9:** Two pairs of shielded 26-AWG, used for data, comprise this type of cable.

The big disadvantage for STP cable is the cost. Because STP is almost exclusively used with IBM's Token Ring and not mass produced for other uses besides data networking, it has a higher cost than UTP.

Installation of STP is also harder than that of UTP. STP uses a ground wire to dissipate the EMI that it collects, as well as connectors that are more proprietary.

The good news is, due to the shielding, you can have higher bandwidth rates than UTP. The bad news is, since STP is used almost exclusively with Token Ring, it normally has a bandwidth of 16Mbps.

The extra shielding does not really help the attenuation problem with twisted-pair cabling.

Shielded twisted pair alleviates some disadvantages of UTP. First, it has shielding which reduces the effect of EMI. STP is also capable of speeds up to 16Mbps, which is faster than the maximum of 10Mbps for Category 3 UTP.

While STP has some advantages over UTP, it also has disadvantages. It is more expensive than UTP and coaxial cable. Because of the extra bulk of the shielding, it is also harder to install. One characteristic it shares with UTP is the attenuation problem that lets it be used only for short distances.

exam preparation pointer

**For the exam, be sure to know the characteristics of STP and also the advantages and disadvantages of using STP.**

**Characteristics of STP:**

- **Medium cost**
- **Ease of installation is medium due to grounding and connectors.**
- **Higher capacity than UTP**
- **High attenuation, but the same as UTP**
- **Medium immunity from EMI**
- **100-meter limit**

**Advantages of STP:**

- **Shielded**

- Faster than UTP and coaxial

**Disadvantages of STP:**

- More expensive than UTP and coaxial
- More difficult installation
- High attenuation rate

# Fiber–Optic Cable

*Fiber-optic cable* is not like the others I have discussed. Instead of using electrical signals to transmit data, it uses *light*. The discussion of fiber-optic cable can quickly get complex. I will go over the basics of this new media. This should be enough so that you are familiar with it and prepared for any question that may arise.

In a fiber cable, light only moves in one direction. For a two-way communication to take place, a second connection must be made between the two devices, which why when you examine fiber cable you notice it is actually two strands of cable. Each strand is responsible for one direction of communication. A laser at one device sends pulses of light through this cable to the other device. These pulses are translated into 1's and 0's at the other end.

The light contained inside the fiber cable cannot escape. No electrical fields are created around the cable, so you could run a bundle of fiber together with no ill effects.

In the center of the fiber cable is a glass strand, or *core*. The light from the laser travels through this glass to the other device. Around the internal core is a reflective material known as *cladding*. No light escapes the glass core because of this reflective cladding. Fiber-optic cable was extremely expensive a few years ago. Gladly, its price has dropped substantially in the years since, and it is becoming much more common in networks today. Most of the cost of a fiber-optic network is for the installation. I have yet to see any books detail the installation of fiber-optic media. At this time the only way to learn about installation is to go to a class, usually lasting a few days with a lot of hands-on learning time.

What do you get for the high cost of installation and cable? High speeds and distances, of course. Fiber-optic cable currently has a bandwidth of more than 2Gbps. That is no typo, that is *gigabits per second*. It is very high speed, indeed.

As stated above, you could run a fiber-optic cable tens of miles, so attenuation is not a problem. There is also no susceptibility to EMI since the transmission occurs over light, not electricity.

Fiber-optic cable comes in two flavors: *single mode* and *multimode*. Single-mode cable only allows for one light path through the cable, where multimode has many paths. Single-mode cable allows for a faster transmission time and longer distances, but of course costs more.

Single mode is normally only used for long distances, as in tens of miles. If you are just connecting nearby buildings, stick with multimode.

You will see fiber cable listed by core and cladding size. An example of this is 62.5 micron core/140 micron cladding multimode. Consult the manufacturer of your network devices to see which size you need.

As you can see, fiber-optic cable has many great advantages. Currently, most installations are using fiber-optic cable for its length capability. Fiber is the perfect media to connect buildings and campuses together. It can also be used in environments with such high EMI that no other cable will do. Now that fiber-optic cable is becoming cheaper, it is found more commonly inside the buildings that it used to just connect. The reason for this is speed. Fiber-optic cable handles speeds far greater than those at which standard LANs operate today. These high speeds hold the promise of teleconferencing and other multimedia network enhancements.

Though fiber-optic cable has dropped in price over the last few years, it is still the most expensive cable type. The installation is also still the most difficult because of the special connectors that are used. Fiber-optic installers still need to go to class to learn to properly install the cable. There is also some limitation on how much the cable can bend due to the light reflected inside.

exam preparation pointer

**For the Networking Essentials exam, be sure to know the characteristics of fiber-optic cable and also the advantages and disadvantages of using fiber-optic cable.**

**Characteristics of fiber-optic cable:**

- **Expensive**
- **Very hard to install**
- **Capable of extremely high speeds**
- **Extremely low attenuation**
- **No EMI interference**

Advantages of Fiber-optic media:

- Fast
- Low attenuation
- No EMI interference

Disadvantages of Fiber-optic media:

- Hard to install
- Expensive

# UNBOUNDED MEDIA

*Unbounded*, or wireless, media does not use any physical connectors between the two devices communicating. Usually the transmission is sent through the atmosphere, but sometimes it can be just across a room. Wireless media is used when a physical obstruction or distance blocks the use of normal cable media.

in the
real world

**While working on deploying a large enterprise network one time, the company I was working for was faced with a problem. It was not uncommon for this company to have two offices near each other. One was usually a retail store while the other was a small administrative office or warehouse. Normally this situation was solved by using fiber-optic cable to connect them, but this time was different. The two offices were across a highway from each other. A wireless media solution was the perfect answer to this problem.**

The three main types of wireless media are *radio wave, microwave,* and *infrared.*

## Radio Waves

Radio waves have frequencies between 10KHz and 1GHz. Radio waves include the following types:

- Short-wave
- Very-high frequency (VHF) television and radio
- Ultra-high frequency (UHF) television and radio

Most radio frequencies in the US and Canada are regulated. To gain permission to use a regulated frequency can take a long time and a large amount of money. The good news is that there are some frequencies that are not regulated and anyone can use. These bands are:

- 902-928 MHz

- 2.4GHz (internationally unregulated)

- 5.72-5.85 GHz

The problem with unregulated frequencies is that they can get saturated. To ease this, there have been limits set on the amount of power that devices can broadcast in these frequencies. While letting more people use the frequencies, this cuts down on the usable range.

There are several different types of antennas to choose from. Some are shown in Figure 3-14. Radio waves can also be broadcast omnidirectionally or in one certain direction.

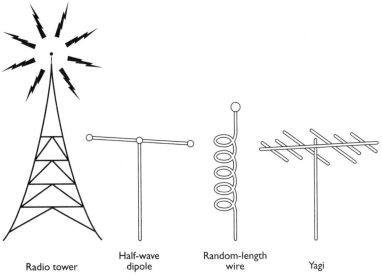

| Radio tower | Half-wave dipole | Random-length wire | Yagi |

**FIGURE 3-14**   **Radio antennas**

Radio wave transmissions can be divided into these three categories:

- Low power, single frequency

- o High power, single frequency
- o Spread spectrum

### *Low power, single frequency*

As the name suggests, this system transmits on one frequency and has low power output. The normal operating range on these type of devices is 20–25 meters. This is generally the cheapest wireless media type, although the price can increase if more complicated and advanced equipment is needed.

Installation can be either simple or more complex, depending on the equipment purchased. Some devices come preconfigured and are simple to install. Other, more custom installations may need a trained technician to do the fine-tuning.

The speed of these units can vary from 1Mbps to 10Mbps, which is about perfect for a small LAN. Attenuation is a problem with these devices due to the low power output that is allowed.

EMI could be a very large problem because of other devices that operate on the same frequencies. Other equipment such as electric motors may also inadvertently produce radio frequencies in your network device's range, causing even more noise-induced problems.

Although they do not have much range, low-power, single-frequency operations do have some benefits. Imagine using it in an office where everyone has a notebook or portable computer. There would be no need for cables or other networking devices.

### *High power, single frequency*

While similar to low power, single frequency, these devices can communicate over greater distances. Transmissions can be either line of sight or bounced off the atmosphere for longer distances. Networks based on this technique would be useful to a mobile sales force or others who travel frequently.

Along with higher power, you get higher costs. Installation is not as easy as with the low-power units, either. High-power, single-frequency waves are also susceptible to EMI.

Characteristics of high power, single frequency:

- o Moderate cost
- o Easier to Install than low-power solutions

- 1Mbps to 10Mbps capacity
- Low attenuation for long distances
- Low immunity to EMI

### Spread spectrum

Spread spectrum systems use several frequencies at once to provide reliable data transmissions that are resistant to interference. Using multiple frequencies ensures more secure transmissions. *Direct-sequence modulation* and *frequency-hopping* are two methods used in spread spectrum communications.

Direct-sequence modulation breaks data into chips and transmits the chips across several frequencies. The receiver knows which data to collect on the different frequencies and assembles the data accordingly. False data can be transmitted to confuse any possible eavesdroppers. To reconstruct the data, the listener would have to know which frequencies to monitor and which data was false. Direct-sequence modulation provides 2–6Mbps transmission rates and operates in unregulated frequencies.

Frequency-hopping uses strict timing to switch frequencies. Both the sender and the receiver are set to change frequencies at a specific time. Bursts of data are sent on one frequency, and then the machines switch to another frequency for the next data burst. It is difficult for unauthorized persons to monitor these transmissions without knowing the timing scheme. This improved security has a price. Frequency-hopping networks achieve a maximum transmission rate of 2Mbps.

exam preparation pointer

**For the Networking Essentials exam, you should be able to compare the types of unbounded media.**

**Characteristics of low power, single frequency:**

- **Low cost for wireless media**
- **Simple installation with preconfigured equipment**
- **1Mbps to 10Mbps capacity**
- **High attenuation, which can limit range to 25 meters**
- **Low immunity to EMI**

**Characteristics of high power, single frequency:**

- **Moderate cost for wireless media**
- **Easier installation than low-power solutions**

- 1Mbps to 10Mbps capacity
- Low attenuation for long distances
- Low immunity to EMI

Characteristics of spread spectrum:

- Moderate cost
- Simple to moderate installation
- 2–6Mbps capacity
- High attenuation
- Moderate immunity to EMI

# Microwaves

Microwaves travel at higher frequencies than radio waves and provide better throughput as a wireless network media. Microwave transmissions require the sender to be within sight of the receiver. These systems use licensed frequencies, which makes them more costly than radio wave systems. Microwaves are utilized on the following two types of communication systems:

- Terrestrial
- Satellite

### Terrestrial microwave

Terrestrial microwave transmissions are used to transmit wireless signals across a few miles. These systems are often used to cross roads or other barriers that make cable connections difficult. Terrestrial systems require that direct parabolic antennas be pointed at each other. Relay towers can be used as repeaters to extend the distance of the transmission. These systems operate in the low gigahertz range and require licensed frequencies. Installation can be difficult because terrestrial microwave transmissions require that the antennas have a clear line of sight.

### Satellite microwave

Satellite microwave transmissions are used to transmit signals throughout the world. These systems use satellites in orbit about 50,000 kilometers (km) above the earth. Satellite dishes are used to send the signal to the satellite where it is then sent back down to the receiver's satellite. These transmissions also use directional parabolic antennas within line-of-site. The large distances the signals travel can cause propagation delays. These delays vary from under a second to several seconds. These delays are roughly the same for transmissions down the street as for transmissions across the world. This equipment is expensive and quite complicated. Launching a satellite into orbit is a task beyond many organizations. These systems can provide average bandwidth but lack advanced security and protection from interference. These systems can provide a good bandwidth connection to link LANs across the world, but this capability comes with (literally) a hefty price.

# Infrared

Infrared frequencies are just below visible light. These high frequencies allow high-speed data transmissions. This technology is similar to the use of a remote control for a television. Infrared transmissions can be affected by objects obstructing the sender or receiver and by interference from light sources. These systems are immune to electromagnetic interference and can be used successfully where certain types of cable media fail. These transmissions fall into the following categories:

o Point-to-point

o Broadcast

## *Point-to-point*

Point-to-point infrared transmissions utilize highly focused beams to transfer signals directly between two systems. Many laptop systems and PDAs (personal data assistants) use point-to-point transmissions. Point-to-point systems require direct alignment between devices. Point-to-point can provide an alternative to terrestrial microwave as well. If two buildings have direct line-of-site availability, point-to-point can utilize high-power infrared beams. This does not require an FCC license and is immune to EMI. These systems are susceptible to interference from anything that can block the path of the beam. This provides a high level of security, as any attempt to interfere with the beam would be noticeable. One must be careful when working with high-power laser beams, as they can cause damage to eye and skin tissue.

## *Broadcast*

Broadcast infrared transmissions use a *spread signal*, one broadcast in all directions, instead of a direct beam. This helps to reduce the problems of proper alignment and obstructions. It also allows multiple receivers of a signal. Some systems utilize a single broadcast transceiver to communicate with many devices. This type of system is easy to install. Broadcast infrared transmissions operate in the same frequencies as point-to-point infrared and are susceptible to interference from light sources. The drawback of this system is that the diffused signal reduces transmission rates to 1Mbps. This system overcomes some of the problems of point-to-point transmissions, but the trade-off is a decrease in speed.

exam preparation pointer

Again, for the Networking Essentials exam, you should be able to compare the types of infrared frequencies.

Characteristics of terrestrial microwave:

- Moderate to high cost
- Moderately difficult installation
- 1–10Mbps capacity
- Variable attenuation
- Low immunity to EMI

Satellite microwave characteristics:

- High cost
- Extremely difficult and complex installation
- 1–10Mbps capacity
- Variable attenuation
- Low immunity to EMI

Point-to-point infrared characteristics:

- Wide range of costs
- Moderately easy installation
- 100Kbps–16Mbps capacity
- Variable attenuation
- High immunity to EMI

**Broadcast infrared characteristics:**

o  Inexpensive

o  Simple installation

o  1Mbps capacity

o  Variable attenuation

o  Moderate immunity to EMI

# DATA TRANSMISSION

Now that you have learned the function of the different media types, when each is best suited, and the considerations for use, I will take the next step and discuss transmission methods.

Data transmissions across the network can occur in two forms, either analog or digital. *Analog* signals exist in an infinite number of values. Just like an analog watch, in which the hands glide across the seconds and minutes, there are many time values displayed. *Digital* signals exist in a finite number of values. Digital watches display the time down to the second or fraction of a second, but these values are always displayed as definite amounts. Analog transmissions are displayed using a sine graph in which the signal slopes from one value to another; as a value increases from 0 to 1, it becomes every value along the way. Digital transmissions are displayed using a graph in which the change from one value to another is instant; the value changes instantly from 1 to 0.

Figure 3-15 shows an example of a digital and analog signal.

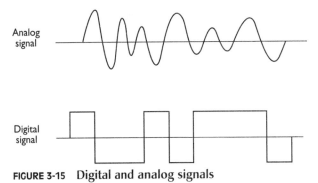

Analog
signal

Digital
signal

**FIGURE 3-15**  **Digital and analog signals**

# Analog Signaling

An analog signal takes the form of a *wave*, which smoothly curves from one value to the next. The analog wave starts at zero, increases to its high peak, recedes past zero to its low peak, and then rises back to zero. This change in the wave is known as the *wave cycle*.

Characteristics of an analog signal include amplitude, frequency, and phase. The *amplitude* is the signal strength and is measured as the distance from the zero baseline to the high peak. Amplitude is measured in several forms depending on the signal type. *Amps* are the measurements used for electric current; sound and light are measured in decibels. *Frequency* is the time it takes the signal to complete its cycle. Frequency is measured in *Hertz*. *Phase* is determined by comparing the cycles of two signals of the same frequency. Phase is measured in degrees. When two signals differ by 180 degrees, this is known as a *phase change*. Each of these characteristics can be used to encode data in an analog signal. The following list shows the different methods by which data is encoded into the analog signal. Different characteristics of the signal can be changed to show different data bits.

o **Amplitude Shift Keying (ASK):** This method of encoding uses amplitude to represent data. Strong amplitude can signify one value while low amplitude signifies another. An example is high amplitude representing 1 and low amplitude representing 0. Figure 3-16 shows an example of amplitude shift keying.

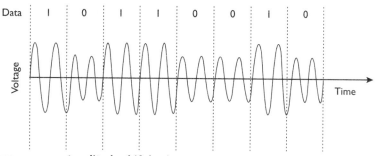

**FIGURE 3-16**   **Amplitude shift keying**

o Frequency Shift Keying (FSK): This method of encoding allows the frequency to represent a data value. For example, FSK uses one frequency to represent 1 and another frequency to represent 0. Figure 3-17 shows an example of frequency shift keying.

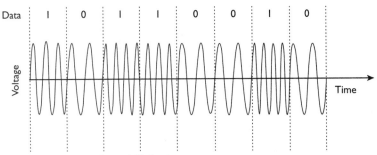

**FIGURE 3-17**  **Frequency shift keying**

o Phase Shift Keying (PSK): In this method, a change (or absence of change) can present a data value. For example, a phase change can represent 1, while the absence of a phase change can represent 0. Figure 3-18 shows an example of phase shift keying.

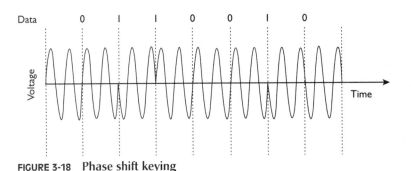

**FIGURE 3-18**  **Phase shift keying**

exam
preparation
pointer

**Be sure to know the advantages of analog signaling for the Networking Essentials exam.**

**Advantages of analog signaling:**

o **Allows multiple transmissions across the cable**

o **Suffers less from attenuation**

Disadvantages of analog signaling:

o Suffers from EMI and noise

o Can only be transmitted in one direction without sophisticated equipment

# Digital Signaling

Unlike analog signals where there is a smooth curve, *digital signals* jump directly to the next value. For example, if the voltage changed from -5 V to 0 V, it would change instantly, not drop off with a curve. When digital signals can exist in only one of two values, they go directly to the next value, typically changing between 0 and 1. The jump from one value to another is known as a *transition*. In digital signaling, transitions give a notched appearance to the graph. Digital signals are synchronized in bits which can be clocked by either sending a separate clocking scheme across the network with the bits, or by using a guaranteed state-change clocking scheme. Data rate is measured in *bits per second* (bps). Also known as *hertz* or *baud*, this rate is sometimes called *baud rate*. Encoding data in a digital signal can be done using several encoding types. The different encoding types can be described as either state-transition encoding or current-state encoding.

*State-transition encoding* uses a change (or lack of a change) in a signal to represent a data value. One way this is done is to let a change in voltage represent a 1. Whenever the voltage changes this is translated to a 1; if the voltage remains the same, the value is a 0. State-transition could also allow that a change in voltage represents a specific value. When the voltages changes from high to low this represents a 1, while a change from low to high represents a 0. State-transition encoding is used in several encoding schemes including:

o **Manchester:** Ethernet utilizes Manchester encoding, which uses a low-to-high or high-to-low mid-bit transition to represent data values.

o **Differential Manchester:** This encoding scheme also uses mid-bit transitions; however, here they are used for clocking. Data is represented by the presence of a transition at the beginning of the bit. Token Ring LANs utilize Differential Manchester.

o **Non-Return-to-Zero:** This scheme is similar to Differential Manchester in that it uses a transition at the beginning of the bit to determine the value. A transition signifies one value while the lack of a transition signifies another value. This method does not use a mid-bit transition for clocking.

*Current-state encoding* is done by examining the current condition of the signal. A specific voltage can represent a specific value. When the signal is received, it is examined and then translated to its corresponding value. The value of a current-state encoded signal is not dependent on the previous value. The following encoding schemes use this method:

o **Return-to-Zero:** This example of current-state encoding translates a high voltage to one value while a low voltage represents another. Return-to-Zero includes a mid-bit transition to 0 for clocking purposes.

o **Unipolar:** This scheme of encoding data uses a 0 level to represent one value, while either a positive or a negative level represents the other value.

o **Polar:** This scheme is similar to Unipolar in that each level represents a specific value. The difference is that in Polar encoding, one of the levels doesn't have to be 0. This scheme allows for a positive and a negative level to each represent a value.

 exam preparation pointer

**Be sure to know the advantages and disadvantages of digital signaling for the Networking Essentials exam.**

**Advantages of digital signaling:**

o **Equipment is cheaper and simpler than analog equipment.**

o **Signals can be transmitted on a cable bidirectionally.**

o **Digital signals suffer less from noise and interference.**

**Disadvantages of digital signaling:**

o **Only one signal can be sent at a time.**

o **Digital signals suffer from attenuation.**

# DATA TRANSMISSION CONSIDERATIONS

There are two other considerations when discussing the transmission of data. The first is *bit synchronization*. The receiving device must know when a signal begins and ends, and how to differentiate it from other signals on the cable. The second is *multiplexing*, which uses a single high-bandwidth channel to transmit lower-bandwidth channels

# Bit Synchronization

Timing is essential if the encoding schemes are going to work. The signal must be examined at the appropriate time to determine what changes have occurred and to interpret the signal correctly. Coordinating timing between the sending device and the receiving device is known as bit synchronization. Bit synchronization can be either asynchronous or synchronous.

*Asynchronous bit synchronization* requires a start signal at the beginning of the message and a stop bit at the end of the message. When the transmission is ready to begin, the start bit is sent to synchronize clocking on the sender and receiver. The stop bit informs the receiver that the transmission has ended. When no message is being sent, there is no synchronization between devices. Asynchronous systems also use *parity* for error checking in transmissions. The parity options available for asynchronous communications are even, odd, and none. *Even parity* specifies that the sum of the bits be an even number. *Odd parity* specifies that the sum be an odd number. *None* specifies that no parity error checking be used. Parity only detects if there is a problem with one bit. If two bits are incorrect, parity will not report an error. The overhead required in asynchronous communications makes it inefficient for sending data at high speeds.

*Synchronous bit synchronization* relies on other methods to coordinate clocks on the sending and receiving devices. Synchronous communications require the sending and receiving systems to agree upon clocking systems that are continuously synchronizing the clocks. The receiver is constantly awaiting data. No start bit is used to prepare the receiver. Several methods can be used to synchronize the clocks on the sender and receiver. These methods are *guaranteed state change*, *separate clock signals*, and *oversampling*.

o **Guaranteed State Change:** Guaranteed state change is the method used often with digital signals. In this method, the clocking scheme is embedded in the data signal, which guarantees that the devices stay synchronized. Guaranteed state change uses regular changes in the voltage to clock the signal. The receiver is expecting the changes and is continually adjusting its clock.

o **Separate Clock Signals:** This method sends data over one wire and the clocking signal over a separate wire. This method is inefficient in the use of available bandwidth. It is most often used in short-distance transmissions such as printing over parallel cable.

○ **Oversampling:** In oversampling, the receiver samples the signal ten times faster than the sending rate. One of the samplings provides data information and the others verify that the clocks are synchronized. With this method, no clocking transition is sent with the data. The sending system doesn't have to include a clocking system and can send straight data signals. However, this method requires the receiver to work much harder to maintain the clocking system.

Some situations require multiple signals to travel across the cable at once, while others may only need one signal at a time. The two different methods of utilizing the cable are *baseband* and *broadband*.

### Baseband transmissions

A transmission of data across network cable has limited *bandwidth,* or capacity. There are two ways of utilizing bandwidth: baseband and broadband transmissions. Baseband transmissions use the entire bandwidth to transmit one signal at a time. The signals can be bidirectional. This method is frequently used in LANs, which use digital signaling to transmit data, but it can be used with analog signaling, as well. Baseband has a limit of 2 km in cable length. Repeaters are often used to extend the distance. A repeater is a device that removes any distortion in the signal and retransmits it.

### Broadband transmissions

Broadband transmissions utilize bandwidth by dividing it into channels. This allows for multiple transmissions at once. Broadband is less susceptible to attenuation and can transmit further than baseband transmissions. The drawback with this method is that transmissions can occur only in one direction. Fortunately, there are ways to overcome this. A *dual-cable configuration* uses one cable to transmit and another to receive. The *split configuration* uses the same cable but different frequencies to transmit signals in both directions. Broadband transmissions are used only by analog signals.

exam
preparation
pointer

**Baseband and broadband will be contrasted on the Networking Essentials exam. Remember that baseband uses a single digital signal that can be transmitted bidirectionally. Broadband can send multiple analog signals at once in only one direction.**

# Multiplexing

In data transmission, you must also consider multiplexing. This is a method of using a single high-bandwidth channel to transmit many lower-bandwidth channels. Many low-bandwidth channels can also be combined to provide a single high-bandwidth channel for transmitting signals. A *Multiplexer/Demultiplexer* (MUX) is the hardware device that allows the channels to be joined and separated. Both broadband and baseband transmissions can benefit from this technique. A commonly known use of this technique is cable TV. Many channels are sent across one cable. The channel changer on the cable box is a demultiplexer that separates the signal. The multiplexing method used depends on whether the transmission is broadband or baseband. These two types of multiplexing are:

o **Frequency-Division Multiplexing (FDM):** This method is used in broadband transmissions to transmit analog signals. The channels are on different frequencies with an area of unused frequency ranges separating them. These unused ranges are known as *guardbands,* and they prevent interference from other channels. This is the form of multiplexing used in cable TV systems.

o **Time-Division Multiplexing (TDM):** TDM uses time slots to separate channels. Each device is given a time slot to transmit using the entire available bandwidth. This is the only technique that can be used to provide multiple channels on a baseband line. There are two types of TDM.

   The two types of time-division multiplexing are:

   o **Synchronous Time-Division Multiplexing:** All the time slots are the same length, and if there is no traffic in a time slot, the bandwidth goes unused.

   o **Statistical Time-Division Multiplexing:** This method utilizes time slots more efficiently by allotting time based on how busy a channel is. As a channel gets busy, more bandwidth is allotted. This method requires expensive equipment known as *Stat MUXes.*

# KEY POINT SUMMARY

The following list outlines what you've covered in this chapter.

o *Network adapters* allow your computers to communicate on the network

o *NDIS* and *ODI drivers* let you use more than one protocol at a time.

- The *ISA bus* transfers 16 bits at a time at up to 8MHz.

- The *MCA bus* transfers 32 bits at a time at up to 10MHz.

- The *EISA bus* transfers 32 bits at a time at up to 8MHz.

- *PCI* is a new bus type that transfers 32 bits at a time at up to 33MHz.

- *PCMCIA* are small cards meant for use in notebook computers.

- *VESA* is an inexpensive bus capable of delivering 32 bits at a time at up to 40MHz.

- *IRQs, DMAs, I/O addresses,* and *shared memory ranges* are all configurable settings on a network adapter and must be unique throughout the computer.

- You can use *hardware jumpers, DIP switches,* or *software* to configure a network card.

- *Resistance, impedance, noise, attenuation,* and *cross talk* must all be considered when choosing a cable type.

- *Coaxial* cable is inexpensive and easy to wire. It has a moderate EMI immunity, but a single cable failure can take down an entire network.

- *Unshielded twisted-pair* (UTP) cable has a low cost and is capable of high speed. It is susceptible to EMI and has a high rate of attenuation.

- *Shielded twisted-pair* cable has a higher cost than UTP but has better EMI immunity.

- *Fiber-optic* cable uses glass and light to transmit data instead of copper and electrical signals.

- *Low-power, single-frequency radio waves* have a low cost, and speeds range from 1Mbps up to 10Mbps. Range is limited to about 25 meters.

- *High-power, single-frequency radio waves* have a higher cost for the same speed, but the range is greatly expanded.

- *Data signaling* uses cheaper and simpler equipment than analog.

- Data signals can be transmitted bidirectionally on the same cable, though only one signal can be sent at a time.

- Digital signaling suffers from *attenuation* worse than analog.

- *Multiple analog signals* can be sent over a single cable at once.

- Analog suffers from *EMI* and *noise interference*.

- *Multiplexing* allows multiple signals to be sent over one digital media.

# APPLYING WHAT YOU'VE LEARNED

Now it's time again to regroup, review, and apply what you've learned in this chapter about network media. The questions in the Instant Assessment section bring to mind key facts and concepts. The Critical Thinking labs provide you with an opportunity to apply the knowledge you've gained in this chapter about network media.

note 
Critical Thinking labs challenge you to apply your understanding of the material to solve a hypothetical problem. The questions are scenario-based, requiring you to decide "why" or "how" or to devise a solution to a problem. You might need to be at a computer to work through some of these labs.

concept link 
Refer to the "Hardware and Software You'll Need" section in the Preface or in Appendix B if you're not sure you have the necessary equipment to do the Critical Thinking labs.

## Instant Assessment

1. Which type of network adapter driver is used by the Microsoft Windows NT operating system?

   **a.** ODI

   **b.** NDIS

   **c.** MAC

   **d.** Network driver

2. MCA was developed by IBM to overcome the limitations associated with:

   **a.** EISA

   **b.** PCI

   **c.** ISA

   **d.** VESA

3. Which type of resource allows your adapter to work directly with the computer's memory?

   **a.** IRQ

   **b.** I/O

**c.** Shared memory address

**d.** DMA

4. Which type of adapter is used with UTP cable?

**a.** BNC

**b.** RJ-45

**c.** AUI

**d.** DIX

5. Electrical signals are not susceptible to which problem?

**a.** Cross talk

**b.** Noise

**c.** Attenuation

**d.** Refraction

6. Which type of cable is used in most home cable television systems?

**a.** Coaxial

**b.** UTP

**c.** STP

**d.** Fiber optic

7. Which of the following is an example of unbounded network media?

**a.** Fiber optic

**b.** Coaxial

**c.** Unshielded twisted pair

**d.** Infrared

8. Token Ring networks use which encoding scheme?

**a.** Return-to-Zero

**b.** Unipolar

**c.** Differential Manchester

**d.** Manchester

**9.** Which type of encoding isn't used by analog signaling?

   **a.** Amplitude Shift Keying

   **b.** Frequency Shift Keying

   **c.** Phase Shift Keying

   **d.** Unipolar

**10.** Which of the following is used to measure coax cable?

   **a.** Gauge

   **b.** Ohm

   **c.** Impedance

   **d.** EMI

**T/F**

**11.** ODI drivers are used by Novell NetWare. _____

**12.** ISA slots are capable of supporting 8- or 16-bit adapters. _____

**13.** Notebook computers may support Types I, II, and III PCMCIA adapters. _____

**14.** Coax cable is expensive due to the complex technology that provides high transfer rates. _____

**15.** Category 3 UTP is capable of supporting 100Mbps transfers. _____

**16.** Fiber-optic cable has a bandwidth of more than 2Gbps. _____

**17.** The use of radio waves can require a special FCC license. _____

**18.** Multiplexing uses a single high-bandwidth channel to transmit many low-bandwidth channels. _____

**19.** Multimode fiber-optic cable is capable of greater distances than single-mode cable. _____

**20.** Coax cable uses BNC connectors. _____

concept link **For answers to these Instant Assessment questions, see Appendix C.**

# Critical Thinking Labs

The following Critical Thinking labs provide you with a practical opportunity to apply the knowledge you've gained in this chapter about network media.

### Lab 3.1 *Overcoming network hardware bottlenecks*

You have just added another fifty clients to your network, and now your server seems to be acting sluggish. You run some tests on the server and find that the CPU can handle the load fine, as can the hard drive subsystem. You pinpoint the bottleneck to be in the network card. Further investigating shows a normal 16-bit ISA network adapter. Which adapter type could you replace it with to improve performance? What factors might influence your decision?

### Lab 3.2 *Managing network card resources*

You are trying to install a network card into a computer with the following hardware: COM1, COM2, LPT1, PS/2 mouse, and an IDE hard drive controller. The NIC supports IRQs 3, 4, 5, 7, and 10. Which IRQ(s) could you use?

### Lab 3.3 *Deciding the correct cable type*

You are consulted to install new network cabling into a building. The building turns out to be a manufacturing center with a lot of heavy equipment in it. EMI could definitely become a problem. Another requirement is to be able to connect the new wiring to the existing administration office 400 yards away. Which cable should you use? Why would you not use the other cable types?

### Lab 3.4 *Troubleshooting drivers*

You are attempting to load a second protocol onto a computer on your network. For some reason the protocol will not bind to the network card. What might you surmise about the driver that the card is using?

### Lab 3.5 *Crossing a highway*

Your company has just purchased a new building. The new building is directly across a busy interstate from the existing building. An unbounded network media is required to cross the road. Security and speed are major factors to consider, and the company is not interested in acquiring special licenses. Which media would you choose and why?

 **For answers to these labs, see Appendix C.**

concept link

# Network Designs

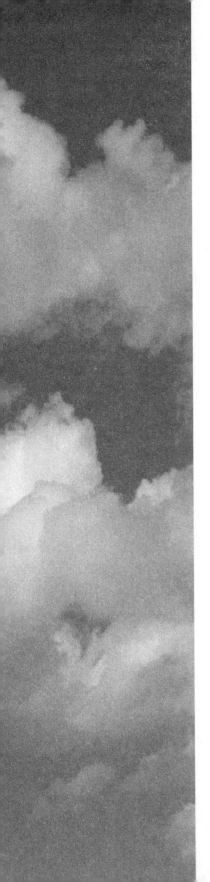

# About Chapter 4

Now that you have learned about the OSI model and its implementations, you can move on to the physical layouts of different network types. This chapter covers network designs, including the topologies and network types used in modern networks. This chapter helps you understand how standards and components combine to create a network.

First you will learn about the four ways you can physically connect your network. The method you choose depends on which type of network you install. You will then learn how these connections are implemented on ARCNET, Ethernet, Token Ring, and FDDI networks.

You will learn about the different variations of these networks. The variations can call for different cable, speed, and topologies. By the end of the chapter, you will be able to describe the standards used in each network type. Given certain criteria, you will be able to determine which network should be used. The material in this chapter is crucial for passing the certification test and is important when implementing a network in the real world.

# PHYSICAL TOPOLOGIES

The way devices on the network are physically connected is known as the *topology*. Topology can include such aspects as the transmission media, adapters, and physical design of the network. Topologies specify which of these devices are used to connect systems on the network. The four main topologies are bus, star, ring and mesh. There are pros and cons for each type of topology, and careful consideration should be used when choosing which type of network to install. The characteristics of your topology determine how the network functions and affects aspects such as installation and troubleshooting of the network. I will explore the layout and components of the four topologies before I discuss the network types that implement them.

# Bus

The *bus* topology is the simplest to install. All devices on the network are connected to one primary trunk cable, as shown in Figure 4-1. The bus topology is a passive technology that requires no special equipment to amplify or regenerate the signal, although amplification can be used to extend the signal. Bus topology is typically used with a contention network. When a device wants to transmit across the bus, it has to determine whether the media is in use. If no other device is transmitting, the signal is sent. Each device receives the signal and then determines whether its address matches that of the recipient. Messages that weren't addressed to the device are disregarded. When dealing with bus networks, it is important to pay careful attention to termination. Each end of the trunk cable needs to be properly terminated. Without termination the signal will bounce back down the cable causing collisions. Bus topologies use coaxial cable. The sections are connected with BNC connectors. T connectors are often used to connect the computer to the trunk cable. The T connector can connect the computer to two sections of cable with the bus extending in both directions. The end devices on the bus have terminators on one connector of the T.

**FIGURE 4-1**  A network set up using bus topology

 **Be sure that you know the advantages and disadvantages of using each of the four topologies for the exam.**

The advantages of using bus include:

o  Easy to install and configure

o  Inexpensive

o  Easily extended

The disadvantages of using bus include:

o Performance degradation

o Weakened signal

o difficult troubleshooting

# Star

The *star* topology uses a separate cable for each workstation, as shown in Figure 4-2. The cable connects the workstation to a central device, typically a *hub*. This configuration provides a more reliable network that is easily expanded. With the star, there is no central point of failure in the cable. If there is a problem with the cable, only the station connected to that cable is affected. To add more workstations, simply connect another hub.

Hubs can be used as more than just a central connection device. When a workstation wishes to transmit, it sends a signal to the hub. How the hub handles the message can vary according to the network and the hub type. A *passive hub* is used to connect computers in a broadcast network. The signal sent to a passive hub is sent to all workstations with no regeneration or amplification. Passive hubs are simple devices that require no external power. One example of a passive hub is a patch panel in a wiring closet. An *active hub* uses an external power source and regenerates the signal before sending it out to all workstations in a broadcast network. Active hubs can be connected while passive hubs typically aren't. Because the active hub regenerates the signal, greater cable distances are allowed. Certain active hubs are capable of switching. A *switched hub* directs the signal directly to the recipient. Switched hubs can greatly reduce network traffic. The more features a hub has, the more inexpensive it becomes. Active hubs also contain diagnostic features to aid in network troubleshooting.

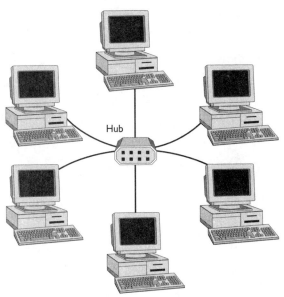

FIGURE 4-2    A network set up with star topology

exam
preparation
pointer  You are likely to see questions about the four topologies on the exam, so be sure to review the advantages of using star.

Advantages of the star topology include:

o  Easily expanded

o  Easier to troubleshoot

o  Multiple cable types supported by hubs

The disadvantages of using star include:

o  Hub failure

o  Requires more cable

o  May require a device to rebroadcast signals across the network

## Ring

The *ring* topology looks like the bus topology with connected ends. Rings differ greatly from the bus in *function*. Ring networks provide high performance for a large number of users. Data flow on a ring network travels from computer to computer in one direction, as shown in Figure 4-3. The signal is actually retransmitted by each system when passed on to its neighbor. This provides a reliable signal that can travel a large network. *Token passing* is frequently used on the ring topology. With this system, a token is passed around the network. The workstation that has control of the token can transmit data. The data travels the ring to its destination. The destination device returns an acknowledgment to the sender. The token is then given to another device, giving it the ability to transmit. This happens much quicker than it sounds, and creates a high-speed, orderly network. Ring networks using the token-passing media access method can provide many advantages over a star or bus for a large network. Because the signal is regenerated by each system, it can travel a longer distance without degrading. Token passing helps to create an orderly network where every device has an opportunity to transmit. Under heavy loads, this provides a smoother functioning network than those using a contention system involving collisions.

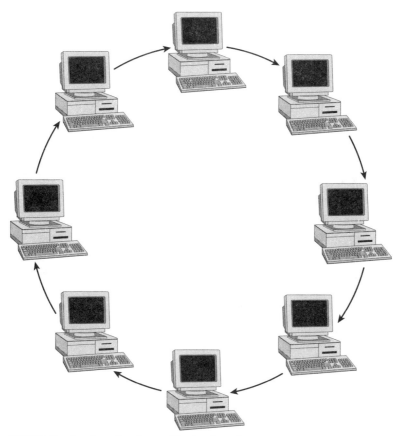

**FIGURE 4-3**   A network set up with ring topology

Again, be sure that you know the differences between the four topologies for the exam.

Advantages of using ring include:

o It provides an orderly network in which every device has access to the token and can transmit.

o It performs well under a heavy load.

The disadvantages of using ring include:

o Malfunctioning workstations and cables create problems for the entire network.

o Changes made when adding or removing a device affect the entire network.

## Mesh

The *mesh* topology provides the highest level of fault tolerance. A true mesh network uses separate cables to connect each device to every other device on the network, providing a straight communications path, as shown in Figure 4-4. This requires a large amount of cable and can quickly become confusing. Few mesh networks are true mesh, instead many use a *hybrid mesh* topology. These hybrids utilize star, ring, or bus topologies with redundant links for added fault tolerance, as shown in Figure 4-5. Because there is a dedicated link between each system in a mesh network, it is easy to troubleshoot cable problems. If two devices can't communicate, there is no guesswork about which cable could be bad. Simply check the cable connecting the two devices. No routing is done in a true mesh network, a message is sent directly from the sender to the recipient. This provides fault tolerance because cable breaks affect only the two devices that are connected to the cable. Mesh networks do provide a high level of fault tolerance for mission-critical projects. They are just too cumbersome to be practical for more than a few stations.

For the exam, be sure to review the advantages and disadvantages of a mesh topology.

Advantages of using mesh include:

o Enhanced fault tolerance provided by redundant links

o Easy to troubleshoot

The disadvantages of using mesh include:

- Difficult to install and maintain
- Costly to provide redundant links

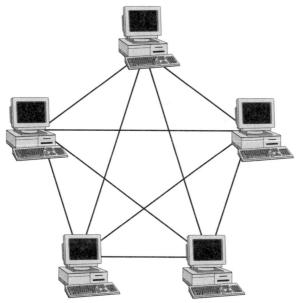

**FIGURE 4-4** True mesh network

# NETWORK TYPES

Now that you've discovered the different physical topologies most common networks use, you can move on to the different network types. Network types combine Physical layer protocols with the physical topology to form the basic network. The different types of networks I discuss in this chapter are:

- ARCNET
- Ethernet
- Token Ring
- FDDI

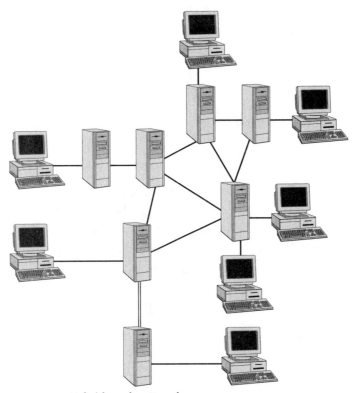

FIGURE 4-5    Hybrid mesh network

Network types are defined by many different characteristics. Maximum number of clients, speed, distance, and media access type are all defined in the network type specification. Physical topology may also be part of the specification, as some network types can only use certain physical topologies. You should consider the many factors when deciding on the correct network type for you and your organization. Costs can vary greatly between the different types, as well as speed and ease of installation.

The first network type that is covered is ARCNET. It is one of the oldest popular network types still in existence. From there you will cover the current most popular network types, consisting of Ethernet, Token Ring, and the new FDDI.

 exam
preparation
pointer

**For the exam, pay close attention to the characteristics of each type. Remember the cable type required and maximum nodes, as well as the different speeds at which the network can operate.**

# ARCNET

*ARCNET* (Attached Resource Computer Network) is the oldest network type I'll discuss. It was created in 1977 by Datapoint Corporation. ARCNET uses token passing in combination with a star/bus topology to transmit data at 2.5Mbps. ARCNET was designed to be a simple, inexpensive, and reliable topology. ARCNET can be a good solution for small LANs. Figure 4-6 illustrates an ARCNET network.

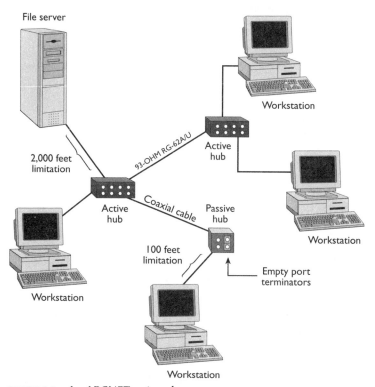

**FIGURE 4-6**  An ARCNET network

exam preparation pointer

**You might see questions on the exam about ARCNET, so be sure to review the characteristics of ARCNET networks:**

*Topology:* **Star or bus**

*Cable types:* **RG-62, 90-ohm or 93-ohm coaxial, UTP, and fiber optic**

*Transmission speed:* **2.5Mbps or 20Mbps for ARCNET Plus**

*Maximum number of network nodes:* **255**

*Maximum number of nodes per segment:* Varies

*Maximum number of segments:* Varies

*Minimum distance between nodes:* Varies

*Maximum network length:* 20,000 feet

*Maximum segment length:*

- o *Coaxial cable:* 2,000 feet
- o *UTP cable:* 400 feet
- o *Fiber-optic cable:* 11,500 feet

## Cabling

ARCNET utilizes UTP or coaxial cable and hubs to connect as many as 255 computers. For a more reliable network, RG-62 93-ohm coaxial cable is used with low-impedance NICs. This allows the signal to travel 2,000 feet to an active hub and 100 feet to a passive hub. Active hubs use external power to regenerate the signal and allow for greater distances than passive hubs that have no power and simply split the signal. Active hubs can be connected because they regenerate the signal; since passive hubs do not have the capability, they should not be connected. Any unused ports on the hubs should be terminated using 93-ohm terminators. When ARCNET is configured in a linear bus, up to eight systems are allowed to share the same cable using BNC T connectors similar to those used in Ethernet. This limits configuration to a trunk length of 1,000 feet and requires termination. ARCNET is limited in distance to 20,000 feet; this is because ARCNET can't have a propagation delay greater than 31 microseconds. An ARCNET token, known as an *invitation to transmit,* or ITT, traveling at 2.5Mbps can travel 20,000 feet in 31 microseconds. ARCNET running over UTP has slightly different capability. ARCNET over UTP calls for 22-AWG or 24-AWG cable with at least two twists per foot. UTP cabling length is limited to 400 feet with no more than thirty-two computers per cable. ARCNET can also utilize fiber-optic cable. Fiber-optic ARCNET networks allow for cable lengths of 11,500 feet, and the total LAN may have a maximum length of 100,000 feet.

## Installing and configuring ARCNET adapters

Unlike most network adapters, ARCNET adapters do not have their physical address coded onto the adapter by the manufacturer. ARCNET adapters use switches to set the physical address, which can vary from 1 to 255. This is done because the ARCNET ITT travels sequentially from device 1 to 2 to 3, and so on. This introduces several considerations for the network administrator. Each device must have a unique physical address; therefore it is important to maintain addressing standards and to carefully track physical addresses. ARCNET networks cannot be interconnected due to the limitation in the number of systems. In addition, for the greatest speed, it is important to have devices with sequential physical addresses located close to one another. The stations on the LAN go through an initialization sequence when the LAN is first activated. During the sequence, the stations broadcast their node ID across the LAN. When a new system joins the network, a reconfiguration burst is sent, and the initialization sequence is performed once again. If a system is detected to be missing from the LAN (such as when it doesn't receive its ITT within 31 microseconds), a reconfiguration is initiated by its neighbor.

 tip **Always keep a record showing which node ID your ARCNET cards are using. It is wise to place a small sticker on the back of each card as well, showing what it is configured for.**

## Troubleshooting

When troubleshooting ARCNET networks, keep several things in mind. Because the physical addresses are set manually, it is possible to have duplicate addresses on the network. Duplicate physical addresses can cause intermittent problems. Make sure you use the correct cable type; Ethernet and television cable look similar, so be sure that you're using RG-62 93-ohm coax cable. Be sure to terminate unused ports on hubs using 93-ohm terminators. Remember not to connect two passive hubs; the signal is not strong enough to be transmitted through two passive hubs without regeneration. Do not exceed the maximum cable length to avoid errors on the network. Exceeding the maximum cable length can cause systems to appear to be disconnected from the network. Also, as with any other adapter, check your hardware resources (DMA, IRQ, I/O settings, and so on) to be sure no conflicts exist.

## The Future of ARCNET

The *ARCNET Traders Association* (ATA) and Thomas-Conrad are attempting to create a future for ARCNET. *ARCNET Plus* will operate at a speed of 20Mbps. ARCNET Plus also allows eight times as many nodes as original ARCNET. ARCNET

Plus equipment is designed to work with the original ARCNET equipment. Each node advertises its transmission capabilities to the other nodes so that if a fast node needs to communicate to a slow node, it steps down to the slower speed for the duration of that session. This will allow ARCNET Plus to work in existing ARCNET networks. Another new feature is the ability to connect with Ethernet, Token Ring, and Transmission Control Protocol/Internet Protocol (TCP/IP) networks using bridges and routers. This is possible because the new version supports the IEEE 802.2 logical link control standard. The ARCNET Plus standard moves ARCNET networks into a more usable realm. The future of ARCNET is still undecided, but ARCNET Plus makes ARCNET an option for today's LANs.

exam preparation pointer  **For the exam, you should be able to compare the network types discussed in this chapter. Be sure to review the advantages and disadvantages of ARCNET.**

**ARCNET's advantages include:**

o **Reliable, mature technology**

o **Uses simple technology that is easily installed**

o **Operates over several cable types**

**The disadvantages of ARCNET include:**

o **Limited to 255 devices**

o **Operates at a low speed of 2.5Mbps**

# Ethernet

*Ethernet* is the most common network. It offers support for a variety of protocols and computer platforms. The Ethernet 802.3 standard was developed by the IEEE 802 Committee. Ethernet is an open network standard developed by Intel, Digital, and Xerox. Ethernet has been successful due to its varied support and its relatively low cost.

## Cabling standards

There are many options for cabling on an Ethernet network. The different cable types allow for a variety of network speeds and cabling lengths. Each type has certain advantages and disadvantages. Ethernet is available in three main standards.

o **10Base-5:** 10Mbps using RG-8 or RG-11 coaxial cable to transmit baseband signals in 500-meter segments. This is also known as *Thick Ethernet.*

o **10Base-2:** 10Mbps using RG-58 coaxial cable to transmit baseband signals on 200-meter segments. This is also known as *Thin Ethernet.*

o **10Base-T:** 10 Mbps using UTP cabling to transmit baseband signals on 100-meter segments. This is also known as *Twisted-pair Ethernet.*

Apart from the three main standards of Ethernet, there are also several variations. These variations aren't as widely used but tend to offer increased speed and distance. Other Ethernet standards include:

o 10Base-FL

o Fast Ethernet

o 100VG-AnyLAN

o Switched Ethernet

**10Base-5**

*10Base-5* is the original Ethernet standard. It became known as Thick Ethernet due to the RG-8 cable used in the standard. The RG-8 cable uses external transceivers and a vampire clamp that fastens directly into the cable, which is wired in a linear bus. The transceiver then connects to a drop cable, which uses a 15-pin DIX connector to connect to the NIC in the workstation. Transceivers must be at least 8 feet apart. This provides the benefit of longer segment lengths (up to 164 feet) for the drop cable because the transceivers provide better signal regeneration. This also allows for the longer segment lengths of up to 500 meters and allows for up to one hundred nodes per segment. Although each segment can be up to 500 meters long, the 10Base-5 network is limited to 2,500 meters in total length. The coax cable must be terminated on both ends with one of the terminators providing a ground. 10Base-5 follows the *5-4-3 rule* — there can be five segments with four repeaters, and only three of the segments can have workstations. Figure 4-7 illustrates a 10Base-5 network.

 exam preparation pointer

**The 5-4-3 rule may be asked about directly on the exam, but will probably be applied in a scenario. Be sure you understand how it effects the design of a network.**

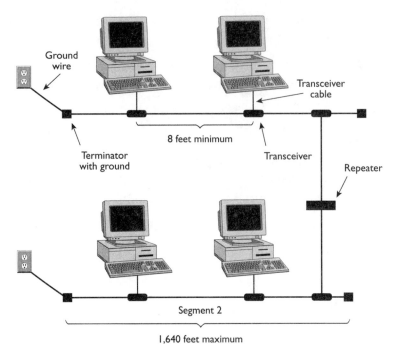

FIGURE 4-7    10Base-5 network

exam
preparation
pointer

You may see questions on the exam concerning 10Base-5 networks, so be sure to review the following summary of 10Base-5 networks:

- *Topology:* Bus
- *Media access method:* CSMA/CD
- *Cable types:* 50-ohm Thicknet coax cable
- *Transmission speed:* 10Mbps
- *Maximum number of network nodes:* 300
- *Maximum number of nodes per segment:* 100
- *Maximum number of segments:* 5; 3 of which can have connected nodes
- *Minimum distance between nodes:* 2.5 meters
- *Maximum network length:* 2,500 meters
- *Maximum segment length:* 500 meters

## 10Base-2

*10Base-2* was developed as one of the alternatives to 10Base-5 because the RG-8 cable used in 10Base-5 is rigid and difficult to work with, and also because the external transceivers were expensive. Because many people did not need the lengths made possible by this cable-and-transceiver combination, people began to look for an alternative. 10Base-2 standard uses RG-58 cable along with T connectors wired in a linear bus configuration. This, thinner cable is much easier to work with and provides a more cost-efficient Ethernet network. The transceiver was moved onto the NIC to provide a simpler network. This, however, limits the distance the signal can travel. Another limitation is the amount of space between the trunk of the bus and the workstation. T connectors are quite small and connect the workstation directly to the trunk. 10Base-2 networks have a maximum length of 925 meters and follow the 5-4-3 rule allowing five segments, four repeaters, with three of the segments supporting as many as 30 devices which must be 1.5 feet apart. The coax cable used is RG-58 50-ohm cable using 50-ohm terminators on each end, one of which is terminated. 10Base-2 is a simple and inexpensive solution for many small networks. Figure 4-8 illustrates a 10Base-2 network.

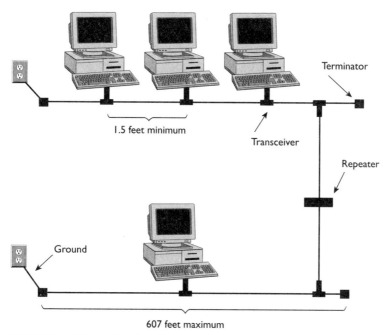

**FIGURE 4-8**    10Base-2 network

Cabling is extremely important on a bus network because one break can take down an entire segment. I suggest buying prefabricated cable, if possible, that has molded connectors instead of crimped connectors. These last longer and hold up better under abuse.

 You may see questions on the exam concerning 10Base-2 networks, so be sure to review the following summary of 10Base-2 networks:

o *Topology:* Bus

o *Media access method:* CSMA/CD

o *Cable types:* 50-ohm, RG–58 coax cable

o *Transmission speed:* 10Mbps

o *Maximum number of network nodes:* 90

o *Maximum number of nodes per segment:* 30

o *Maximum number of segments:* 5; 3 of which can have connected nodes

o *Minimum distance between nodes:* 0.5 meters

o *Maximum network length:* 925 meters

o *Maximum segment length:* 185 meters

### 10Base-T

*10Base-T* is quite different from the other Ethernet standards. This standard utilizes 22-AWG UTP cable with RJ-45 jacks arranged in a star configuration. This uses much more cable but also provides for a more stable and easily maintained network. This configuration eliminates the single point of failure problem associated with the bus configuration. Each device has a separate UTP cable connecting it to the hub. The workstations must be at least 2 feet apart and no more than 328 feet from the hub. Several hubs can be connected for a larger network. 10Base-T works well for a growing network. This network standard must also follow the 5-4-3 rule, which allows for five segments, four connected hubs, and three populated segments with up to 512 devices. There is a limit of 1,024 total devices on the network. To overcome the problem of exceeding the 5-4-3 rule, networks can be *segmented*. In segmentation, the smaller networks are connected using bridges or routers, allowing for a large overall network. Figure 4-9 illustrates a 10Base-T network.

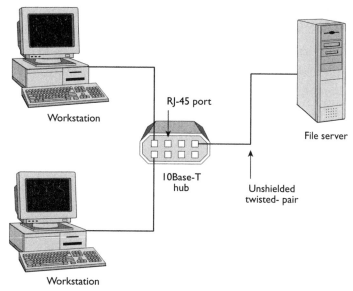

**FIGURE 4-9** 10Base-T network

You may see questions on the exam concerning 10Base-T networks, so be sure to review. The following is a summary of 10Base-T networks:

- *Topology:* Star
- *Media access method:* CSMA/CD
- *Cable types:* Categories 3-5 UTP
- *Transmission speed:* 10Mbps
- *Maximum number of network nodes:* 1,024
- *Minimum number of nodes per segment:* 1
- *Maximum number of segments:* 1,024
- *Maximum distance between nodes:* 2.5 meters
- *Maximum network length:* No maximum length
- *Maximum segment length:* 100 meters

### 10Base-FL

Another lesser-known Ethernet standard is *10Base-FL*. This standard operates over fiber-optic cable at 10Mbps using baseband signaling. Data is transmitted as light instead of electrical signals. Fiber-optic cabling provides a better signal that can travel farther than an electrical signal. This network utilizes hubs and star wiring. Both active and passive hubs can be used. *Active hubs* are capable of retransmitting the signal while *passive hubs* just split the signal, directing it to every port on the hub. Active hubs use electricity and can provide valuable troubleshooting and diagnostic information. Fiber-optic cable allows a network segment of up to 2,000 meters. The maximum number of segments on a 10Base-FL network is 1,024. Each network can support 1,024 nodes, and up to four hubs can be connected.

 **You may see questions on the exam concerning 10Base-FL networks, so be sure to review. The following is a summary of 10Base-FL networks:**

exam
preparation
pointer

o *Topology:* Star

o *Media access method:* CSMA/CD

o *Cable types:* Fiber optic

o *Transmission speed:* 10Mbps

o *Maximum number of network nodes:* 1,024

o *Maximum number of nodes per segment:* 1

o *Maximum number of segments:* 1,024

o *Minimum distance between nodes:* No minimum distance

o *Maximum network length:* No maximum length

o *Maximum segment length:* 2,000 meters

## Future Cabling Standards

All of the standards mentioned earlier are only capable of 10Mbps. Networks today are starting to require higher speeds due to multimedia applications and the increase of users. One of Ethernet's greatest advantages is its ability to evolve and expand. By adding new standards that enhance the existing Ethernet topology, administrators do not have to totally overhaul a network when new requirements are needed.

### Fast Ethernet

Recently there has been increasing interest in *Fast Ethernet,* which can transmit at either 10Mbps or 100Mbps. Fast Ethernet can transmit across UTP or fiber optics. The three standards developed are dependent on the type of cable used.

- *100Base-TX* using two-pair Category 5 UTP and STP cable

- *100Base-T4* using four-pair Category 3 through 5 UTP cable

- *100Base-FX* using fiber-optic cable

These standards allow for several options with Fast Ethernet. For 100Mbps Fast Ethernet, the adapters and hub must be capable of 100Mbps transfer rates. If any 10Mbps adapters are detected, the entire network will run at 10Mbps. Fiber optics provide for greater cable lengths at 100Mbps than UTP cable. With UTP, you are limited to two hubs between workstations, and the hubs must be connected using a 5-meter cable. Fiber optics allow a distance of 400 meters between hubs. This standard allows for a slow implementation of Fast Ethernet. You could upgrade your network cable and later replace the adapters with those capable of either speed. When you are ready to make the full commitment to 100Mbps, you can add the higher-speed hubs. This standard is appealing due to the increased speed and backward compatibility.

exam preparation pointer

**You may see questions on the exam concerning Fast Ethernet, so be sure to review. The following is a summary of Fast Ethernet networks:**

- *Topology:* Star

- *Media access method:* CSMA/CD

- *Cable types:* 100Base-TX: Category 5 UTP
  *100Base-T4:* Categories 3-5 UTP
  *100Base-FX:* Fiber optic

- *Transmission speed:* 100Mbps

- *Maximum number of network nodes:* 1,024

- *Maximum number of nodes per segment:* 1

- *Maximum number of segments:* 1,024

- *Minimum distance between nodes:* 2.5 meters

- *Maximum network length:* No maximum length

- *Maximum segment length:*
  - *100Base-TX:* 100 meters
  - *100Base-T4:* 100 meters
  - *100Base-FX:* 2,000 meters

### 100VG-AnyLAN

*100VG-AnyLAN* uses voice-grade fiber optic, as well as Categories 3, 4, or 5 twisted -pair cable to provide a possible transmission rate of 100Mbps. If twisted pair is to be used, two pairs of wires are necessary. This standard was developed by Hewlett-Packard and AT&T. 100VG-AnyLAN uses hubs in a star topology. Several hubs can be connected to allow for growth. The media access method used by 100VG-AnyLAN is different from the methods used by standard Ethernet or Token Ring but can be integrated into both types of networks. A *demand priority method* is used, in which computers that want to transmit send a demand to the hub. The hub allows the computer to transmit. This method allows the hubs to control the media access, preventing packets from being broadcast to the entire network. This method also allows prioritization so the more important items are transmitted first.

100VG-AnyLAN can be integrated into a Token Ring network, as well as Ethernet. 100VG-AnyLAN NICs can transmit Token Ring frames when using the correct driver. A bridge is used to allow 100VG-AnyLAN and Token Ring to coexist.

The length of a 100VG-AnyLAN network varies according to the type of cable used. Category 3 UTP is limited to 100 meters, Category 5 UTP allows for 150 meters, and fiber-optic cable can reach lengths of 2,000 meters.

exam preparation pointer

**Remember that 100VG-AnyLAN is a proprietary network from Hewlett-Packard. Equipment for this type of network cannot work with existing standard Ethernet equipment.**

**Also, you may see questions on the exam concerning 100VG-AnyLAN networks, so be sure to review the following summary of 100VG-AnyLAN networks:**

- *Topology:* Star
- *Media access method:* Demand priority
- *Cable types:* Fiber optic, Categories 3–5 UTP, and STP
- *Transmission speed:* 100Mbps
- *Maximum number of network nodes:* 1,024
- *Maximum number of nodes per segment:* 1
- *Maximum number of segments:* 1,024
- *Minimum distance between nodes:* 2.5 meters
- *Maximum network length:* No maximum length

- *Maximum segment length:*
  - *Category 3 UTP:* 100 meters
  - *Category 5 UTP:* 150 meters
  - *STP:* 100 meters
  - *Fiber optic:* 2,000 meters

**Switched Ethernet**

Bridges are used in standard Ethernet to reduce the traffic in a segment of the network and to connect segments containing multiple hubs. This accomodates more than four hubs across the entire network and helps reduce network traffic, but it can cause other problems as well. If the bridge is too busy, it can drop packets causing lost communications. *Switches* are used to help solve this problem. Switches use software to learn the node address of every workstation on its ports. When a packet is directed at a workstation, the switch receives the packet and sends it directly to the destination port, helping prevent network collisions and allowing for a more orderly network. The problem with this is when most of the traffic is directed to a few machines. This can cause collisions when multiple messages are being sent to one machine, such as a server. To help solve this problem, full-duplex Ethernet may be used. This method uses both pairs in twisted-pair cable simultaneously. One pair sends while the other pair monitors the cable for collisions. This method puts a lot of strain on the adapters (bus-mastering adapters are recommended) but can be used to provide a collision-free network.

## Frame Types

Packets can be sent across an Ethernet network in one of several *frame types*. These frame types are actually syntax for the messages being transmitted. If two systems are using different frame types, they're speaking different languages and don't understand each other. IEEE developed the standards for the various frame types used across Ethernet networks. The most common are *802.3, 802.2,* and *Ethernet_II.*

- Ethernet_802.3: This frame type was developed and used by NetWare for its IPX/SPX protocol before the IEEE finished developing the standard. The frame size used in 802.3 is between 64 and 1,518 bytes and includes *cyclic redundancy check* (CRC) for error checking. This frame type, which doesn't fully comply with the standards developed by IEEE, is used primarily by NetWare 2.2 and 3.11.

- Ethernet_802.2: This frame type differs slightly from 802.3 and is fully IEEE compliant. It contains three additional one-byte values. These values add flow control, error checking, and reliability to the previous 802.3 frame type. These packets also range from 64 to 1,518 bytes. This is the default frame type for NetWare 3.12 and 4.1.

- Ethernet_II: This frame type can be used by both Internetwork Packet Exchange/Sequenced Packet Exchange (IPX/SPX) and Transmission Control Protocol/Internet Protocol (TCP/IP). This frame type doesn't identify the length of the packet, but the type. This is used to specify whether the packet is IPX/SPX or TCP/IP.

exam preparation pointer

**Understanding that computers using different frame types cannot communicate with each other is extremely important. You are almost guaranteed to see questions concerning this on the exam.**

**Also, be sure to remember which frame types are the default for different versions of NetWare. There is usually an exam question concerning problems connecting to a server from one particular workstation that has to do with frame types.**

### Installing and configuring Ethernet adapters

Ethernet adapters are easily installed and configured. When installing Ethernet adapters be sure to use the proper resources, such as IRQ, I/O settings, DMA, and so on. Some adapters use a switch to specify whether the transceiver is external or internal; this needs to be configured properly for your setup. Many of the current adapters have connections for the three main standards of Ethernet. They have the 15-pin *DIX connector*, a *coax connector*, and an *RJ-45 connector* for UTP cable. When using coax cable, it is important to connect the trunk using a T connector, which connects to either another cable segment or to a terminator.

### Troubleshooting

Different devices need to be examined when troubleshooting the different Ethernet standards. 10Base-5 problems can often be attributed to a problem with the transceiver or vampire clamp. Problems can also be due to a problem with termination or grounding. A damaged cable can cause problems across the network, as well. 10Base-2 problems can also be associated with incorrect termination, a bad connector, or a damaged cable. Problems with these network types can be more difficult to track down because an error in one place causes problems all over. 10Base-T networks are a bit easier to troubleshoot. If a cable is damaged, only the connected workstation is affected. The hub can also be a source of problems in a 10Base-T network. There can be a problem with the port. This would only affect devices attached to that particular port. The hub could also malfunction causing problems for all affected devices. Even if a hub fails, this is easier to diagnosis than a crimped portion of coax cable.

**exam preparation pointer**

**For the exam, you should know which type of media access that Token Ring, Ethernet, and EtherTalk use.**

- **Ethernet uses CSMA/CD.**

- **Token Ring uses token passing.**

- **EtherTalk uses CSMA/CA.**

Another common problem with Ethernet is *collisions*. The type of media access that Ethernet employs causes collisions. In a contention-based network, any device can transmit whenever it needs to. The advantage of this system is that it allows equal access to the network media, but at the expense of possible collisions. Collisions occur when two devices try to transmit at the same time and disrupt each other's signaling. During a collision, no data is being transmitted. As the number of collisions increases, the amount of time data is transmitted is reduced. On a large network, with many devices attempting to transmit, things can be slowed considerably. On modern contention-based networks, devices listen for other signals on the media before transmitting. Collisions are not totally eliminated, but they are reduced. This is known as *Carrier Sense Multiple Access,* or CSMA.

**exam preparation pointer**

**Be sure to review the advantages and disadvantages of Ethernet for the exam.**

**Advantages include:**

- **Flexible standard allowing a variety of equipment**

- **Inexpensive network option (10Base–2 provides the least expensive Ethernet option)**

- **High–speed network that can operate at 10 or 100 Mbps**

- **Easily expanded**

**Disadvantage of Ethernet:**

o **Performance degradation under high network load**

# Token Ring

*Token Ring* is a reliable network based on some of the best standards available. It uses token-passing in a physical star configuration connected in a ring using hubs. For this reason, Token Ring holds up well under heavy network traffic. This standard was developed by IBM and was certified by the IEEE Committee as the IEEE 802.5 standard. IBM continues to be the leader in components for Token Ring networks, although many other vendors produce the components. Token Ring transmits at 1, 4, or 16Mbps using proprietary equipment. Because Token Ring uses the token-passing method of media access, it allows devices to have varying priority in accessing the network media. This can be beneficial for servers that need frequent access to the network. The IEEE 802.5 Token Ring standards allow for 250 devices, but a more practical limit is 96 stations and twelve MAUs. Token Ring is a much more expensive network than Ethernet or ARCNET.

exam preparation pointer

You may see questions on the exam about Token Ring, so be sure to review to following summary of Token Ring networks:

o *Topology:* Physical star, logical ring

o *Media access method:* Token passing

o *Cable types:* STP, UTP, and fiber optic

o *Transmission speed:* 4 or 16Mbps

o *Maximum number of network nodes:*

　o *UTP:* 72

　o *STP:* 260

o *Maximum number of nodes per segment:* Varies according to the hub.

o *Maximum number of segments:* 33

o *Minimum distance between nodes:* 2.5 meters

o *Maximum network length:* No maximum length

o *Maximum segment length:*

　o *UTP:* 45 meters

　o *STP:* 101 meters

o *Frame size:*

    o *4Mbps:* 4K

    o *16Mbps:* 16K

## Hardware

Token Ring is a bit more complex in its cabling scheme than Ethernet and ARC-NET. Token Ring uses a physical star to connect systems in a logical ring, as shown in Figure 4-10. This is not as difficult to understand as it first sounds. This simply means that systems are connected to a central device using separate cables. This is called the *physical star* configuration. Inside the central device, the ports are connected in a ring. The ring configuration does have one major weakness: there is a single point of failure. If there is a break in the ring, the entire ring goes down, as shown in Figure 4-11. To help overcome this, Token Ring hubs can detect a break in the ring and disconnect that portion of the ring, allowing them to route the ring around the failed area. Figure 4-12 illustrates a logical ring on a Token Ring network.

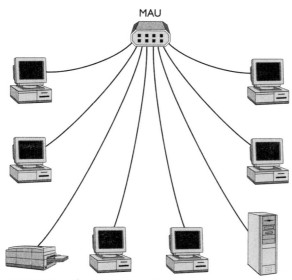

**FIGURE 4-10**   Physical Token Ring star

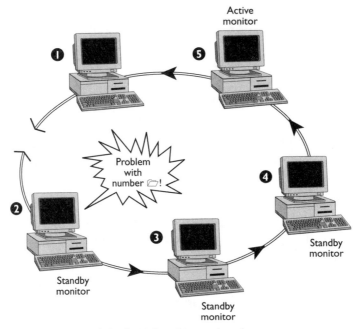

**FIGURE 4-11**    Break in the Token Ring network

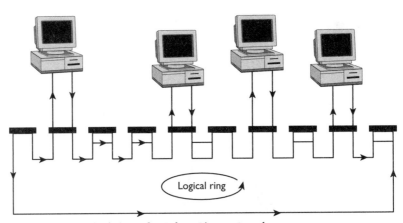

**FIGURE 4-12**    Logical ring of a Token Ring network

### Hubs

There are several hardware components used in a Token Ring network:

o **Multistation Access Unit (MAU):** A MAU (pronounced *mow*, as in "cow") is a Token Ring hub. This device is sometimes known as an *IBM 8228* MAU and an *MSAU*. Devices connect to the hub in a physical star. The MAU internally links the workstations into a ring. MAUs have special ring-in and ring-out ports used to connect several MAUs to the ring. The ring out on one MAU is connected to a ring in on the next MAU. This continues until the ring out on the last MAU is connected to the ring-in on the fist MAU, forming a ring.

o **Controlled Access Unit (CAU):** A CAU (pronounced *cow*) is an intelligent MAU.

o **Lobe Access Module (LAM):** A LAM (pronounced *lamb*) allows intelligent expansion of CAUs.

### Cables

Following are the seven types of cable that can be used with IBM Token Ring:

o **Type 1:** STP cable made of two twisted pairs of solid-core, 22-gauge AWG copper wire surrounded by a braided shield. This type of cable is run to wiring closets. It is also used to connect terminals to distribution panels. It is run through conduit, walls, and so on.

o **Type 2:** STP cable similar to Type 1 but uses four twisted pairs of telephone wires. This allows hookup of data and telephone equipment with one cable. This cable is used to connect terminals to distribution panels located in the same area.

o **Type 3:** UTP cable made of 22- or 24-gauge wire with four pairs, each twisted two times every 12 feet. This cable is subject to cross talk and is limited to shorter distances than Type 1 and 2.

o **Type 5:** Fiber-optic cable with either a 62.5- or 100-micron diameter. Type 5 cable is used only on the main ring path.

o **Type 6:** STP cable made with two 26-gauge AWG stranded-core copper wires twisted together in a shielded jacket. Type 6 STP is much easier to work with but is limited in distance and is typically only used as a patch cable or as an extension in a wiring closet.

- Type 8: STP cable made with two 26-gauge AWG stranded-core wires twisted together. Type 8 cable is run under carpets.

- Type 9: STP cable made with two 26-gauge AWG stranded-core copper wires twisted together in a shielded jacket. Type 9 cable is fire retardant and designed for use in ceilings with ventilation systems.

### Connectors

The different cable types also use different types of connectors. STP cables are connected to the MAU using a *hermaphroditic* connector, and to the NIC using a 9-pin AUI connector. A special patch cable using hermaphroditic connectors on both ends is used to connect the ring-in and ring-out ports on the MAU. STP is the most frequently used cable type, but there are also allowances for Category 5 UTP and fiber-optic cable. When a computer enters the Token Ring network, a click can be heard as the station inserts into the ring.

## *Installation and configuration of Token Ring adapters*

One of the reasons for Token Ring's high price is the cost of the adapters. Token Ring adapters are more intelligent than other network adapters. For this reason, there are several important factors to consider when configuring Token Ring adapters. Some of the older Token Ring adapters use switches to configure the resource settings, as well as the buffer size and ring speed. It is important for these items to be configured properly. If one of the settings is incorrect, the adapter won't work reliably. Newer adapters have a BIOS on-board, which stores the configuration parameters. These cards can typically handle either Plug and Play or manual resource settings. *Ring speed* is an important consideration. Many adapters can operate at either 4 or 16Mbps. If the adapter is configured for the wrong speed, this can cause problems for that workstation and others on the ring.

## *Troubleshooting*

The first station to be activated in a Token Ring network becomes the *active monitor*. The other workstations are known as *standby monitors* and are potential active monitors. The active monitor has several responsibilities. It creates the token and initiates the process of identifying devices on the network. Every seven seconds a token is sent from the active monitor to its *nearest active upstream neighbor* (NAUN). The token is received from the *nearest active downstream neighbor* (NADN) and passed on to the nearest active upstream neighbor. This continues until every station has identified itself to the others on the network. During this process, each computer learns the address of the active monitor and its nearest upstream and downstream neighbors. Some of the other responsibilities of the active monitor also include dealing with lost tokens, exterminating tokens that have finished their trip around the ring, checking for more than one active monitor, and correcting problems that occur with a short ring that can't hold the token. By using some software network analyzers, you watch these processes. When an error occurs, the analyzers may help you locate the device causing the error. Using analyzing software can be especially useful if a device starts *beaconing*.

Token Ring networks are better for high-utilization networks due to their media access type. Token passing is considered deterministic because a device is guaranteed to have network access.

Token passing has more overhead than CSMA and therefore is slower on a network with little congestion. On a congested network it can perform significantly higher than CSMA, though if the network gets too congested, devices will start reporting errors. These errors show up as "congestion errors" and can bring an already busy network to a crawl.

 A common problem with Token Ring is a card set for 4Mbps that is put on a 16Mbps ring. Depending on the type of card installed, it may either remove itself from the network, or begin beaconing and take the entire ring down.

The process of monitoring its neighbors allows computers in a Token Ring network to participate in a community watch program. If a computer doesn't hear from its neighbor every seven seconds it assumes there is a problem and alerts the authorities. The workstation sends its address, the address of its nearest active upstream neighbor, and the type of error known as a *beacon*. This process is known as beaconing. Beaconing helps identify fault domains, which are areas on the ring with a problem. Once a workstation has identified a fault domain, it is responsible for removing the packets belonging to the failing workstation from the network. When a computer beacons the network, all systems on the network exit the ring and perform diagnostics to determine if they are responsible for the errors. The failing system tries to repair itself; this is known as *autoreconfiguration*. The failing system will remain disconnected from the ring if it cannot repair itself. Beaconing and autoreconfiguration allow a Token Ring network to attempt to diagnose and repair itself.

exam preparation pointer

**You should know the advantages and disadvantages of using Token Ring for the exam.**

**Advantages of Token Ring include:**

o **Performs well under heavy load**

o **Uses intelligent adapters for self-diagnosis and repair**

o **High-speed network capable of 4 or 16Mbps**

**Disadvantages of Token Ring include:**

o **Expensive**

o **Difficult to troubleshoot**

# FDDI

*Fiber Distributed Data Interface,* or FDDI, is a token-passing ring network similar to Token Ring, but running over a fiber-optic cable. Unlike Token Ring, FDDI allows several devices to transmit at once. Instead of using hubs, FDDI uses concentrators to connect devices. Because FDDI utilizes fiber-optic cable, it is capable of transmitting at the rate of 100Mbps. Figure 4-13 shows an FDDI network.

FDDI uses a token-passing network over the ring, but the method used in FDDI is much different from Token Ring. FDDI allows many frames to be transmitted simultaneously. This is possible because the station that controls the token can send several frames without waiting for the previous frame to complete its journey around the ring. When one station finishes sending its frames, it passes the token to the next station. The second station can begin transmitting without waiting for the frames sent by the first station to completely circle the ring. This process continues around the ring, allowing a constant stream involving several frames circulating around the ring. This provides a method of token passing that is much quicker than Token Ring.

FDDI has other options for further increasing the speed of the network. Another method is known as *synchronous frames*. This method assigns transmission times to certain devices that do not require a token. During this time, only the device specified is allowed to transmit. *Multiframe dialogs* are another option that can be used in FDDI. Multiframe dialogs utilize *limited tokens*. Limited tokens are tokens that allow a device only to transmit with the sender. This allows two devices to transmit to one another without interference.

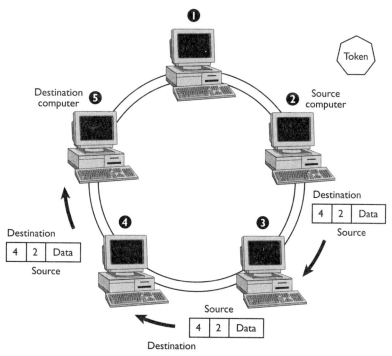

**FIGURE 4-13** An FDDI network

Another way in which FDDI creates a faster, more reliable network is to utilize two rings that run counter to one another. This provides fault tolerance on the network. If the cable is damaged, a connection is made between the two rings before and after the break; this is known as *wrapping*. It enables packets to loop back around the ring. Wrapping forces the packets to travel twice the distance (one trip on the first ring, another on the second), but enables the packets to reach their destination. This eliminates a single point of failure in the cable, which was a weakness in Token Ring. However, a workstation connected to both rings can bring them both down. Figure 4-14 illustrates a broken FDDI network.

There are several adapters and concentrators used in FDDI to allow for a single- or dual-ring configuration. *Class A* systems are those that are configured to connect to only one ring. *Class B* systems can be connected to both rings. Because a workstation can bring down the ring, be sure that systems connected to both rings are highly reliable.

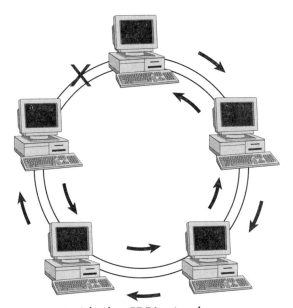

**FIGURE 4-14**   A broken FDDI network

 For the exam, be sure to review the following summary of FDDI networks:

- *Topology:* Ring
- *Media access method:* Token passing
- *Cable types:* Fiber optic
- *Transmission speed:* 100Mbps
- *Maximum number of network nodes:* 500

- *Maximum number of nodes per segment:* No maximum number of nodes per segment
- *Maximum number of segments:* No maximum number of segments
- *Minimum distance between nodes:* No minimum distance
- *Maximum network length:* 100 kilometers
- *Maximum segment length:* No maximum segment length

## Cabling

As you have learned, fiber-optic cable is quite different from traditional network media. Instead of using electrical signals to transmit data, it uses *light*. I will review the basics of this new media so that you understand the way it functions and can troubleshoot problems that may arise.

As stated above, fiber-optic cable uses light instead of electricity. In a fiber cable, light only moves in one direction. For two-way communication to take place, a second connection must be made between the two devices. This is why when you look at fiber cable you will notice it is two strands connected together. A laser at one device will send pulses of light through this cable to the other device. These pulses are translated into 1's and 0's at the other end.

The light contained inside the fiber cable cannot escape. No electrical fields are created around the cable, so you could run a bundle of fiber together with no ill effects.

In the center of the fiber cable is a glass strand, or *core*. The light from the laser travels through this glass to the other device. Around the internal core is a reflective material known as *cladding*. This way all light is reflected through the glass since no fiber installation will be an exact straight line with no light leaving the internal glass core. This cladding allows a little more flexibility in installation of cabling.

### Single mode and multimode fiber

Fiber-optic cable comes in two flavors, *single mode* and *multimode*. Single-mode cable only allows for one light path through the cable, where multimode has many paths. Single-mode cable allows for a faster transmission time and longer distances, but of course costs more.

Single mode is normally only used for long distances, as in tens of miles. If you are just connecting close buildings, stick with multimode.

You will see fiber cable listed by core and cladding size. An example of this would be 62.5-micron core/140-micron cladding multimode. Consult the manufacturer of your network devices to see which size you need.

### Installation and configuration of FDDI networks

Fiber-optic cable was extremely expensive only a few years ago. The price has dropped substantially in recent years, and fiber-optic cable is becoming much more common on networks today. Most of the cost of a fiber-optic network is in the installation. I have yet to see any books go over the installation of fiber-optic media. At this time, the only way to learn is to attend a class, usually lasting a few days with a lot of hands-on learning time.

What do you get for the high cost of installation and cable? High speeds and distances, of course. Fiber-optic cable currently has a bandwidth of more than 2Gbps. That is no typo; that is *gigabits per second*. It is high speed, indeed. FDDI has a bandwidth of 100Mbps.

As stated above, you could run a fiber-optic cable tens of miles, so attenuation is not a problem. There is also no susceptibility to EMI since the transmission occurs over light, not electricity. This allows the greatest distance of any bound network media. FDDI is limited to a distance of 200 kilometers.

### Troubleshooting

The major component to examine when troubleshooting a FDDI network is cabling. FDDI cable can be quite difficult to slice connectors to. Unless you're an expert with special equipment, buying precut cable lengths with attached connectors will save you a lot of headache. Remember to be careful when installing fiber-optic cable. Too sharp a bend can cause problems with the signal. Be sure to use the proper cable type for the distance the signal needs to travel. Multimode fiber should only be used for distances less than 2 kilometers. FDDI inherently has a delay factor of up to 4 milliseconds. This is unavoidable. There is equipment available to test fiber-optic cable. An *optical time domain reflector* (OTDR) is an expensive device that can be used to test cable.

 exam preparation pointer

**Again, it will be important for the exam that you can compare all the network types I've discussed.**

Advantages of FDDI:

o **FDDI is the fastest network and is capable of 100Mbps transfers.**

- o Fiber-optic cable allows signals to travel great distances, up to 200 kilometers.
- o Dual rings provide a higher level of fault tolerance.

Disadvantages of FDDI:

- o Expensive cable and equipment is required.
- o Workstations can be a single point of failure for both rings.
- o FDDI requires a high level of expertise to install, troubleshoot, and maintain.

# KEY POINT SUMMARY

Now that you have covered topologies and the networks that use them, take a moment to review.

- o The four topologies used in networking are *bus*, *star*, *ring*, and *mesh*.
    - o In a *bus* topology all devices are connected to a primary trunk cable. Each end of the trunk cable requires termination to prevent the signal from bouncing back down the cable.
    - o In a *star* topology all devices connect to a central device, typically a hub. This removes the dependency of the entire network on one cable.
    - o A *ring* topology looks like bus topology with the ends connected. Ring differs greatly in function. Because data moves in one direction and the network is more orderly, it functions well under a heavy load.
    - o A *mesh* topology is based on the simple idea of connecting each device directly to every other device. This provides a straight, dedicated data link. Unfortunately, due to the cable requirements, this network can quickly become confusing and difficult to maintain.
- o The four major network types are ARCNET, Ethernet, Token Ring, and FDDI.
    - o *ARCNET* was developed in the 1970s and was designed to be a simple, inexpensive network. This network operates at 2.5Mbps using token passing over coax or UTP cable. ARCNET networks can use hubs in a star configuration. They can also be configured to use the bus topology.

ARCNET adapters use switches to set their physical address. ARCNET Plus was designed as an update to ARCNET and operates at 20Mbps.

o *Ethernet* is currently the most common network type. There are several options for Ethernet, all of which use the CSMA/CD media access method.

o *10Base-5* is the earliest Ethernet standard. This is known as *Thicknet* because of the thick coax cable used. It operates at 10Mbps and is configured in a bus topology.

o *10Base-2* is similar to 10Base-5. 10Base-2 utilizes thinner coax cable to operate at 10Mbps. 10Base-2 is sometimes known as *Thinnet* because of the cable used. 10Base-2 also operates in a bus topology using terminators at each end.

o *10Base-T* operates a bit differently. UTP cable is connected to hubs to form a star network. 10Base-T provides a more reliable 10Mbps Ethernet option. UTP cable is connected to hubs to form a star network. 10Base-T provides a more reliable 10Mbps Ethernet option.

o *100VG-AnyLAN* provides another 100Mbps option that is quite different from the others. 100VG-AnyLAN is capable of operating in Ethernet and Token Ring networks. This network standard operates over voice-grade UTP, STP, and fiber-optic cable. The demand priority media access method is used, in which the workstation informs the hub (or bridge) of a need to transmit. The hub then directs the frames to the recipient.

o Ethernet uses a variety of *frame types* to transmit data.

   o *Ethernet 802.3* was used by Novell before the standard was completed. This frame type is the default used by NetWare 2.2 and 3.*x* networks with IPX/SPX.

   o *Ethernet 802.2* is in full compliance with the IEEE standards. This is the default frame type for IPX/SPX on NetWare 3.12 and 4.*x*.

   o Ethernet_II is used with TCP/IP networks. It provides support for multiple protocols.

o *Token Ring* networks provide a reliable option for large networks. Token Ring uses the token-passing media access method with the ring topology. *MAUs* (Token Ring hubs) are used to form a physical star with a logical ring. Token Ring networks can operate at either 4 or 16Mbps and operate over UTP, STP, or fiber-optic cable. Token Ring adapters are more intelligent and can do some self-diagnosis and repair. This makes Token Ring a more expensive network option.

o *FDDI* uses fiber-optic cable in a ring topology with token passing. FDDI operates at 100Mbps and can support two counter-rotating rings. FDDI provides more fault tolerance than Token Ring. It has the ability to detect a break in the cable and loop the two rings together. This eliminates the cable as a single point of failure. However, a defective workstation connected to both rings can bring both rings down.

# APPLYING WHAT YOU'VE LEARNED

It is now time to test your knowledge of topologies and network types. The following Instant Assessment questions will test what you remember from this chapter and are a good indicator of any weak areas before moving on. The Critical Thinking labs provide you with an opportunity to apply the knowledge you've gained in this chapter about network media.

 note **Critical Thinking labs** challenge you to apply your understanding of the material to solve a hypothetical problem. The questions are scenario based, requiring you to decide "why" or "how" or to devise a solution to a problem. You might need to be at a computer to work through some of these labs.

 concept link **Refer to the "Hardware and Software You'll Need" section in the Preface or in Appendix B if you're not sure you have the necessary equipment to do the Critical Thinking labs.**

## Instant Assessment

**1.** Which media access method is used by Ethernet networks?

   **a.** CSMA/CD

   **b.** CSMA/CA

   **c.** Token passing

   **d.** Polling

2. Which media access method is used by Token Ring networks?

   **a.** CSMA/CD

   **b.** CSMA/CA

   **c.** Token passing

   **d.** Polling

3. Which media access method is used in ARCNET networks?

   **a.** CSMA/CD

   **b.** CSMA/CA

   **c.** Token passing

   **d.** Polling

4. Which physical topology requires termination?

   **a.** Bus

   **b.** Star

   **c.** Ring

   **d.** Mesh

5. Which physical topology uses direct connections to each device?

   **a.** Bus

   **b.** Star

   **c.** Ring

   **d.** Mesh

6. Which physical topology connects workstations to a central device?

   **a.** Bus

   **b.** Star

   **c.** Ring

   **d.** Mesh

7. Which physical topology allows only a one-way flow of data across the media?

   **a.** Bus

   **b.** Star

**c.** Ring

**d.** Mesh

8. Which frame type is used on NetWare 3.12 networks?

    **a.** Ethernet_802.3

    **b.** Ethernet_802.2

    **c.** Ethernet_II

    **d.** IEEE

9. Which Ethernet standard operates at 10Mbps over UTP cable connected to a hub?

    **a.** 10Base-5

    **b.** 10Base-2

    **c.** 10Base-T

    **d.** 10Base-FL

10. At what speed do ARCNET networks operate?

    **a.** 2.5Mbps

    **b.** 4Mbps

    **c.** 10Mbps

    **d.** 16Mbps

11. Which media access method is used by 100VG-AnyLAN?

    **a.** CSMA/CD

    **b.** CSMA/CA

    **c.** Token passing

    **d.** Demand priority

12. Token Ring MAUs use which type of connector?

    **a.** BNC

    **b.** RJ-45

    **c.** 9-pin AUI

    **d.** hermaphroditic

**13.** What is the maximum number of nodes on an ARCNET network?

    **a.** 90

    **b.** 100

    **c.** 255

    **d.** 300

**14.** Which standard defines Token Ring networks?

    **a.** IEEE 802.2

    **b.** IEEE 802.3

    **c.** IEEE 802.5

    **d.** ATA

**15.** Which network type utilizes two counter-rotating rings?

    **a.** ARCNET

    **b.** Ethernet

    **c.** Token Ring

    **d.** FDDI

 

**T/F**

**16.** 100VG-AnyLAN can be integrated into Ethernet and Token Ring networks. _____

**17.** Token Ring operates over a physical star and a logical ring. _____

**18.** The mesh topology is ideal for a network with many nodes spread across a large building. _____

**19.** Bus networks require termination on each end of the trunk cable. _____

**20.** ARCNET adapters use switches to set their physical address. _____

**21.** Ethernet_802.2 and Ethernet_802.3 are compatible frame types. _____

**22.** Fast Ethernet equipment is compatible with 10Mbps Ethernet networks. _____

**23.** Problems with a Class A FDDI workstation can bring down both FDDI rings. _____

**24.** Beaconing is used in Token Ring networks to help diagnose problems on the network. _____

**25.** Token Ring and Ethernet can use the same physical topology. _____

concept link    **For answers to these Instant Assessment questions, see Appendix C.**

# Critical Thinking Labs

The following Critical Thinking labs provide you with a practical opportunity to apply the knowledge you've gained in this chapter about network media and topology.

### Lab 4.6 *Planning network cabling*

Your company is relocating to a new building that was prewired with Category 5 UTP cable by the previous occupants. There will initially be 150 clients and three servers on your network. The expected growth rate of the company will add twenty clients a year for the next four years. You have been asked to recommend a reliable, inexpensive network that can be easily expanded to accommodate future growth. What type of network do you recommend?

### Lab 4.7 *Troubleshooting connectivity*

Your network uses Windows 95 clients to connect to NetWare 3.12 servers. A new workstation is having problems connecting to the servers. However, the client can access other Windows 95 clients on the network. What is the most probable reason that this client cannot connect to the server?

### Lab 4.8 *Troubleshooting token ring connectivity*

You are installing a new 16/4 Token Ring adapter in a new workstation. The network is being slowly upgraded from a 4Mbps network to a 16Mbps network. The workstation is successfully configured and tested in your lab. When delivered to the customer's office the system loses all network connectivity. The cable and port being used were working moments before on his old system. What is the most likely cause of the problem?

### Lab 4.9 *Troubleshooting a token ring LAN*

You notice the speed of your Token Ring LAN has slowed considerably. Upon further examination, it is discovered that a system is beaconing the LAN. Where would you look to find the source of the problem?

### Lab 4.10 *Finding a conflict*

A workstation on your ARCNET network is having problems connecting to the network. The user is having trouble retrieving data from other systems on the network. This problem began when new workstations were added to the network. You also notice that the problem does not occur while the new part-time secretary is out of the office. What problem would cause these symptoms?

concept link

**For answers to these labs, see Appendix C.**

# Connectivity

In the third part of this book, you get to put your knowledge of the OSI model to use while learning about network protocols. It is important to know when to use each protocol before you take the Networking Essentials test.

In Chapter 6 you learn how to connect these different networks to make large internetworks. I cover the different devices this involves, as well as when and why to use them.

The information in this part is some of the most important for helping you prepare for the test. Be sure to study these chapters carefully and follow the exam preparation pointers throughout the chapters to help you prepare.

# Network Protocols

# About Chapter 5

Chapter 5 introduces the protocol suites used for network communications. Protocols in the suites are designed to be modular — they fit into the layers of the OSI model — and they define how communications occur. Protocol suites are groups of protocols that work together to provide a solution for implementing the OSI model and supplying network communications.

In this chapter, you'll see how the different protocols combine to form a suite of protocols that work at the various layers of the OSI model. Knowing the OSI layer at which a protocol functions can help you understand how it works. I will discuss which protocols are routable and suitable for large networks. All of this can help with troubleshooting network communications. If you understand the protocols and how they work together, you will know where to look when a problem occurs.

The protocol suites discussed in this chapter include TCP/IP, IPX/SPX, NetBEUI, AppleTalk, DNA, and DLC. These are the major suites of protocols used in today's networks. By the end of this chapter, you will have a deeper understanding of how these protocol suites enable devices on the network to communicate.

# How Protocols Work

*Protocols* are how computers on a network communicate. They are comparable to human language. Each language has a set of written rules that must be followed for communications to be successful, and protocols serve this function for network communications.

Data communications protocols are very complicated and can sometimes vary between manufacturers. Protocols may determine packet size, information in the headers, and how data is stored in the packet. Both sides of the conversation must understand these rules for a successful transmission. Therefore, a common language must be agreed on between communicating devices. If neither device has a common protocol installed, they cannot communicate.

Most protocols actually consist of several protocols grouped together in a suite. One protocol usually only covers one aspect of communications between devices. For example, the TCP/IP suite has multiple protocols, including one for file transfer, another for e-mail, and a third for routing information.

As I discuss the different protocol suites in this chapter, you will see how they relate to the OSI model. Be sure that you understand the OSI model before diving into this chapter! Before discussing the first suite of protocols, I define the difference between routable and nonroutable protocols, and connectionless versus connection oriented. Protocols can have different capabilities depending on the need they fill. Some protocols were designed before large networks were common, or were designed for maximum performance, not reliability. The different capabilities and limitations should be fully understood when deciding which protocol or suite to implement.

## Routable Protocols

Many networks today consist of connected LANs. These LANs are often connected using *routers*. One consideration of connecting LANs is the ability of protocols to work properly across the router to the different networks. A protocol with the ability to communicate across the router is known as a *routable protocol*. This type of protocol has become increasingly important and may dictate the choice of protocols used in an organization.

Routable protocols are usually more complicated than *nonroutable protocols* because they need extra layers to handle the routing features. While discussing the protocols in this chapter, you will learn which protocols can be routed and which cannot. In the case of routable protocols, you'll see precisely which protocol in the suite handles the routing.

## Nonroutable Protocols

Some protocols cannot be routed and are limited to smaller LANs. Usually these are older protocols that were devised before networks grew as large as they are today. Though there are not many nonroutable protocols left, some are still used.

Besides being simpler than routable protocols, nonroutable protocols are also usually faster and provide better transfer speeds, due to less overhead.

## Connectionless Protocols

*Connectionless protocols* are similar to mailing a letter. Once you give the letter to the post office to be sent, you have no real feedback as to whether it arrived safely or not. Connectionless protocols send out data across the network with no feedback as to whether it arrived at the destination device.

Connectionless protocols are faster than connection-oriented ones due to less overhead. They are used mainly when there is a need to send data to multiple computers at once, or where high speed is needed, such as in video or audio.

## Connection-Oriented Protocols

If you need to ensure that certain data arrives at its destination, then a *connection-oriented protocol* can be used. The protocols send acknowledgments to show that data was received successfully. This is similar to receiving a delivery receipt from a package you have shipped to someone.

exam preparation pointer

**For the Networking Essentials exam, you should fully understand TCP/IP, IPX/SPX, DLC, and NetBEUI. The other protocols mentioned are here for your information.**

# POPULAR PROTOCOL SUITES

A *protocol suite* is a collection of protocols that work together to form a single system to handle networking devices. The purpose of a protocol suite is to handle the underlying network functions of which user applications can take advantage. For example, the *Simple Mail Transfer Protocol* (SMTP) is responsible for e-mail in a TCP/IP network. This does not mean there is an SMTP application that the user uses for mail; rather it means an application that the user uses can interface with the underlying SMTP and send mail.

The protocol suites normally have many protocols with different capabilities, so the needs of the user's applications are met. A suite may have more than one protocol for the handling of files. One might be optimized for speed, whereas the other has a higher reliability rate. Some protocol suites are dependent on the network equipment used. For example, Digital Network Architecture is used when connecting to Digital Equipment Corporation's mainframe computers. Other suites such as TCP/IP and IPX/SPX can be used with many types of equipment.

Protocol suites can usually be loosely mapped to the OSI model, though some can be mapped closer to the model than others. This relationship normally depends on when the protocol suite was developed as to how well it maps to the OSI model.

The protocol suites in this chapter are the most commonly used in networking today, and they provide all the services that network applications might require.

## TCP/IP Protocol Suite

The *Transmission Control Protocol/Internet Protocol* (TCP/IP) protocol suite, also known as the *Internet Protocols*, is a suite of industry-standard protocols. The TCP/IP suite is made up of many protocols, not just TCP and IP, and has a broad feature set due to its large number of open-standard protocols. Over the years the individual components have evolved to handle almost any need a network user may have.

The TCP/IP protocols were originally designed for a large network that served as a Department of Defense (DoD) experiment to test the idea of keeping communications open even during times of war. This experiment was done by a branch of the Department of Defense known as Advanced Research Projects Agency, or ARPA. The initial network was called *ARPANet*. ARPANet has evolved over the last twenty to thirty years and is now known as the *Internet*.

TCP/IP has also evolved over the years, and today it is the main protocol used on the worldwide Internet (due to its being included in the UNIX operating system, which was the main operating system for early users of the Internet). TCP/IP has also become the protocol of choice for most companies for the following reasons: no one company has control of the usage of standards; almost any network software or equipment is capable of running over it; and, unlike other protocols such as NetBEUI, it is routable, which enables you to connect multiple LANs into one large internetwork.

 web links

**For more information on TCP/IP, you can visit** http://www.inter-nic.net. **There you will find RFCs (Request For Comments) and other documents that discuss the TCP/IP protocols in great detail.**

## TCP/IP and the OSI model

The original designs for TCP/IP were started long before the OSI model was developed; instead of OSI's seven-layer model, TCP/IP was based on a DoD model with four layers. The four layers can be loosely matched to the OSI model in the following ways:

o Network Access layer: This layer corresponds to the Physical and Data Link layers of the OSI model. When TCP/IP was developed, it was made to use existing standards for these two layers so it could work with such protocols as Ethernet and Token Ring. Over the years, TCP/IP has been shown to run over almost any type of network connection from FDDI to radio wave.

o Internet layer: This layer of the DoD model roughly matches up with the Network layer of the OSI model. Both of these layers are responsible for moving data to other devices on the network. *Internet Protocol* (IP) is mainly responsible for this job.

o Host-to-Host layer: This one is similar to the Transport layer of the OSI model. The job of both of these layers is to communicate between peers on the network. As a result, almost all devices on a TCP/IP network are considered hosts, whether they're workstations, servers, or network-attached printers.

o Process/Application layer: This fourth layer does the same job as the top three layers of the OSI model, which is to provide network services.

Figure 5-1 shows how the TCP/IP protocol suite relates to the OSI model.

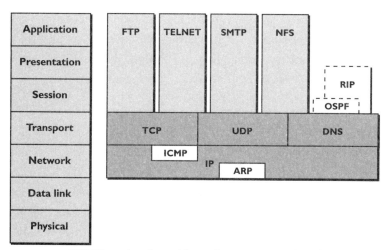

**FIGURE 5-1** TCP/IP protocols and how they correspond to the OSI model

## TCP/IP addressing

Before two computers on a network can communicate, they need to know how to contact each other. Just as every computer has a hardware address called a MAC address that is encoded into the network card, computers also have what is called a *logical address*. This is an address that is usually set by the administrator, though it is sometimes automatically set by the network protocol suite used.

Every host on a TCP/IP network is given an *IP address*. This address is a unique 4-byte address in dotted notation — for example, 56.88.1.231. IP addresses are handed out by a single organization, called interNIC, so each computer has its own unique address; however, organizations should request their IP addresses from the Internet provider to which they are connecting.

IP addresses are divided into classes. IP address classes are used to segment the pool of addresses into sizes corresponding to various organization sizes. When an organization requests a range of IP addresses, they receive a block from one of these classes:

Class A: Class A addresses have one byte for the network and three bytes for the host. For example, the address 56.88.1.231 has a network number of 56, and the remaining numbers signify the host. The first byte of Class A network addresses is always between 1 and 127.

Class B: Class B addresses have two bytes for the network address and the remaining two for the host address. With this arrangement each Class B network can have more than 65,000 hosts. The first byte of Class B addresses is always between 128 and 191.

Class C: Class C addresses are the most common. They use the first three bytes of the address for the network portion and the final byte for the host. This allows for a great number of network addresses given out, with more than 250 hosts on each network. Class C addresses always have the first byte as between 192 and 223.

 note **The network addresses of 128 and 224 and up are used for special purposes and experimentation.**

An organization may segment the addresses given to them by using a subnet mask. A large organization may receive a Class A address that allows for sixteen million hosts. Since the organization could not theoretically use this many addresses for hosts, they can segment the Class A address into many networks, with a smaller amount of hosts per network.

concept link

**The details of splitting TCP/IP addresses into networks and host addresses are beyond the scope of this book. For an excellent tutorial on this procedure, see *TCP/IP MCSE Study Guide* by Greg Bulette. (IDG Books Worldwide, Inc., 1998)**

Besides the IP address, the subnet mask completes a computer's address on a TCP/IP network, and thus is required. The subnet mask is responsible for separating the IP address into the host portion and the network portion.

As I mentioned previously, a Class A address has one byte for the network and three bytes for the host. It has the subnet mask of 255.0.0.0. The 255 in the first byte signifies that it is a network address. A Class B address has two bytes for the network and two for the host. It has a subnet mask of 255.255.0.0.

Subnet masks can get very complicated if you venture outside the standard masks assigned. Table 5-1 shows the standard masks.

**TABLE 5-1**    STANDARD SUBNET MASKS

| SUBNET MASK | NETWORK CLASS |
| --- | --- |
| 255.0.0.0 | Class A |
| 255.255.0.0 | Class B |
| 255.255.255.0 | Class C |

## What's in the TCP/IP suite?

The Internet Protocols are made up of a lot more than just TCP and IP, though these are the main two. The following sections cover the main protocols in the TCP/IP suite, but they are by no means the entire suite. It would take many books to cover all the included protocols.

### Internet Protocol

The *Internet Protocol* (IP) is a connectionless protocol that sits in the Network layer level of the OSI model. The job of IP is to address and route packets accordingly through the network. An IP header is attached to each packet (also referred to as a *datagram*) and includes the source address, destination address, and other information used by the receiving host. Another job of IP is to fragment and reassemble packets that were split up in transit. Some types of networks can support larger packets than other types, and packets may become fragmented when going to a network that cannot support the current packet size. The packet is split up, and then each piece gets a new IP header and is sent on its way to the final destination. When the final host receives the packets, it is up to IP to put all the pieces back together to form the original data.

### Internet Control Message Protocol

The *Internet Control Message Protocol* (ICMP) provides error reporting for IP. Since IP is connectionless, and there is no error checking happening, it cannot detect when an error occurs on the network. It is up to ICMP to report errors back to the host that sent the IP packet. For example, if a device cannot forward an IP packet on to the next network in its journey, then it will send back a message to the source of that packet using ICMP to explain the error. Some common types of errors that ICMP can report are Destination Unreachable, Congestion, Echo Request, and Echo Reply (used with the PING command).

The popular Ping utility uses the ICMP Echo and Echo Request messages. A Ping session is shown in Figure 5-2.

```
Command Prompt                                          _ □ ×

D:\>ping nash-pdc.usps.gov

Pinging nash-pdc.usps.gov [56.88.1.231] with 32 bytes of data:

Reply from 56.88.1.231: bytes=32 time=10ms TTL=127
Reply from 56.88.1.231: bytes=32 time<10ms TTL=127
Reply from 56.88.1.231: bytes=32 time<10ms TTL=127
Reply from 56.88.1.231: bytes=32 time<10ms TTL=127

D:\>_
```

**FIGURE 5-2** A Ping session

 **note** Ping is an unofficial acronym for Packet Internet Groper. It is unofficial because the name Ping existed long before the Packet Internet Groper name.

## RIP and OSPF

*Routing Information Protocol* (RIP) and *Open Shortest Path First* (OSPF) are two routing protocols in the Internet Protocol suite. RIP, similar to NetWare's RIP, uses the number of routers (hops) between the originating computer and the destination to decide the best way to route a packet. OSPF uses much more information than just the number of hops to make a decision. Usually OSPF is configured to figure in the hop count, the speed of the connection between the hops, and the load balancing to calculate the best way to route packets.

## Transmission Control Protocol

*Transmission Control Protocol* (TCP) is a connection-oriented protocol that corresponds to the Transport layer of the OSI model. TCP opens and maintains a connection between two communicating hosts on a network. When an IP packet is sent between them, a TCP header that contains flow control, sequencing, and error checking is added to the packet. Each virtual connection to a host is given a port number so datagrams being sent to the host go to the correct virtual connection.

A port is similar to a mailbox. When data is delivered to a computer via the network, it must be sent to a process on the computer. A computer may have multiple processes running on it, such as an Internet Web server, a mail server, and a file-sharing service. Each service that expects data from the network will register itself onto a port number. For example, an Internet Web server uses port 80, while a mail server usually uses port 25. Inside of the header of the network packet is the port number for which the data is intended.

## User Datagram Protocol

The *User Datagram Protocol* (UDP) is a connectionless transport protocol and is used when the overhead of TCP is not needed. UDP is just responsible for transporting datagrams. UDP also uses port numbers similar to TCP, except that they do not correspond to a virtual connection, but to a process on the other host. For example, a datagram may be sent to a port number of 53 to a remote host. Since UDP is connectionless there is no virtual connection setup, but there is a process on the remote host "listening" on port 53.

## Address Resolution Protocol

Suppose that a computer needs to communicate with another computer on a network. The source computer has the IP address of the destination computer, but not the MAC address that is needed to communicate at the Physical layer of the OSI model. *Address Resolution Protocol* (ARP) handles the conversion of the address by sending out a discovery packet.

The discovery packet is sent out to the broadcast MAC address so every device on the network receives it. In the packet is a request for the owner of the IP address. When the receiving computer with that IP gets the discovery packet, it replies to the originator to let the originator know that it owns that IP. ARP maintains a list of IP and MAC addresses so a discovery packet is not needed every time communication takes place.

note ▼ **The opposite of ARP is RARP (Reverse Address Resolution Protocol).**

### Domain Name System

*Domain Name System*, or DNS (not to be confused with Microsoft domains), is the system that converts user-friendly names such as `http://www.idgbooks.com` to the correct IP address. DNS is a distributed database hierarchy maintained by different organizations. There are a number of main DNS servers that point clients to the more specific servers at each company.

To resolve the aforementioned name to the correct IP address, a client first goes to one of the main DNS servers, which tells the client which the server to contact for the `idgbooks.com` domain. The client then goes to that server to resolve the full name to an IP. This way the main servers only need to point a client to a closer server. (This is just as well, as the main servers could not possibly handle the load needed to resolve every computer name on the Internet to an IP address.) Administrators at IDG Books can then make changes to their computer names any time they want without having to constantly update a main server.

### File Transfer Protocol

*File Transfer Protocol* (FTP) is the file-sharing protocol most commonly used in a TCP/IP environment. This protocol allows users to remotely log on to other computers on a network and browse, download, and upload files. One of the main reasons FTP is still very popular is that it is platform independent. There are FTP servers and clients for almost every operating system on the market. An FTP session is shown in Figure 5-3.

```
Command Prompt - ftp nash-pdc.usps.gov                    _ □ ×

D:\>ftp nash-pdc.usps.gov
Connected to nash-pdc.usps.gov.
220 nash-pdc Microsoft FTP Service (Version 3.0).
User (nash-pdc.usps.gov:(none)): anonymous
331 Anonymous access allowed, send identity (e-mail name) as password.
Password:
230-Welcome to the NASH-PDC FTP Server.  Any
 problems/questions please contact Jason Nash.

.All uploads go in the Incoming directory.
230 Anonymous user logged in.
ftp> _
```

**FIGURE 5-3**  An FTP session

### Simple Mail Transfer Protocol

Internet e-mail is very popular now. *Simple Mail Transfer Protocol* (SMTP) is
responsible for making sure that e-mail is delivered. SMTP only handles the delivery of mail to servers and between servers. It does not handle the delivery to the
final e-mail client application.

### Dynamic Host Configuration Protocol

Once your network becomes large, keeping up with IP addresses and settings can
become an ordeal. *Dynamic Host Configuration Protocol* (DHCP) takes over the
job of assigning addresses and configuring computers on the network. Instead of
configuring each device on the network manually, the administrator does it once
for the entire network on the DHCP server. The DHCP server is given a range of IP
addresses to hand out to network devices. The range of IP addresses is also configured for the network they will be given out on. When a computer comes online to
the network, it sends out a DHCP request. The nearest DHCP server responds with
all the information to set up TCP/IP on the new client.

exam
preparation
pointer

For the Networking Essentials exam, know that DHCP is responsible for automatic IP addressing. Questions may present a scenario
where an administrator needs an easier way to manage network
addressing and configuration. Be aware that DHCP can provide all
configuration settings — not just an IP address, but also a subnet
mask, default gateway, and so on.

## Telnet

*Telnet* allows a user to remotely log in to another computer and run applications. The computer at which the user is physically working effectively becomes a *dumb terminal* — no processing is done on that computer; it is only used for display. Telnet clients are available for almost every operating system on the market today. Windows 95 and Windows NT come with a Telnet client out of the box. Figure 5-4 shows a Telnet session.

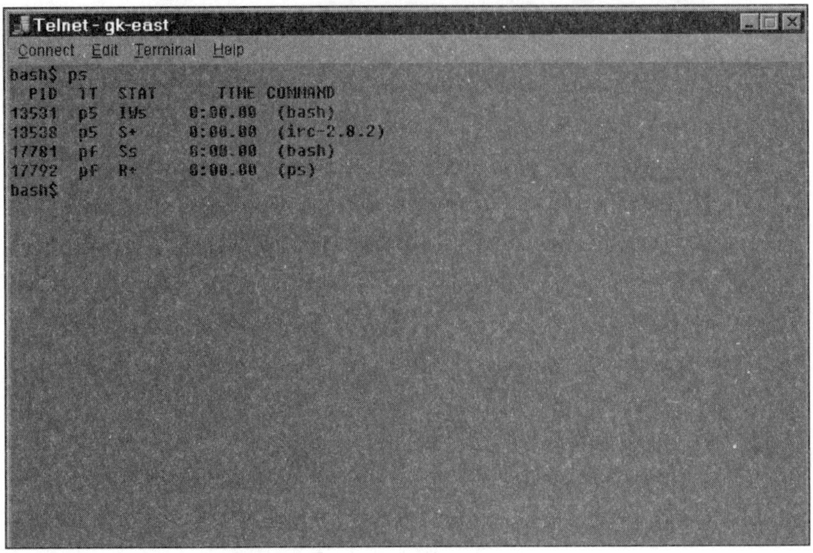

```
Telnet - gk-east
Connect  Edit  Terminal  Help
bash$ ps
  PID  TT  STAT      TIME  COMMAND
13531  p5  IWs    0:00.00  (bash)
13538  p5  S+     0:00.00  (irc-2.8.2)
17781  pf  Ss     0:00.00  (bash)
17792  pf  R+     0:00.00  (ps)
bash$
```

**FIGURE 5-4**  A Telnet session

## Network File System

The *Network File System* (NFS) was developed by Sun Microsystems. It is a more advanced way to share files and disk drives than FTP and Telnet. While FTP and Telnet require you to use a separate client, NFS allows users to connect to network drives and use them as if they were local hard drives. This is similar to mapping drives in NetWare or Windows NT. Now that NFS is available for public use, it has become very popular.

# IPX/SPX Protocol Suite

The *Internetwork Packet Exchange/Sequenced Packet Exchange* (IPX/SPX) protocol suite was developed and maintained by Novell, Inc. Like TCP/IP, the name comes from the two main protocols in the suite, IPX and SPX, even though there are many other protocols in the suite. It was developed in the early 1980s and derived from work that Xerox had done on a protocol named *Xerox Network System* (XNS).

The IPX/SPX protocol suite handles everything from file and disk sharing to message and application services. Most of the IPX/SPX functionality is aimed toward requesting and receiving services from a large server. While TCP/IP has many peer-to-peer functions, IPX/SPX has none, as Novell did not need this ability because their networks use the server-centric NetWare operating system. A main goal of the NetWare and IPX/SPX development was user friendliness. The IPX/SPX protocols and network applications are written so the network environment is comfortable for users — so comfortable that they sometimes cannot tell if they are accessing network resources or local ones. One example of this is the ease of mapping a network drive to a server. To a user the newly mapped drive looks like a local hard disk. Figure 5-5 demonstrates the mapping feature.

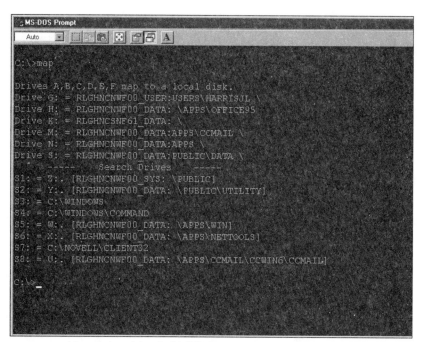

**FIGURE 5-5** Mapping a drive in NetWare

The IPX/SPX suite is also very functional because it is modular. That is, pieces can be removed and replaced by protocols from other suites. As an example, you could remove the main IPX/SPX protocols and replace them with *User Datagram Protocol* (UDP) and TCP. This type of modular design allows the protocol suite to be very adaptable to other needs and permits IPX/SPX to use other types of networks, such as AppleTalk.

One very important feature of the IPX/SPX protocol suite is its ease of use and administration. Unlike TCP/IP, IPX/SPX needs no manual addressing for workstations to function. The only real addressing needed is on the NetWare server, and that is just to pick a network address not found on any other connected network. This information is automatically passed on to the NetWare client.

exam preparation pointer

**The Microsoft version of the IPX/SPX suite is called NetWare Link (NWLink). You may see this on the exam and should know it refers to the IPX/SPX protocols.**

The IPX/SPX suite is relatively new, whereas TCP/IP is extremely old in the world of computers and networking. Because IPX/SPX was created around the time the OSI model was conceived, it can easily be mapped to the model. You will learn the individual protocols by OSI model layer. Figure 5-6 shows how each of the IPX/SPX protocols compares to the OSI model.

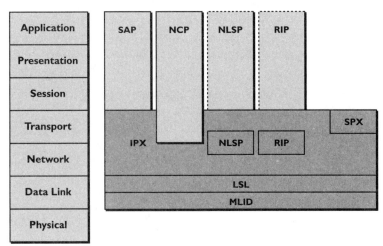

FIGURE 5-6  IPX/SPX and the OSI model

## Lower-layer protocols in the IPX/SPX suite

The layers discussed in this section correspond to the Data Link layer of the OSI model. There are no protocols in the Physical layer of the IPX/SPX suite because it can utilize any popular physical network type, such as Ethernet, Token Ring, or FDDI. The protocols that work at the Data Link layer are responsible for media access and interfacing to the network card. There are two protocols in this layer: *Multiple Link Interface Driver* protocol and *Link Support Layer* protocol.

### Multiple Link Interface Driver

Corresponding to the MAC sublayer function of the Data Link layer, the Multiple Link Interface Driver (MLID) protocol is concerned with media access. Remember from previous chapters that media access is the arbitration method devices use to decide who can transmit on the media. Examples are:

- Token passing
- Polling
- Contention

MLID is a network interface board driver specification — the piece of software that makes the network card in a computer work. Such drivers are written to a certain specification called the *Open Datalink Interface* (ODI) specification. The ODI spec was written by Novell to allow third-party vendors to create network card drivers that work with their NetWare operating system. Each network card requires a separate MLID driver.

The MLID software driver is usually named after the network card it supports. For example, the 3Com 3C509 network card has the MS-DOS MLID driver of `3c509.com`, and the Novell/Eagle Ne2000 card has the `Ne2000.com` driver.

The following shows how MLID driver loading appears onscreen:

```
C:\FS_CNECT>smc8000
SMC Ethernet Adapter DOS ODI Driver v4.04 (940314)
(C) Copyright 1992-94 Standard Microsystems Corp. All Rights
  Reserved.

Adapter 8216C, Int 10, Port 280, Mem D0000, Node Address
  C0682EBB L
Max Frame 1514 bytes, Line Speed 10 Mbps
```

*(continued)*

```
Board 1, Frame ETHERNET_802.3, LSB Mode
Board 2, Frame ETHERNET_II, LSB Mode
Board 3, Frame ETHERNET_802.2, LSB Mode
Board 4, Frame ETHERNET_SNAP, LSB Mode


C:\FS_CNECT>
```

### Link Support Layer

The other piece that makes up the IPX/SPX protocol suite's Data Link layer is the Link Support Layer (LSL) software. It functions as the interface between MLID and the upper-layer protocols.

The Link Support Layer is responsible for making sure data goes to the correct upper-layer protocols, should multiple protocol stacks be loaded.

 **note** **Neither the MLID nor the LSL software are tied to a specific protocol. You could load TCP/IP or IPX/SPX protocol stacks using these software drivers.**

On an MS-DOS workstation, the LSL software is loaded by the file named Lsl.com. It is loaded before MLID. The following shows how the LSL software loading appears onscreen:

```
C:\FS_CNECT>lsl
NetWare Link Support Layer v2.16 (950417)
(C) Copyright 1990-1995 Novell, Inc. All Rights Reserved.

The configuration file used was "C:\FS_CNECT\NET.CFG".
Max Boards 4, Max Stacks 4


C:\FS_CNECT>
```

## *Middle IPX/SPX suite protocols*

The middle protocols in the IPX/SPX suite map to the Network and Transport layers of the OSI model, and are responsible for transferring data between devices on the network, as well as carrying some routing functionality.

The protocols in this section are:

o  IPX

o  SPX

o  NLSP

o  RIP

## Internetwork Packet Exchange

The *Internetwork Pack Exchange* (IPX) protocol corresponds to the Network layer of the OSI model. IPX is responsible for connectionless data service. It handles the routing of data across an internetwork, as well as the logical network addressing.

In a NetWare network most data transfers between clients and servers are handled by the IPX protocol. However, this protocol is not used when a client must cross a router to get to a server, or during printing (in these instances, the SPX protocol is used).

An IPX address is a combination of the physical MAC address on the network card and a logically assigned network address. An example of this is 123456789ABCD. IPX also uses socket numbers to successfully deliver data to the correct upper-layer process on the destination device. Socket numbers are the IPX/SPX equivalent of TCP/IP port numbers.

IPX decides the best route to a remote device by using one of the built-in routing protocols covered in this section.

The MS-DOS driver for the IPX protocol is `Ipxodi.com`. It is loaded last. The following shows how `Ipxodi.com` loading looks onscreen:

```
C:\FS_CNECT>ipxodi

NetWare IPX/SPX Protocol v3.02 (950808)
(C) Copyright 1990-1995 Novell, Inc. All Rights Reserved.

GET LOCAL TARGET STACKS 5
SPX CONNECTIONS 60
SPX LISTEN TIMEOUT 2000
SPX ABORT TIMEOUT 3000
Bound to logical board 1 (SMC8000) : Protocol ID 0

C:\FS_CNECT>
```

**Sequenced Packet Exchange**

*Sequenced Packet Exchange* (SPX) makes up for the inherent unreliability of IPX. Where IPX is a connectionless datagram protocol, SPX is connection oriented, with sequencing and error control. SPX rides on top of IPX to add this extra functionality in a similar way that TCP rides on top of IP in the TCP/IP suite.

SPX is mainly used when a connection is made across an internetwork device such as a router, or to a print server to service a printing request. SPX uses acknowledgments to ensure delivery, where IPX does not.

SPX also establishes virtual circuits, called *connections*, between devices. Each connection has its own connection ID to distinguish it. Connection IDs can be tied to upper-layer processes.

On an MS-DOS client, the SPX protocol is supplied via the NetWare shell requester. One such requester is Vlm.exe. The following shows how Vlm.exe loading appears onscreen:

```
C:\VLM>vlm
VLM.EXE    - NetWare virtual loadable module manager v1.20 REV
 B (951002)
(C) Copyright 1993, 1994, 1995 Novell, Inc. All Rights
 Reserved.
Patent pending.

The VLM.EXE file is pre-initializing the VLMs
The VLM.EXE file is using extended memory (XMS)


C:\VLM>
```

**Routing Information Protocol**

One protocol that IPX can use to decide the best route through an internetwork is the *Routing Information Protocol* (RIP). RIP is a very simple routing protocol that uses the distance vector method to calculate hop count (basically, it counts the number of times a piece of data crosses a router before reaching its destination) and then chooses the route with the least number of hops. This may sound adequate at first; however, just imagine a short route of only two hops, but the links between them are slow modems. While this route was chosen, another route with three hops over high-speed links was turned down. No consideration is given for the speed of the links over which the data would travel, just the number of hops.

Another problem with distance vector routing protocols is that devices using this method occasionally (every 30 or 60 seconds) broadcast their routing information. On a small network with a few internetworking devices this may be negligible, but it can quickly become a problem on a very large network, as large networks typically have a large number of segments and routers. If there are six routers between two ends of the network, it takes 30 to 60 seconds for each router to pass the information. This could result in 3 to 6 minutes elapsing before the farthest end is notified of the change.

 **You may also notice that RIP is in the TCP/IP suite, as well as the IPX/SPX suite. The IPX/SPX RIP is based on the TCP/IP RIP, but it has been modified to work for IPX.**

### Network Link Services Protocol

*Network Link Services Protocol* (NLSP) is a more advanced routing protocol than RIP. Instead of using a simple distance vector scheme, it uses a *link state routing* mechanism to choose the best route. In a link state routing protocol, the best route is chosen using more information than just hop count. Things such as latency and speed of the links between the internetwork devices come into the picture.

Another advantage of a link state routing protocol is that it only broadcasts routing information when a change occurs, not at a preset interval. Because of this, NLSP uses far less bandwidth than a distance vector protocol and can keep up with a changing network better. NLSP does not need to wait 30 or 60 seconds before sending out updates — it does it as needed.

 **Under the new NetWare 4.1 operating system, an administrator has the choice of either using NLSP or RIP.**

## *Upper-layer IPX/SPX protocols*

The two upper-layer protocols in the IPX/SPX suite for use with NetWare are *NetWare Core Protocol* and *Service Access Protocol*. They cover multiple layers of the OSI model: Netware Core Protocol corresponds to the Transport, Session, Presentation, and Application layers, and Service Access Protocol corresponds to the Session and Application layers.

### NetWare Core Protocol

NetWare Core Protocol (NCP) is the "language" spoken between a NetWare client and a server. This protocol handles most network services, including file services, printing, file locking, resource access, and synchronization.

NCP functions at the following four layers of the OSI model:

- **Transport layer:** Connection services with segment sequencing, error control, and flow control
- **Session layer:** Session control
- **Presentation layer:** Character translation
- **Application layer:** Application and service interface to the end-user application

NCP is a high-level language built into NetWare and is used inside any lower-level protocol that accesses the server. This way you use NCP whether your clients and servers are using IPX/SPX or TCP/IP, though it is most often used with IPX/SPX. Developers can use NCP to make requests and send replies between a client and a server. The commands are grouped into requests and replies. The NCP commands are mainly concerned with file, directory, and printer access.

An example of a communication using NCP commands would be the Get Nearest Server command, issued by a client upon booting in a NetWare environment. In this communication, a workstation has just booted and needs to know the name of a file server. The workstation sends out a Get Nearest Server query to everyone on the network. Any servers that hear this request will send back an NCP command of Get Nearest Server Reply with its name and network address. Figure 5-7 shows a data decoder demonstrating this type of communication.

### Service Access Protocol

Servers using the IPX/SPX protocol are easy to set up and maintain, thanks to the Service Access Protocol (SAP). At a set interval, each computer sharing a resource on the network sends out a SAP packet containing information about the resource and where it is located.

While the SAP feature is very useful and makes the network easy to configure, it can also become a problem. While allowing clients to find servers without having to manually configure every client for each server, the SAP packets can quickly overrun a large network. Steps must be taken to filter out the excessive SAP packets and keep them down to a manageable level.

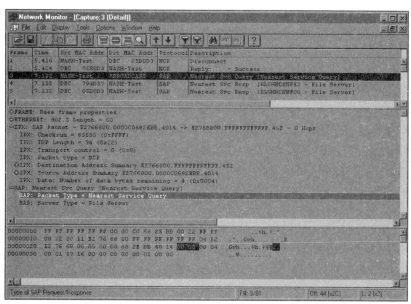

**FIGURE 5-7**  Get Nearest Server Request in NCP

## Microsoft protocols

Microsoft network operating systems can use many different protocols to function. This contrasts with many network systems which require a set suite of protocols. Though Microsoft can use many standard protocol suites, there are some protocols that Microsoft uses almost exclusively. These are described in the following paragraphs.

## NetBEUI

*NetBIOS Extended User Interface* or NetBEUI (pronounced *net-buoy*) is a small, very fast protocol used in Microsoft networks. It has some advantages and some disadvantages that must be considered for its use. The main advantages of NetBEUI are its speed and ease of configuration. NetBEUI is one of the fastest, if not *the* fastest, protocols you can use to share files. Configuration is simple because all that is needed is a computer name — no network or logical addresses are required.

exam
preparation
pointer  **Know for the exam that NetBEUI is a small, fast, nonroutable protocol used in small Microsoft workgroup networks.**

concept link

The main disadvantage of NetBEUI is that it cannot be routed across a large internetwork. If your network is separated by internetwork devices such as routers (which will be covered in Chapter 6), a computer using NetBEUI as its only protocol will not be able to access resources on the other side of these devices.

Another disadvantage of NetBEUI is that it is only used on Microsoft networks. There is very limited support, if any, for this protocol on other vendor's operating systems.

### NetBIOS

NetBEUI stands for NetBIOS Extended User Interface. Originally Network Basic Input/Output System (NetBIOS) and NetBEUI were considered the same protocol, but that is no longer the case. NetBIOS has been "separated" from NetBEUI and is now a distinct Session layer protocol that can be used on top of other Transport layer protocols.

NetBIOS was originally developed by IBM and acts as an interface for applications to the network. It was made so that developers could easily use this interface to write network-aware applications.

NetBIOS is still very prominent today, even without NetBEUI. Most Microsoft systems use NetBIOS commands for communications. Most file sharing and administration done on Microsoft networks use the NetBIOS interface on top of TCP/IP or IPX/SPX.

### Server Message Block

The *Server Message Block* (SMB) protocol is a Presentation layer protocol used by Microsoft networking software to communicate. Once a communication channel has been established with a protocol such as TCP/IP, a NetBIOS session is made between the devices. The SMB commands flow over this NetBIOS session. SMB is similar in function to Novell's NCP protocol. That is, it provides the communication and commands between the client and server to handle resource requests and replies.

# The AppleTalk Protocol Suite

*AppleTalk* was developed by Apple Computers for use with their Macintosh brand of computers. AppleTalk is a large suite of protocols that make up an easy-to-configure and easy-to-use networking system. Originally designed with their LocalTalk cabling architecture in mind, it has expanded to support other network types such as Ethernet and Token Ring.

The original AppleTalk specification greatly limited the size and type of network on which it could run. Its design was meant for use in a small workgroup type of environment, not large enterprise-wide networking. Apple revised the specification in 1989 to allow for larger, more robust networks. The second version, named Phase 2, allowed use of other network protocol suites such as TCP/IP.

Original AppleTalk networks could not be internetworked because of the address space used. Phase 2 added support for a network address along with a node ID to allow for larger networks.

AppleTalk is very modular and can be mapped to the OSI model quite easily. Figure 5-8 shows the AppleTalk suite in relation to the OSI model.

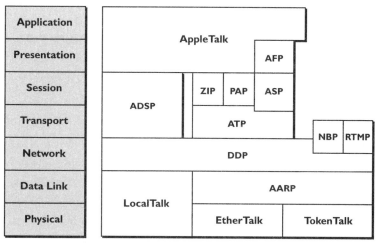

**FIGURE 5-8** AppleTalk protocols and how they correspond to the OSI model

The AppleTalk suite is made up of so many protocols that sometimes the number can seem overwhelming. One good thing about the protocols is that the naming helps you understand the function more than almost any other suite. First I discuss the Physical layer protocols and move on from there.

## *LocalTalk, EtherTalk, and TokenTalk Link Access protocols*

The *Link Access protocols* allow the AppleTalk suite to operate with different network media types. The *EtherTalk* (ELAP) and *TokenTalk* (TLAP) protocols let you build AppleTalk networks on the popular Ethernet and Token Ring network protocols.

*LocalTalk* (LLAP) is a proprietary design made by Apple Computers. LocalTalk uses twisted-pair cable with a bandwidth of 230.4Kbps and is based on the CSMA/CA contention system. With a maximum length of 300 meters and only 32 devices, it was well suited for a small workgroup network when it was first utilized. Unlike other types of networks, with these small workgroup networks, all device addressing was done dynamically by the devices themselves. When a device first came online, it communicated with the other network devices to find an unused ID.

LocalTalk fit the Macintosh reputation very well with its ease of setup and use, although speed and network size later caused this network type to become very unpopular.

## *AppleTalk Address Resolution Protocol*

Ethernet and Token Ring use preconfigured hardware addresses on network cards. *AppleTalk Address Resolution Protocol* (AARP) allows the upper-layer protocols to use these addresses instead of the dynamically configured LocalTalk addresses.

## *Datagram Delivery Protocol*

*Datagram Delivery Protocol* (DDP) is a connectionless Network layer protocol. It provides connections between two sockets. Like ports in TCP/IP, sockets are addresses on the communicating devices for upper-layer processes. Devices not only need a network and node address to make a full connection but also a socket number to know for which process on a device the data is destined.

To route data across an internetwork, DDP uses *Routing Table Maintenance Protocol*, *Zone Information Protocol*, and *Name Binding Protocol* to determine the best path.

### Routing Table Maintenance Protocol

Routing Table Maintenance Protocol (RTMP) is the AppleTalk equivalent of the RIP routing protocol. It uses a distance vector algorithm to decide the best path to send data.

### Zone Information Protocol

Because networks can become very large and overwhelm users trying to find the resources they need, AppleTalk employed a concept known as *zones*. Zones allow administrators to selectively group services together so they are easier for users to find. Instead of seeing every service on a network, a user may be given a list of zones to choose from. An administrator could put all local resources in one zone to allow users easy access. The Zone Information Protocol (ZIP) is used by routers to resolve zone and network names and assign service providers to zones. ZIP uses DDP for communications between devices.

### Name Binding Protocol

Using the network and node IDs in AppleTalk to reach resources is neither user friendly nor intuitive. With the use of the Name Binding Protocol (NBP), administrators can assign more user-friendly names to resources on the network. With this, users can connect to a server by a name such as `ACCTING_SERVER` instead of the ambiguous device address.

Remember that in AppleTalk, device addresses are dynamic. The main job of the Name Binding Protocol is to keep up with the dynamic changes in device addresses and hide them from the user. Lower-level protocols in the AppleTalk suite still use the real device addresses, but they are translated to friendly names by this protocol for the upper-layer services.

## AppleTalk Transaction Protocol

The *AppleTalk Transaction Protocol* (ATP) provides a connectionless Transport layer protocol, but instead of being strictly for data like others of this type, it is for transactions. Reliability is added using acknowledgments and retransmissions. If an acknowledgment isn't received in a set time, a packet is re-sent.

A *transaction* consists of a request and a reply. For example, an entry into a database is a transaction. In this example, a request would be made to the database, and a reply would be sent back stating whether the request was successful or not. If no reply was sent back, the transaction would be considered a failure.

ATP also handles the fragmentation and reassembly of packets that are too large for lower-level protocols. Packets that were part of a larger message can be selectively re-sent.

### AppleTalk Session Protocol

As you learned above, the AppleTalk Transaction Protocol was not meant for data. The *AppleTalk Session Protocol* (ASP) on top of ATP allows reliable data transport. ASP provides and maintains connections between service requesters and providers.

Multiple sessions can be maintained between devices. Only workstations can initiate ASP connections — servers cannot.

### Printer Access Protocol

Though the name of this protocol implies only printer service, it can be used for more. *Printer Access Protocol* (PAP) is a Session layer protocol similar to ASP. It provides printing services to clients by setting up connections, transmitting data, and tearing down those connections. Unlike ASP, either a client or server can initiate a Printer Access Protocol connection.

### AppleTalk Data Stream Protocol

*AppleTalk Data Stream Protocol* (ADSP) is a newer protocol than some of the others about which you have learned. It is a replacement for ASP, PAP, and ATP.

ADSP uses byte-streaming connections instead of transactions like ATP. *Streaming* is a fast way to transfer data, as it is a constant flow without any stops or starts. This provides far greater bandwidth and performance, especially over slower network links. Connections between devices are set up as an open link that through which either end can send data. Since ADSP is layered on top of DDP, the data is actually sent as datagrams.

### AppleTalk Filing Protocol

The *AppleTalk Filing Protocol* (AFP) allows users to access resources on their workstations as if they were local. It translates local requests into the necessary network formats understood by AppleShare file servers. It can also handle file format changes.

AppleTalk Filing Protocol is also responsible for the login and authentication of user names and passwords. It handles the encryption and verification of the passwords over the network.

### AppleShare

*AppleShare* is actually three different client/server applications that provide access to network resources.

- AppleShare File Server: Allows users to share and retrieve files using AppleTalk Filing Protocol (AFP). Also handles user authentication.

- AppleShare Print Server: This service uses NBP to resolve names of printers so that PAP can connect to them. The AppleShare Print Server also manages print spooling and network printing.

- AppleShare PC: The AppleShare PC service allows MS-DOS workstations to save files on the AppleShare server and print to AppleShare printers. A special client on the MS-DOS workstation is needed.

# Digital Network Architecture Protocols

The *Digital Network Architecture* (DNA) was developed by Digital Equipment Corporation (DEC) in 1974. It is used when connecting to DEC's mainframe computers. It has been revised many times over the years and is currently in its fifth revision, called Phase V. Equipment by DEC that operates within the specifications of DNA are referred to as *DECNet products*.

Through the different revisions of DNA over the years, DEC has striven to move to standards-based protocols and can be mapped very well to the OSI model.

### Low-level DNA protocols

The protocols that DNA utilizes at the Data Link and Network layers of the OSI model are mostly standard. They are responsible for the media access and formatting the data into frames for transmission. Only one is proprietary. Figure 5-9 shows the relationship that DNA has to the lower layers of the OSI model.

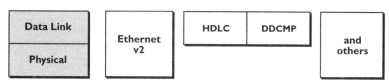

**FIGURE 5-9** DNA and OSI low-level protocols

### Ethernet version 2

The Ethernet protocol was originally developed by DEC, Intel, and Xerox. It was updated later to version 2, which is the standard Ethernet that other networks use.

Characteristics of Ethernet version 2:

o Manchester encoding

o Bandwidth of 10Mbps

o CSMA/CD for media access

The later IEEE 802.3 standard was developed from the Ethernet v2 standard but with one important format change, involving the packet header information, that made it incompatible with the earlier standard.

### High-level Data Link Control

*High-level Data Link Control* (HDLC) is a Data Link protocol that defines the format for data frames and how to transfer them from one station to another.

Characteristics of HDLC:

o Provides both synchronous and asynchronous transmission

o Includes LLC flow control

o Specifies data frame structure and command syntax

### Digital Data Communications Message Protocol

*Digital Data Communications Message Protocol* (DDCMP) is a protocol from the original DNA specifications. It is responsible for transmitting data to end stations. It is proprietary to DEC and is included in Phase V as an option to retain compatibility with older versions of DNA. A frame in DDCMP is known as a *message*.

Characteristics of DDCMP:

o Designed for WAN links

o Allows synchronous or asynchronous transmission

o Permits either full- or half-duplex communications

o Permits either point-to-point or multipoint connections

o Includes Data Link layer flow control and error checking

## Middle-layer DNA protocols

As mentioned previously, protocols in DNA closely match the OSI model. These next protocols handle routing and data transmission. Figure 5-10 shows the middle layers of the OSI model in relation to the DNA protocol suite.

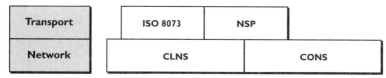

**FIGURE 5-10**   DNA and OSI middle-layer protocols

### Connectionless Network Services

*Connectionless Network Services* (CLNS) is a Network layer protocol. It is used more often than its connection-oriented partner, *Connection-Oriented Network Service* (CONS).

   CLNS includes the following three protocols:

- ISO 8473: A connectionless network services protocol that handles the communications between end systems

- ISO 9542: A routing protocol that handles communications from end systems (ES) to intermediate systems (IS). This is known as an *ES-IS routing protocol*. An ES would be a workstation and an IS would be a router.

- ISO 10589: The ISO 9542 protocol handles the routing from an end system to the router, and ISO 10589 handles the routing between intermediate systems. This protocol is more complicated because it has to make decisions on the best routes, unlike ISO 9542, which just has to find the closest router.

### Connection-Oriented Network Service

Where CLNS is connectionless, CONS is connection oriented. Unlike most other Network layer protocols, the connection-oriented nature of this protocol adds reliability. It is made up of the following protocols:

- ISO 8208: ISO version of the X.25 packet switching protocol.

- ISO 8878: Connection-oriented implementation of the X.25 protocol.

   CONS is not used as often as CLNS.

### Connection-Oriented Transport Protocol specification

*Connection-Oriented Transport Protocol* (ISO 8073) is a generic Transport layer protocol. It provides the basic Transport-level services of flow control, error control, and packet sequencing.

### Network Services Protocol

*Network Services Protocol* (NSP) was an original part of the DNA specification and the only proprietary protocol in the middle layers. It is a full-duplex, connection-oriented protocol that is capable of prioritizing messages based on needs. It also implements flow control to handle the number of outstanding messages appropriately during times of congestion.

## High-level DNA protocols

At the top three layers of the OSI model, DNA provides a full set of service applications. Services range from session control and file services to messaging. Figure 5-11 shows the high-level DNA protocols.

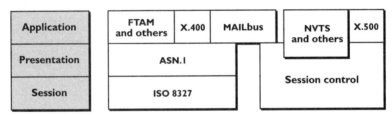

**FIGURE 5-11**  DNA and OSI high-level protocols

### Session Control

The *Session Control* protocol acts as an intermediary between the Application and Transport layers of the OSI model. It is used in protocol stacks that are not OSI compliant.

Functions of the Session Control protocol:

o Provides address-to-name resolution

o Routes messages to the correct lower-level protocol stacks

o Manages connections and assigns IDs to these connections

### ISO 8327

*ISO 8327* is a generic Session layer protocol. It handles half-duplex data transfer, connection establishment, and connection release, all of which are basic Session layer jobs. Flow control and error checking are accomplished using *checkpoints*, also known as *bookmarks*. If an error is encountered, the session can be rolled back to the last successful checkpoint.

### Abstract Syntax Notation Character Code Translation Scheme

The *Abstract Syntax Notation Character Code Translation Scheme* (ASN.1) Presentation layer protocol uses *Basic Encoding Rules* (BER) to translate to and from different character sets and data structures.

### File Transfer Access Method

*ISO 8571*, or *File Transfer Access Method* (FTAM), is an OSI-compliant file access protocol. FTAM is not a complete protocol itself, but requires other protocol implementations to be complete. One such protocol is *Digital Access Protocol*.

### Digital Access Protocol

Digital Access Protocol (DAP) is a proprietary data transfer protocol that is used with FTAM. It allows for file management tasks such as deletion, retrieval, and storage. It supports heterogeneous file systems (many different computer platforms) and database indexing.

### Network Virtual Terminal Service

*Network Virtual Terminal Service* (NVTS) provides terminal emulation over the network. It translates the data into a format that can be sent over the wire and then handles the translating of the data back to its original form for the host or for display on a workstation.

### X.400

*X.400* is a messaging standard that allows different e-mail systems to communicate seamlessly. The DNA family of message products is called *DEC MAILbus*. Other popular enterprise-wide e-mail packages, such as Microsoft Exchange Server, also support X.400.

### X.500

*X.500* is an international address-to-name resolution and directory services standard. By supporting a standard directory services protocol, DNA can fit into larger enterprise-wide directory services.

## Data Link Control

*Data Link Control* (DLC) is a nonroutable data transfer protocol designed to connect terminals to mainframe computers. It is also frequently used to connect networked computers with Hewlett-Packard network printers. It is not a full protocol suite and cannot be used for normal client/server interaction. Specifically, you could not use DLC to share files.

exam preparation pointer

**For the exam, know that DLC is mainly used for Hewlett-Packard network printers and that it cannot be used for data communications.**

# WIDE AREA NETWORK PROTOCOLS

The preceding protocols you've learned about enable clients to talk to servers, usually over a LAN. However, suppose your company just merged with another that had a remote office in another state. You need to engineer a way to connect your network to their network. It is not as simple as getting some sort of network connection, such as a telephone line, and then using IPX/SPX or TCP/IP over it. You need technology to handle the movement of data across these WAN connections.

In this section, I cover current popular technologies used by companies to send data across WANs. Before you start learning these new protocols, you need to quickly go back over switched, dedicated, and virtual circuit connections (see Chapter 2).

## Connection Types

The best WAN connection would simply be one long wire between sites. This would give you unrestricted, dedicated bandwidth. The main problems with this are, of course, cost and feasibility. Instead of having a dedicated cable, companies buy or lease connections from some sort of service provider. Examples of a service provider are a regional telephone company or a long-distance provider.

Leased connections can take two different forms: *dedicated* or *switched*.

## Dedicated connections

In a dedicated connection, you have full use of the connection as if it were a physical cable. The difference is that the service provider owns and manages the "cable." No one else can use the line that you have leased.

The cost of a dedicated connection usually is high. You pay the same amount whether you use the bandwidth or not.

## Switched connections

As you read earlier in this book, switched connections allow several people to use a connection at once. Switched connections take special hardware to manage the connections but give you the benefit of lower cost for the connection.

Another advantage of switched connections is that you are normally only charged for the bandwidth used, not the total capable bandwidth. A drawback to this is that bandwidth could be limited due to the possible number of people sharing the connection.

Two forms of switching are *packet switching* and *circuit switching*.

### Packet switching

Packet switching takes the total message and divides it into smaller chunks. These chunks are then routed through the network the best way possible to reach the destination.

Packet switching can also use *virtual circuits*, which are logical circuits set up between devices. There is no real physical connection, just an open channel between the devices.

### Circuit switching

You use a circuit switching network all the time, but may not know it. Each time you make a telephone call, a "virtual" circuit between you and the other end is set up dynamically for you to use. Only you are using the circuit at that given time. When the call is over, the circuit is torn down and can be used by someone else.

The advantage of circuit switching is you get the features of a dedicated service without the price.

# Popular WAN Protocols

WAN protocols allow you to route data over a large internetwork. They do not replace the upper-layer protocol suites such as IPX/SPX or TCP/IP; they carry these protocols through the internetwork so they may deliver the data.

Some WAN protocols such as X.25 have been around for many years and are still used today, while others are very new and still changing.

The protocols covered are:

o Public switched telephone network

o SLIP and PPP

o X.25

o Frame relay

o ISDN

o ATM

o Switched Multimegabit Data Service

o Synchronous Optical Network

## *Public switched telephone network*

The *public switched telephone network* (PSTN) has been around for a long time and is a very popular way to move data across an internetwork. You may also hear this referred to as *plain old telephone system* (POTS). In the United States, the PSTN is handled by *Regional Bell Operating Companies* (RBOC) and other long-distance providers.

When the local telephone company installs the telephone lines to your office, they bring the connection to the *demarc point*. The demarc point is the spot where the phone company connects to your location. Usually it is an outside box out of which the interior phone lines run. Anything beyond the demarc point is your responsibility. Most often companies will contract the same phone company to handle all inside wiring, but that wiring is still not the phone company's responsibility.

The local telephone company is responsible for all communications between your demarc point and their local *central office* (CO). The connection between the CO and your demarc point is known as the *local loop*. This local loop is usually made up of UTP cable or, if you are lucky, fiber optic. The central offices are then connected to each other through high-capacity trunk lines. Long-distance carriers also tie into this large network of COs to offer long-distance service.

Calls made over the PSTN use circuit switching. The call travels over a dedicated wire to the CO, but once there, a switched circuit is set up to the CO to which the call is destined. Once the call is completed, the circuit is torn down.

Using the PSTN, you can get several different connection types. They are:

- Dial-up connections
- Dedicated leased line
- Switched-56
- T-carrier System
- Integrated Services Digital Network (ISDN)

### Dial-up connections

The simplest and most common connection over the PSTN is the *dial-up connection*. You make one of these connections each time you call up your Internet provider. Using a normal modem, speeds can reach up to 56Kbps (but usually don't due to imperfect local loop conditions).

### Dedicated leased lines

*Dedicated leased lines* are a step up from a normal dial-up connection. Leased lines are either *analog* or *digital*.

Analog leased lines are basically just a dial-up connection that is connected all the time. They use standard modems at each end, and are susceptible to the same speed-limiting problems as normal dial-up connections. These lines are somewhat expensive, but because they are dedicated they can usually be tuned and cleaned up to provide higher speeds than normal telephone lines.

Digital leased lines are faster than analog lines. Their speeds can range from 2Kbps all the way to 56Kbps. Because of digital transmission they are less susceptible to interference and can truly reach the 56Kbps speeds. They also are not as error prone as analog lines. Digital leased lines are usually called *Digital Data Service* (DSS) lines. They require special digital equipment to be used, which is called *Channel Service Unit/Data Service Unit* (CSU/DSU). (Occasionally you will hear it referred to as a Customer Service Unit/Data Service Unit.) The CSU/DSU is connected to the digital line and to your LAN. Figure 5-12 shows a dedicated leased line setup.

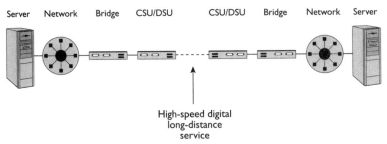

Server    Network    Bridge    CSU/DSU         CSU/DSU    Bridge    Network    Server

High-speed digital
long-distance
service

**FIGURE 5-12**    CSU/DSU diagram

DDS lines are relatively expensive, especially compared to some newer technologies, discussed in the following sections.

### Switched-56

*Switched-56* is the answer to the high cost of a dedicated leased line connection. Switched-56 provides 56Kbps speeds over a switched connection, not a dedicated connection. Users are only charged for the time that is used, not for when the connection sits unused.

A different CSU/DSU is used than with a standard dedicated 56Kbps line.

### T-carrier system

When you have need for bandwidth larger than what 56Kbps connections provide, another option is available. Originally designed in the 1960s to handle multiple voice calls at once, the *T-carrier system* is now used in data communications. The T-carrier system uses devices called *multiplexers*, or MUXes, to combine multiple communications into one. At the other end, another MUX separates the different communications. Figure 5-13 shows an example of combining signals with a MUX.

The basic T-carrier system is a *T1*. A T1 is composed of twenty-four 64Kbps channels that can be combined for a total bandwidth of 1.544Mbps. One big feature of this system is that the channels can be split so that some are used for voice traffic and some for data.

These 64Kbps channels are called *Digital Signal Level 0* (DS-0) signals. A full T1 line is also known as a *DS-1*, or in European, an *E-1*.

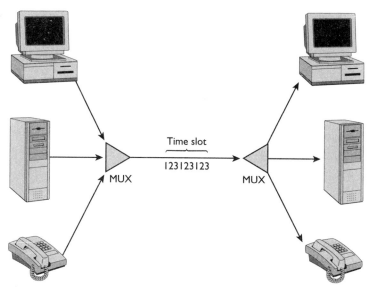

**Figure 5-13** **Combining multiple signals with a MUX**

Table 5-2 shows the different T-carrier lines available.

| TABLE 5-2  T-CARRIER SYSTEMS | | | |
|---|---|---|---|
| *DIGITAL SIGNAL* | *CARRIER* | *SPEED (MBPS)* | *CHANNELS* |
| DS-0 | N/A | 0.064 (64Kbps) | 1 |
| DS-1 | T1 | 1.544 | 24 |
| DS-2 | T2 | 6.312 | 96 |
| DS-3 | T3 | 44.736 | 672 |
| DS-4 | T4 | 274.760 | 4,032 |

By far the most common T-carrier line used is the T1. If you need more speed, you can go to a larger carrier. T3s are becoming more popular, due to the falling cost of bandwidth and the increasing needs of users. It is not uncommon for a large company or university to have one or more T3s connected to the Internet.

T1 lines use standard copper cable, whereas the T3 and T4 lines use fiber optic. (T2s are not offered to the public.)

Suppose that you need higher speed than a 56Kbps line can provide, but do not need or cannot afford a full T1 line. The middle connection is called a *Fractional T1* (or *Fractional T3* if you need more than a T1). With this line, you can get as many of the DS-0 lines as you need without getting all twenty-four in a DS-1. As your network bandwidth grows, you can easily request more bandwidth.

T-carrier system connections are expensive and require skilled people for the installation. A special CSU/DSU and a router or bridge is required on both sides of the connection.

## SLIP and PPP

*Serial Line Internet Protocol* (SLIP) is an older protocol used to handle TCP/IP traffic over a dial-up or other serial connection. SLIP is a Physical layer protocol that doesn't provide error checking, relying on the hardware (such as modem error checking) to handle this. It also only supports the transmission of one protocol, TCP/IP.

A later version of SLIP, called *Compressed SLIP* (CSLIP), became available. Though the name says compressed, the protocol actually just reduces the amount of information in the headers, and does not compress the transmission.

*Point-to-Point Protocol* (PPP) is much more robust than its earlier cousin, SLIP. PPP provides a Physical and Data Link layer functionality that fixes many problems with SLIP. Basically, your modem is transformed into a network card, as far as upper-level protocols are concerned.

At the Data Link layer, PPP provides error checking to ensure the accurate delivery of the frames that it sends and receives. PPP also keeps a Logical Link Control communication between the two connect devices by using the *Link Control Protocol* (LCP).

Besides being less prone to errors, PPP also lets you use almost any protocol you want over the link. TCP/IP, IPX/SPX, NetBEUI, and AppleTalk can all be sent over the modem connection. PPP also supports the dynamic configuration of the dialed-in computer. Unlike SLIP, where your addresses and other information have to be hard-coded ahead of time, PPP allows the client computer to receive its information from the host it dials into.

Most Internet dial-up connections today are made using PPP over modem or ISDN.

## X.25

*X.25* was developed in 1974 by the CCITT as a Network layer packet-switching pro-tocol. It specifies how internetwork devices connect over a packet-switched net-work, giving users an alternative to dedicated connections.

X.25 consists of three levels that can be mapped to the bottom three layers of the OSI model:

**Level 1 (X.21):** Physical layer protocol that defines rules for connectivity and data transmission standards.

**Level 2 (LAPB):** Provides Data Link layer connection-oriented data transmission using the *Link Access Procedures Balanced* (LAPB) protocol.

**Level 3 (X.25):** Defines how packets are sent between *Data Terminal Equipment* (DTE) and *Data Circuit-Terminating Equipment* (DCE). X.25 relies on other protocols for switching and routing functionality.

X.25 was developed before the PSTN was as error free as it is today. For this reason it has a high-error control system built-in and is kept fairly low speed (the maximum speed of an X.25 network is 64Kbps).

The physical connection of an X.25 network requires you to lease a line to the switched network through an X.25 provider. A hardware *Packet Assembler/Disassembler* (PAD) is needed to handle the packet switching.

X.25 is no longer a good choice when building an internetwork. Other tech-nologies such as frame relay and ATM make more sense today.

## Frame relay

*Frame relay* is based on X.25 but with less overhead. As technology increased, the need for tight error control was diminished. Frame relay took the features of X.25 and stripped out the error control and accounting. The assumption is that most connections now are made over fiber optic, which provides an extremely low error rate.

Unlike X.25, which had dynamically routed packets, frame relay uses *Permanent Virtual Circuits* (PVC) to establish connections ahead of time. Packets can now just have the PVC number attached to them and be sent through the frame relay network. With the removal of the error control and the use of PVCs, frame relay can reach speeds of 1.544Mbps.

A nice feature of frame relay is its ability to guarantee bandwidth and then occasionally exceed that amount when needed. When you have a frame relay connection installed, you determine your *Committed Information Rate* (CIR). This becomes your guaranteed bandwidth. You may also occasionally exceed that bandwidth limit if your provider's network is capable of delivering it.

Frame relay is a very economical choice for the bandwidth received, so, not surprisingly, it's a very popular WAN protocol right now.

The physical connection requires a frame relay CSU/DSU and a bridge or router.

### Integrated Services Digital Network

*Integrated Services Digital Network* (ISDN) has been around for a number of years, but has just recently become affordable. ISDN allows you to send voice, data, and video over normal copper telephone lines by sending digital signals instead of analog.

ISDN uses 64Kbps channels, called *B channels*, for data transfer. It also has a 16K channel, called the *D channel*, for call setup and control information. It is also possible to send X.25 data over the D channel.

There are two types of ISDN:

**Basic Rate Interface (BRI):** BRI is intended for home users and small offices. It consists of two B channels and one D channel for a total data bandwidth of 128Kbps. Each B channel can be used separately. You could use one for data while the other is handling a voice call.

**Primary Rate Interface (PRI):** PRI is mainly for larger organizations that need high bandwidth connections. It provides twenty-three B channels and one D channel for a capacity of 1.544Mbps, the same as a T1 line. Again, the B channels can either be used for voice or data.

ISDN was not originally designed to be set up as a continuous connection service, but rather a fast dial-up service. Depending on your location, ISDN service may be billed by the minute or at a flat-rate pricing.

The physical connection is through standard telephone lines. An ISDN adapter (sometimes called an ISDN modem) is required to dial in or out.

### Asynchronous Transfer Mode

*Asynchronous Transfer Mode* (ATM) is a new packet-switching technology aimed at real-time applications, such as voice and video over data lines. ATM uses a different type of switching called *cell switching*. It uses a fixed packet size of only 53 bytes, 5 of which are header information. Each of these 53-byte packets are called *cells*. With the use of fixed-size packets, routing and switching can be done much faster by the networking hardware. Speeds of ATM can reach 622Mbps!

ATM uses switches to quickly move the cells across a network. When a connection needs to be made to a distant device over ATM, a virtual connection is set up through the switches. As you may have guessed, 5 bytes of header on a cell is not enough to define the source and destination. To set up a connection, a special cell is sent through the network to the remote device. This path is recorded by the switches along the way and is given a connection number. For the duration of the virtual connection, the cells only need this connection number in the header to designate their path through the network.

ATM hardware is still very expensive and complicated. As it becomes more popular, the price will drop, and others will be able to enjoy its speed.

## Switched Multimegabit Data Service

*Switched Multimegabit Data Service* (SMDS) is a combination of X.25 and ATM. It was designed by Bell Communications Research and released in 1991. It uses cells like ATM and creates virtual circuits like X.25.

SMDS can provide high-speed connections ranging from 1.544Mbps to 45Mbps.

## Synchronous Optical Network

*Synchronous Optical Network* (SONET) specifies how to deliver voice, data, and video over WAN connections at speeds in excess of 2Gbps. It is a Physical layer standard that defines the transfer of data over fiber-optic media.

SONET links are rated in what are called *optical carrier levels* (OC). The base OC-1 is rated at 51.8Mbps. Each additional OC level is calculated by taking the level and multiplying it by the OC-1 speed. For example, an OC-3 would be $3 \times 51.8$Mbps, for a speed of 155.52Mbps. Currently the highest defined level is OC-4.

SONET is considered to be the underlying architecture for most ATM implementations at telephone companies.

# KEY POINT SUMMARY

In this chapter you learned the different network and WAN protocols common in the networking world. Though sometimes these protocol suites can be complicated and confusing, the summary below should point out the main ideas from this chapter:

o *Routable protocols* can be used across an entire internetwork.

o *Nonroutable protocols* cannot operate across a router.

o *Connectionless protocols* do not check if data arrived successfully. They are faster than connection-oriented protocols due to less overhead.

o *Connection-oriented protocols* are more reliable due to the use of acknowledgments, which ensure that data has arrived successfully.

o The *TCP/IP* suite of protocols is very popular due to its ability to run on almost any computing platform. TCP/IP is also extremely well suited to large, enterprise-wide internetworks.

o TCP/IP uses *IP addresses* to designate hosts on the network. They must be unique through the entire network.

o The *IPX/SPX* suite of protocols was created by Novell, Inc., to be used with their NetWare network operating system.

o *NetBEUI* is a small and efficient protocol used on Microsoft networks. It is nonroutable and intended for small workgroup-size networks.

o *AppleTalk* was created by Apple Computers to be used on their Macintosh line of computers.

o *DLC* was designed for use with IBM mainframe computers, but is now also used to print to network printers.

o The *public switched telephone network* is a popular way to connect networks due to the low cost.

o *Dial-up connections* between networks are inexpensive but limited to a maximum of 56Kbps speed.

o *T-carrier systems* allow networks to be connected over telephone lines at a much higher speed than dial-up connections.

o The most popular T-carrier system is the *T1*, with a speed of 1.544Mbps.

- *X.25* was developed in the 1970s and was used as a packet-switching network protocol.

- *SLIP* was an early dial-up networking protocol that could only be used with TCP/IP. It has no error checking or flow control.

- *PPP* is a newer dial-up networking protocol that can be used with almost any network protocol available. It has error checking and flow control to maintain a good connection status.

- *ATM* is a new packet-switching technology with speeds up to 622Mbps.

# APPLYING WHAT YOU'VE LEARNED

Now it's time again to regroup, review, and apply what you've learned in this chapter about network protocols. The questions in the Instant Assessment section bring to mind key facts and concepts. The Critical Thinking labs provide you with an opportunity to apply the knowledge you've gained in this chapter about network protocols.

note    Critical Thinking labs challenge you to apply your understanding of the material to solve a hypothetical problem. The questions are scenario based, requiring you to decide "why" or "how" or to devise a solution to a problem. You might need to be at a computer to work through some of these labs.

concept link    Refer to the "Hardware and Software You'll Need" section in the Preface or in Appendix B if you're not sure you have the necessary equipment to do the Critical Thinking labs.

## Instant Assessment

**1.** Which of the following is an example of an IP address?

   **a.** 9.67.43.8

   **b.** http://www.idgbooks.com

   **c.** 00-C0-6D-10-47-8D

   **d.** 0384CD:2766801

**2.** The Ping utility uses which protocol?

   **a.** TCP

   **b.** IP

   **c.** IDP

   **d.** ICMP

**3.** Which protocol is responsible for converting IP addresses to MAC addresses?

   **a.** TCP

   **b.** ARP

   **c.** UDP

   **d.** DNS

**4.** At which OSI layer does IPX function?

   **a.** Physical

   **b.** Data Link

   **c.** Network

   **d.** Transport

**5.** Which IPX/SPX protocol is responsible for advertising available network resources?

   **a.** RIP

   **b.** SAP

   **c.** NCP

   **d.** SPX

**6.** Which of the following is a proprietary network protocol?

   **a.** LocalTalk

   **b.** EtherTalk

   **c.** TokenTalk

   **d.** NetBEUI

**7.** Which protocol is used for communication with Hewlett-Packard network printers?

   **a.** DNA

   **b.** DLC

   **c.** IPX

   **d.** IP

**8.** Which protocol allows dynamic addressing for remote access?

   **a.** SLIP

   **b.** PPP

   **c.** ISDN

   **d.** ATM

**9.** What is the main protocol suite used on the Internet?

   **a.** TCP/IP

   **b.** IPX/SPX

   **c.** NetBEUI

   **d.** DNA

**10.** Which protocol is used to deliver e-mail to servers on the Internet?

   **a.** UDP

   **b.** FTP

   **c.** POP

   **d.** SMTP

|  | T/F |
|---|---|
| **11.** DNS is used to translate friendly names to MAC addresses. | ____ |
| **12.** An MLID is a driver that operates at the Data Link layer of the OSI model. | ____ |
| **13.** NetWare Core Protocol is designed to function on four layers of the OSI model. | ____ |
| **14.** NetBEUI is a routable protocol. | ____ |
| **15.** ATM is a packet-switching technology used for real-time applications. | ____ |
| **16.** LocalTalk devices use dynamic physical addressing. | ____ |
| **17.** UDP is a connection-oriented protocol. | ____ |
| **18.** RIP and OSPF are routing protocols used to transmit data across large networks. | ____ |

**19.** TCP/IP is the protocol of choice for the Internet because         \_\_\_\_
it was used on early NetWare networks.

**20.** X.25 is a switching protocol used in WANs since the 1970s.         \_\_\_\_

concept link        **For answers to these Instant Assessment questions, see Appendix C.**

# Critical Thinking Labs

The following Critical Thinking labs provide you with a practical opportunity to apply the knowledge you've gained in this chapter about network protocols.

### Lab 5.11 *Expanding the network*

You administrate a network that currently has NetBEUI as its primary protocol. Your company is expanding and will soon be moving to a large office building with multiple floors. You have decided to split your network up with internetworking devices to handle the increased volume. Should you change your protocol choice? What protocol(s) could you possibly change to? Why?

### Lab 5.12 *Adding protocols*

Your company has just received a new UNIX server that uses TCP/IP as its only protocol. You need to let your clients easily access the data that is on the server. Which protocol might you use to handle this? Why?

### Lab 5.13 *Adding NetWare protocols*

The Microsoft clients currently on your network use NetBEUI, but a NetWare server was just added to work as a file server. What are your options for protocol choices?

### Lab 5.14 *New network printer*

A new Hewlett-Packard printer was just connected to your LAN. What changes must be made to the clients to allow them to print to it?

### Lab 5.15 *Remote connectivity*

Your company has recently decided to allow remote access for users that travel. There is a limited number of IP addresses available, so the company has decided to assign them dynamically to users when they are connected. Users will also need to use NetBEUI to access their printers remotely. Which protocol would users need to use to access the network?

concept link

**For answers to these labs, see Appendix C.**

# Connecting Networks

# About Chapter 6

**N**etworks can only grow so large before you'll encounter certain problems.

Eventually the congestion from all the devices transmitting becomes too large, or the maximum number of devices per segment is met. This chapter covers what it takes to extend your network to handle more data and larger amounts of clients.

Chapter 6 also delves into the idea of connecting networks to other networks. Many things must be considered when this is done. Hardware must be selected, and which protocols to use must be decided. Some of the networking hardware that I cover includes repeaters, hubs, and bridges. I also cover internetworking hardware, such as routers and Channel Service Unit/Data Service Units (CSU/DSUs). The communication needs of the two networks must be calculated to make the right choices on which equipment and services to use.

# LAN CONNECTIVITY DEVICES

Eventually your LAN may reach its limit on distance or number of nodes that you can have on a segment. This may happen when your network segment is too long, causing client connection errors or abundant collisions on an Ethernet network. When this happens, you may turn to hardware devices such as *bridges* or *repeaters* to extend your network and allow for expansion.

## Repeaters

One of the easiest devices you can use to extend the distance of a network is a repeater. Going back to the Physical layer of the OSI model, remember that an electrical signal diminishes over distance due to attenuation. Repeaters work at the Physical layer to regenerate the electrical signal on the network media. At this layer they do not understand things such as protocols, packet addresses, or anything concerning the data it carries. They simply understand the electrical signal of 1's and 0's.

Repeaters are normally two-port boxes that connect two segments. As a signal comes in one port, it is regenerated and sent out the other port. Usually the repeater does more than just amplify the electrical signal. The signal is read as the binary 1's and 0's and retransmitted as the 1's and 0's so the noise in the signal can be cleaned out. Repeaters send and receive data at the speed of the network, but signal regeneration does take a small amount of time. Figure 6-1 illustrates a repeater regenerating a signal.

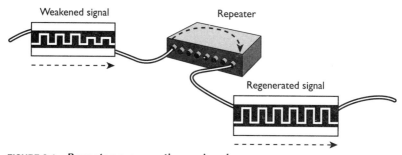

**FIGURE 6-1   Repeater regenerating a signal**

As you can see, repeaters do not have a lot of built-in intelligence. For this reason, they cannot connect dissimilar network types. A repeater cannot convert the CSMA/CD media access of Ethernet to the polling of a Token Ring network.

One thing that repeaters can do, however, is convert the type of cable being used on a similar network. For example, you could have an Ethernet segment with UTP cable connected to an Ethernet network using thinnet cable by using a repeater. The essential thing to remember about this situation is that the type of media access cannot change between the segments.

Most network types have a limit to the number of repeaters that can be used to connect segments. In Ethernet, this rule is called the *5-4-3 rule*. In this rule, you may have a total of five Ethernet segments, four repeaters, and three populated segments. The extra two segments that cannot be populated are used for distance to reach other locations. Figure 6-2 illustrates the 5-4-3 rule.

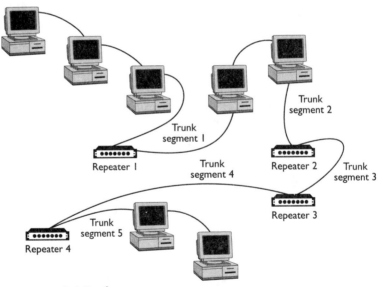

**FIGURE 6-2**  5–4–3 rule

Any more segments or repeaters would cause timing problems and would affect the collision detection used by Ethernet.

exam
preparation
pointer

Repeaters are a very inexpensive and easy way to extend a network. For the exam, you should know the advantages and disadvantages of adding repeaters.

Advantages of repeaters:

o Repeaters easily extend the length of a network.

o They require no processing overhead, so very little, if any, performance degradation occurs.

o You can connect segments from the same network type that use different types of cable.

Disadvantages of repeaters:

o Repeaters cannot be used to connect segments of different network types.

o They cannot be used to segment traffic on a network to reduce congestion.

o Many types of networks have limits on the number of repeaters that can be used at once.

## Bridges

Where repeaters do not do any type of filtering of traffic that they pass, bridges do. Consider an example: You are in a large conference room with two meetings going on. People are talking and discussing ideas at each meeting, and they are doing it loudly. Eventually each party has trouble hearing the people in their group. A good solution would be to put some sort of barrier between the groups to block the noise. Now, suppose they occasionally needed to pass information between the two groups. The perfect solution would be something that blocked the noise but did allow needed information to flow through—maybe a person to run back and forth.

With bridges, you can apply this idea to networking. Bridges work at the Data Link layer of the OSI model and, like a repeater, attach two different network segments and pass data. What it does that a repeater does not is filter the data on whether it needs to be passed. Suppose you have a workstation and a server on one side of a bridge that are communicating. Does the data they are sending need to pass through the bridge? No. The bridge knows this and blocks the traffic. If this had been a repeater, the data would have been passed only to help congest the other network segment.

As an example, Figure 6-3 below shows a sample network with a bridge in the middle.

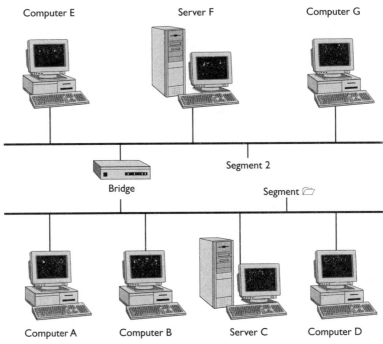

**FIGURE 6-3   Bridged network**

If you should decide to use bridging, be sure to think about its placement on the network. If all clients access the same server and you put the bridge between the server and the clients, you will get no benefit. Place the bridge for maximum effectiveness. The optimum situation would be to block about seventy percent of the traffic from coming to the segmented LAN.

exam
preparation
pointer

**Bridges are more intelligent than repeaters and have certain advantages over them. Bridges also come with some very important considerations that must be dealt with when implementing them in a network. You should review these for the exam.**

**Advantages of bridges.**

o **Bridges extend network segments by connecting them together to make one logical network.**

- o They segment traffic between networks by filtering data if it does not need to pass.

- o Like repeaters, they can connect similar network types with different cabling.

- o Special *translational bridges* can connect different network types together.

Disadvantages of bridges:

- o Bridges process information about the data they receive, which can slow performance.

- o Bridges pass all broadcasts.

- o They cost more than repeaters due to extra intelligence.

There are two main types of bridges, *transparent* and *source-route*. A translational bridge is used to connect dissimilar network types.

## Transparent bridges

Transparent bridges use hardware network card addresses to know which data to pass and which should be filtered. If you remember from before, each network card has a unique address assigned to it at manufacture. Bridges use this information to decide which frames are passed and which are not. Computer addresses are stored in a table, one for each port. When data is received, the destination address is checked and compared against this table.

Looking back at Figure 6-3, you can assume the bridge has just been powered up and initialized. Currently, the MAC address table is empty and will stay that way until someone transmits. First, Computer A transmits data to Server C. The bridge intercepts this message on port 1, which is connected to segment 1. Since the data came from port 1 and was transmitted by Computer A, that must mean Computer A is on the port 1 segment. However, the bridge does not know which segment Server C is on yet, so the data is simply passed to the other segment. Table 6-1 shows the current MAC address table of the bridge.

| **TABLE 6-1** BRIDGE MAC LIST | |
| --- | --- |
| *SEGMENT 1* | *SEGMENT 2* |
| Computer A | |

Server C receives the message sent by Computer A and replies. The bridge receives the message from Server C from segment 1. Server C's MAC address is then added to the list for segment 1, and the data is not passed across the bridge because it knows both computers are on the same segment. Table 6-2 shows the updated MAC address table.

**TABLE 6-2** BRIDGE MAC LIST

| SEGMENT 1 | SEGMENT 2 |
| --- | --- |
| Computer A | |
| Server C | |

If a computer such as Computer G from segment 2 on port 2 sends data to Server C, the bridge now knows to pass the data through. Eventually, if all computers transmit, the full MAC address table will be filled by the bridge.

Table 6-3 shows the final MAC address table. Once the table is fully filled out the bridge knows exactly when to pass data and when to filter it.

**TABLE 6-3** BRIDGE MAC LIST

| SEGMENT 1 | SEGMENT 2 |
| --- | --- |
| Computer A | Computer E |
| Computer B | Server F |
| Server C | Computer G |
| Computer D | |

Since bridges pass data depending on hardware MAC addresses, what happens when a broadcast is sent? By default, bridges pass broadcast messages without hesitation.

Observe Figure 6-4, and imagine what would happen if Computer A sent out a broadcast message to the other computers on the network.

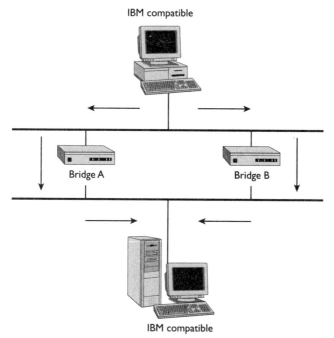

IBM compatible

**FIGURE 6-4**   **Broadcast on a bridged network**

The broadcast is sent out, and the two bridges both receive the same message at the same time. Each bridge then passes the broadcast message to the other segment. It is not passed once, but once by each bridge which creates two broadcast messages. Now Bridge A receives Bridge B's broadcast, and Bridge B receives Bridge A's broadcast. They each resend the broadcast they receive repeatedly. This is what is known as a *broadcast storm*. Figure 6-5 illustrates a broadcast storm. To make things even scarier, imagine a third bridge in this scenario. With a third bridge on the network between the two segments, at each cycle each bridge would receive multiple broadcasts. The number of broadcasts would increase indefinitely.

A protocol has been developed to keep network nightmares like this from happening. It is called the *Spanning Tree Protocol*. This protocol checks for network loops each time a bridge is initialized and closes these loops. No more than one bridge may connect two network segments together. At a set interval the bridges will send out a packet checking to make sure the one working bridge is still active. If not, one of the disabled bridges takes over and connects the two segments.

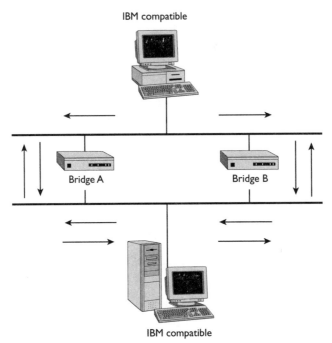

**FIGURE 6-5** Broadcast storm

## *Source-route bridges*

While most networks use transparent bridges, Token Ring networks use a different type of bridge called a source-route bridge. Instead of depending on MAC addresses, they use information in the token ring frame to determine whether to pass the data or not.

Before a connection is made to a remote computer in a source-routed network, the source computer sends out an *explorer packet*. An explorer frame's job is to go through the network remembering each bridge it passed through getting to the destination computer. When a bridge on a Token Ring network receives an explorer frame, it adds its bridge ID to the list of IDs in the packet and automatically forwards it to all connected segments. Eventually this one explorer frame may turn into many explorer frames since one Token Ring segment may connect to many others. When the destination computer receives an explorer frame, it flips the list of bridge IDs in the packet around so the path back is reversed and sends the explorer frame back. The frame then takes the exact route back that it took to get to the destination.

When the source computer receives back all the explorer frames that were sent back from the destination computer, it looks for the one with the shortest bridge ID list. This is the list that it attaches to the rest of the packets destined for that computer (and that network). On a very large network, the number of explorer frames that can be created from the initial frame can become enormous. Eventually on a large network, you must use some sort of filtering for these explorer frames so they do not completely clog the bandwidth.

### Translational bridges

Unlike repeaters, a translational bridge allows you to connect dissimilar networks together. Translational bridges have a port for the two different network types. The process that translational bridges use to pass data depends on which two types of networks they are connecting. They handle the conversion of the frames from one type to another and take into account the media access method.

There are many translational bridges for connecting Ethernet, Token Ring, and FDDI to each other, and they can be purchased to suit the types of networks that are being connected.

## Ethernet Hubs

*Ethernet hubs* are basically just multiport repeaters for UTP cable. Hubs range in size from four ports up to several hundred and are specific to the network type.

Some hubs are just repeaters; they work the same way and follow the same rules. Hubs just repeat the signal given to them, and no intelligence is built into the system. You can only have up to four hubs between any two points on a network to follow the 5-4-3 rule. There are two types: *passive* and *active*.

There are some hubs that have the intelligence of a bridge built-in. They are called *switches*.

exam
preparation
pointer

**Hubs are an integral part of many networks. The lists below should help you decide when to use a hub and when another device may be more beneficial.**

**Advantages of hubs:**

- **Hubs need almost no configuration.**
- **Active hubs can extend maximum network media distance.**
- **No processing is done at the hub to slow down performance.**

Disadvantages of hubs:

- Passive hubs can greatly limit maximum media distance.
- Hubs have no intelligence to filter traffic, so all data is sent out all ports whether it is needed or not.
- Since hubs can act as repeaters, networks using them must follow the same rules as repeaters.

 tip Some hubs have ports for other types of cable such as coaxial and AUI. This allows you to connect your UTP network to another type of segment.

### Passive hubs

Passive hubs provide no signal regeneration. They are simply cables connected together so that a signal is broken out to other nodes without regeneration. These are not used often today because of the loss of cable length that is allowed.

### Active hubs

Active hubs act as repeaters and regenerate the data signal to all ports. They have no real intelligence to tell whether the signal needs to go to all ports, it is blindly repeated.

### Switches

Switches are multiport bridges. They filter traffic between the ports on the switch by using the MAC address of computers transmitting through them. Switches can be used when greater performance is needed or when collisions need to be reduced. Figure 6-6 illustrates a switched network.

Switches are the key to a large and fast Ethernet network. As you've learned, Ethernet can be congested under moderate load. With the use of switches, the load can be cut down dramatically. Consider the following example: Two comput-ers are connected to a switch. If the switch already has its MAC address list com-pleted, it can properly filter data. When the first computer sends something to the second computer, the bridge knows which ports each is off of and only sends data to those ports. No other port on the switch is affected by the transmission. Using a switch is like having a dedicated connection between the two transmitting devices.

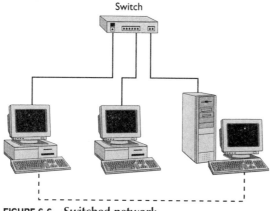

**FIGURE 6-6** Switched network

 *tip* Switches can be an inexpensive way to add bandwidth to a congested network. Connecting a server to a switching hub can provide a boost to clients that access that server since the server is not affected by other traffic on the network.

# INTERNETWORKING DEVICES

Now that you know how to extend and expand the capacity of a LAN, look at the devices you use to connect LANs. Several pieces of hardware that enable you to connect LANs include:

o Modems

o Multiplexers

o Routers

o Brouters

o CSU/DSUs

o Gateways

Table 6-4 shows how these devices relate to the OSI model.

| TABLE 6-4 HOW INTERNETWORKING DEVICES RELATE TO THE OSI MODEL | |
| --- | --- |
| DEVICE | OSI LAYER |
| Repeater | Physical |
| Bridge | Data Link |
| Router | Network |
| Gateway | All seven layers |

exam preparation pointer

**The information in Table 6-4 is the most important information contained in this chapter. The exam always has questions asking which layer a certain device operates at. Be sure to know them for the exam.**

## Modems

*Modems* are small devices that connect networks, though at a slow speed, over normal telephone lines. Modems handle the conversion of signals between computers and telephone lines. They're needed because computers are all digital, using 1's- and -0's encoding in an electric signal to communicate. Telephone lines are analog in nature and do not understand the digital 1's-and-0's approach. Figure 6-7 illustrates LANs that are connected by modems.

Modems convert signals through a process called *modulation* and *demodulation* (which is where the name comes from, MODulation/DEModulation). Modulation is converting the digital computer signals to analog telephone signals. Demodulation is the opposite conversion, analog to digital.

With a modem you can connect networks together over inexpensive telephone lines. Because of their low speed, modems should not be used to connect networks that frequently need to exchange information.

Most analog modems operate at speeds from 14.4Kbps up to a theoretical limit of 56Kbps, and have the capability of compression.

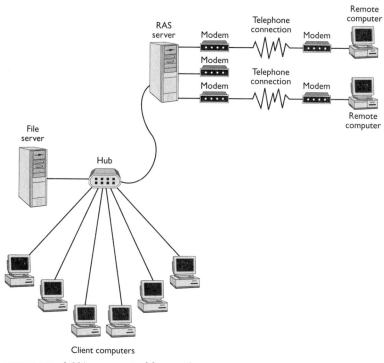

**FIGURE 6-7** LANs connected by modems

Common modem protocols as defined by ITU:

- **V.32**: 9600bps Communications speed
- **V.32bis**: 14.4Kbps Communications speed
- **V.34**: 28.8Kbps Communications speed
- **V.42**: Modem error control
- **V.42bis**: Compression protocol
- **V.17**: Faxing capability

Windows NT provides the necessary software to connect LANs through a modem. By dialing in to a Windows NT server, computers with Remote Access Service installed act as routers to move data through the modem connection.

Modems can be an inexpensive way to connect networks together. But you get what you pay for in slow performance. Know the advantages and disadvantages of using modems for the exam.

Advantages of modems:

o Inexpensive hardware and telephone lines

o Easy to set up and maintain

o Mature standards and multiple vendors

Disadvantages of modems:

o Very slow performance

## Multiplexers

*Multiplexers* (or MUXes) are what you use to send multiple signals across one transmission media. Multiplexing (or MUXing) takes the different signals and combines them to form one single signal. One popular example of MUXing is cable television. Each individual television channel is one signal. With the use of MUXes, the cable company can take all those different signals and send them through one piece of coaxial cable. Without multiplexers you would need one piece of cable coming into your home for each channel.

Multiplexers have no real intelligence in them as to what data to send across the link they are connecting. In most modern networks, they have been replaced by routers and are only seen in older networks. They are popular with central networks where remote terminals connect to a large mainframe, since no real intelligence is needed.

## Routers

*Routers* are used to connect complicated networks with many segments. They do more than just filter traffic; they make intelligent decisions on the path of the data. Routers can use either MAC addresses or administratively assigned logical addresses (such as IP addresses) to handle data routing. This allows you to segment your network into what are called *subnets*. A subnet is a network connected to another network via a router. Figure 6-8 shows a network divided into subnets using routers.

Routers operate at the Network layer of the OSI model.

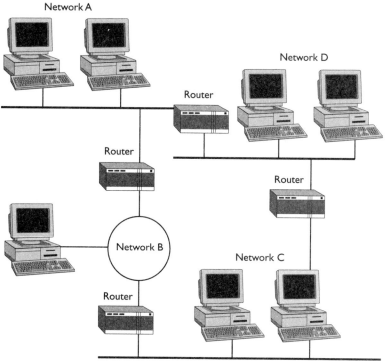

**FIGURE 6-8**   A network divided into subnets by routers

 tip

*Bridging routers*, or *brouters*, offer the best of both worlds between bridges and routers. Remember that some protocols are nonrouteable, such as NetBEUI. What if your network consisted of NetBEUI traffic and TCP/IP traffic? In this scenario you could use a brouter to route the TCP/IP, and bridge the NetBEUI traffic.

 exam preparation pointer

Routers have become very popular in the last few years, as they are a powerful way to connect networks together. Know the advantages and disadvantages of routers for the exam.

Advantages of routers:

o They use the highest level of intelligence to route data accordingly.

o Routers can also act as a bridge to handle nonroutable protocols such as NetBEUI.

**Disadvantages of routers:**

○ Higher level of intelligence takes more processing time, which can affect performance.

○ Routers are very complicated, which makes installation and maintenance difficult.

# CSU/DSU

If you use a modem to connect to an analog telephone line, what do you use to connect to a digital line such as a 56Kbps or T1? The answer is a *Channel Service Unit/Data Service Unit* (sometimes called a Customer Service Unit/Data Service Unit).

The CSU portion of the CSU/DSU handles line management and *loop-back testing* (used to test connectivity to the local telephone company's central office). The DSU portion handles the interface to your hardware, as well as the data formatting into frames to be sent out.

Most CSU/DSUs are leased from the telephone company you are getting service from. They will also usually install and configure the device for your line, as well.

# Gateways

*Gateways* can operate at all seven layers of the OSI model. Their function is to do any necessary conversion of protocols between networks. Gateways are customized and designed to perform a specific function and are used on a case-by-case basis.

Gateways may do anything, from converting protocols to converting application data. There is no limit. One example of a gateway is for e-mail. Most large companies upgrade their e-mail system at one time or another. During the upgrade process, there will normally be two e-mail systems, the original system and the new system, running at once. Users will still need to mail others on the old system after they are upgraded. To accomplish this, you can install an e-mail gateway between the two systems until the migration to the new system is finished. This gateway would be written just to connect the two specific mail systems together.

**in the real world**   **While writing this book, I am on contract to a large company that is considering an e-mail migration. The migration will take months to finish, and during the process there will be two e-mail systems running as in the earlier example under Gateways. Their old system is Lotus' cc:Mail, and they are considering an upgrade to Microsoft Exchange Server. To handle the transfer of mail between them during the upgrade, we are using a gateway that does conversion between the two systems. Any user on either system can mail anyone on the other system. Other e-mail enhancements such as file attachments work, as well.**

# KEY POINT SUMMARY

In this chapter you learned how you can extend and expand your network many different ways. Below are the key points to remember about each device:

- *Repeaters* operate at the Physical layer of the OSI model. They regenerate the signal to extend the distance of a network. Repeaters can be used to connect the same type of networks using different cable media.

- Advantages of using repeaters:

  - Repeaters easily extend the length of a network.

  - There is no processing overhead, so very little, if any, performance degradation occurs.

  - You can connect segments from the same network type that use different types of cable.

- Disadvantages of using repeaters:

  - Repeaters cannot be used to connect segments of different network types.

  - Repeaters cannot be used to segment traffic on a network to reduce congestion.

  - Many types of networks have limits on the number of repeaters that can be used at once.

- *Bridges* operate at the Data Link layer of the OSI model. They use MAC addresses (in the case of *transparent* bridges) to filter traffic between segments. They may be used to connect two segments with different cable types, assuming the network type (for example, Ethernet, Token Ring) is the same.

  - Special bridges called *translational* bridges may be used to change the network type, along with the cable type.

  - Advantages of using bridges:

    - Bridges extend network segments by connecting them together to make one logical network.

    - Segment traffic between networks by filtering data if it does not need to pass.

    - Like repeaters, they can connect similar network types with different cabling.

    - Special translational bridges can connect different network types together.

  - Disadvantages of using bridges:

    - Bridges process information about the data they receive, which can slow performance.

    - Bridges pass all broadcasts.

    - Bridges cost more than repeaters due to extra intelligence.

- *Hubs* are used to group computers together in the star topology. They act as multiport repeaters that split or regenerate a signal to all connected devices. Normal hubs have no other intelligence to help filter traffic.

  - Advantages of using hubs:

    - Hubs need almost no configuration.

    - *Active hubs* can extend maximum network media distance.

    - No processing done at the hub to slow down performance.

  - Disadvantages of using hubs:

    - *Passive hubs* can greatly limit maximum media distance.

    - Since hubs use no intelligence to filter traffic; all data is sent out all ports whether it is needed or not.

- Since hubs can act as repeaters, networks using them must follow the same rules as repeaters.

- *Modems* can be used as an inexpensive way to connect LANs together. Though they are inexpensive, they are also slow. Their speeds usually range from 14.4Kbps to 56Kbps.

  - Advantages of using modems:

    - Inexpensive hardware and telephone lines

    - Easy set up and maintenance

    - Mature standards and multiple vendors

    - The disadvantage of using a modem is that modems give *very slow performance*.

- *Multiplexers* are used to combine multiple signals into one to be transmitted over a single cable or media.

- *Routers* are used to segment a network into *subnets*. They operate at the Network layer of the OSI model. Routers use *logical addresses* (such as an IP address) to handle the routing of data. Unlike bridges, which simply passes or filters data, routers make intelligent decisions about the path data should take. They forward the data to the next closest hop on its journey.

  - Advantages of using routers:

    - Use the highest level of intelligence to route data accordingly

    - Can also act as a bridge to handle nonroutable protocols such as NetBEUI

  - Disadvantages of using routers:

    - Poor performance due to more processing time

    - Difficult installation and maintenance

- *Customer Service Unit/Data Service Units* connect networking devices to digital telephone lines. They are normally connected to a bridge or router using a line such as a 56Kbps leased line or a T1 connection.

- *Gateways* operate at all seven layers of the OSI model. They are used to convert between different protocol and data types.

# Applying What You've Learned

Now it's time again to regroup, review, and apply what you've learned in this chapter about connecting networks. The questions in the Instant Assessment section bring to mind key facts and concepts. The Critical Thinking labs provide you with an opportunity to apply the knowledge you've gained in this chapter about connecting networks.

 note **Critical Thinking labs challenge you to apply your understanding of the material to solve a hypothetical problem. The questions are scenario based, requiring you to decide "why" or "how" or to devise a solution to a problem. You might need to be at a computer to work through some of these labs.**

 concept link **Refer to the "Hardware and Software You'll Need" section in the Preface or in Appendix B if you're not sure you have the necessary equipment to do the Critical Thinking labs.**

## Instant Assessment

1. Which layer of the OSI model do repeaters function at?

   **a.** Physical

   **b.** Data Link

   **c.** Network

   **d.** Transport

2. Which type of bridge is used on Token Ring networks?

   **a.** Transparent

   **b.** Source-routing

   **c.** Translation

   **d.** Spanning Tree

3. Multiport bridges used in Ethernet networks that filter traffic between ports by using the MAC address of the computers are known as:

   **a.** Switches

   **b.** Transparent bridges

**c.** Translation bridges

**d.** Source-routing bridges

4. Which layer of the OSI model do routers function at?

   **a.** Physical

   **b.** Data Link

   **c.** Network

   **d.** Transport

5. What type of device is used to connect T1 and ISDN lines?

   **a.** Modem

   **b.** CSU/DSU

   **c.** Gateway

   **d.** Router

6. Routers that transport NetBEUI traffic to connected subnets are known as:

   **a.** Bridges

   **b.** Multiplexers

   **c.** Brouters

   **d.** Gateways

7. Transparent bridges use which type of address when determining whether to filter data?

   **a.** MAC address

   **b.** Network address

   **c.** Computer name

   **d.** Workgroup name

8. Which ITU modem protocol defines the 28.8Kbps communications speed?

   **a.** V.14

   **b.** V.42bis

   **c.** V.32bis

   **d.** V.34

9. Which device is used to separate several signals that are transmitted across the same cable?

   **a.** Modems

   **b.** CSU/DSU

   **c.** Multiplexers

   **d.** Routers

10. Which connectivity device can operate on all seven layers of the OSI model?

    **a.** Routers

    **b.** Hubs

    **c.** Bridges

    **d.** Gateways

T/F

11. The Ethernet 5-4-3 rule allows for four repeaters to connect five segments, three that are populated.    _____

12. Repeaters use built-in tables to direct data to the recipient.    _____

13. Bridges help reduce network traffic by segmenting the network and passing along only the data destined for the segment.    _____
    _____

14. Bridges operate on the Transport layer of the OSI model.    _____

15. Source-route bridges send out an explorer packet to determine the path to its destination.    _____

16. Broadcast storms occur when two bridges are looped, causing the broadcasts to be constantly repeated by both bridges.    _____

17. The Spanning Tree Protocol is used by bridges to create routing tables.    _____

18. Passive hubs filter and rebroadcast signals.    _____

19. Routers use intelligence to route data across subnets to its destination.    _____

20. Gateways are capable of converting protocols to allow dissimilar networks to communicate.    _____

concept link

**For answers to these Instant Assessment questions, see Appendix C.**

# Critical Thinking Labs

The following Critical Thinking labs provide you with a practical opportunity to apply the knowledge you've gained in this chapter about connecting networks.

### Lab 6.16 *Extending the network*

You are in charge of an Ethernet network that uses the bus topology. You are currently close to the maximum number of client workstations allowed on a single segment. Which network device would be the best choice to extend your network? What if your main protocol was TCP/IP?

### Lab 6.17 *Troubleshooting Ethernet*

A new hub was added to your 10Base-T network, but now the collision count per second is extremely high. Plugging in a new hub did not help. How could you begin to troubleshoot this problem?

### Lab 6.18 *Troubleshooting broadcast storms*

After installing a new router on your network, you have been hit with a number of broadcast storms. The protocol configuration in the router seems to be correct, but isolating that segment causes the storms to stop. What could be the problem?

### Lab 6.19 *Connecting distant LANs*

You have decided to connect the network used by the HR department in your company to the network used by Accounting. HR has a thinnet Ethernet network using coaxial cable and Accounting is using a 10Base-T Ethernet network running over UTP cable. The signal is not currently strong enough to cover the distance effectively. What device would you use to connect the networks?

### Lab 6.20 *Ethernet bridging*

Would you want to use a source-route bridge on an Ethernet network? Why or why not?

concept link

**For answers to these labs, see Appendix C.**

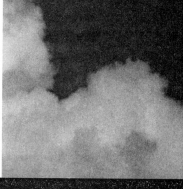

# Administration and Troubleshooting

**A**light at the end of the tunnel! The final part in this book starts with the day-to-day administration tasks you may be asked to perform. Here I cover important topics such as backup strategies, data protection, and security concerns. The information in Chapter 7 will help you whether you plan to take the Networking Essentials test or not. Every administrator should know this information.

Chapter 8 covers troubleshooting. Microsoft is notorious for using troubleshooting questions on its test so do not tread lightly on that last chapter of the book! Be sure to learn the important troubleshooting ideas and procedures, as they are extremely important, and your knowing them will greatly affect your score on the exam. Cover the labs in Chapter 8 and make sure that you understand them in full detail.

Chapter 9 is an optional chapter that explains how to add optional network services to your LAN. This information may not be on the exam, but it is useful if you want more value from your network.

# Administration

# About Chapter 7

Now that you've covered the theories and technologies used in choosing and installing a network, it's time to move on to administration and maintenance of your network.

I will cover the different types of Microsoft networks and the way each is configured and managed. You will learn about user accounts and the policies used to control them.

This chapter also discusses the tasks you must perform to maintain the network, and also the tools that can make this job easier. You will discover that there are two types of security used on networks and when each is used. I will discuss ways to safeguard data from disaster, both internal and external. You will learn the benefits of performance monitoring and some of the essential items to monitor. By the end of the chapter, you will be familiar with the tasks involved in network administration and some of the tools used to perform these tasks.

# USER AND SECURITY ADMINISTRATION

Installation and configuration of the network is just the beginning of the job for the network administrator. Once the network is in place, there are many maintenance tasks involved in network administration. Users come and go, and new network resources are added, involving network reconfiguration. Other tasks involve providing a fault-tolerant network that can survive the inevitable device failure. I will discuss various responsibilities of managing the network and tools available to make the job easier. Before I begin discussing these tools, I'll begin with a quick overview of the basics of Microsoft networks and their components. Once I cover the components, I'll discuss the tools available to help manage these components and secure the network.

## Microsoft Networks

Microsoft networks come in two forms: *workgroups* and *domains*. When a computer is configured for networking, a computer name must be supplied along with a workgroup or domain name. It is important to maintain a standard naming scheme.

Standardizing the naming scheme can make it much easier to locate network resources. Another important reason for a naming scheme is to make sure all of your computers have unique names. Workgroups and domains should be given names, which identify either location or function (a combination can also be used). One example of this is to name all workgroups according to department; for example, ACCOUNTING, MARKETING, and HR. Inside the workgroups, you need naming standards to specify each machine. An example of this is to name the computers the job title of the user; for example, RECEIVABLES, PAYABLES, BILLING, and so on. It is important to remember that workgroups, domains, and computers must have names that are unique on the network.

The naming of your servers and workstations should follow some sort of standard defined by your organization. Each computer in a Microsoft network, either a server or a workstation, has a NetBIOS name. This name is how the server is known on the network. It is very common to see servers named after movie characters, pets, or any other convenient name that an administrator may think of. This may work in a small network with only a few servers. But if this network grows, trying to remember what a server does or where it is located by these types of names can become a big headache.

The idea behind a naming scheme is to sort out the confusion of many different servers for users. If users cannot locate the resources they need, the network is not helping them. The method you use in your naming convention is based on and decided by your company or organization. Some people suggest using a name that denotes the server's function, though that may be a bad idea since servers now do many things. Another more practical method is to use the location. Servers rarely move location, and if they do, they are probably serving new users who do not know the original name.

**in the real world**    **One company I have worked for used the location and server type to define the name. The first six letters denoted the city and state, while the last 6 gave the server type and number (in case there were multiple servers of that type). For example, a Windows NT Server running Microsoft Exchange in Raleigh, North Carolina, was given RLGHNC-NTX000. The RLGHNC was for Raleigh, North Carolina. NTX000 showed that it was an NT Server running Exchange (The *X* is for Exchange) and that it was the first server of this type. This naming scheme was used in a network with many thousands of servers.**

The key to the scheme is being consistent and making the names unique. One you have decided on a scheme, you should stick with it and make sure servers not under your control also use it. This may become a management issue that has to be issued as a policy or procedure.

Shared resources should also have a naming scheme. This way it will be easier for users to move from one server to another if they change locations. Once you do this, you will find this greatly helps your administration efforts, as well.

Now take a look at workgroups and domains.

## *Workgroups*

Workgroups help organize computers in a peer-based network according to department or function. Networks can have a large number of workgroups. Each computer can be a member of one workgroup. Figure 7-1 shows Network Neighborhood viewing a workgroup. When users on a Microsoft network browse the network, they first see all the computers in their workgroup that have sharing enabled. They can then browse the entire network to see a list of workgroups on the network, as shown in Figure 7-2. Each workgroup is browsable. Any computer can join a workgroup by simply specifying the workgroup name. A server is not required in a workgroup but can be present. Workgroups require each user to manage their own resources and users. Microsoft Windows 95, Windows for Workgroups, and Windows NT Server and Workstation are capable of joining a workgroup.

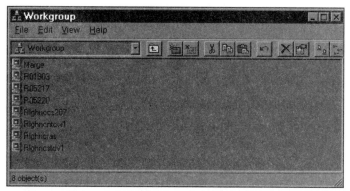

**FIGURE 7-1**    Network Neighborhood viewing a workgroup

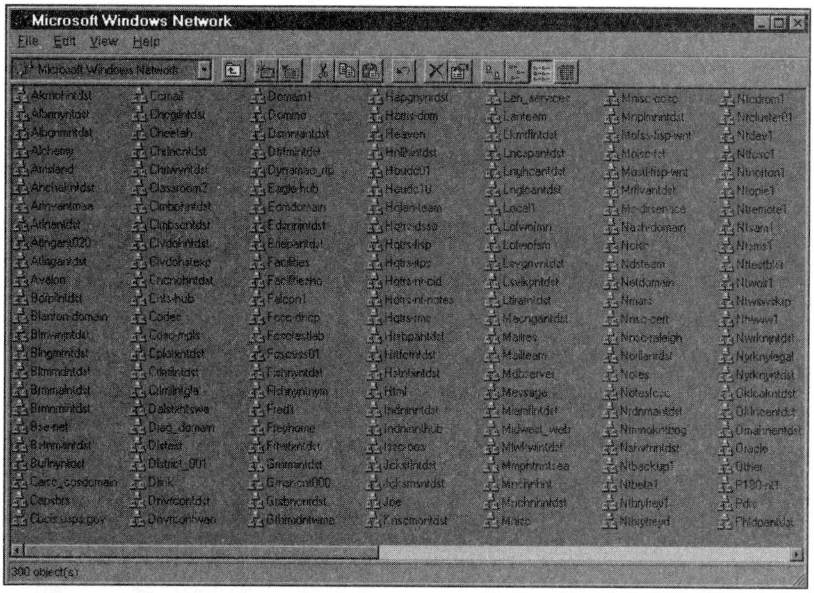

**FIGURE 7-2**    Network Neighborhood viewing entire network

## *Domains*

Domains are server-based networks that provide a higher level of security and central administration that isn't available with workgroups. The *primary domain controller*, or PDC, is a Windows NT server that validates accounts as users log on to the network. *Backup domain controllers* (BDCs), also Windows NT servers, can assist with logons if the PDC is unavailable. A user must have an account on the domain before he can log on to it. Once a user logs on to the domain, network resources are granted based on that account's *user rights* and *permissions*.

A domain provides a central database of users and groups, which can be granted rights to resources throughout the domain. Domains provide centralized administration and accounts for the network. Windows 95, Windows for Workgroups, and Windows NT Server and Workstation are capable of joining a domain.

exam
preparation
pointer

**For the Networking Essentials exam, be sure that you know the differences between workgroups and domains.**

**Workgroups have the following characteristics:**

o  **Peer-based networks**

o  **No central administration**

o  **Used to organize resources**

**Domains have the following characteristics:**

o  **Require a Windows NT server to function as a PDC**

o  **Provide central administration of users and resources**

o  **Require an account to log on to the network**

## Users

Anyone who accesses resources on a network needs a *user account*. User accounts identify the user to the network, and it allows rights to be granted to that specific user. User accounts can be created and administered for one computer or for an entire domain. Domains make it easier to maintain proper user accounts throughout the network. User Manager for Domains is a utility in the Administrative Tools program group that is provided with Microsoft Windows NT Server to manage user accounts for the domain. Non-domain user accounts are managed using User Manager on Windows NT Server and Workstation. Figure 7-3 is a screen shot of User Manager for Domains.

When an account is created on any Windows NT computer, it is assigned a number that identifies it. This number is called a *security identifier* (SID). SIDs are very large numbers that theoretically should be unique in the universe. All rights given to the user are identified with that account number. When an account is deleted, the number is lost. If a new account is created, even with the same user name, a new number, or SID, is assigned. This means that an account cannot be recreated if it is deleted. Instead, the new user account will then need to be assigned the necessary permissions.

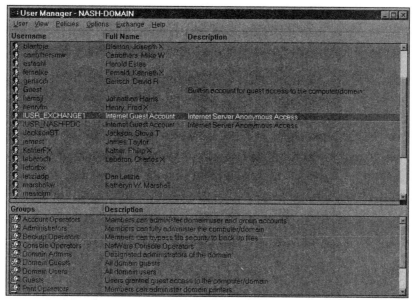

Figure 7-3 User Manager for Domains

Users can be joined to form *groups*. Access to network resources can be granted to both users and groups. User groups are useful for combining users in the same department or with a similar function. When resources are shared, the group can be granted access instead of requiring that each user account be granted access. As users join and leave the department, this makes the job of maintaining rights and accounts much simpler.

exam preparation pointer

**You will probably see some questions on the exam regarding user accounts. Be sure to know the characteristics of user accounts:**

o **Domain accounts are created using Account Manager for Domains.**

o **User accounts require certain rights to create, edit, and delete user accounts.**

o **They are associated with an account number, making it impossible to recreate if deleted.**

## Creating user accounts

There are some rules to keep in mind when creating user accounts. In Windows NT a user account can be up to twenty characters using any combination of letters, numbers, and symbols except for /, \, :, ;, |, =, +, *, <, and >.

User accounts are most often created by the administrator, but in certain circumstances another person can be delegated the duty. The following list shows the standard information needed to create a user:

o **Username:** Short name that signifies the user (for example, nashwj). This is the name that the person sitting at the client computer will use to log on to the network.

o **Password:** Password provides security for the user account.

o **Full Name:** Full name is usually needed for an account for informational purposes.

o **Description:** Description usually contains information pertaining to the user's role in the company.

o **Home directory:** The home directory is a private directory on the server to which users normally save their work.

o **Login scripts:** Script name that is executed upon the user logging in. This normally sets up the network environment for the user and attaches them to resources.

Not all these options may be available in every network operating system. Other options, such as the times that a user is allowed to log in or which computers they are allowed to log in from, may also be available.

Most network operating systems have a graphical utility to add and manage users. In Windows NT this is User Manager for Domains, and with NetWare it is SysCon or NWAdmin. Figure 7-4 shows getting to User Manager for Domains from the Start menu.

Using the User Manager for Domains is easy. First open up the User Manager for Domains application, located in the Administrative Tools program group. From the menu bar at the top, select User, and then select New User. A window appears asking for the information needed to create the user. Figure 7-5 shows creating a new user.

When creating a new user, several properties can be included with the user name. The information needed on the New User Properties screen is as follows:

o Username

o Full Name

o Description

o Password (and confirmation)

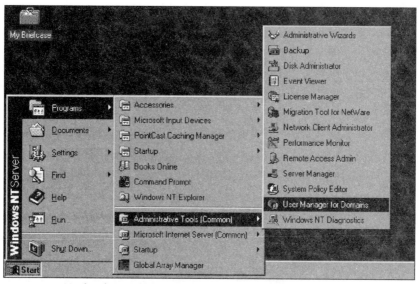

**FIGURE 7-4**   Navigating to User Manager for Domains from the Start menu

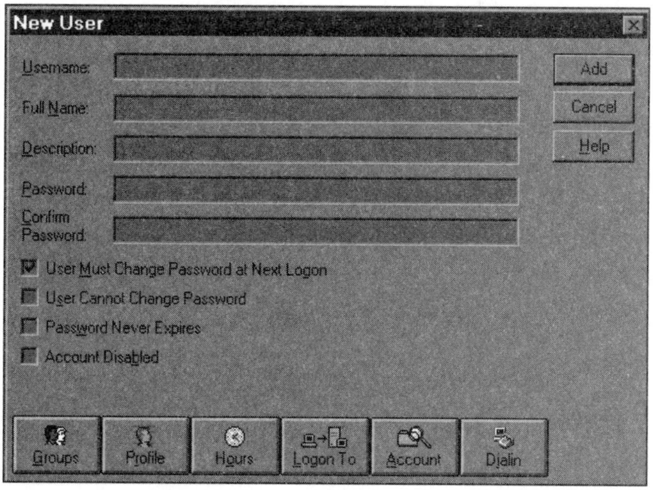

**FIGURE 7-5**   Creating a new user using the User Manager for Domains utility

- User Must Change Password at Next Logon
- User Cannot Change Password
- Password Never Expires
- Account Disabled

tip

**Do not check the User Must Change Password at Next Logon and User Cannot Change Password check boxes at the same time. If both boxes are checked, the user is forced to change his or her password when he or she first logs on. However, the conflict is that the user is not allowed to change it. This guarantees confusion for the users as they will not be allowed to log in until an administrator (or Account Operator) acknowledges and corrects the problem.**

When creating accounts for users that require the same groups and access, there are several options for simplifying the process. Windows NT allows you to rename and copy existing accounts. You may wish to set up a template account and use the copy function to create the new account. This would enable you to define the groups and rights once and to add the specific user information instead of creating an entirely new account each time.

With Windows NT User Manager, you can also set more options than the standard ones listed previously:

o **Logon times:** Limit the hours that users may access the network.

o **Home directory:** Access to the users' private files.

o **Expiration date:** Limit the account's life on the network. This option is especially useful for intern or temporary accounts.

Windows NT also allows for further controls on the user account. *User profiles* allow administrators to set standard desktops and define further levels of security for users. An administrator may use these profiles for new users that are not yet capable of having full access to their computers.

Profiles can be set to maintain the following information:

o Printer connections

o Windows sizes and positions

o Desktop settings such as colors

o Mappings to network resources

Profiles may be set so they are either mandatory or not. Mandatory user profiles are hard coded by the administrator, and the settings cannot be changed by the user. Normal user profiles can be changed by the user and are created to store their settings from session to session.

## *Special accounts*

Network operating systems usually come with at least a few special accounts that are created when the software is installed. The first account is usually some sort of administrator account.

### Administrator account

In Windows NT the administrative account is known as *Administrator*. Under NetWare the account is *Supervisor* or *Admin*, and in UNIX it is *root*. Normally this user cannot be deleted and should have a very good password assigned to it that contains numbers and symbols. The password should be changed often, but not forgotten.

 **A standard recommendation in a secure environment is to rename this account and its description, and create a dummy account called "Administrator" with no rights and no privileges throughout the system. That way, just in case the hacker manages to break in to what they thought was the administrative account, it has actually been denied privileges to do anything on the computer or network.**

Normally these accounts have the ability to:

o Start the network

o Set the security parameters

o Create other accounts

### Guest account

Another account created automatically by Windows NT is the *Guest* account. This can allow you to share resources to users on your network that may not be authenticated through a user account.

By default, the Guest account is disabled under Windows NT Server and enabled under Windows NT Workstation.

## *Accounts policies*

User accounts can be given *policies* that limit user rights. These are accessed through the Policies menu and then the Accounts menu options in User Manager for Domains.

Policies provide many controls on user accounts. They can be used to manage passwords, including setting length, duration, and uniqueness. This helps maintain security, because by restricting the passwords users can use, you force users to put more effort into creating passwords. Users can also be locked out after a number of incorrect password attempts. This prevents an unauthorized person from simply guessing the password until they discover it.

Policies can also be used to set user rights for such things as to which computers someone can log on and which administrative rights, if any, they are granted. One way this can be used is to give someone rights to manage a shared printer. Remote access rights can be set to specify whether the user has the right to dial into the server from a remote location. Logon times can also be set to prevent users from logging on to the network after hours. *Auditing* allows an administrator to track successful and failed attempts by the user to log on to the network, access resources, shut the system down, and so on. This can help inform the administrator of possible security problems on the network.

exam preparation pointer

**For the exam, remember that account policies are used to specify the following:**

- **Set password criteria such as password length, duration, and uniqueness**
- **Assign user rights such as to which computers a user can log on**
- **Allow users to access the computer remotely**
- **Set logon times during which the user has access to the network**
- **Allow for auditing of events such as logons, file access, and so on**

## Passwords

The network is only as secure as the user's password. Anyone with access to the user's password has access to all the data on the system, as well as the network resources shared to the user. That is why users must carefully choose their passwords. Users should follow some basic rules when deciding on a password.

- Do not use obvious passwords such as your birth date, spouse's name, children's name, or your type of car.
- Memorize your password. Do not write it down, and especially do not write it on a sticky note and stick it to your monitor.

o Be sure to change your password often in case someone does compromise your account.

Also, as mentioned earlier, policies can be used to help manage passwords. They can be used to control password length, duration, and uniqueness. Data with a higher sensitivity level requires a higher level of password control. Users can be forced to change their passwords often. This decreases the likelihood of an unauthorized user gaining access to their password. Forcing users to log on to change their password also helps prevent an unauthorized user from gaining access to the system. Windows 95 computers do not require a user to know the correct user name and password to gain access to the system. Windows 95 is a less secure operating system that allows anyone to type a new user name and password to gain access to the system (users can also simply cancel the logon screen). This allows any user to gain access to data stored on the system. The security requirements of the data can dictate which operating system is used. Windows NT requires the correct user name and password before a user can access the system.

The account policy editor in User Manger, shown in Figure 7-6, enables you to set these policies.

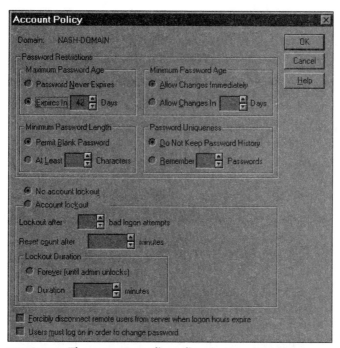

**FIGURE 7-6**   The accounts policy editor in User Manager

exam preparation pointer **You will probably see questions about passwords on the exam, so remember that the following restrictions and demands can be placed on user passwords:**

- **Minimum password length**
- **Password duration**
- **Password uniqueness**
- **Whether users must log on to change the password**

# Group Accounts

A large company network can have thousands of accounts that must be managed. At some point the overhead of handling security and access to resources becomes too much of a burden for the support staff. By implementing groups, you can cut out a lot of the simple administration that takes so much time.

A *group* is a special account that contains other accounts. Groups allow the administrator to logically group users together for the purpose of administration. If everyone in the accounting department needs access to the same database, what sense does it make to manually assign each one individual rights to that database? What if the database moves and now you must reassign everyone the new rights? With a group you only need to make one change to affect hundreds or thousands of users. Almost every network operating system supports these types of accounts.

 **The planning of your group organization should begin when the network is first designed. Groups should be the primary way you handle the security and resource access on your network.**

Groups can be used to:

- Grant access rights to resources such as files and printers
- Give users the ability to perform system functions such as backups, reboots, and changing configuration settings
- Simplify communications by cutting down the number of messages or broadcasts that must be sent across the network

## *Types of groups*

Windows NT has two different types of groups. These are *local groups*, *global groups*, *special groups*, and *built-in groups*.

### Local groups

Local groups are created and stored on a local computer's security database. They are used to group users together on a single server or domain and cannot be shared with other servers or domains.

### Global groups

Global groups allow you to share group information between domains and servers. In a network that uses Windows NT and domains, these groups allow you to assign rights to users in other domains by simply giving the rights to the group, not each user individually.

### Special groups

Special groups are used by Windows NT to handle users dynamically. Two examples of these special groups are the *Interactive group* and the *Network group*. Administrators cannot control the membership of these groups. Windows NT does it automatically. The Interactive group is composed of users who are physically working on the computer's console. The Network group's members are using the computer's resources from across the network.

### Built-in groups

Windows NT, NetWare, and most other network operating systems have some groups that are automatically made when the software is installed. Some examples of groups in Windows NT include:

o **Administrators:** This group includes network administrators with full rights to the server.

o **Operator-type groups:** These groups grant the members system functions such as the ability to backup and restore data.

o **System groups:** Groups that are used by Windows NT itself to manage data. The *Replicator group* is used to help replicate data between servers on the network.

## *Creating groups*

Groups are created in a way similar to user accounts in Windows NT. This is done through the User Manager for Domains utility. In the User Manager for Domains, select the User menu option, and then choose New Local Group. Figure 7-7 shows a new local group created in User Manager.

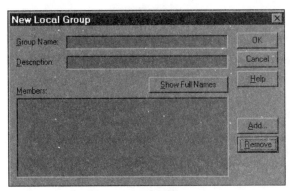

**FIGURE 7-7    Creating a new local group**

The following two fields should be filled when creating the group:

o **Group Name:** The group name must be unique among other group names and user names. The same symbols that are prohibited in user accounts are also prohibited in group names.

o **Description:** This field describes the purpose of the group.

After filling out the two fields above, the next step is to add members. This is done by clicking the Add button and choosing the users which you would like to be members of this group.

## Security Types

There are two main types of security available for use on the network. The type of security you use depends largely on the type of network and the operating system. Workgroups depend on *share-level* security while domains employ *user-level* security.

Share-level security involves assigning a password to resources shared on the network. All a user needs to access the resource is the password. The same resource can be shared with different permissions and different passwords. The level of access to the resource depends on which password one uses to access it. This allows the resource to be shared as *read-only*, and the password for this share is given to the users who need to view the resource. The resource could then be shared as full-access. The users that use the password assigned to the *full-access* share could delete, change, and read the data. This allows the data to be shared with different levels of access for a variety of users on the network. This method of security can be difficult to maintain. Users may have to remember several passwords in order to access all the resources needed to perform their jobs. You will also need to tell everyone the new password should the resource password be changed. Users who should not have access to a resource may learn the password. Once this occurs, the password must be changed, and all users must learn the new password. Windows 95 can only use share-level security when in a peer-based network.

Most networks share data with user-level security. User-level security requires the proper user name and password to access a resource. When resources are shared, permission is granted to certain users or groups of users. Only those user accounts can access the resource. Microsoft Windows NT Server and Workstation use user-level security when in workgroups and domains. When the computers are in a domain, accounts from the PDC can be granted access to shared resources. In addition, a local accounts database can be used in a workgroup. User-level security can be used on a computer running Windows 95 when it is a member of a domain or configured as a Client to a NetWare server. User-level security not only provides a higher level of security, it also allows a wide variety of permissions. A Windows 95 computer using share-level security has only two options: read and full control. User-level security provides read, write, add, change, delete, and so on. The added security and flexibility makes user-level security the preferred method for networks over about ten computers.

exam preparation pointer

**Be sure to know the differences between the two levels of security for the exam:**

- **Share-level security only relies on a single password to access a resource and is used in workgroups.**

- **User-level security requires a user name and password to log on to the resource. User-level security is used in domains, especially Windows 95 computers in a domain and Windows NT workstations and servers in a workgroup or domain.**

## Auditing

Auditing can help you track events on your network to ensure security. This can include things such as users logging on and off the system, access to files and/or directories, as well as system reboots.

Audit logs can be a great tool to help administrators find unauthorized access, as well as simple security mistakes that the administrator may have overlooked. Common events that can be audited are:

- Success and failure of user logons and logoffs

- Connections to network resources such as disk shares and printers

- System reboots

- Password changes

- Opening, closing, or changing of a file

- Any permission changes or user rights changes

- Creation or deletion of user or group accounts

Windows NT and NetWare support auditing, and Windows NT provides the Event Viewer to show the audit log. Figure 7-8 shows the audit log in Event Viewer.

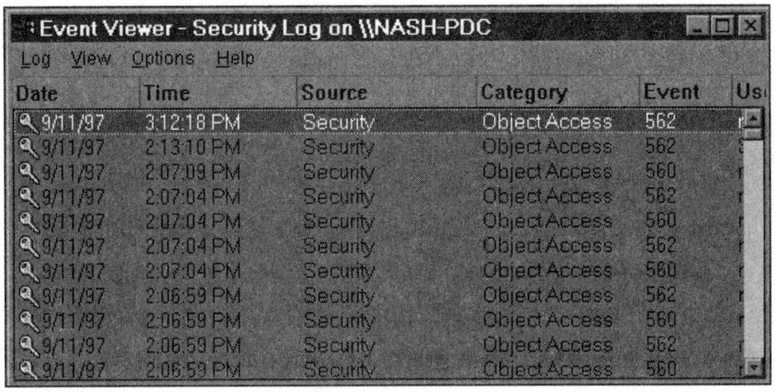

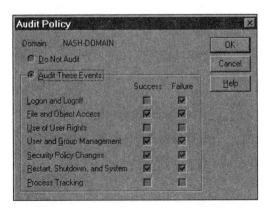

**FIGURE 7-8**   Event Viewer showing the audit log

In Windows NT, auditing is enabled through User Manager for Domains. This is done by choosing Policies from the menu bar and then selecting Audit from the menu. Select the Audit These Events option to enable auditing. To view the logs, you must use Event Viewer from the Administrative Tools group in Windows NT. Figure 7-9 shows auditing being enabled in User Manager for Domains.

**FIGURE 7-9**   Enabling auditing in User Manager for Domains

# SAFEGUARDING DATA

Data saved on the servers often takes months or years to obtain and is impossible to replace, so you must take measures to safeguard against threats. Threats to network data can vary. Employees and outsiders can purposely or accidentally delete or damage files. Hard drives or disk controllers can fail, causing lost or corrupt files. Forces of nature also pose a threat; fires, floods, and other natural disasters can cause damage to equipment and loss of data. Therefore, it is very important to have disaster recovery plans in place to safeguard the data. Methods that make your network fault tolerant include *data backups*, *redundant data*, and *uninterruptible power supplies*.

## Backups

Tape drives, recordable CD-ROM drives, and other removable disk drives can be used to back up and archive data. These devices enable you to back up certain files, directories, or entire disk drives depending on what data is most critical and how often it changes. You can back up remote data and data saved on other systems across the network.

 **When performing backups across the network, be aware of the bandwidth this requires. Backups performed across the network are typically scheduled to occur at night when there is more available bandwidth.**

Several methods are used for backing up data, and most effective backup plans utilize several methods. The method used varies according to the amount of data that needs to be saved and the amount of time you want to spend backing up and restoring data.

- **Full backup:** A full backup is used to back up all selected files. This process marks the files as archived.

- **Incremental backup:** Incremental backups are used to back up selected files that have been changed since the last backup. The files are then marked as archived.

- **Differential backup:** Differential backups are used to back up selected files that have changed since the last backup. This method does not mark files as archived.

- **Copy:** Copying backs up selected files without marking them as archived.
- **Daily copy:** Backs up selected files that have changed during the day without marking them as archived.

One way these types can be utilized in a backup plan is to perform a full backup of the network on the weekend. During the week, differential backups are performed. This plan provides a full backup that can be used to restore the entire system to the version obtained on the weekend. Each differential backup contains all files that have changed since the full backup was performed. If the system needs to be restored on Thursday, the full backup from the weekend will first be restored. Then the differential backup performed Wednesday night will then be restored. At this point, the entire system will be at the level obtained the previous night. The only drawback to performing differential backups nightly is that as the week progresses and more files are changed, the backup process takes longer. The benefit is the quicker rate of restoring the system. Some administrators prefer incremental backup because they are quicker. You should note that when restoring incremental backups, each backup should be restored in the proper order. This ensures that all files are restored to the latest version.

note **Backup software is included with some operating systems such as Microsoft Windows NT and Windows 95. Many third-party companies also provide backup software with a wide range of functionality. Backup software can be used to schedule the various backup types and perform them unattended throughout the day and night.**

Carefully testing and documenting your backup procedure is important. When testing the backup process, you should back up data as you normally do, delete the data, then restore from the backup. The data should be tested to ensure its usability. This should be done regularly to ensure that the equipment is functioning properly. You don't want to discover that a device is malfunctioning when you really need to restore lost data. Creating two copies of each backup is a good idea. One copy should be stored on-site, the other stored in a remote location. This helps ensure a natural disaster doesn't destroy the original data and all backups. Documentation helps ensure the backups are occurring according to schedule. Documentation also helps ensure that the correct backups are being restored to the system.

**TO ACHIEVE A SUCCESSFUL BACKUP PLAN, FOLLOW THESE STEPS:**

**1.** Determine which data on your network needs to be backed up.

**2.** Develop a schedule to show when certain data should be backed up. Not all data changes daily, or at all. Use this information to make an efficient and secure backup schedule.

**3.** Assign the duties of backing up data to a dependable person.

**4.** Select the hardware that will be used to handle the data backup. The type of drive you choose will depend on the amount of data you have to be backed up, as well as the amount of money you wish to spend.

**5.** Use the previously mentioned list to determine the backup methods that will be used each day.

**6.** Test the backup system. Be sure to do one complete backup and restore (to a test server) to make sure the hardware is working correctly.

**7.** Identify on-site and off-site storage locations for the tape media.

**8.** Keep a log of backups, and clearly mark all tapes so they can be found easily when needed.

 *tip* **Be sure to test your backup hardware. There is no worse feeling for a network administrator than to find out the backup you thought you had is not good.**

## Redundant Systems

Another fault-tolerant system that can be utilized in combination with backups is *redundancy*. With redundancy, data is duplicated or spread across drives. Redundant systems can help quickly restore the system in case of a device failure. There are several types of redundancy used in today's networks. *Redundant arrays of inexpensive disks* (RAIDs) provide for several levels of redundancy with varying levels of fault tolerance. RAIDs use a combination of hard drives to provide a higher level of fault tolerance or to provide greater speed when accessing data on the drive. The levels of RAID listed below are the most commonly used today. They also happen to be the ones that Windows NT Server supports in software.

## RAID 0

RAID 0 utilizes *disk striping*. Striping divides data into 64K blocks and spreads the blocks across each drive or partition. All the devices combine to create one logical device. This does not provide fault tolerance because the data is not duplicated. If one device fails, all data is lost. The amount of storage space used is 100 percent. Figure 7-10 illustrates disk striping.

RAID 0 does provide a few benefits. Small partitions can be combined to form one logical device. In addition, disk access rates are increased if multiple disk controllers are used. This allows several devices to read and write data simultaneously. Microsoft Windows NT is capable of configuring RAID 0 through Disk Administrator.

## RAID 1

RAID 1 utilizes *disk mirroring*. Disk mirroring duplicates all data and partitions to a separate physical disk. This provides two full copies of the system and all data. If one drive fails, the duplicate can be used in its place. This provides quick restoration of the system without restoring several backups. The weakness of disk mirroring is that both drives use the same controller. If the controller fails, then both copies of the data are unusable. Figure 7-11 illustrates disk mirroring.

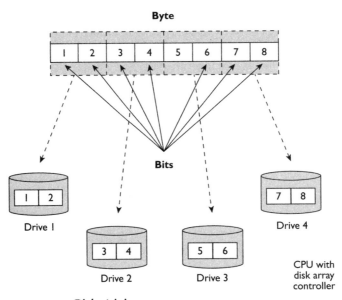

**FIGURE 7-10**   Disk striping

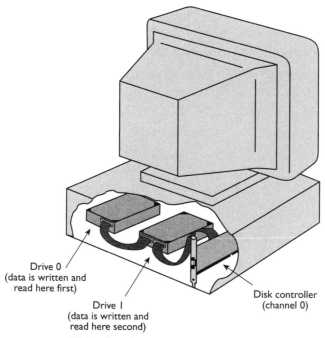

Drive 0
(data is written and
read here first)

Drive I
(data is written and
read here second)

Disk controller
(channel 0)

**FIGURE 7-11   Disk mirroring**

RAID 1 can also utilize *disk duplexing*. Disk duplexing is simple disk mirroring with separate controllers. This provides a higher level of fault tolerance. Microsoft Windows NT comes with the software necessary to create a mirror set. Figure 7-12 illustrates disk duplexing.

The drawback to disk mirroring and duplexing is the cost. The duplicate drive provides no extra storage space. Duplexing is more expensive because of the extra controller that is used. Usable storage space versus storage space purchased is 50 percent. Due to the cost of mirroring and duplexing, RAID 1 is rarely used for all disks in the server. RAID 1 is primarily used only for system disks.

## *RAID 5*

After RAID 1, the next type of RAID configuration that is commonly used is RAID 5. RAID 2, 3, and 4 are just variations that are not usually used due to their limitations. RAID 5 utilizes disk striping with parity. Data blocks are striped to several disks with a parity stripe written in varying locations. The data and parity are always written on different disks. The parity stripe contains information that can be used to reconstruct data. RAID 5 can combine three to thirty-two drives in an array. Because the parity is spread across several disks, if any one disk goes down it can be replaced and the data reconstructed. The level of fault tolerance this provides often makes it worth the amount of disk space lost to parity. RAID 5 can be controlled through special hardware or software. Windows NT contains Disk Administrator, which is capable of configuring software RAID 5. This is currently the preferred redundancy system.

Figure 7-13 illustrates RAID 5.

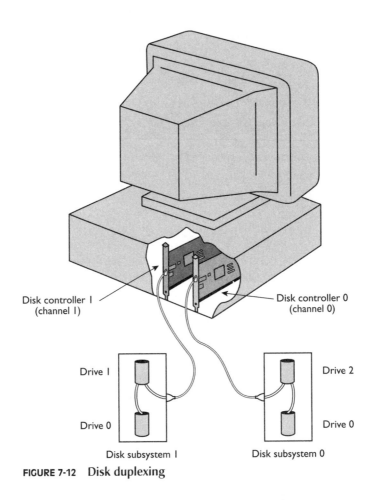

FIGURE 7-12    **Disk duplexing**

## Uninterruptible Power Supplies

An uninterruptible power supply (UPS) can be used to safeguard against power outages. A UPS is a battery that operates between the power outlet and the computer. The size of the battery varies, and it is important to purchase a UPS that is powerful enough to support the equipment that is attached.

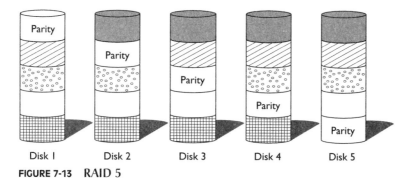

Disk 1    Disk 2    Disk 3    Disk 4    Disk 5

**FIGURE 7-13** RAID 5

The UPS sends valuable information such as power conditions and available battery life to the computer. In case of a power failure, the UPS can alert the user and the system when battery life is low. This can allow the computer to go through an orderly shut down, writing data to the disks and avoiding corrupt data.

Some operating systems such as Windows NT include software that is capable of communicating with the UPS. There is also third-party software available that can communicate with UPSes over a serial connection that provides greater functionality.

# PERFORMANCE

Monitoring performance of the network and servers alerts you to trends in the network and possible problems. Performance monitoring includes monitoring the performance of systems as well as performance of the network. Components monitored on computers include memory usage, CPU utilization, and available disk space. By monitoring these components, you can plan for upgrades or off-load some tasks to another computer. This helps ensure that your servers are being used efficiently. Monitoring also alerts you to a server that is overloaded and providing slow access to the users.

When monitoring the network, pay attention to the amount of bandwidth being utilized. You can also detect which segments of the network have the highest utilization. This helps you effectively segment and maintain the network. Packet-loss alerts you to possible problems with cables, connectors, or other equipment. By monitoring the network, you learn which areas need upgrades and where there may be failing components.

Some network operating systems such as Windows NT include performance-monitoring software. You can also find many third-party software products available to aid in performance monitoring. The *Simple Network Management Protocol* (SNMP) can be a very useful tool for doing performance monitoring on your network. Most network devices now include SNMP as a support protocol. With a good SNMP management software system, you can obtain almost any statistical information you desire.

Performance monitoring is a valuable tool for the network administrator. It alerts you to problems that are currently occurring. By monitoring trends, you can properly prepare for the future of your network.

Figure 7-14 shows Performance Monitor.

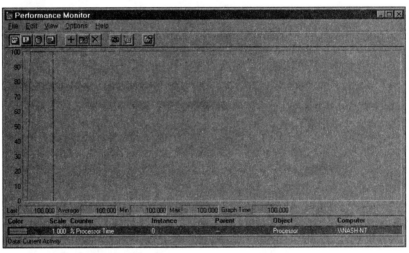

**FIGURE 7-14** Performance Monitor

# KEY POINT SUMMARY

In this chapter you learned several important tasks of the network administrator.

- Workgroups have the following characteristics:
  - Peer-based networks
  - No central administration
  - Used to organize resources

- *Domains* have the following characteristics:

    - Require a Windows NT server to function as a *primary domain controller* (PDC)

    - Provides *central administration* of users and resources

    - *More secure*, requires an account to log on to the network

- Users are the most important part of the network, and there are several ways to give users rights and secure the network.

- *User accounts* have the following characteristics:

    - *User name:* Short name that signifies the user (for example, nashwj).

    - *Password:* Password that provides security for the user account.

    - *Full name:* Full name is usually needed for an account for informational purposes.

    - *Description:* Description usually contains information pertaining to the user's role in the company.

    - *Home directory:* The home directory is a private directory on the server to which users normally save their work.

    - *Login scripts:* Script name that is executed upon the user logging in.

- *Profiles* can be set to maintain the following information:

    - Printer connections

    - Window sizes and positions

    - Desktop settings such as colors

    - Mappings to network resources

- User accounts are managed using account policies. Account policies are used to specify the following:

    - Set *password criteria* such as password length, duration, and uniqueness

    - Assign *user rights* such as which computers a user can log on to

    - Allow users to access the computer *remotely*

    - Set *logon times* during which the user has access to the network

    - Allows for *auditing* of events such as logons, file access, and so on

- The *Administrator* and *Guest* accounts are special accounts that are automatically created on Windows NT computers. These accounts have been included for specific purposes.

- The Administrator and Guest accounts have the following rights:
    - Start the network
    - Set the security parameters
    - Create other accounts
- A guest account allows access for users who don't have an account.
- One of the most important features controlled with account policies is *passwords*. The following restrictions and demands can be placed on user passwords:
    - Minimum password length
    - Password duration
    - Password uniqueness
    - Whether users must log on to change the password
- Windows NT computers use *user groups* to help manage users. Groups can be used to:
    - Grant access rights to resources such as files and printers
    - Give users the ability to perform system functions such as backups, reboots, and changing configuration settings
    - Simplify communications by cutting down the number of messages or broadcasts that must be sent across the network
- There are two types of groups:
    - *Local groups* are used to assign permissions to users on the local computer.
    - *Global groups* are used to assign permissions to groups of users across the domain.
- There are special groups built into Windows NT computers to help with administrative tasks. These groups include:
    - *Administrators:* Network administrators with full rights to the server.
    - *Operator-type groups:* These groups grant the members system functions such as the ability to back up and restore data.
    - *System groups:* Groups that are used by Windows NT itself to manage data. The *Replicator group* is used to help replicate data between servers on the network.

- Security on Microsoft networks can be handled in two ways: *share-level* and *user-level.*

  - Share-level security has the following characteristics:

    - Used on Windows 95 computers in a workgroup

    - Access is determined according to the password entered.

    - Requires users to remember several passwords to access all of the needed resources

  - User-level security has the following characteristics:

    - Used on Windows NT computers when in a domain or workgroup; used on Windows 95 computers in a domain.

    - Access is determined by the user account used.

- *Auditing* can help maintain security by tracking possible attempts at inappropriate access. Auditing is used to track the following events:

  - Success and failure of user logons and logoffs

  - Connections to network resources such as disk shares and printers

  - System reboots

  - Password changes

  - Opening, closing, or changing of a file

  - Any permission changes or user rights changes

  - User or group accounts that are created or deleted

- Data backups are important for a fault-tolerant network. There are several types of backups to help safeguard important data:

  - *Full backup:* A full backup is used to back up all selected files. This process marks the files as archived.

  - *Incremental backup:* Incremental backups are used to back up selected files that have been changed since the last backup. The files are then marked as archived.

  - *Differential backup:* Differential backups are used to back up selected files that have changed since the last backup. This method does not mark files as archived.

  - *Copy:* Copying backs up selected files without marking them as archived.

  - *Daily copy:* Backs up selected files that have changed during the day without marking them as archived.

- Successful backup plans contain the following components:
  - Determine which data on your network needs to be backed up.
  - Develop a schedule to show when certain data should be backed up. Not all data changes daily, or at all. Use this information to make an efficient and secure backup schedule.
  - Assign the duties of backing up data to a dependable person.
  - Select the hardware that will be used to handle the data backup. The type of drive you choose will depend on the amount of data you have to be backed up, as well as the amount of money you wish to spend.
  - Use the list above to determine the backup methods that will be used each day.
  - Test the backup system. Be sure to do one complete backup and restore (to a test server) to make sure the hardware is working correctly.
  - Identify on-site and off-site storage locations for the tape media.
  - Keep a log of backups and clearly mark all tapes so they can be found easily when needed.

- There are several types of *redundant drive systems* which help provide enhanced fault tolerance:
  - *RAID 0* consists of *disk striping* with no redundancy.
  - *RAID 1* provides for *disk mirroring* and *duplexing*. Mirroring and duplexing are used to create exact copies of a drive. Mirroring relies on the same controller, while separate controllers are used for duplexing.
  - *RAID 5* is the preferred redundancy system. RAID 5 utilizes disk striping with *parity*. This allows the data to be recreated even if one disk fails.

- An *uninterruptible power supply,* or UPS, is a large battery which can provide power to systems during power loss. Software that communicates with the UPS can perform an orderly shutdown of the system when battery power is getting low.

- *Performance monitoring* is used to alert you to trends and problems on the network. This can help with planning upgrades and ensuring that all systems are configured for maximum performance.

- *Simple Network Management Protocol* is used for performance monitoring. SNMP software allows for detailed monitoring of many network components.

---

# APPLYING WHAT YOU'VE LEARNED

Now it's time to regroup, review, and apply what you've learned in this chapter about administration. The questions in the Instant Assessment section bring to mind key facts and concepts. The Critical Thinking labs provide you with an opportunity to apply the knowledge you've gained in this chapter about administraton.

 **note** Critical Thinking labs challenge you to apply your understanding of the material to solve a hypothetical problem. The questions are scenario-based, requiring you to decide "why" or "how" or to devise a solution to a problem. You might need to be at a computer to work through some of these labs.

 **concept link** Refer to the "Hardware and Software You'll Need" section in the Preface or in Appendix B if you're not sure you have the necessary equipment to do the Critical Thinking labs.

## Instant Assessment

**1.** Which of the following is not a characteristic of a workgroup?

  **a.** Peer networking

  **b.** No central administrator

  **c.** Used to organize resources

  **d.** Utilizes a PDC

**2.** Which of the following is not a valid character for use in user names?

  **a.** &

  **b.** @

  **c.** #

  **d.** *

**3.** Which operating system must use share-level security in a workgroup?

  **a.** Windows NT Server

  **b.** Windows NT Workstation

  **c.** Windows 95

  **d.** NetWare Server

**4.** Which of the following is set with user profiles?

    **a.** User name

    **b.** Password length

    **c.** Network mappings

    **d.** Desktop settings

**5.** Which of the following is set with policies?

    **a.** Printer connections

    **b.** Password length

    **c.** Network mappings

    **d.** Desktop settings

**6.** Which of the following restrictions cannot be placed on user passwords in Windows NT?

    **a.** Minimum password length

    **b.** Maximum password length

    **c.** Password duration

    **d.** Password uniqueness

**7.** Which type of backup is used to back up selected files that have changed since the last backup and doesn't mark them as archived?

    **a.** Full backup

    **b.** Incremental backup

    **c.** Differential backup

    **d.** Copy

**8.** Which type of backup is used to back up all selected files without marking them as archived?

    **a.** Full backup

    **b.** Incremental backup

    **c.** Differential backup

    **d.** Copy

9. Which type of backup is used to back up selected files that have changed since the last backup and marks them as archived?

   **a.** Full backup

   **b.** Incremental backup

   **c.** Differential backup

   **d.** Copy

|  | T/F |
|---|---|
| 10. Computers logging onto a workgroup require accounts on the workgroup. | ____ |
| 11. Primary domain controllers are used to process user logons and domain accounts. | ____ |
| 12. Windows NT allows user accounts to be disabled after a specified number of unsuccessful logon attempts. | ____ |
| 13. Profiles are used to specify user settings such as desktop preferences and network mappings. | ____ |
| 14. Administrators can require a minimum password length for user accounts. | ____ |
| 15. The Administrator account on Windows NT Server is disabled by default. | ____ |
| 16. Auditing can be used to track logon attempts on the network. | ____ |
| 17. Share-level security is the only option for Microsoft clients in a domain. | ____ |
| 18. Global groups can be used throughout the domain. | ____ |
| 19. Copying a file marks it as archived. | ____ |

concept link        **For answers to these Instant Assessment questions, see Appendix C.**

# Critical Thinking Labs

The following Critical Thinking labs provide you with a practical opportunity to apply the knowledge you've gained in this chapter about administration.

### Lab 7.21 *Security planning*

You are the administrator of a small company network that is migrating to Microsoft networking products. Your users typically work on documents that they maintain and control security. You also do not currently have a central file server. Would you choose to implement workgroups or domains? Why?

### Lab 7.22 *Windows NT administration*

Create a user account under Windows NT for yourself. Make sure that your password must be changed at next logon and it never expires. Next, make yourself a member of the Administrators group so you can change the configuration of your computer.

### Lab 7.23 *Monitoring users*

You are suspicious that a user has gained access to the account files on your network. You need to find a way to catch the user and document them for your report to management. Which Windows NT feature could you use?

### Lab 7.24 *Sharing resources*

In Windows 95, share a directory with read permission and again with full permission using share-level security.

### Lab 7.25 *Backup strategies*

The data on your server undergoes many changes daily. You want to quickly back up the data several times a day. Which backup method would you choose?

### Lab 7.26 *Security considerations*

You have just installed a Microsoft network using workgroups. Which type of security will you use on the Windows NT Workstation computers in the workgroup? Why would you choose this type?

concept link

**For answers to these labs, see Appendix C.**

# Troubleshooting

# About Chapter 8

Chapter 8 prepares you for when things go wrong on your network. Troubleshooting skills are very important — you should learn them as soon as possible. It is well known that Microsoft likes to put questions geared toward troubleshooting scenarios on its exams, so be sure to pay close attention to this chapter. You should be intimately familiar with which tools to use in which scenarios and the steps to follow to use them. Any hands-on experience with setting up a network and troubleshooting hardware problems will help you with this exam, in addition to strengthening your skills for your future as an administrator.

Troubleshooting is one of the hardest things to teach, but this chapter introduces you to helpful software and also provides some good advice. When troubleshooting, remember to pay careful attention to the symptoms of the problem, only try one thing at a time to correct the problem (so you'll know if it worked or not), and keep documentation. When the problem arises again, why reinvent the wheel?

This chapter covers the software and hardware needed to successfully troubleshoot the most common problems you will see on a network as an administrator. It also contains tips for minor adjustments you can try when troubleshooting.

# TROUBLESHOOTING BASICS

Network troubleshooting is a skill that can take a long time to master. With all the parts of a network that must work together perfectly for everything to function as expected, it is no surprise that troubleshooting can be tedious. You should first try the following steps to help resolve a problem. You will be amazed at the number of problems you can solve with these.

o  **Make sure the problem is not user error.** It is not uncommon for a user to complain of a problem they think has to do with the network but turns out to be a simple configuration setting on their workstation.

o  **Check simple physical connections.** Cables come unhooked all the time. Before delving too deep into troubleshooting, check their connection to the network. Most network cards have a link light that shows whether they are talking to a hub or MAU. These can save you hours of trouble.

o  **Restart the computer.** It is amazing how many things are fixed by a simple reboot. It is always worth a shot.

If these simple steps do not solve the problem, then more serious actions may need to be taken. Also, check to see if more than one computer is affected. Multiple computers having the same problem usually point to a network error.

Everyone has their own method of troubleshooting. Some methods are better than others. For the Networking Essentials exam, you should be familiar with the Microsoft approach to problem troubleshooting. Microsoft recommends a structured approach for troubleshooting that involves five steps:

1. Set the problem's priority.

2. Collect information.

3. Determine possible causes.

4. Isolate the cause.

5. Study the results.

## Set the Problem's Priority

Priority can be a big issue when it comes to resolving a network problem. Everyone wants his or her computer fixed right away. Sometimes this is possible and sometimes it is not. You have to prioritize problems based on things such as the time necessary to fix the problem, importance, and who has the problem.

For example, you would not want to fix a problem that takes two hours first, while waiting to fix a problem that could be done in a few minutes. You may also need to prioritize a problem with the accounting systems before a problem with a secretary's workstation, because the accounting problem affects everyone.

Not all problems can be resolved as soon as they are found; you may have to schedule time to fix the problem. If a production server or central piece of network equipment must be reset or reconfigured, this can affect everyone on the network. Most work of this nature must be handled after hours.

in the
real world

**It is not uncommon for me to have to set priorities in my job. Sometimes I am responsible for changes that need to be made to the e-mail system, but they require a reboot of the main server. This has to be scheduled for after hours when everyone is off the system. No one said that being an administrator was a 9-to-5 job!**

## Collect Information

Once you have decided which problem to concentrate on, you must then collect information to help isolate the trouble. If you have a *baseline performance chart* for your network — and you should — you can use it to compare against the current network operations. A baseline performance chart is a set of statistics you have taken over a period of time showing your network functioning normally. If you've documented things well, you may be able to track through previous logs for an answer if this problem has happened before. If the problem is with a specific user, you can question them.

Users are a good source of information, since they are using the network all the time. A simple question such as "What problems have you noticed with the network?" may yield all sorts of information.

- The network is sluggish today.
- I cannot map a drive to the server.
- I cannot print.
- I get an error when I run my application.

Once you have questioned the users, you may need to ask yourself and other technical support staff questions to further isolate the problem. Some examples are:

o How many users were affected?

o Is there any correlation between the affected users?

o Is this an intermittent problem?

o Was a new piece of equipment added to the network?

o Any other work being done to the building?

o Have we had this problem before?

o Have any software configuration changes been made lately?

The key question to ask when a problem arises on a network is "What changed?" Whether the problem is with one user or one hundred, the question should always be asked, as 99 percent of the time something was added, removed, or reconfigured prior to the problem starting.

 **tip**

**Always be sure to check for any other work being done on the building or completed right before the problems started. I have been on many client sites where a problem that appeared on the network had nothing to do with the networking staff or hardware changes. Things such as a change in the electrical system or new lighting can adversely affect the network.**

If the cause of the problem is not immediately evident after checking for network changes or questioning the user, the next step is to isolate the problem. To isolate the problem, you should start removing or replacing components to narrow down the field with which you are working. If a computer cannot connect to a server, you might try it on a different workstation. This way you are isolating either the workstation or the server from the problem. It is much easier to troubleshoot a small piece of network than it is to troubleshoot the entire company LAN. After you isolate the problem down to a specific area, you can then focus on the smaller parts, such as:

o Clients

o Adapters

o Cable

- o  Hubs
- o  Connectors
- o  Servers
- o  Internetwork devices
- o  Protocol configuration

## Determine Possible Causes

Hopefully at this point you should be starting to determine the source of the problem. You may not know the exact problem but instead have a small list of possible causes. The next step is to try out your possible causes.

## Isolate the Problem

At this point, try your most likely solution to see if it fixes the problem. For example, if you suspect a bad LAN cable, replace the cable and retest the workstation to see if a connection can be made.

## Study the Results

Carefully study the results for each fix you try. See if the problem was fixed or changed in any way. If the problem was not fixed by your solution, keep trying the ideas on your list until either it is fixed or you run out of ideas. Even if a solution does not fix the problem entirely, it may help you further pinpoint the real issue. If you run out of ideas, you may need to start back at collecting information to see if you overlooked anything.

# CLIENT HARDWARE TROUBLESHOOTING

Client hardware commonly becomes faulty and causes errors. The good news is that it is usually easy to pinpoint the exact issue and resolve it.

If only one workstation on your network is affected by a problem, odds are the problem is at the workstation itself. While sometimes frustrating because all the other workstations on your network are functioning fine, this can also make the job easier, since the problem is already isolated.

Some places where common workstation problems occur are:

o Network adapters

o Protocol configuration

o Application configuration

# Network Adapters

The most common workstation-related network problem involves the network adapters. Problems occur when adapters are incorrectly configured or when adapters malfunction.

## *Network adapter configuration*

When configuring a network adapter, you must be sure that the settings such as IRQ, I/O address, and shared memory range are unused by anything else in the computer. One sign of a conflict with another device is that the other device also doesn't function. A device that is conflicting with another may also seem erratic. The careful eye may notice that the troubled network adapter card does not function when another device, such as a scanner or modem, is being used. The simple solution to this problem is to change one of the conflicting devices to another unused setting.

 tip    **On an MS-DOS or Windows 95 computer, you can run** Msd.exe **to get a list of IRQs being used. Under Windows NT you can find detailed information on the resources being used by looking in Windows NT Diagnostics from the Administrative Tools group.**

 concept link    **You can refer back to Chapter 3 for information on the different network adapter configuration settings. Just remember that they must be unique and not shared by other cards or devices in the computer.**

When checking the configuration of a network card, also pay close attention to the transceiver type that is selected. A common problem with a computer that cannot make a connection to a server is that its transceiver type setting is wrong. For example, it may be set to use the AUI port when you should be using the UTP port.

### Malfunctioning network adapter

Spotting a malfunctioning network adapter is generally easy, because most have diagnostic LEDs on the back to help you diagnose problems. Two common lights are the *link light* and the *data transmission light*. The link light shows that the network card has made a connection to a hub (or, as in the case of Token Ring, a MAU). If you see the link light is not illuminated, you may need to check the network card, cable, or sometimes the port on the hub. The data transmission light shows when, and if, data is being sent and received by the network card.

# NETWORK TROUBLESHOOTING

Once you've determined that a problem is with the network and not isolated to one workstation, the number of possible causes of the problem increases greatly. Thankfully, several hardware devices exist to help you find the problem. Also, some common problems are easily solved, and I discuss those in this section.

## The Right Tool for the Job

A number of hardware devices can help you pinpoint your problem on the network. Some of the most common ones are:

- Digital volt meters (DVMs)
- Time-domain reflectometers (TDRs)
- Advanced cable testers
- Oscilloscopes
- Network monitors
- Protocol analyzers

**For the exam, be sure to know exactly when and why to use a particular hardware troubleshooting device.**

### Digital volt meters

The *digital volt meter* (DVM) is a basic electronic measuring device. Though usually used to check the amount of voltage going through a circuit, it can help you pinpoint certain types of cable problems. For instance, you can use a DVM to check for continuity on a network cable, to see if there are any breaks in the physical media. By connecting the DVM to the ground mesh and the central core, you can check for a short in the cable that may cause disturbances in the communications.

### Time-domain reflectometers

Whereas a DVM can only tell you if a break exists in the cable, a *time-domain reflectometer* (TDR) can tell you exactly where the break occurred. The TDR uses a sonar-like pulse that is sent down the cable. The signal bounces back from a break in the cable. The TDR calculates the time the signal took to go down the cable and back, and then computes the distance.

TDRs are great to use when a new network is being installed and also after the installation, when a break can be hard to troubleshoot.

### Advanced cable testers

*Advanced cable testers* work beyond the lower levels of the OSI model to give you real insight into how your network is functioning. They can display all sorts of information, including:

o Frame counts

o Congestion errors

o Network utilization

o Late collisions

o CRC errors

o Network-level statistics

o Protocol statistics

o Information concerning which applications are using the network

By using these statistics, you can watch for network errors such as collisions caused by excessive cable length or congestion errors due to an overloaded network. Normally, problems resulting from these statistics are segment- or network-wide and affect all users.

 web links

**For an example of an advanced cable tester, be sure to check out** `http://www.fluke.com`.

## Oscilloscopes

*Oscilloscopes* are used to show voltage over time. While used frequently in diagnosing problems with electrical equipment, they can also test for faulty network cable. Oscilloscopes can be used to check for:

o Shorts

o Crimps in the cable

o Breaks in the cable

o Attenuation

## Network monitors

*Network monitors* are software programs that track and show information about a network. They can generate reports showing utilization, errors, and overall traffic patterns on your network — reports that are very beneficial, as they show your network growth over time. By watching the growth, you can predict when problems may arise and take proactive steps before they do.

## Protocol analyzers

*Protocol analyzers* can do the job of network monitors, and much more. A protocol analyzer often proves to be an important tool when debugging problems on a network. Also called *network analyzers* or *sniffers*, protocol analyzers can be hardware only or a combination of hardware and software. They collect information by examining all data going across the network and decoding the information for display. Figure 8-1 shows a protocol analyzer.

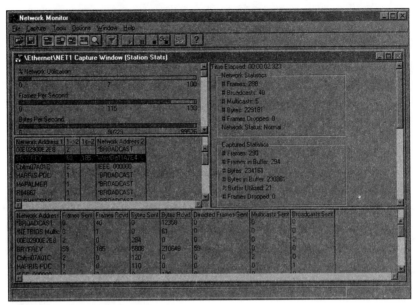

**FIGURE 8-1**   A protocol analyzer

Some problems that protocol analyzers can find are:

o Bad network cards

o Cable problems

o Bottlenecks

o Configuration errors in protocols

Protocol analyzers are excellent tools for finding most problems on a network. They can look at the network packet by packet and tell you exactly what is being transmitted. You may even use them to debug network applications by looking at the "conversation" going on.

 tip **Many administrators constantly keep a protocol analyzer working on their network. Most analyzers allow you to set threshold levels for errors and other conditions — such as maximum number of collisions per second or network utilization — and alert you when those thresholds are reached.**

Some popular protocol analyzers are Network General's Sniffer, Hewlett-Packards's Network Advisor, Novell's LANalyzer, and Microsoft's Network Monitor.

Many common protocol analyzers run on a normal workstation computer. They use the workstation's network hardware to access and monitor the network. The correct choice of network card is important in the computer that will be running the protocol analyzer software, as the network card must function in what is called *promiscuous mode*. Normally, the MAC address on a network frame header is checked at the Data Link layer. If the MAC address is found to be different from the computer reading it, it is discarded. A network card running in promiscuous mode passes all frames up to the higher-level processes, whether the frame was intended for it or not.

 **Some network cards will hide certain errors from protocol analyzers, because they sense the errors and discard the frames before the frames can be given to the upper-level processes. 3Com network cards would commonly do this, as do most PCMCIA cards.**

Most Token Ring network cards cannot run in promiscuous mode. This is common with cards that have an IBM chipset. Special Token Ring cards can be bought that do allow promiscuous-mode operation.

## Common Network Problems and Solutions

Some fairly common problems don't require the use of the aforementioned hardware devices. Be sure to check for these potential problems before you waste a lot of time.

### Cable problems

Many problems you will encounter will be Physical layer problems having to do with cables. Common cable problems include:

o A break in the cable

o A cable short

o A faulty connector

Cable should be one of the first things checked when troubleshooting a network problem. Something as simple as a piece of thinnet Ethernet cable getting disconnected will take down the entire LAN segment.

The first step in working with a cable problem is to make sure that, in fact, it is a cable issue. The easiest way to check is to keep a notebook computer handy that you can attach to the LAN over the questionable cable.

The next step is to ask if anyone has moved equipment or furniture recently. Many times cables are broken when being moved or having things moved on top of them.

If the network uses a bus topology, you can use a terminator to segment the network in half and start isolating the faulty cable. While this may cause disruption to the other users, it can quickly solve the problem.

### Network adapters

Network adapters rarely quit working suddenly. The more usual situation is that a new piece of hardware was added to the computer. The first step should be to check for conflicting IRQs, I/O addresses, and shared memory ranges.

You can check the link lights and data transmission lights on the network card to see if it is talking to the hub or the rest of the network.

Network adapter drivers can cause many problems should they become corrupted or get replaced by a wrong version. The simple solution is to reinstall the drivers. An easy way to totally reconfigure the network under Windows 95 is to remove the network card from the Network properties menu, then reboot the system. When the computer comes back up, you can manually read the card. Figure 8-2 shows the Network properties window.

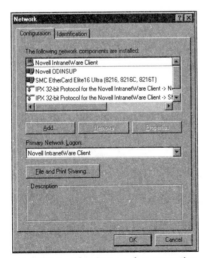

**FIGURE 8-2**  **The Network properties window**

Incorrect protocol settings can keep a workstation from attaching to a network server. The most common solution is to check the frame type, mainly with IPX/SPX. Be sure you are using the same frame type on your workstations as on your servers. Figure 8-3 shows the frame type settings for IPX/SPX.

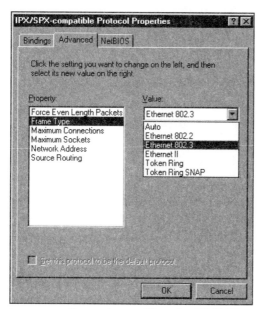

**FIGURE 8-3**   **Frame type settings for IPX/SPX**

Also check your IP address, subnet mask, and default gateway (typically a router functions as the gateway between subnets). An incorrect setting on any of these can keep your workstation from participating on the network. Figure 8-4 shows the IP address configuration screen from Windows 95.

## Network protocols

Protocols can be especially hard to troubleshoot. They are designed to overcome any network problems that arise. Sometimes you may not know network problems such as a faulty connector exist until the protocol slows down and users start complaining.

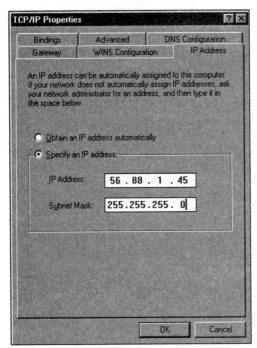

**FIGURE 8-4**   IP address settings in Windows 95

Some questions to ask at this point are:

o If the computer receives an error while connected to the LAN, does the computer function offline?

o Has the traffic on this part of the network increased substantially?

o Is there any connection between the devices that are getting the error?

To further troubleshoot protocols, other tools such as a protocol analyzer or network monitor may be needed.

### Network traffic congestion

Network congestion is usually noticed by users, though it should not be. A good network administrator has a protocol analyzer or other sort of network monitor tracking the network traffic trends. Congestion should be cleared up before it is a problem. Figure 8-5 shows the Windows NT Performance Monitor tracking network utilization.

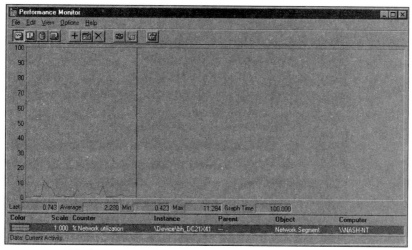

**FIGURE 8-5**   Windows NT Performance Monitor showing network utilization

Once you have decided to head off the congestion problem, you can use several hardware devices to help. Bridges can be used to filter traffic, and routers can split the network into logical segments.

## Broadcast storms

Broadcast storms are a condition where there are so many broadcasts, the entire network slows down. Remember that broadcasts are read by every device on the network, so not only is network access slow, but the computers will be slow as well. Broadcast storms can be caused by several conditions. A bad network adapter can send out infinite numbers of broadcasts with no reason. This condition is called *jabber*. Malfunctioning or badly planned bridges can also cause broadcast storms.

Most routers do not pass broadcasts, so they can provide some level of protection. The best bet is to find the offending device by the use of a protocol analyzer and remove it.

## Network-intensive applications

Use of new applications may contribute to new congestion problems. A new breed of applications known as *push applications* can cause a lot of network traffic. These applications constantly receive information from a server and provide real-time information, such as news, stock quotes, sports scores, and so on.

Another problem to watch out for on your network is gamers. Many popular games now support playing against other people over a network. The only real solution to this problem is to ban the applications. Some of the new push applications are utilizing special server software that caches information and sends it to the client so that each client does not have to get the same data over and over.

 **When the popular game Doom first appeared on networks, it caused many problems. The initial release used broadcast packets for all communications. As you may have guessed, this brought many corporate networks to their knees.**

### Power problems

Most problems having to do with power can be solved with an uninterruptible power supply. Fluctuations and power surges can all be handled by a good UPS.

Most UPS systems also come with software that shuts down your server in case of a total power failure. This allows your applications running on the server to be shut down gracefully, so as not to lose any data.

# TROUBLESHOOTING RESOURCES

Sometimes a problem may be extremely hard to pinpoint and solve. When this is the case, you may need to turn to outside information to help you through the process. Luckily, some excellent resources exist for troubleshooting any problem a network engineer or administrator may run into:

- Microsoft download library
- Microsoft TechNet
- Microsoft Knowledge Base
- Vendor support Web sites
- Newsgroups
- Online services such as MSN and CompuServe
- Publications

## Microsoft Download Library

A quick way to get file updates for Microsoft products is through their download library. The download library is available by dialing into their electronic bulletin board system at (206)936-6735.

 **The Microsoft software library is also available by using FTP to reach** ftp://ftp.microsoft.com **and looking in the** /softlib **directory.**

## Microsoft TechNet

For the Microsoft networking professional, TechNet is an essential tool that should be in your troubleshooting kit. TechNet is a subscription-based service, where each month you receive a CD containing all sorts of documents and file updates to help you with any problems you may encounter with Microsoft products. There are excellent articles, white papers, and documents to help with planning, engineering, troubleshooting, and deployment. TechNet has an easy-to-use interface that lets you browse and query the information contained on the CD.

 TechNet is well worth the cost of a subscription. You can subscribe by calling (800)344-2121. For more information go to http://www.microsoft.com/technet.

**If you pass an operating system exam for Microsoft, you will receive a free copy of TechNet. If you go on to become an MCSE, you will receive a year's subscription!**

## Microsoft Knowledge Base

The next best resource from Microsoft after TechNet is the Knowledge Base. It contains many articles describing problems having to do with any of Microsoft's applications and their resolutions. These articles are written by developers and support engineers from within Microsoft. A copy of this Knowledge Base is sent to you on TechNet (though it is not as up-to-date). These are the same Knowledge Base articles that Microsoft's Product Support engineers use to resolve your problems when you call.

 **The Microsoft Knowledge Base is available at** http://www.microsoft.com/kb.

## Vendor Support Sites

Almost every vendor in the networking field now has a support site on the Internet. Normally these can be reached by going to `http://www.company_name.com`.

## Newsgroups

Newsgroups can be a good way to reach a large number of people who may be able to help you find the answer to a problem. Quite often, someone has had the same problem as you, and the answer to your question is already there.

There are many Microsoft-specific newsgroups, as well. They usually start with `microsoft.public.product_name`.

 **web links**  **The Web site** `http://www.dejanews.com` **is an excellent newsgroup search engine. You can use it to search through past articles to try to find help with any problem that may have been answered previously.**

## Online Services

Online services can be a good source for technical information. Though not as important as they once were due to the number of companies with excellent Web sites, they can still be your best bet for information. CompuServe, America Online, and the Microsoft Network are all good choices if you are looking for an online service to join.

## Publications

There are many publications that deal with the networking industry. A lot of them can be had for free. Some publications are done weekly, and others are monthly. Some good examples of publications are *LAN Times*, *LAN Magazine*, *Windows NT Magazine*, *Communications Week*, *InfoWorld*, and *PC Week*.

 **web links**  **Check out the following Web sites for more information about the publications referenced in this section:**

- `http://www.lantimes.com`
- `http://www.infoworld.com`

- `http://www.pcweek.com`
- `http://www.winntmag.com`
- `http://www.mcpmag.com`
- `http://www.news.com`

# KEY POINT SUMMARY

This is one of the most important chapters in the book, especially where the exam is concerned. Pay close attention to the summary provided below so that you will not have any surprises on the exam.

Microsoft recommends five steps for troubleshooting:

- **Set the problem's priority.** The priority you set for a problem may factor in things such as available time, importance, and who has the problem.
- **Collect information to identify the symptoms.** Data can be collected by questioning the user and using performance-monitoring tools.
- **Develop a list of possible causes.** After collecting information, you can use the data to develop a list of possible causes.
- **Test to isolate the cause.** Testing the individual components can help locate the failed component.
- **Study the results of the test to identify a solution.** By studying the results of the testing you can often identify the problem and find a solution.

- If only one client is experiencing problems, troubleshooting should be focused on the client.
- Network adapters should be checked for proper resource settings. Checking the lights on a network adapter can be useful when troubleshooting.
- Protocol configuration should be checked to make sure it matches with the rest of the network.
- Application configuration should also be checked to make sure it is set up correctly to work over the network.
- There are several devices that can help you with network troubleshooting:
    - *Digital volt meters* measure voltage on the cable.

- *Time-domain reflectometers* are used to test whether a signal travels the entire length of the cable. This can help detect breaks in the cable.
- *Advanced cable testers* are used to gather several different kinds of data about the network; this can include utilization, collisions, frame count, and so on.
- *Oscilloscopes* show voltage over time.
- *Network monitors* show utilization, errors, and traffic.
- *Protocol analyzers,* known also as *sniffers*, can help identify problems such as bad network cards, cable problems, bottlenecks, and configuration problems.

- There are several resources to advise you with troubleshooting, including:
  - Microsoft download library
  - Microsoft TechNet
  - Microsoft Knowledge Base
  - Vendor support Web sites
  - Newsgroups
  - Online services such as MSN and CompuServe

# APPLYING WHAT YOU'VE LEARNED

Now it's time again to regroup, review, and apply what you've learned in this chapter about troubleshooting. The questions in the Instant Assessment section bring to mind key facts and concepts. The Critical Thinking labs provide you with an opportunity to apply the knowledge you've gained in this chapter about troubleshooting.

 note

**Critical Thinking labs challenge you to apply your understanding of the material to solve a hypothetical problem. The questions are scenario based, requiring you to decide "why" or "how" or to devise a solution to a problem. You might need to be at a computer to work through some of these labs.**

 concept link

**Refer to the "Hardware and Software You'll Need" section in the Preface or in Appendix B if you're not sure you have the necessary equipment to do the Critical Thinking labs.**

## Instant Assessment

1. Which of the following is not a step in the Microsoft preferred-structure approach?

    **a.** Establish priority

    **b.** Reload the operating system and all applications

    **c.** Collect information

    **d.** Test to isolate the cause

2. Which IRQ is used by the system timer?

    **a.** 0

    **b.** 2

    **c.** 5

    **d.** 7

3. Which IRQ is used by LPT1?

    **a.** 0

    **b.** 2

    **c.** 5

    **d.** 7

4. Which device shares IRQ 4 with COM1?

    **a.** COM2

    **b.** COM3

    **c.** COM4

    **d.** LPT2

5. Which IRQ is used by COM2?

    **a.** 0

    **b.** 2

    **c.** 3

    **d.** 4

6. Which diagnostic device is used to test whether a signal travels across a cable?

    **a.** Digital volt meter

    **b.** Time-domain reflectometer

    **c.** Oscilloscope

    **d.** Protocol analyzer

7. Which diagnostic device is used to test the voltage of a cable?

    **a.** Digital volt meter

    **b.** Time-domain reflectometer

    **c.** Oscilloscope

    **d.** Protocol analyzer

8. Which diagnostic device is known as a sniffer?

    **a.** Digital volt meter

    **b.** Time-domain reflectometer

    **c.** Oscilloscope

    **d.** Protocol analyzer

9. Which of the following is not detected by a protocol analyzer?

    **a.** Bad network cards

    **b.** Cable problems

    **c.** Configuration errors in protocols

    **d.** Cable voltage

10. If only one system on the network is having problems, which component would you examine first?

    **a.** Servers

    **b.** Hubs

    **c.** Adapters

    **d.** Internetworking devices

| | T/F |
|---|---|

11. When collecting information to aid in troubleshooting, it is      ____
    important to note what last changed on the system.

12. Client problems can include failing network adapters, protocol      ____
    configuration, and application configuration.

13. User error is rarely seen on modern networks.      ____

14. COM2 and COM4 share IRQ3.

15. Digital volt meters are only useful for measuring voltage on      ____
    network cable.

16. Problems with cable on a thinnet Ethernet network affect the      ____
    entire network.

17. Incorrect protocol settings only affect transmissions through      ____
    a router.

18. Broadcast storms slow network access only for the      ____
    sending device.

19. A user must be present to shut down a system during a      ____
    power outage.

20. Slow network access can be caused by overloading the network.      ____

 concept link      **For answers to these Instant Assessment questions, see Appendix C.**

## Critical Thinking Labs

The following Critical Thinking labs provide you with a practical opportunity to apply the knowledge you've gained in this chapter about troubleshooting.

### Lab 8.27  *Planning the user environment*

A user on the network is complaining that his print jobs are going to the wrong printer. What is the quickest way to eliminate user error as the cause of the problem?

### Lab 8.28  *Detecting conflicts*

A user on your network is complaining that every time he uses his modem his serial mouse freezes. What is the likely cause of the problem?

### Lab 8.29 *Troubleshooting physical connections*

A user suddenly began having problems connecting to the network after redecorating his office. When his workstation is plugged into the Ethernet cable in his neighbor's office, it works properly. What would you suspect as the problem and what equipment could be used to verify the problem and locate the exact location of the problem?

### Lab 8.30 *Locating answers to problems*

A Windows NT computer is returning a specific error code when the messenger service fails to start. You can find no information about this specific error code in Windows NT Help or in your copy of the Resource Kit. Which resources would you use next to discover the meaning of the error code?

### Lab 8.31 *Configuring TCP/IP*

A user on the network is complaining about her new workstation. She can access resources that are on her floor but not those on the floor above her. The floors are separated by a router. TCP/IP is the only protocol installed on the network, and no other user is experiencing problems. What is the most likely cause of her problem?

concept link   **For answers to these labs, see Appendix C.**

# Adding Services to Your Network

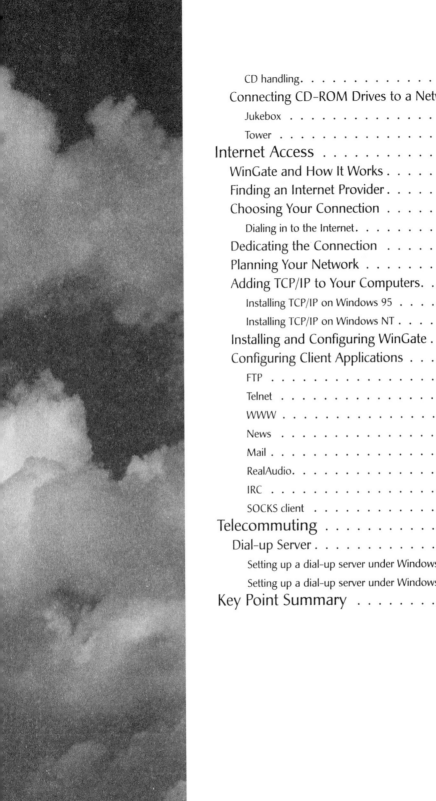

# About Chapter 9

This is an optional chapter that is not required reading to prepare for the Networking Essentials exam. This chapter will walk you through adding some simple, but effective, network services to a small LAN — a small office LAN you are building or your own personal network at home. The solutions given below use the easiest and most inexpensive methods available so that you may enjoy these services on the smallest of LANs.

This chapter will cover the addition of many useful services to your network. These services supplement the file sharing that is inherent in almost all network systems.

The following network services will be covered:

- Network printing
- Network faxing
- Sharing CD-ROMs
- Internet access
- Telecommuting

Some of these services are built into your network operating system, while others require third-party products.

# NETWORK PRINTING

The first network service I will discuss is probably the most popular. This section will cover the installation, maintenance, and management of network printers, print servers, and queues. If you are not familiar with any of these terms, don't be scared. They will be covered soon! The first thing to understand is the difference between local and network printing.

## Printing Terminology

Before I can really begin to discuss printing, I need to cover the terms you will encounter when reading about network printing. One problem with network printing terminology is that the meanings sometimes change depending on the network software used.

The printing terms to know are:

o Print job

o Print queue

o Print server

o Printer

When a user chooses to print a document or graphic, the data is sent across the network to the server and stored there in a file. The file includes the document or graphic data to be printed as well as any formatting or commands that need to be sent to the printer. The size of the document does not matter; it is all held in that one file. This request and data is referred to as a *print job*.

The queue is the area on the *print server* (or workstation, if printing is local) where the print job is stored. Under Novell NetWare, this is by default a directory on the SYS volume under the SYSTEM directory. Microsoft's Windows NT uses the SYSTEM32\SPOOL directory. Occasionally, a print job will be corrupted and you may need to clear out the spool directory.

A *print server* services print queues. The print server process takes print jobs from the queue and sends them to the physical print device.

So you thought you knew what a printer was? You may not. Depending on which network operating system you use, the term *printer* may describe a software object or the physical printer that puts words to paper. Under NetWare and most other operating systems, the term printer refers to the physical device. When using Windows NT, the term server refers to the object that users connect to. The physical printer is called the *print device*. This is important to remember when setting up Windows NT printing.

## Local versus Network Printing

Before networks were common, printers were attached directly to the computers that needed them. Printing was a simple task. An application would send the data to be printed to the printer port on the computer, which would in turn send it through the cable to the printer. This process was easy to set up and easy to troubleshoot if something went wrong.

Networked printing can complicate this procedure. Printing directly to a network printer can be similar to the stand alone procedure, but when the network is client-server the process can be complex. The application must send the print request to the network requester software. The network requester software then "talks" through the network to the server. The server accepts the data to be printed and places it in a print queue where it stays until the physical printer is ready for it. Many things can go wrong in this process, and it can sometimes be hard to track down the exact problem.

in the
real world

**While network printing provides the advantage of enabling all of your users to print to shared printers, it can have some disadvantages to users and network administrators. Some users may not trust the network to handle their print requests. Hearing a printer start up and print their document as soon as they give the command can be reassuring. As a network administrator, you will find that printing is an extremely important, and sometimes personal, service for your users. Network printing is also harder to set up than local printing. It is very easy to just attach a printer to a personal computer and configure it to print. Sometimes setting up printers off a server can be a hassle – and time consuming.**

## Advantages of network printing

There are many more advantages to network printing than there are disadvantages, however. The main advantages are:

o Reduction in number of printers required

o Print spooling

o Improved print management and security

o Flexibility

### Reduction in number of printers required

Probably the most compelling reason to use network printing is the reduction in the number of printers needed. If you use conventional local printing, each user who needs to print must have his or her own personal printer. This scenario can be very expensive and hard to maintain. Each user may have a different configuration, or a user may have different requirements that require a special printer. Why buy five expensive color printers for a department when everyone could share one?

### Print spooling

*Print spooling* enables a user to continue working while the printer does its job. If an application sends data directly to a printer, the computer must wait until that job is completed before it can enable the user to move on. If the document is large or a graphic is complex, the user may be forced to wait for a lengthy amount of time.

Print spooling is the process of storing the print job data in a temporary location while it is being printed. Once the entire print job is put into that temporary location, the computer and user can continue working on other tasks. The printer can print the job whenever it needs to or is available. Print spooling does not speed up the printing process, but it does enable the user to continue working.

Most new operating systems support spooling on local printing. MS-DOS uses RAM to spool the data. Windows and Windows NT use files on the local hard disk to store the data. Network printing has even better spooling than local printing. When a network printing user spools the print job, it goes to the file server. Being low on local hard disk space is a very common problem that can cause local printing to fail. This happens much less often with network printing since servers normally have abundant disk space.

If a user is trying to print a large or complex job to a network printer, he or she can log off the workstation without waiting for the job to finish. Since the spooled information is on the server, the local workstation is no longer needed. This also helps if the printer is offline or out of paper, since the job will get printed as soon as the problem is remedied.

### Improved printer management and security

Printer management is also easier with networked printing. Most printer configuration changes can be done from one computer instead of on each individual workstation.

Printer security is usually simple to administer with network printing. Access to the networked printers is controlled by the user's own login. The network administrator can define the different levels of access. For example, most users will simply be given the right to send print jobs to the printers while others may be allowed to administer the printers.

### Flexibility

Network printing provides for greater flexibility and options. For example, you may set up a separate print queue that is only serviced after business hours. Users can still send data to the queue at any time, but it will only be printed at night. This enables users to send very large jobs that would tie up the printer for a long time and have them printed at off-peak hours. You may also give print queues higher priorities for different users. If you only have one printer, you can have it service multiple queues. One of those queues could have a high priority and only be accessible by Vice Presidents. This way their jobs get printed first.

# Printer Interfaces

There are several different ways to attach printers to computers. The interface is used to transmit data to, and sometimes from, the printer. Some interfaces simply require the user to plug in a cable, while others may need an administrator to configure it for that particular network. The three main types of printer interfaces are:

o Parallel

o Serial or RS-232

o Network interface

The following sections will cover each of these interfaces in detail.

## *Parallel interfaces*

The parallel printer interface is the most commonly used connection today. The original parallel interfaces were unidirectional. They could only send data to a printer; they could not send any information back to the printer. This was not a major problem for printers at that time, but it has become a problem recently. Printers today need the capability of sending back error and information messages to the computer and the printing application. The bidirectional parallel port has also been used for other peripherals. SCSI adapters that plug into the parallel port are common now, as are Ethernet cards.

Parallel ports are also quicker than serial ports at transmitting data. This is due to the way that they function. As the name implies, the data is sent in parallel, eight bits at a time instead of a single bit at a time. Each data path has a separate physical wire in the cable to use. Bidirectional parallel ports have a total of sixteen wires for data transfer.

The one peculiar thing about the parallel interface is its physical connectors. The connector on the workstation or client device is different than the one on the printer. The computer interface is a 25-pin female connector. Table 9-1 shows the pin-outs for the workstation connector.

| TABLE 9-1 | 25-PIN PARALLEL PIN-OUTS |
|-----------|--------------------------|
| PIN | SIGNAL |
| 1 | Strobe |
| 2 | Data Bit 0 |
| 3 | Data Bit 1 |
| 4 | Data Bit 2 |
| 5 | Data Bit 3 |
| 6 | Data Bit 4 |
| 7 | Data Bit 5 |
| 8 | Data Bit 6 |
| 9 | Data Bit 7 |
| 10 | Acknowledge |
| 11 | Busy |
| 12 | Paper End |
| 13 | Select |
| 14 | Auto Feed |
| 15 | Error |
| 16 | Initialize Printer |
| 17 | Select Input |
| 18 | Data Bit 0 Return |
| 19 | Data Bit 1 Return |
| 20 | Data Bit 2 Return |
| 21 | Data Bit 3 Return |
| 22 | Data Bit 4 Return |
| 23 | Data Bit 5 Return |
| 24 | Data Bit 6 Return |
| 25 | Data Bit 7 Return |

Figure 9-1 shows the 25-pin interface.

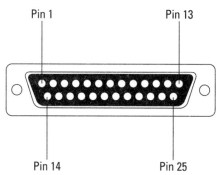

**FIGURE 9-1**   **The 25-pin parallel interface**

If you have ever seen an external SCSI-1 connector, then you have seen the 36-connector parallel connector for printers. A company named Centronics originally designed it, and the connector is now named after it. Table 9-2 shows the Centronics connector pin-outs.

| TABLE 9-2 | CENTRONICS PIN-OUTS |
|-----------|---------------------|
| *PIN* | *SIGNAL* |
| 1 | Strobe |
| 2 | Data Bit 0 |
| 3 | Data Bit 1 |
| 4 | Data Bit 2 |
| 5 | Data Bit 3 |
| 6 | Data Bit 4 |
| 7 | Data Bit 5 |
| 8 | Data Bit 6 |
| 9 | Data Bit 7 |
| 10 | Acknowledge |
| 11 | Busy |
| 12 | Paper Out |

*(continued)*

| **TABLE 9-2** CENTRONICS PIN-OUTS *(continued)* | |
|---|---|
| *PIN* | *SIGNAL* |
| 13 | Select |
| 14 | Auto Feed |
| 15 | Ground |
| 19–30 | Ground |
| 31 | Initialize |
| 32 | Fault |
| 33 | Ground |
| 34 | Select |

Figure 9-2 shows the 36-connector Centronics interface.

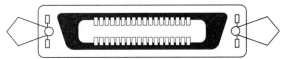

**FIGURE 9-2**    The Centronics interface

Most computers have a limit of three parallel ports. Each parallel port uses an input/output (I/O) address, and two use an interrupt request (IRQ). Table 9-3 shows the resources each uses. Parallel ports are referred to as LPT (line printer) ports on MS-DOS computers.

| **TABLE 9-3** PARALLEL PORT RESOURCES | | |
|---|---|---|
| *PARALLEL PORT* | *I/O ADDRESS* | *IRQ* |
| LPT1 | 3BCh | 7 |
| LPT2 | 378h | 5 |
| LPT3 | 278h | None |

## *Serial or RS-232*

The serial port interface is also known as the *RS-232 interface*. The serial interface sends data one bit at a time. It also uses start and stop bits to handle the flow of information. For this reason it is referred to as an asynchronous interface. Because computers transmit data in parallel, serial ports require that the data be converted. This conversion is done using a universal asynchronous receiver/transmitter chip also known as a UART chip. This chip is also responsible for converting serial data to parallel form. Data sent across a serial port uses start and stop bits. These bits are used to signal when a data byte begins and ends. Parity can also be used for error checking to ensure data reliability. Due to the overhead caused by the translation of data from parallel to serial form, serial communications are slower than parallel. The benefit of parallel over serial connections is the distance allowed. Serial cables can have greater cable lengths with no loss of signal. Table 9-4 shows a standard transmission of data across a serial port. This is a typical transmission that occurs with every byte that is transmitted.

**TABLE 9-4**

| BITS TRANSMITTED | PURPOSE |
|---|---|
| 111111111 | Mark bits that are sent continuously when no transmission is occurring |
| 0 | Start bit that signals the beginning of a transmission |
| 10101001 | Byte that is transmitted. The length can vary but is usually either 7 or 8 |
| 11 | End bits that mark the end of a transmission |

The physical serial interface is either a 25-pin connector or a smaller, 9-pin connector. Table 9-5 shows the pin-outs of the 25-pin connector.

| **TABLE 9-5**   25-PIN SERIAL PORT PIN-OUTS | | |
|---|---|---|
| *PIN* | *SIGNAL* | *ABBREVIATION* |
| 1 | Chassis/Frame Ground | GND |
| 2 | Transmitted Data | TX or TD |
| 3 | Receive Data | RX or RD |
| 4 | Request to Send | RTS |
| 5 | Clear to Send | CTS |
| 6 | Data Set Ready | DSR |
| 7 | Signal Ground | GND |
| 8 | Data Carrier Detect | DCD or CD |
| 9 | Transmit + | TD+ |
| 10 | Unused | |
| 11 | Transmit - | TD- |
| 12–17 | Unused | |
| 18 | Receive + | RD+ |
| 19 | Unused | |
| 20 | Data Terminal Ready | DTR |
| 21 | Unused | |
| 22 | Ring Indicator | RI |
| 23 | Unused | |
| 24 | Unused | |
| 25 | Receive - | RD- |

Figure 9-3 shows the 25-pin interface.

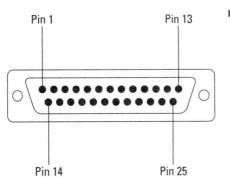

Pin 1          Pin 13

Pin 14          Pin 25

**FIGURE 9-3**   The 25-pin serial interface

| TABLE 9-6 | 9–PIN SERIAL PORT PIN-OUTS | |
|-----------|---------------------------|---------------------|
| *PIN* | *SIGNAL* | *ABBREVIATION* |
| 1 | Data Carrier Detect | DCD |
| 2 | Receive Data | RD |
| 3 | Transmit Data | TD |
| 4 | Data Terminal Ready | DTR |
| 5 | Signal Ground | GND |
| 6 | Data Set Ready | DSR |
| 7 | Request to Send | RTS |
| 8 | Clear to Send | CTS |
| 9 | Ring Indicator | RI |

Figure 9-4 shows the 9-pin interface.

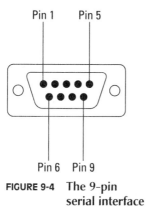

**FIGURE 9-4** **The 9–pin serial interface**

Most computers can use four serial, or *COM*, ports. If more than two ports are used, then IRQs must be shared. It is important to be cautious when configuring ports to share IRQs. If two devices attempt to use the same IRQ simultaneously, problems could occur causing one or both of the devices to fail. This problem has caused a problem for many people that use a serial mouse and an external modem. When the modem is initialized, the mouse freezes. Table 9-7 shows the resources used by each serial port.

| **TABLE 9-7** PARALLEL PORT RESOURCES | | |
|---|---|---|
| *PARALLEL PORT* | *I/O ADDRESS* | *IRQ* |
| COM1 | 3F8h | 4 |
| COM2 | 2F8h | 3 |
| COM3 | 3E8H | 4 |
| COM4 | 2E8H | 3 |

### Network interface

Printers can also be connected directly to the network using a network interface. The network interface is really just a network adapter designed for printers. These come with a variety of connector types to enable the printer to be easily connected to the existing network.

The network interface also provides for the configuration of a number of protocols to enable the printer to function with computers on the network. The network interface cards have a processor and RAM; they receive data from the network and pass it on to the printing device. Software from another computer is used to configure the network interface. This provides more flexibility in installation and configuration. The printer can be configured and utilized by any computer on the network. This also enables the printer to be connected using the network cable, which is capable of greater speeds than parallel or serial cables.

The adapter and software are often proprietary to the type of printer being used. One of the most commonly known devices is the Hewlett-Packard Jet Direct card.

## Setting Up Network Printing

Setting up network printing can be either simple or complicated, depending on the network operating system and how you perform your setup. I will discuss adding printing in NetWare and Windows NT environments.

### NetWare

There are clearly many options for configuring printers and queues in NetWare. The print server services the print queue, and each printer must have a corresponding queue. The queue can exist on the print server and on other file servers throughout the network. There can be a one-to-one relationship between queues and printer as well as a many-to-one relationship. It is possible for multiple printers to share a single queue, and multiple queues can be configured for only one printer. Each printer must be set up individually and pointed to the appropriate queue.

### NetWare print servers

As I said earlier, a print server is a process that takes print jobs from a queue and sends them to a physical printer. NetWare supports running the print server process a few different ways. The server can be run on any one of the following devices:

o  File server

o  Dedicated workstation

o  Nondedicated workstation

o  Dedicated print server devices

If you have a small network, the easiest way to add printing functionality is to load the printer server process, `Pserver.nlm`, on the NetWare file server. To do this you can simply hook the printer to the file server computer's serial or parallel interface ports. Under NetWare 3.12 the `Pserver.nlm` can support up to sixteen printers, with five of them directly on the file server. NetWare 4's `Pserver.nlm` can handle up to 255 printers, with up to seven of them directly connected to the file server.

Loading the print server on the file server can make things much simpler, but at a cost. Parallel ports are very CPU intensive and can greatly hinder the file server if they are used often. Physical location can also be a problem. Most often the file server is not readily accessible by end users, but if you have a printer attached to it they must be able to get to that.

A solution to the location problem may be a dedicated workstation as print server. All you need to do for this is to connect a printer to the computer, and run `Pserver.exe`. This file can support up to sixteen printers with five of them connected directly to the workstation. Another great feature of this setup is that you do not incur any performance penalties. You also do not need a large computer to act as a print server.

note  **NetWare 4.1 does not support dedicated print servers. You can use them only on NetWare 3 networks.**

The next type of print server that NetWare supports is the nondedicated workstation print server. This setup is supported under NetWare 3 and 4. The appeal of a nondedicated setup is that any computer on your LAN can act as a print server. All you need to do is attach a printer to the computer and load either `Rprinter.exe` for NetWare 3 or `Nprinter.exe` for NetWare 4. These two files enable the `Pserver.nlm` process on the file server to access and use the local printer on the workstation. This setup is good because you can put a printer anywhere it is needed, but at the cost of a performance penalty on that workstation.

The final type of print server is quickly becoming the most popular. Many printer manufacturers are putting the print server functionality directly in the printer, or offering small boxes that act as a print server. Intel was one of the first to offer small print server boxes. They enable you to attach four printers to the box and not be required to use any of your workstations. These devices enable `PSERVER.NLM` to connect to them and use the attached printers. They enable you to put printers anywhere that you have a LAN cable.

The print server configuration you use depends on a few different considerations. The first is performance. Serial and parallel ports are much slower than printers connected directly to the LAN. A LAN-attached printer also frees up the CPU time on your workstations and servers. Cost is, of course, a consideration. Small, dedicated workstations used to be the choice since they could be built inexpensively. But now that small, print server boxes are getting cheaper, they have all but replaced these dedicated boxes.

 **The best type of print server to use is one of the new small print server boxes directly connected to the LAN. Most new printers have these built in. If you add a large amount of memory to your printer to help it buffer the print jobs, you can get a fast, easy to maintain, and fairly inexpensive solution.**

### Configuring print servers in a NetWare environment

Configuring print servers in NetWare is fairly simple. You need to set up the connections between the print server(s) and print queue(s). In NetWare, you set up print servers and print queues, and then connect them. As you will learn, this is handled behind the scenes in Windows NT.

PCONSOLE is used to manage and configure printers in NetWare. The options available in PCONSOLE vary in NetWare version 3.*x* and 4.*x*. Table 9-8 covers the options shown under NetWare 3.*x*.

**TABLE 9-8** PCONSOLE IN NETWARE 3.*x*

| *OPTION* | *FUNCTION* |
| --- | --- |
| Change Current File Server | Used to change the default print server and attach additional file servers. This provides management of multiple queues and servers in one session. |
| Print Queue Information | Brings up a list of defined queues which may be examined or deleted and provides for the creation of new queues. |
| Print Server Information | Brings up a list of defined print servers which may be examined or deleted and provides for the creation of new servers. |

The options available under PCONSOLE in NetWare 4.*x* vary somewhat. These options are shown in Table 9-9:

**TABLE 9-9** PCONSOLE IN NETWARE 4.*x*

| *OPTION* | *FUNCTION* |
| --- | --- |
| Print Queues | Brings up a list of the print queues which may be examined or deleted and provides for the creation of new queues. |
| Printers | Brings up a list of the printers which may be examined or deleted and provides for the creation of new printers. |
| Print Servers | Brings up a list of the print servers which may be examined or deleted and provides for the creation of new print servers. |
| Quick Setup | Provides for the easy creation of new printers and print servers. There may be some customization required afterwards. |
| Change Context | Used to change your default NDS context; provides for the management of queues and print servers in more than one NDS context. |

The options in NetWare 3.*x* and 4.*x* function in much the same way. Many of the options in PCONSOLE, especially the Print Servers and Print Queue options, involve working with objects. The objects can be managed using the keys listed in Table 9-10.

**TABLE 9-10    KEYS USED IN PCONSOLE**

| KEY | FUNCTION |
| --- | --- |
| Insert | Creates a new object |
| Delete | Deletes an object |
| F5 | Tags object; used when deleting multiple objects |
| F3 | Renames an object |
| Enter | Edits an existing object |

### Creating print components

Now that you have covered the tools used to create network printing components in NetWare, look at the process of creating these components.

**TO CREATE PRINT SERVER USING PCONSOLE, FOLLOW THESE STEPS:**

**1.** Select Printer Servers in NetWare 4.x or Print Server Information in NetWare 3.*x.*

**2.** Press Insert.

**3.** Name the server.

Once the print server has been created, a printer needs to be configured. The process for configuring the printer varies under NetWare 3.*x* and 4.*x.*

**TO DEFINE PRINTERS UNDER NETWARE 3.*X*, FOLLOW THESE STEPS:**

**1.** Highlight the printer name under Print Server Information in PCONSOLE and press Enter.

**2.** Select the Print Server Configuration option; up to sixteen printers can be configured per server.

**3.** Highlight a slot and press Enter.

**4.** Name the printer.

**5.** Choose the type field and select the appropriate printer type. Available options include local parallel, local serial, remote parallel, remote serial, and so on.

**6.** Select the appropriate resources used by the printer port; when using a serial port, you must also choose the appropriate settings for parity, stop bits, data bits, and so on.

**7.** Pressing the ESC key exits the configuration utility and prompts to save the values.

NetWare 4.*x* handles printers as objects and therefore requires a different configuration method.

**TO CONFIGURE A PRINTER UNDER NETWARE 4.*x* , FOLLOW THESE STEPS:**

**1.** Select the Printers option in PCONSOLE.

**2.** Using the Insert key, enter the name of the printer.

**3.** Highlight the printer name and press Enter.

**4.** Choose the corresponding print server from the list.

**5.** Select the correct printer type.

**6.** Edit the resources field to show the resources used by the printer port.

Once the print server has been created and defined, it is necessary to assign the appropriate print queue to the printer.

**TO ASSIGN THE APPROPRIATE PRINT QUEUE TO THE PRINTER, FOLLOW THESE STEPS:**

**1.** In PCONSOLE, choose the configuration menu for the print server.

**2.** Select the Queues Serviced by Printer option.

**3.** Choose the appropriate printer.

**4.** Press the Insert key to see a list of queues.

**5.** Select the queue that the printer will utilize.

**6.** If you wish, change the priority of the queue.

**7.** Press Enter to save the configuration.

## Windows NT

Network printing is installed and managed in a much different way. Any printer installed on Windows NT can easily be shared to other users on the network. Wizards are used to guide users through the process of installing and configuring the printer. NT enables several print devices to be configured and shared as one printer. This is known as *printer pooling* and provides for easy expansion of network printing capabilities. You do not need to worry about making queues and printers and print servers, and then connecting them together. All of this is handled by Windows NT.

### Printer folder

Printers are configured in Windows NT in the Printers folder.

**TO CONFIGURE A PRINTER IN THE PRINTERS FOLDER, FOLLOW THESE STEPS:**

**1.** From the Start button choose Settings and Printers. Double-click the Add Printers icon to activate the Add Printer Wizard.

**2.** You will be prompted as to whether the printer is to be connected as a Network Printer or to My Computer. When configuring a print server, click the radio button next to My Computer. Figure 9-5 shows the option displayed after double clicking the Add Printer icon.

**3.** Click Next. You will be prompted to specify the port used by the printer. Ports can be added and configured using the buttons in this section. There is also a checkbox used for specifying whether printers will be pooled. If you are pooling printers, you can select multiple ports for each of the connected devices. Figure 9-6 shows the options available for selecting the ports.

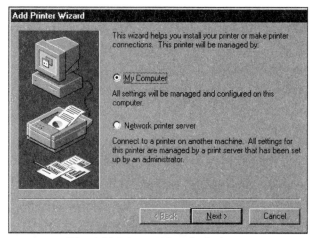

**FIGURE 9-5**    The Add Printer Wizard window

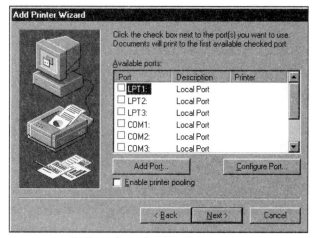

**FIGURE 9-6**    Options for selecting the ports

**4.** Click Next. You are prompted to choose the appropriate printer driver. Windows NT comes with drivers for many printers, and there is also an option to add a driver not included with NT. Clicking the Have Disk button leads to a prompt for the location of the printer driver. Figure 9-7 shows some of the printer drivers available with Windows NT.

**5.** Click Next. You are prompted to name the printer and to decide whether you want the printer to be the default printer for the computer. Figure 9-8 shows the options configured on this screen.

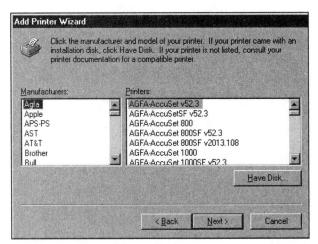

**FIGURE 9-7    Printer driver selection**

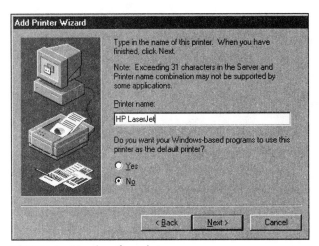

**FIGURE 9-8    Naming the printer**

**6.** Click Next. You will be prompted to determine whether the printer is shared or used strictly as a local printer. If you select the radio button next to Shared, you are prompted for a share name for the printer. You can then choose the operating systems that will print to the printer. Figure 9-9 shows the options, which are configured at this stage.

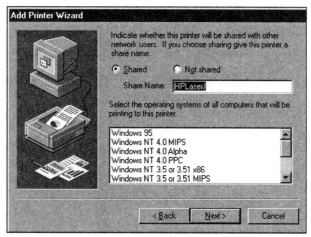

**FIGURE 9-9** **Sharing network printers**

**7.** Click Next. You will be prompted to print a test page. This test page is used to confirm that the printer has been installed correctly and is working properly. The driver for the printer is then installed. If you have elected to enable other operating systems to print to the device, there will be prompts for the location of the drivers for the corresponding print drivers for the operating system.

## Managing printers

Once the printer has been installed, it can then be managed in the Printers folder. The Printers folder contains the Add Printer icon and icons for all printers that have been installed on the computer. Right-clicking the icon for the printer brings up a menu which can be used to manage the printer. Figure 9-10 shows the options available.

**FIGURE 9-10** **Options for printers**

The Properties option on the menu contains several tabbed pages used to configure the printer. Figure 9-11 shows the tabs available on the Properties page.

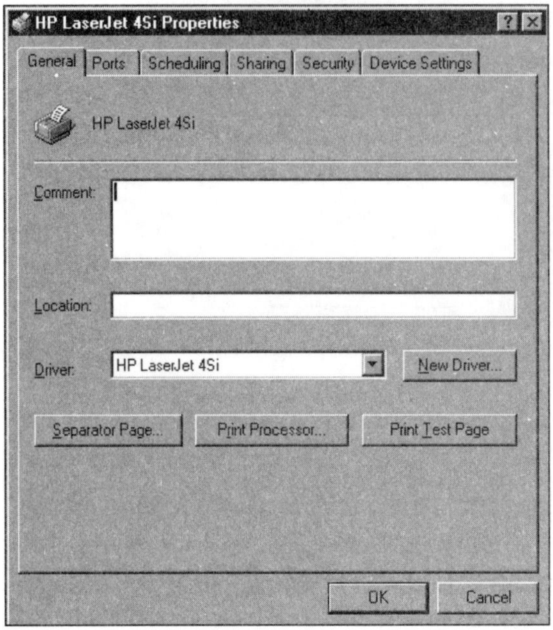

**FIGURE 9-11    Properties options**

Table 9-11 lists the options from the property page.

| **TABLE 9-11** | PROPERTY PAGE OPTIONS |
| --- | --- |
| *TAB* | *FUNCTION* |
| General | Used to specify comments and a physical location of the printer. The printer driver is specified here. The Separator Page, Print Processor, and Print Test Page options are set here. |
| Ports | Used to specify the port used by the print device and whether printer pooling is enabled. Ports are added, deleted, and configured here. |
| Scheduling | Used to specify when the printer is available, the priority of the printer, and how spooled documents are printed. These options are used to produce more efficient printing. |
| Sharing | Used to specify whether the printer is shared on the network, the share name, and the operating systems which can print to the printer. |

| Tab | Function |
| --- | --- |
| Security | Used to set permissions and auditing for the printer. |
| Processing | Used to set the show status option. |
| Help | Used for getting help with printing problems. |
| About | Shows the driver version installed. |

### Print queues

Double-clicking the printers icon in the Printers folder shows the documents present in the printer's queue. The printer queue is created automatically when the printer is installed in NT. Properties of the documents are also displayed. Printing can be paused in this window. Documents can be deleted or jobs can be restarted. This enables a document that is causing a problem and hanging the queue to be deleted without affecting other documents waiting to be printed. Figure 9-12 shows the properties that are displayed from the print queue.

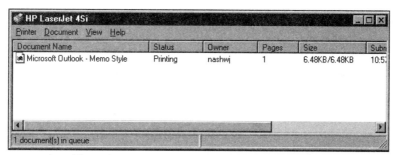

**FIGURE 9-12** The print queue

### Connecting to a shared printer

Connecting to a shared printer from a Windows NT computer is also very easy. The easiest way to do this is from the Add Printer Wizard again. You can connect to printers shared from Windows NT, Windows 95, or NetWare servers this way.

**TO CONNECT TO A SHARED PRINTER, FOLLOW THESE STEPS:**

**1.** Double-click the My Computer icon from the desktop.

**2.** Double-click the Printers folder.

**3.** Double-click the Add Printers icon.

**4.** When the Printer Wizard appears, choose Network Printer Server, as shown in Figure 9-13.

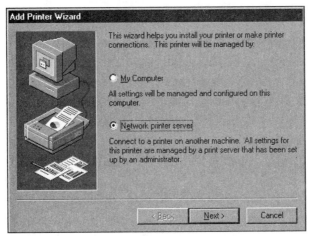

**FIGURE 9-13**    **Choosing a network printer server**

**5.** Click Next. You will see a browse window, as shown in Figure 9-14.

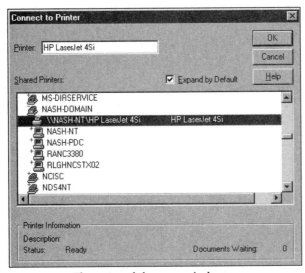

**FIGURE 9-14**    **The network browse window**

**6.** Your browse window may not be as complicated as the one shown. Navigate through the browse window until you find the computer that is sharing the printer you need.

**7.** When you find the computer you are looking for, click it to show its shared printers. Your window should look similar to Figure 9-15.

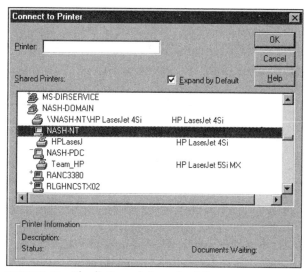

**FIGURE 9-15**  The listing of shared printers

**8.** Highlight the printer you want to connect to and click OK.

**9.** You will be prompted to make this new printer the default printer, as shown in Figure 9-16.

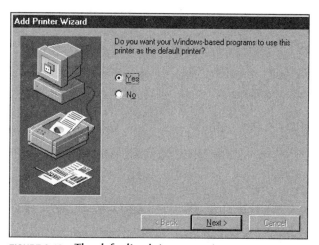

**FIGURE 9-16**  The default printer prompt

**10.** Make your selection and click OK.

**11.** You will see the final screen telling you that you are done adding the printer. Click Finish.

 **Once you have selected the printer to connect to, you may be prompted to install a driver for it depending on what operating system is hosting the driver. If the printer is being shared from a Windows NT computer, you can most likely use the driver on the print server. If the printer is shared from a Windows 95 computer, you will need to install a driver.**

## Windows 95

Setting up shared printers under Windows 95 is very similar to doing it under Windows NT. Once you configure the printer locally, it is just a matter of a few steps to share it to the entire network.

**TO CONFIGURE A SHARED PRINTER UNDER WINDOWS 98, FOLLOW THESE STEPS:**

**1.** Double-click the My Computer icon on your desktop.

**2.** Double-click the Printers folder. You will see the window shown in Figure 9-17.

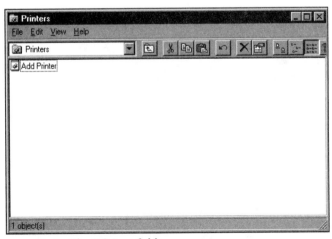

**FIGURE 9-17**    The Printers folder

**3.** Double-click the Add Printer icon. You will see the Add Printer Wizard start up, as shown in Figure 9-18.

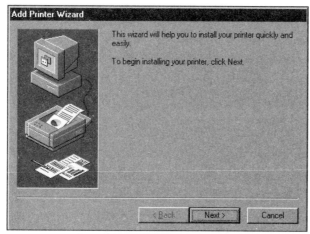

**FIGURE 9-18** The Add Printer Wizard window

**4.** Click Next. You will be prompted for the type of connect, as shown in Figure 9-19.

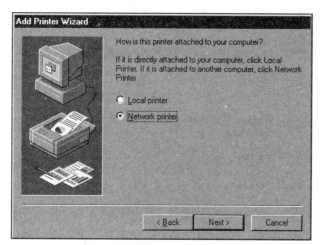

**FIGURE 9-19** Choosing the connection type

**5.** Choose Local Printer and click Next. You will see the printers list, as shown in Figure 9-20.

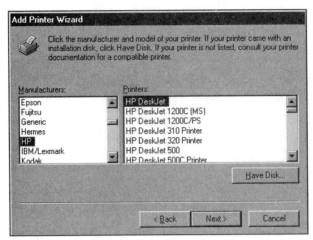

**FIGURE 9-20    The printer list**

**6.** Choose the manufacturer and model of the printer you want to install and click OK. You will see a list of ports, as shown in Figure 9-21.

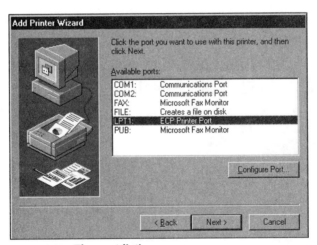

**FIGURE 9-21    The port listing**

**7.** Choose the port to which the printer you want to install is connected. Click Next.

**8.** You will be prompted for the printer name, as shown in Figure 9-22. Enter the name you want the printer known as. Click Next.

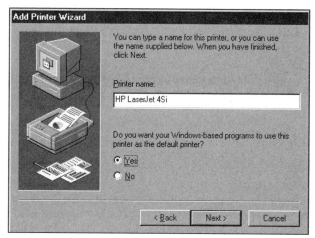

**FIGURE 9-22**    Choosing the printer name

**9.** You will be prompted to print a test page, as shown in Figure 9-23. If you want to, and it is always a good idea, choose Yes.

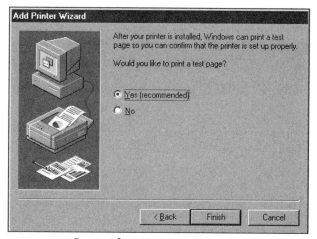

**FIGURE 9-23**    Prompt for a test page

**10.** Click Finish to install the printer.

Connecting to a network printer through Windows 95 is also easy. Again, you use the Add Printer Wizard to do the job.

### TO CONNECT TO A PRINTER SHARED FROM WINDOWS 95, WINDOWS NT, OR NETWARE, FOLLOW THESE STEPS:

**1.** Double-click the My Computer icon on your desktop.

**2.** Double-click the Printers folder.

**3.** Double-click the Add Printer icon. You will see the Add Printer Wizard welcome screen, as shown in Figure 9-24.

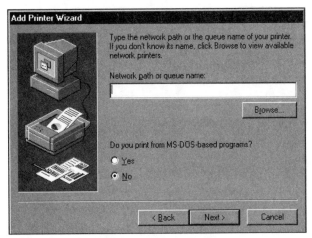

**FIGURE 9-24** Choosing a network printer

**4.** Click Next. Choose Network Printer.

**5.** Click Next. You will be prompted for the location of the shared printer. The easiest way to do this is to click the Browse button and search for the printer.

**6.** If you clicked the browse button, you will see a browse window similar to the one shown in Figure 9-25.

**7.** Navigate through the network and find the computer that is sharing the printer you need.

**8.** Once you have found the computer, click it to show all of the shared printers it has. You will see them listed, as shown in Figure 9-26.

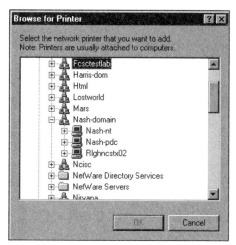

**FIGURE 9-25    Browsing the Network**

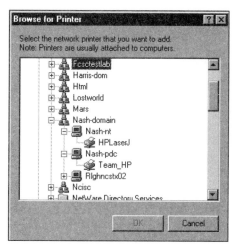

**FIGURE 9-26    Listing of shared printers**

**9.** Once you have chosen the printer you want, click OK. The queue name for the printer will be put into the blank.

**10.** If you will need to print from MS-DOS applications under Windows 95, answer Yes to that question, and click Next. If you don't need to print from MS-DOS applications, skip to Step 13.

**11.** You will see the window shown in Figure 9-27. Click the Capture Printer Port button.

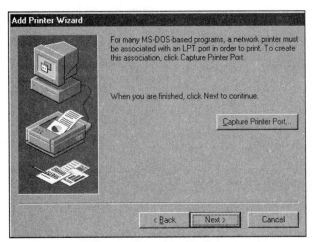

FIGURE 9-27    Setting up MS–DOS printing

**12.** You will be prompted to specify the port you want to capture. Any information sent to this port by an application will actually be sent to the network printer. This window is shown in Figure 9-28. Choose the port you want to capture and click OK.

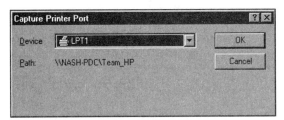

FIGURE 9-28    Capturing a printer port

**13.** Click Next. You will see a list of printers that you can install, as shown in Figure 9-29.

**14.** Choose the printer driver that corresponds to the type of printer you are connecting to.

**15.** Click Next. You will see the window shown in Figure 9-30. Enter a name for the printer, then select whether you want the printer to be set as default or not.

**16.** Click Next. You will be prompted to print a test page, as shown in Figure 9-31. It is usually a good idea to print a test page. Choose whether to or not, and click Finish.

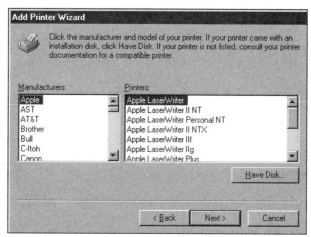

**FIGURE 9-29** Listing of printer drivers

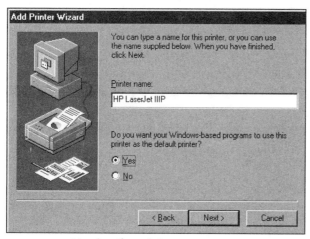

**FIGURE 9-30** Naming the printer

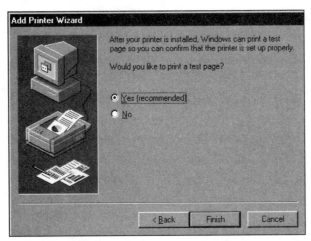

**FIGURE 9-31**    Printing a test page

# Increasing Printing Speed

When network printing is too slow and causes a problem for the users (not to mention a headache for the administrator), it may become necessary to optimize or upgrade network printing. There are several options to increase printing speed on the network.

## *Optimizing network printing*

Network printing can be optimized to provide for faster printing with existing equipment. One way to handle this is to use *printing priorities*. Printers can be set with a variety of priorities to accommodate groups of users that require quicker printing of their documents. Users can print to the device configured with the higher priority, and their documents will print first. This technique can also be used to print long documents that aren't needed immediately. These documents can be printed to a device with a lower priority and printed when other documents aren't waiting.

Spooling of documents can be used to optimize network printing, as well. If the printer is configured to print spooled documents first, the documents that are spooled quickest will be printed quickest. Configuring printing so that printing occurs as soon as the first page is spooled also decreases printing time.

### *Upgrading network printing*

If optimization has been done and printer speeds are still too slow, upgrades to the network printing system may be required. There are several options for upgrading the printing system.

Memory upgrades can increase printer performance. The increased memory will help the printer process and print the jobs quicker. When planning a memory upgrade, consult your printer documentation. It is important to know how much memory the printer can hold and how much is currently installed.

Installation of a network interface is another way to improve printer performance. Moving the printer to the network media provides a faster path to the printer and removes bottlenecks that can occur at the print server. Network interfaces also enable the printer to communicate using a variety of protocols, which can enable a wide range of users to connect to the printer.

Printer pooling can also be used to upgrade network printing. Also, a new printer can be installed and configured to use the same print queue as an existing printer. Two printers provide load balancing and improve printing speeds.

Sometimes the best way to upgrade the printing process is to buy a better printer. Newer printers are much quicker than their older counterparts and can handle options that some older printers cannot. New printers are more likely to be color capable and have a built-in network interface. If a specialized page size is required, a new printer may be required to print on that page size. The old printer can still be utilized on the network, but a new printer can handle more of the printing load.

## Printer Maintenance

Different printer types require different types of maintenance. Cleaning is a big part of maintenance. Printing with ink and toner can be a messy job, and it's important that the printer be carefully cleaned and maintained to ensure a long life. The following guidelines should be used along with the printer documentation to determine the best cleaning method and components needed for your particular printer. When encountering problems with printers, it is important to make sure that the components have been properly cleaned and maintained. You can also use your printer documentation for troubleshooting tips. To better understand cleaning and maintenance, you must first understand how the printer functions. This can help with troubleshooting printing problems, as well.

## Laser printers

*Laser printers* use heat and pressure to fuse the toner powder onto your paper to print. The following is an overview of the laser printer print process:

1. An electric current is carried across a wire, known as the *primary corona wire*, and places a static electric charge on a photosensitive drum called the *electrophotostatic* (EP-S) drum.

2. A laser beam casts light on the image areas of the EP-S drum. This changes the electric charge on the area.

3. The drum is rotated, and the charged image areas pick up the toner particles.

4. A sheet of paper passes over the transfer corona wire which puts an electric charge on the paper. The paper and the drum now have an opposite charge.

5. This difference in charge causes the paper to pick up the toner particles from the drum.

6. High temperatures and pressure in the fusing unit then fuse the toner to the paper.

These components can be replaced individually in some of the older printers and are combined in the newer printers. The combined equipment provides for smaller printers, but at the cost of maintenance. Now instead of just replacing a drum, you may end up replacing a lot more, which will cost more. A diagram of a laser printer is shown in Figure 9-32.

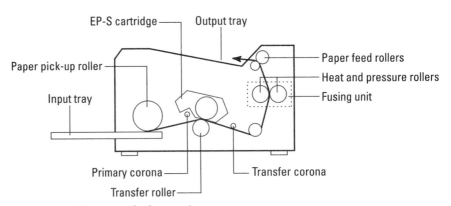

**FIGURE 9-32**   Diagram of a laser printer

The high temperatures and pressure used in laser printers affect what media can be passed through it. Anything that melts can do damage to the laser printer. As a guideline, you should follow these rules:

o Do not use anything with adhesives. Use only labels specially made for laser printers.

o Do not use thermal paper.

o Do not use carbon paper.

o Do not use envelopes with transparent windows.

o Double check with your printer manufacturer to make sure that transparencies are OK.

### Routine maintenance

After using your laser printer for a while, the stray toner particles and pieces of paper that gather in the printer may cause problems. You should carefully clean the laser printer from time to time. Your printer documentation should have information on how to clean your specific printer.

 caution **Be careful when working with laser printers since they can be very hot. Unplug the printer in advance before cleaning it to give it time to cool.**

At a minimum, you should occasionally open the printer and blow out any toner dust that you see.

### Troubleshooting laser printers

Normally, laser printers will print thousands of pages without a single problem. But with that heavy a workload, anything can break. Table 9-12 lists many common problems you may find with your laser printer, as well as common solutions.

| **TABLE 9-12**  COMMON LASER PRINTER PROBLEMS AND SOLUTIONS | |
| --- | --- |
| *PROBLEM* | *SOLUTIONS* |
| Inconsistent vertical shading | Remove the toner cartridge from the printer and shake it from side to side to evenly distribute the toner. |
| Light printing | Clean the corona wire. You may also need to adjust the darkness level on your printer. Replace toner cartridge. |

*(continued)*

**TABLE 9-12**   COMMON LASER PRINTER PROBLEMS AND SOLUTIONS *(continued)*

| PROBLEM | SOLUTIONS |
|---------|-----------|
| Blurred vertical lines | Replace the fuser roller cleaning pad. |
| Faded blotches and spots | Clean the transfer corona wire. |
| Fading across the page | Clean the transfer corona wire. |
| Streaks and marks on the leading edge of the paper | Clean the paper separator and any other paper guides in the printer. |
| Page is totally black. | Replace the primary corona wire. Check the printer drum. |

## Dot matrix printers

Most people are familiar with *dot matrix printers*. They print on paper by using small pins to push ink onto paper from a ribbon. Most print heads have either nine or twenty-four pins on them. The more pins they use, the more detail they can print. Since dot matrix printers are fairly simple, maintenance and troubleshooting are easy.

### Routine maintenance

Normally, all it takes to clean a dot matrix printer is a damp cloth. Just wipe off the outside and inside of the printer to remove any dust or pieces of paper. If there is a lot of dust, you can use a small vacuum cleaner to get it out.

Occasionally you will need to clean the print head of the printer. Usually you can tell it is time to do this because your print outs are starting to look smudged. First, you must remove the print head. You need to check your printer documentation on how to do this. Next, clean the small pins with a cotton swab and alcohol.

### Common dot matrix problems and solutions

Table 9-13 lists the most common problems associated with dot matrix printers, as well as their solutions.

| **TABLE 9-13** COMMON DOT MATRIX PROBLEMS AND SOLUTIONS | |
|---|---|
| *PROBLEM* | *SOLUTION* |
| Light print out | Check your ribbon to see if it is jammed or needs to be replaced. If that is not the problem, adjust the print head so it is closer to the paper. |
| Smudged characters | Check to see if your ribbon is twisted. You may need to move the print head away from the paper. Also check to see if the print head needs to be cleaned. |
| Paper jam | Adjust the tractor pull mechanism to make sure that the paper is held tight, but not too tight. |
| Incomplete characters | Clean or replace the print head. |
| Overlapping lines of text | Check for paper jams. |

## Ink-jet printers

A new and popular type of printer, especially for home and small offices, is the *ink-jet printer*. Ink-jet printers use liquid ink to print. They can do black and white or color. They use small nozzles to "squirt" the ink onto the paper. Most new ink-jet printers are self-cleaning as long as they are used properly. Problems can arise if power is removed from the printer without it shutting down. This can leave the print head and liquid ink exposed to air, which lets it dry.

### Routine maintenance

As stated above, if you do not let the printer shut itself down properly, ink can dry out and damage the print head. If this happens you may be able to use a built-in head cleaning routine. Check your printer documentation to see if you have this option. Other than that, the only real maintenance is to occasionally open up the printer and wipe it out with a damp cloth.

If you plan to store the printer for a long time, consider putting an empty ink cartridge in it instead of a full one.

# NETWORK FAXING

The next logical step for many people is from printing to faxing. Luckily, if your network uses Windows 95, you can add shared faxing very easily. Included with Windows 95 is a faxing feature that lets you fax documents with your fax modem as easily as you print them. But — and this may be new to you — the faxing software in Windows 95 also allows you to share this capability with other network users. To start the process, you first need to install the fax software for Windows 95.

### TO INSTALL THE FAX SOFTWARE FOR WINDOWS 95, FOLLOW THESE STEPS:

**1.** Click Start, then Settings, and then Control Panel.

**2.** Double-click the Add/Remove Programs icon. You will see a window similar to the one in Figure 9-33.

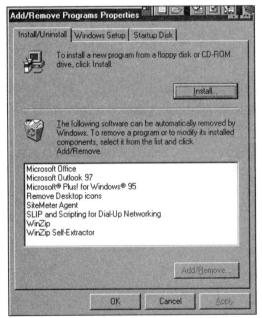

**FIGURE 9-33** The Add/Remove Programs dialog box

**3.** Click the Windows Setup tab. You will see a window similar to the one in Figure 9-34.

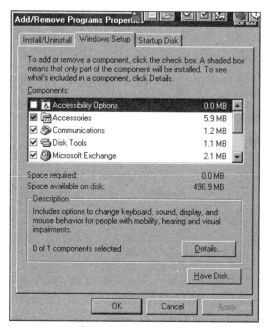

**FIGURE 9-34** The Windows Setup tab

**4.** Scroll down and find the Microsoft Fax box. Check the box and click OK.

Once the fax software has been installed, you may notice a small difference on your computer. If you open the Printers folder again, you will see that a new printer has been added. Figure 9-35 shows the Printers folder.

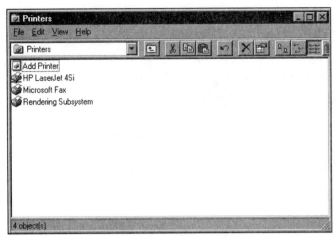

**FIGURE 9-35**  The Printers folder

Now that the fax software is installed, it must be configured. While you can do this manually through the Mail and Fax icon in Control Panel, it is easier to do with a wizard. To invoke the wizard, all we need to do is try and use the new fax software.

---

**TO CONFIGURE THE FAX SOFTWARE WITH THE WIZARD, FOLLOW THESE STEPS:**

**1.** Open WordPad by clicking Start, then Run, typing in WordPad, and pressing Enter. From WordPad, click File, then Print. Choose Microsoft Fax as your printer. This is shown in Figure 9-36.

**2.** The Inbox Setup Wizard will start, as shown in Figure 9-37.

**3.** Choose the Modem connected to my computer option and click Next.

**4.** If you do not have a modem driver installed in Windows 95, you will see the Modem Wizard start, as shown in Figure 9-38. If you already have a modem installed, choose the modem you want to use, click Next, and go to Step 6.

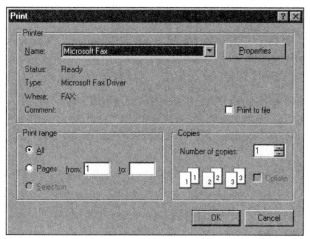

**FIGURE 9-36**    Printing in WordPad

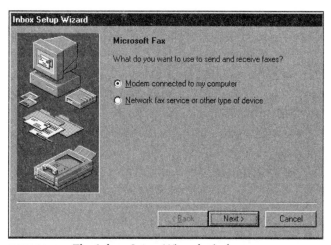

**FIGURE 9-37**    The Inbox Setup Wizard window

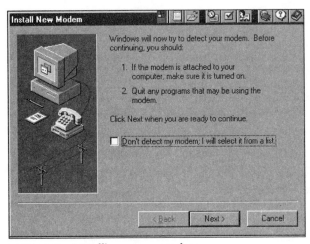

**FIGURE 9-38    Installing a new modem**

**5.** Click Next to have Windows 95 detect your modem.

**6.** Once you have completed the modem wizard process, you will see the window shown in Figure 9-39.

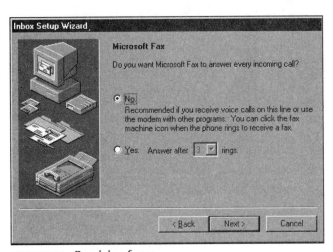

**FIGURE 9-39    Receiving faxes**

**7.** Choose whether you want the modem to receive every call or only receive calls manually.

**8.** Click Next, and you will see the window shown in Figure 9-40.

**9.** Enter your information into the blanks and click Next.

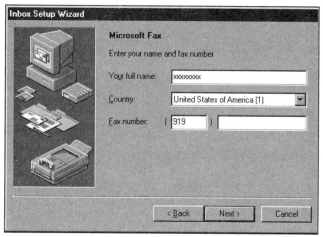

**FIGURE 9-40** Entering personal information

Your fax software is now installed. To use it you will need to open the Inbox application on your desktop. You can use this software anytime by just "printing" to the fax device.

Next, you need to make sure that you can share printers.

**TO SHARE A PRINTER, FOLLOW THESE STEPS:**

**1.** Double-click the Network icon from Control Panel.

**2.** Click the File and Print Sharing button. You will see a window, as shown in Figure 9-41.

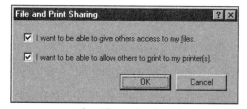

**FIGURE 9-41** The File and Print Sharing button

**3.** Check the I want to be able to allow others to print to my printer(s) checkbox. Click OK.

**4.** Click OK again. (You may be required to reboot.)

Now, the next step is to share that fax with other network users.

**TO SHARE A FAX, FOLLOW THESE STEPS:**

**1.** Open Control Panel.

**2.** Double-click on the Mail and Fax icon.

**3.** You should see a list of services, as shown in Figure 9-42.

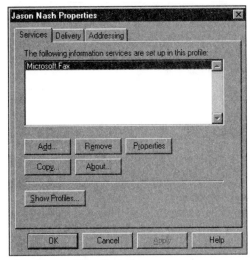

**FIGURE 9-42**    **List of services**

**4.** Highlight the Fax service and click Properties.

**5.** Click the modem tab. This tab is shown in Figure 9-43.

**6.** Check the Let other people on the network use my modem to send faxes box.

**7.** If you want to set a password or other security, click the Properties button.

**8.** Click OK.

**9.** Click OK again.

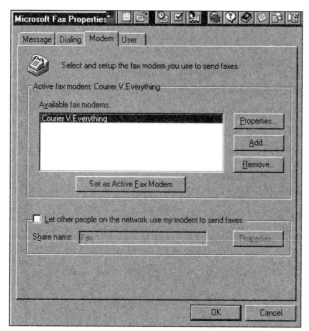

**FIGURE 9-43** The Modem tab

Your fax is now shared on the network. Only one more series of steps to go. These show you how to connect to the shared fax server from across the network.

**TO CONNECT TO A SHARED FAX SERVER, FOLLOW THESE STEPS:**

**1.** Go to the workstation computer, and install the fax software as shown above. Then start the configuration wizard by printing to the fax device.

**2.** When the Inbox Setup Wizard starts, choose Network fax service or other type of device.

**3.** Click Next. You will see the Add a Fax window, as shown in Figure 9-44.

**4.** Choose network fax server and click Next.

**5.** You will see the window shown in Figure 9-45. In the path field, enter `\\COMPUTERNAME\fax`. `COMPUTERNAME` is the name of the computer you installed the fax modem on.

**6.** Enter the name and click Next. You should then see a window similar to the one shown in Figure 9-46.

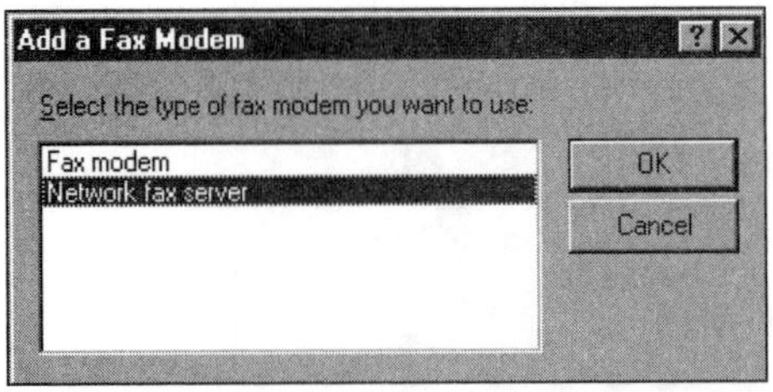

**Add a Fax Modem**    [? |X]

Select the type of fax modem you want to use:

```
Fax modem
Network fax server
```
[OK]
[Cancel]

**FIGURE 9-44**   The Add a Fax Modem window

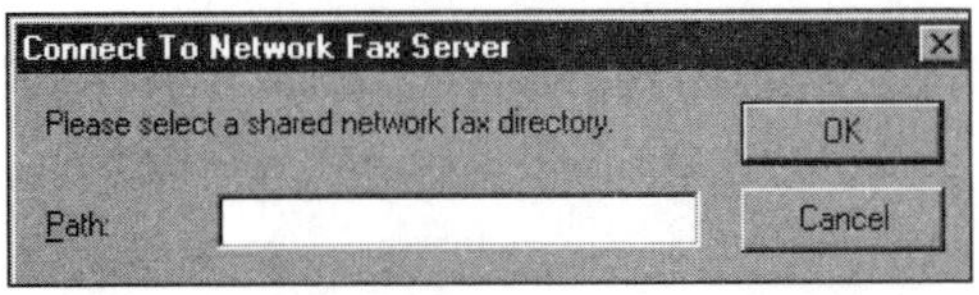

**Connect To Network Fax Server**    [X]

Please select a shared network fax directory.    [OK]

Path:    [                    ]    [Cancel]

**FIGURE 9-45**   Connecting to a network fax server

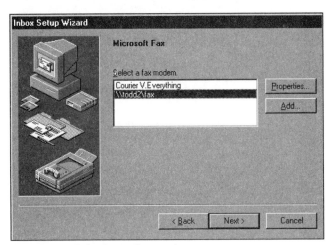

**Inbox Setup Wizard**

**Microsoft Fax**

Select a fax modem.

```
Courier V.Everything
\\todd2\fax
```
[Properties...]
[Add...]

[< Back]   [Next >]   [Cancel]

**FIGURE 9-46**   Selecting a fax modem

**7.** Choose the path that you just entered in the previous window. Click Next.

**8.** Enter your information into the next screen and click Next.

Like a local fax modem device, you print to the fax device in your printing listing. The fax software handles routing your fax through the network and out your fax modem.

# SHARING CD-ROMS

"Floppy disk? What's that?" With the advance of CD-ROMs into the computing community, it won't be long until you hear those words. CD-ROMs enable you to easily store large amounts of data in a small physical medium that lasts for many years. With these great features, it is no wonder people want access to CD-ROMs on a network.

Sharing one CD-ROM on a network is pretty simple. You can do that easily with Windows 95 or Windows NT. But what if you want a lot of CD-ROMs available? Before going over the different ways to share CD-ROM media, first look at the hardware you will need.

## CD-ROM Drive Characteristics

When you go to buy a CD-ROM drive or tower, you will see many different pieces of information concerning them. Exactly what does all this mean to you? It all depends on what you will be using the CD-ROM to store. Most of the specifications you hear concern the speed of the drive. When shopping for CD-ROM hardware pay close attention to the following characteristics:

- Speed
- Access time
- Buffer space
- Interface
- External or internal configuration
- Installation
- CD handling

The following sections discuss each of these different characteristics. Recommending what you should shop for is difficult, however, since this technology is changing so quickly that any recommendations would quickly be obsolete.

### *Speed*

How fast will it go? Originally, CD-ROM drives could transfer data from the CD-ROM to the computer at speeds up to 150 kilobytes (K) per second. These drives are known as *single-speed CD-ROM drives*. Long gone are the days of everyone having a single-speed drive. New drives are many times faster than these older ones.

The speed at which the CD-ROM can get data from the CD to the computer is known as the *data transfer speed*. These are measured in multiples of 150K per second. For example, you may see a drive that says it is a *quad-speed drive*, or *4X*. This means that it can transfer four times as much data in the same amount of time as an original single-speed CD-ROM.

### Access time

The next consideration in deciding on a CD-ROM is its *access time*. Access time is the amount of time it takes the laser of the drive to reach the location where the data is stored on the CD-ROM. This time also includes the delay when the drive has to decide where the data is stored. The lower the access time, the better the CD-ROM will handle requests from different users accessing different data on the CD-ROM.

Access times are getting faster all the time. Currently, a very good access time would be less than 150ms. This number may fluctuate depending upon where the data is stored on the CD-ROM. If the data is on the outside edge of the CD-ROM, the laser takes longer to get to it.

### Buffer space

Most CD-ROM drives now have a buffer. Most low-end CD-ROMs have either 64K or 128K of memory on the drive. High-speed drives have as much as 1024K, or 1 megabyte. If data is held in the buffer and the CPU needs it, sending it from that buffer is much quicker than getting it from the CD-ROM.

### Interface

CD-ROMs normally use one of three types of interfaces. These are:

o  EIDE

o  SCSI

o  Proprietary

These interfaces can play a large role in your hardware decision buy, especially if you want to share a large number of CD-ROMs from one computer.

### EIDE

*Enhanced Integrated Device Electronics* (EIDE) is a relatively new standard for CD-ROMs. Hard drives have been using IDE for many years. EIDE is the cheapest type of interface for CD-ROMs. Most home-level CD-ROM drives use this interface. The main problem with EIDE CD-ROMs is a limit of EIDE itself. You can only put two, or sometimes four, drives in one computer.

### SCSI

The *Small Computer Systems Interface* (SCSI) has been around for many years. Normally, SCSI is only used in large workstations or servers. It is much more expensive than EIDE, but it also has many more features and enhancements.

First, SCSI can handle from seven to fifteen devices on each controller. You can put multiple controllers in one controller. If you use SCSI CD-ROM drives, you can easily build a large CD-ROM server.

Next, SCSI is very fast. The new ultra-wide SCSI supports up to 40MB per second. New CD-ROM drives are starting to support this standard. While one CD-ROM may not be able to use all of this bandwidth, fifteen at one time can use the extra breathing room.

### Proprietary

While proprietary interfaces were very common in the early days of CD-ROM drives, they are much less so now. Proprietary interfaces usually limit you to one or two CD-ROM drives per computer, and they were known to hinder performance. Stay away from proprietary controllers and drives.

## External or internal placement

Most CD-ROM drives can either be put into the computer or reside in a case that sits outside the PC. The two types of drives have no functional differences.

Internal drives are very common in home computers and as single drives in servers to handle software installation. Adding an internal EIDE drive is easy.

Most often, external drives use the SCSI interface since it is easy to implement. EIDE was made for internal hard drives and is much harder to implement for external devices. External placement makes more sense if you plan to use many drives. It would be next to impossible to find a computer case that would accommodate the maximum number of drives you could use with a SCSI interface, while it is very easy to chain seven or fifteen external drives.

External drives give you the advantage of disk space, and you can add an external CD-ROM to almost any computer. But the external device does use space on your desk! External drives also cost about $100 more than internal drives.

### Installation

Most new CD-ROM drives are very easy to install. For EIDE drives, you usually need to set only one jumper. SCSI drives are slightly harder to install since they have other settings that need to be addressed. Windows NT and Windows 95 support EIDE and SCSI CD-ROMs right out of the box. NetWare supports SCSI CD-ROMs with the addition of a few *NetWare Loadable Modules* (NLMs).

### CD handling

CD-ROM drives handle discs in two different ways. Some drives use a plastic case, called a *caddy*, into which you insert the disc; you then insert the caddy into the drive. The advantage of this setup is that it lets you leave the discs in the caddy so that they are not damaged. This may be a good idea in a network environment where other people may handle your discs.

The alternative to caddies is a drive that extends out a tray into which you place the disc. This keeps you from having to worry about caddies, but at the cost of an exposed disc.

## Connecting CD-ROM Drives to a Network

CD-ROMs on a network function the same as those in a small PC. The difference is that the drives are set up to share data. In most cases you want to share many discs at one time. If you want to share just one disc, any PC with a CD-ROM drive can do this using peer-to-peer networking software. To handle large amounts of data, you would usually choose one of two devices. You would use either a *jukebox* or a *CD tower*.

### Jukebox

CD-ROM jukeboxes are similar to the jukeboxes that play 45s. A CD-ROM jukebox has one or more CD-ROM drives and a library of CDs to choose from. Depending on what data the user requests, the jukebox chooses the appropriate disc from its library and puts it in a drive.

Jukeboxes are cheaper than towers, but at the cost of performance. If you have many users trying to access different data at the same time, the jukebox will spend more time shuffling discs than it will sending out data. Nowadays, you most often see small jukeboxes used in personal computers as CD-ROM changers.

### Tower

The best solution to sharing large amounts of CD-ROM data on a network is a CD-ROM tower. A CD tower has many drives in one case. Each CD-ROM you want to share has its own drive. This allows the tower to read and send out data from any CD-ROM at any time.

Almost all CD-ROM towers use SCSI as their back-plane interface. This enables them to support many drives at one time. The use of SCSI also makes it easy to connect these towers to computers. Just plug the tower into your server's SCSI port, load the correct driver, and you're set.

New, smarter towers are becoming very common. These are stand alone boxes that do not need to be connected to a computer. They are connected directly to a network. To use these you normally need to load some special software on your network server that lets the CD-ROMs appear as if they are shared from the server, even though they are not.

# INTERNET ACCESS

A connection to the Internet is quickly becoming a requirement for networks today. The main problem is getting that connection. This section shows you how to add an Internet connection to a small network. Large networks can afford to get a direct connection using a high-speed, dedicated connection. Normally, small networks can only afford a single dial-up connection.

 web links

**The method described in this chapter requires a third-party utility to connect your LAN to the Internet. This product is called WinGate and is available at** `http://www.wingate.net`. **WinGate is shareware and therefore may require you to pay the author if you continue to use it. Luckily, the authors have been kind enough to let you have a single computer license for free. This means that you can let one other computer connect to the Internet through WinGate for free.**

## WinGate and How It Works

WinGate is a very simple and cost-effective way to add Internet access to a small network. With WinGate you need only a dial-up connection to the Internet. In addition, you will need only one IP address for the computer that is dialing up to the Internet, rather than one for every computer that will connect to the Internet.

WinGate functions as a *proxy server*. A proxy server does not allow client computers to directly connect to the Internet through them. Instead, the client computer connects to the proxy, and the proxy then connects to the resource on the Internet. This way only one computer is actually connecting to the Internet, and you do not need extra IP addresses or special Internet accounts. One thing that you cannot do with a proxy is to allow other computers on the Internet to connect to computers on your LAN. Computers on the Internet do not know how to reach your LAN workstations, since all connections are actually made by the computer running WinGate.

Most Internet applications work through a proxy. The following is a list of the most common ones:

o WWW

o FTP

o Telnet

o IRC

o RealAudio/RealVideo

o Mail

o News

As you can see, almost any application you may want is supported. The main applications that do not work are games. Games normally use the UDP protocol instead of the TCP protocol. A UDP connection normally comes from the server (the computer hosting a game) and not the client. As you saw earlier, a computer on the Internet cannot connect to a computer on your LAN.

## Finding an Internet Provider

Before you can connect to the Internet, you need to find an *Internet service provider*, or ISP. ISPs are companies that handle connecting people to the Internet. Some ISPs connect large companies to the Internet while others handle small offices and single users. Choosing a good ISP is the key to making a good Internet connection.

Here are a few key points to think of when shopping for Internet providers:

o **Bandwidth:** Most Internet providers today support 56Kbps or faster modems. If your network has five or fewer users, 56Kbps may meet your needs.

o **Reliability:** If your company will use the Internet connection heavily, you need to make sure your ISP is reliable. Some ISPs provide service level agreements (SLA) to show how reliable the connection will be.

o **Growth:** If you company grows, your Internet connection will most likely grow as well. Make sure the ISP you choose can handle your future growth. Eventually you may want to upgrade your connection or have your ISP host a web server for you. Make sure the ISP can handle what you plan.

To find your area ISPs, you can check local computer trade papers, or the newspaper. Some ISPs are nationwide and cover a large area. They are larger than local ISPs, so it may be hard to get customized or personal service, but they are normally very reliable and offer better technical support.

# Choosing Your Connection

Before you start looking for an Internet service provider, you should have a good idea of the type of connection you will need. The connection you need depends on how you plan to use the Internet. Since I am discussing small LANs here, I will focus on dial-up and ISDN connections. Large companies may have their own dedicated high-bandwidth connections, which are more complex than those discussed in this chapter.

## *Dialing in to the Internet*

If your network is very small, you may be able to use a *dial-up* Internet connection with a modem. This connection is usually adequate to serve up to four or five people. Depending on whether you plan to use this connection twenty-four hours a day or only on demand, it may be a very inexpensive solution.

Most ISPs now provide unlimited dial-up accounts for less than $30 per month. These are not intended to be connected twenty-four hours per day, seven days per week. If you need to connect to the Internet only occasionally, this may work for you. You can configure the WinGate computer to dial up when a computer attempts to connect to the Internet, and then hang up after a set amount of idle time passes.

If you need higher speed than a modem can provide, you may need a dial-up ISDN account. As you learned in Chapter 5, Integrated Services Digital Network allows for high-speed connections over normal telephone lines. With an ISDN connection, you can connect to the Internet at 128Kbps. Unlike the current 56Kbps modems, ISDN provides speeds of 128Kbps in both directions, not just when downloading to your LAN. Dial-up ISDN accounts are becoming more common for use with ISPs. Before, the only way you could connect to an ISP with ISDN was with an expensive dedicated connection. An ISDN connection can easily handle ten to twenty users.

## Dedicating the Connection

If your Internet connection needs to be available any time, you need a dedicated connection. Dedicated Internet connections are more expensive than dial-up connections, costing anywhere from $150 up. Dedicated connections can use either modems or ISDN, depending on what you need and want to spend.

The first step to adding an Internet connection to your LAN is to add the TCP/IP protocol to your workstations.

## Planning Your Network

Before you run off to install the TCP/IP protocol on your network, you should plan ahead. Before you start planning, you need to have some information about your ISP account. At a minimum, you will need the IP address of your DNS server. I said above that you only needed one IP address, which is for the computer that will run WinGate. This is half-true; you will only need one registered IP address. All of the computers on your network will need IPs, but you can choose which ones they will be since they will only be used between the computer running WinGate and the other computers on your LAN.

Luckily, there is a range of IP addresses set aside for this purpose. You can use the entire 192.168.0.0 range of IP addresses for your LAN. I suggest using 192.168.0.1 for your WinGate computer and the rest for your workstations. The subnet mask to use with this range is 255.255.255.0.

To help you with the administration of the IP addresses, you could make a HOSTS file to map these addresses to computer names. Below is a sample of our HOSTS file.

```
192.168.0.1      ANGIE
192.168.0.2      Jason
192.168.0.3      Win95-CD
192.168.0.4      NT_Server
```

This HOSTS file lets me type in the computer name instead of the IP address if I need to do any testing. Check with your operating system to see where you need to store the HOSTS file.

# Adding TCP/IP to Your Computers

Computers on the Internet use the TCP/IP protocol. Therefore, you will need to make sure any computer that needs Internet access supports this protocol. Most popular operating systems now come with TCP/IP. You just need to install the protocol and configure it. The following sections walk you through installing TCP/IP.

### Installing TCP/IP on Windows 95

Windows 95 is shipped with a TCP/IP stack included. You just need to install it. Before you do that, you may want to make sure someone hasn't installed it for you.

**TO CHECK IF TCP/IP IS INSTALLED, FOLLOW THESE STEPS:**

**1.** Open Control Panel by clicking Start⇒Settings⇒Control Panel.

**2.** Double-click the Network icon.

**3.** You will see a list of installed network options. If TCP/IP is installed, you do not need to install it again.

Figure 9-47 shows the list of protocols.

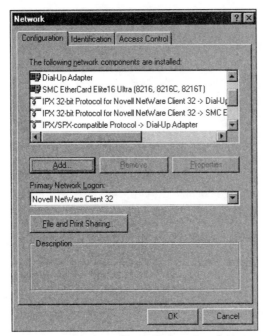

**FIGURE 9-47**   Listing of installed protocols

If TCP/IP is not installed, you will need to install it now.

**TO INSTALL TCP/IP, FOLLOW THESE STEPS:**

**1.** Click Start⇒Settings⇒Control Panel.

**2.** Click the Network icon.

**3.** When you see the Network window, click the Add button.

**4.** Select Protocol.

**5.** Choose Microsoft from the Manufacturers list.

**6.** Select TCP/IP from the Protocols list. Click OK.

The TCP/IP protocol is now installed.

**TO CONFIGURE TCP/IP FOR YOUR NETWORK, FOLLOW THESE STEPS:**

**1.** Highlight the TCP/IP protocol in the Installing Components list.

**2.** Click Properties.

**3.** Click the IP Address tab.

**4.** In the IP Address fields, enter the address you have chosen for this computer.

**5.** In the subnet mask field, enter 255.255.255.0.

**6.** Click the DNS Configuration tab.

**7.** Choose the Enable DNS option.

**8.** In the DNS Search Order field, add the IP address of the computer that will run the WinGate software.

**9.** Click OK.

**10.** You should see the Installed Components list again. Click OK. (You may be required to reboot the computer.)

Figure 9-48 shows the TCP/IP IP Address configuration window. Once you have installed and configured TCP/IP on the workstation and rebooted, you should test it. To do this, you may want to ping the computer that is running WinGate. To do this, open an MS-DOS prompt and type **ping 192.168.0.1** (assuming that the WinGate computer is using the 192.168.0.1 IP address).

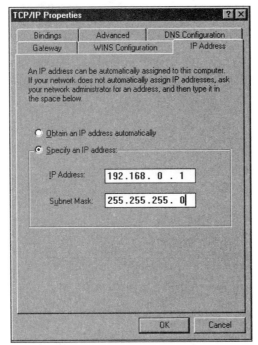

**FIGURE 9-48**   The TCP/IP Properties window

## *Installing TCP/IP on Windows NT*

Microsoft also included a TCP/IP stack in its Windows NT operating system. The installation and configuration process is the same on Windows NT Workstation as it is on Windows NT Server.

### TO ADD TCP/IP, FOLLOW THESE STEPS:

**1.** Click Start⇒Settings⇒Control Panel.

**2.** Double-click the Network icon.

**3.** Click the Protocols tab.

**4.** Click Add.

**5.** Choose TCP/IP Protocol from the list and click OK.

**6.** When you return to the Network properties window, click OK.

**7.** The network bindings will be recalculated. You may need to configure TCP/IP now.

Figure 9-49 shows the Network Properties window. Now that TCP/IP has been installed, you will need to configure it.

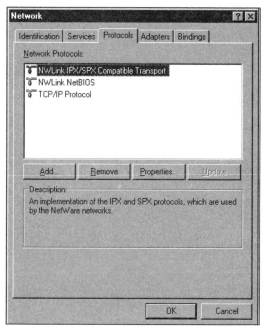

**FIGURE 9-49** The Network window

**TO CONFIGURE TCP/IP, FOLLOW THESE STEPS:**

**1.** Click the Protocols tab.

**2.** Highlight the TCP/IP protocol.

**3.** Click Properties.

**4.** Choose the Specify IP Address option.

**5.** In the IP Address field, enter the IP you have chosen for this computer.

**6.** In the Subnet Mask field, enter 255.255.255.0.

**7.** Click the DNS tab.

**8.** Click the Add button.

**9.** Enter the IP address of the computer that will run WinGate.

**10.** Click OK.

**11.** Click OK again at the Network properties window. (You may be required to reboot.)

Figure 9-50 shows the IP address configuration screen.

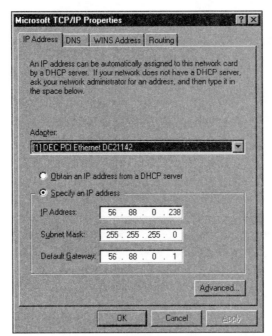

**FIGURE 9-50**    Configuring the IP address
in Windows NT

Now that you have installed TCP/IP on your workstations, you can install and configure WinGate.

## Installing and Configuring WinGate

The first step in installing WinGate is to get it. Go to `http://www.wingate.net` and download the correct version for your operating system. It will run on either Windows 95 or Windows NT.

 note    **At the time of this writing, the current version of WinGate was 2.0e. These instructions were written for that version.**

**TO INSTALL AND CONFIGURE WINGATE, FOLLOW THESE STEPS:**

**1.** Once you have downloaded the WinGate software and unzipped it, you can install it. From Windows Explorer, click the Wg2ent.exe file. You will see the "Welcome to WinGate 2.0" screen, as shown in Figure 9-51.

**FIGURE 9-51**    Welcome to WinGate 2.0

**2.** Click the Install WinGate 2.0e for Windows NT (or Windows 95), then click Next. You will see the Select Installation Directory window, as shown in Figure 9-52.

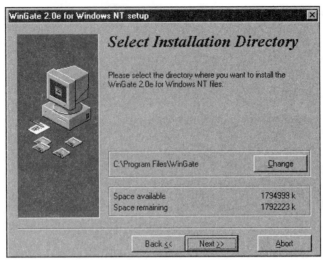

**FIGURE 9-52    The Select Installation Directory window**

**3.** If you want to use the default directory, click Next. You will see the license window, as shown in Figure 9-53.

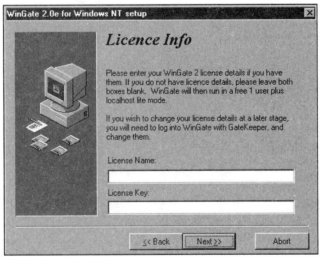

**FIGURE 9-53    The license window**

**4.** Leave the fields blank and click Next. You will see the Basic Services window, as shown in Figure 9-54.

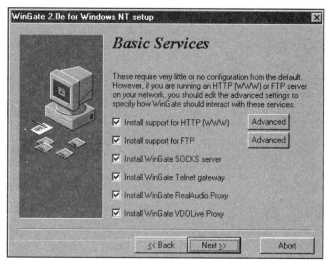

**FIGURE 9-54**   The Basic Services window

**5.** Normally, you would leave all of the choices checked. If you do not want to support a particular service, uncheck it now. Click Next. You will see the Mail Settings window, as shown in Figure 9-55.

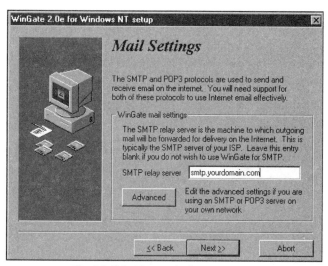

**FIGURE 9-55**   The Mail Settings window

**6.** In the SMTP Relay Server field, put the IP address or name of your ISPs SMTP host. Click Next. You will see the News and IRC Settings window, as shown in Figure 9-56.

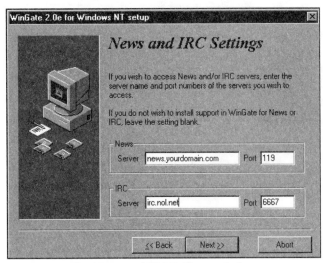

**FIGURE 9-56**   The News and IRC Settings window

**7.** In the News field, put the news server IP address or name that you received from your ISP. In the IRC server field, put the name of the IRC server you wish to use. If you are unsure of an IRC server, you may try `irc.nol.net`. Click Next. You will see the DNS Settings window, as shown in Figure 9-57.

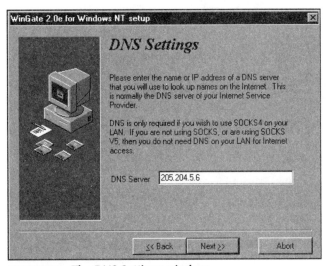

**FIGURE 9-57**   The DNS Settings window

**8.** In the DNS Server field, put the IP address of your ISP's DNS server. Click Next. You will see the Cache Settings window, as shown in Figure 9-58.

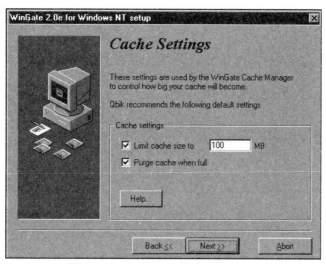

**FIGURE 9-58** The Cache Settings window

**9.** WinGate uses a cache manager to cache frequently accessed Web pages. You choose the settings you want on this screen. Choose the amount of space you want to set aside for caching and click Next. You will see the WinGate Client Utility window, as shown in Figure 9-59.

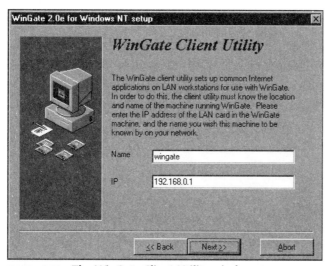

**FIGURE 9-59** The WinGate Client Utility window

**10.** Enter the name and IP address of the computer you are installing WinGate on. Click Next. You will see the Begin Installation window, as shown in Figure 9-60.

**FIGURE 9-60**    The Begin Installation window

**11.** If you do not need to go back and correct any settings you have made so far, click the Begin button to install WinGate. When the install has finished you will see the Installation Complete window, as shown in Figure 9-61.

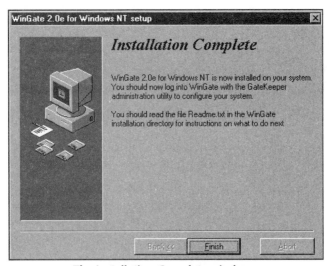

**FIGURE 9-61**    The Installation Complete window

**12.** Click Finish.

**13.** Now that WinGate has been installed, you need to configure it just a little bit more before you can use it. To do this, click Start⇒Programs⇒WinGate 2.0, and choose GateKeeper. GateKeeper will prompt you for a login. Figure 9-62 shows the login screen.

**FIGURE 9-62** The GateKeeper login

**14.** Press Enter to log in with a blank password. You will be asked if you want to continue without a password. Click OK. After you log in you will be required to create a password. The Change Password screen is shown in Figure 9-63.

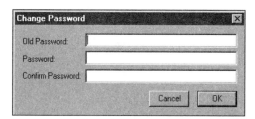

**FIGURE 9-63** Changing the password

**15.** Leave the Old Password field blank, and enter a password that you choose in the other two fields. Then click OK. Once you have changed the password, you will be shown the main GateKeeper screen, as shown in Figure 9-64.

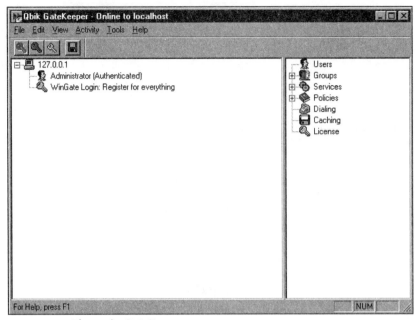

**FIGURE 9-64**   The main GateKeeper screen

By default, you can manage the WinGate computer with GateKeeper only from the computer it is running on. If you want to manage WinGate from another computer you must enable this feature.

**TO MANAGE WINGATE FROM ANOTHER COMPUTER, FOLLOW THESE STEPS:**

**1.** Click the + (plus) symbol next to the Services option in the right window pane. It will expand, as shown in Figure 9-65.

**2.** Double-click the Remote Control Service option. You will see the window shown in Figure 9-66.

**3.** Uncheck the Bind to specific interface option.

**4.** Click OK.

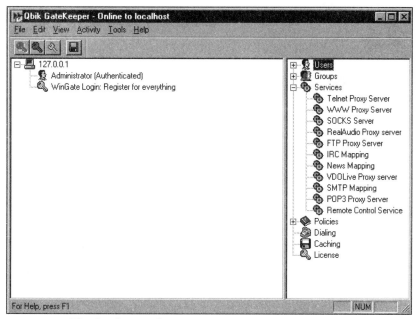

**FIGURE 9-65**    The Services options

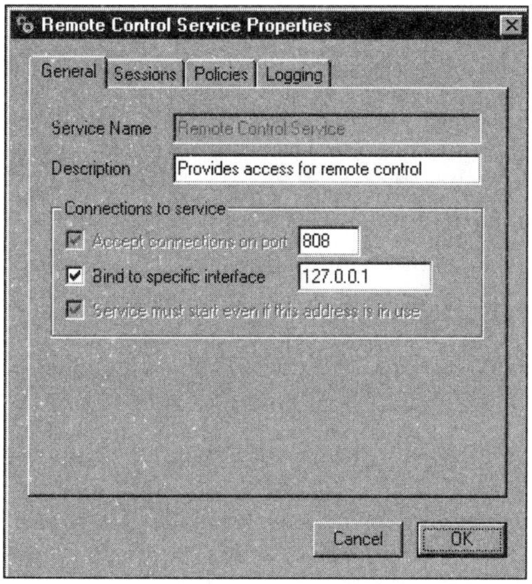

**FIGURE 9-66**    The Remote Control Service
Properties window

Now that WinGate has been installed and configured, you will need to set up your client applications to use the new proxy.

# Configuring Client Applications

Almost any application that your network clients might use can be configured to use the proxy. If your application does not have support for a proxy server built in, you can possibly use what is known as a *SOCKS* client. Next, I will cover the following applications and how to configure them for the proxy:

- FTP
- Telnet
- WWW
- News
- Mail
- RealAudio
- IRC
- SOCKS client

## *FTP*

Like most clients you will find, the way to configure your FTP client may depend on who made it. As an example, we will cover configuring a popular client, WS_FTP, as well as doing command line FTPs through the proxy.

### WS_FTP

WS_FTP is a well-known shareware FTP client that uses a graphical interface. It also supports many different types of network proxies.

 web links   **You can obtain the free trial version of WS_FTP from** `http:\\www.ipswitch.com`.

**TO CONFIGURE WS_FTP TO USE WINGATE, FOLLOW THESE STEPS:**

**1.** When you load WS_FTP you will see a window similar to the one in Figure 9-67.

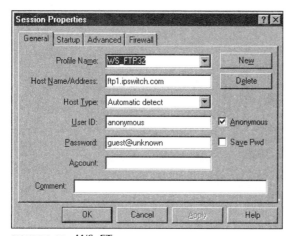

**FIGURE 9-67** WS_FT

**2.** Create a new connection by clicking New.

**3.** Enter all relevant information for the connection that you are creating.

**4.** Click the Firewall tab. You will see the window shown in Figure 9-68.

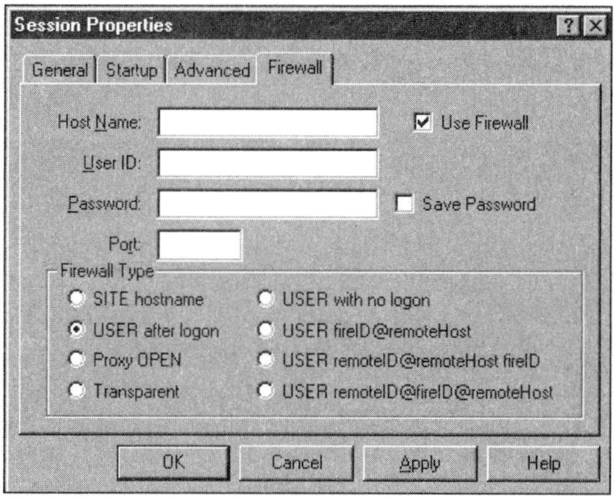

**FIGURE 9-68** Firewall options

**5.** Click the Use Firewall box.

**6.** In the Host Name field, enter the IP address of the computer running WinGate.

**7.** Make sure that the USER with no logon option is selected.

**8.** After you have made your selections, the Firewall tab should be similar to the one shown in Figure 9-69.

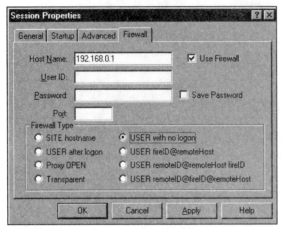

**FIGURE 9-69**  Configured firewall options

**9.** Click OK.

**10.** Click the Save button to save your connection.

Once you have configured the connection, test it by connecting to the server.

**Command-line FTP**

Even though graphical utilities are usually preferred to command-line programs, you may one day need to use the command-line FTP. Changing the command-line FTP to use the proxy is simple.

**TO CHANGE THE COMMAND-LINE FTP TO USE THE PROXY, FOLLOW THESE STEPS:**

**1.** Open FTP by clicking Start, Run, and then typing **FTP IP_OF_WINGATE_COMPUTER**.

**2.** You will see the FTP program, as shown in Figure 9-70.

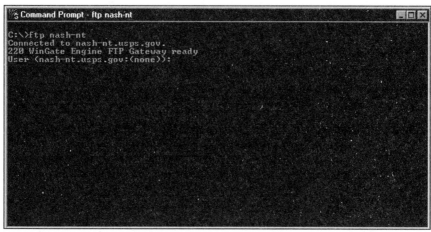

**FIGURE 9-70**   FTP

**3.** Normally, at the User prompt you would enter your user name, or *anonymous*, to the server. But since you have only connected to the WinGate computer and not the actual server, you cannot do this. At the User prompt, enter `anonymous@ftp.microsoft.com`. User name is the name you want to log in as, and server name is the FTP site to which you want to connect. Press Enter.

**4.** Figure 9-71 shows a connection to `ftp.microsoft.com` as anonymous.

**FIGURE 9-71**   FTP connection

**5.** At the password prompt, enter your password (or e-mail address for anonymous) just like you normally would. Press Enter. You are now connected to the FTP site just as you would normally be.

## Telnet

Using Telnet with WinGate is also easy.

### TO CONNECT WITH TELNET, FOLLOW THESE STEPS:

**1.** Open your Telnet application. For this example we will use the normal Windows Telnet, as shown in Figure 9-72.

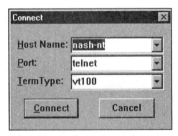

**FIGURE 9-72** Telnet

**2.** Click Connect, then Remote System. You will see the window shown in Figure 9-73.

**FIGURE 9-73** Remote system

**3.** In the Host Name field, enter the IP address of the computer running WinGate.

**4.** Click OK.

**5.** You will see the WinGate prompt, as shown in Figure 9-74.

**FIGURE 9-74**    WinGate prompt

**6.** At the WinGate prompt, type in the host name to which you want to connect.

**7.** Press Enter. You will be connected just as you would without WinGate.

## WWW

Almost all Web browsers support the use of a proxy server. For this example we will use the version of Microsoft Internet Explorer included on the CD-ROM in this book.

concept link

**For information on installing Microsoft Internet Explorer, refer to Appendix F.**

You have two choices of proxy types when using Internet Explorer. You can either use an HTTP proxy or a SOCKS proxy. The steps below show you how to configure these settings.

**TO CONFIGURE INTERNET EXPLORER FOR A HTTP PROXY OR A SOCKS PROXY:**

**1.** Open up Internet Explorer.

**2.** Click View⇒Internet Options.

**3.** You will see the window shown in Figure 9-75.

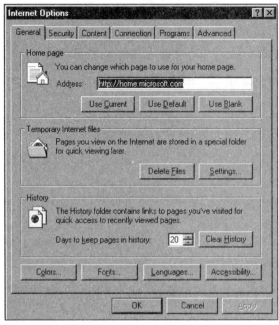

**FIGURE 9-75**    The Internet Options window

**4.** Click the Connection tab. It is shown in Figure 9-76.

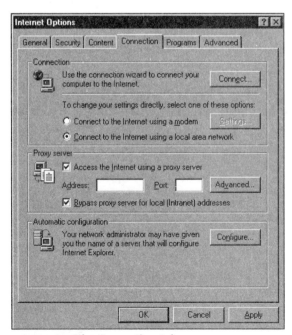

**FIGURE 9-76**    The Connection tab

**5.** Check the box that says Access the Internet using a proxy server.

**6.** Click the Advanced button.

**7.** As shown in Figure 9-77, this window lets you choose many different types of proxy servers.

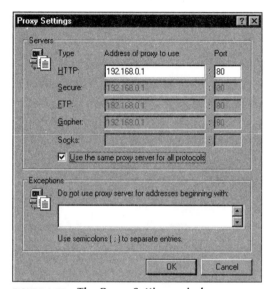

**FIGURE 9-77** The Proxy Settings window

**8.** You can either use the HTTP proxy or the SOCKS proxy. To enable the SOCKS proxy, put the IP address of the WinGate computer in the Socks field.

**9.** To use the HTTP proxy, enter the IP address of the computer running WinGate in the HTTP field. Then check the Use the same proxy server for all protocols box.

**10.** Click OK.

## News

Configuring news clients could not be easier. All you need to do is enter the IP address of the WinGate server in the news client where you would normally put the IP address of the news server. When the client connects to WinGate, it will automatically be rerouted to the news server you defined. The following steps are for use with Outlook Express, which is included with Internet Explorer version 4.0.

**TO CONFIGURE NEWS CLIENTS WITH OUTLOOK EXPRESS, FOLLOW THESE STEPS:**

**1.** Open Outlook Express.

**2.** Click Tools⇒Accounts.

**3.** You will see a list of accounts in a window similar to the one in Figure 9-78.

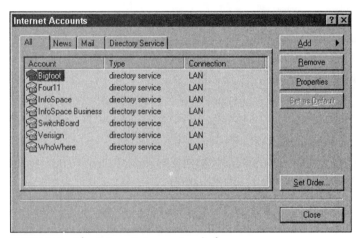

**FIGURE 9-78** The Internet Accounts window

**4.** Click the News tab.

**5.** To set up an account to use WinGate, click Add, and then News.

**6.** You will see the first window in the wizard to create a news account. This is shown in Figure 9-79.

**7.** In the Display name field, enter the name to use to post a message.

**8.** Click Next.

**9.** Next, you will be prompted for your e-mail address so that others can reply to your posts. Enter this and click Next.

**10.** The next screen, shown in Figure 9-80, prompts you for your news server address.

**11.** Enter the IP address of the computer running WinGate.

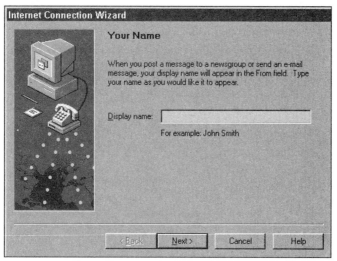

**FIGURE 9-79**    The Internet Connection Wizard window

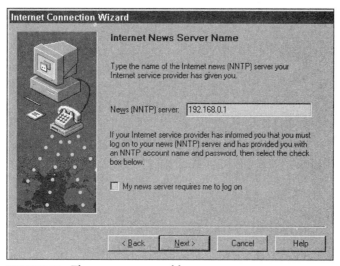

**FIGURE 9-80**    The news server address

**12.** Click Next.

**13.** Enter the account name you want to be shown for this account. Enter anything you want.

**14.** Click Next.

**15.** The next window will prompt you for a connection type. This is shown in Figure 9-81.

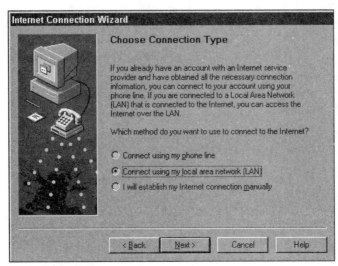

**FIGURE 9-81**    The connection type

**16.** Choose Connect using my local area network, and click Next. You will be shown the final window in the wizard.

**17.** Click Finish.

**18.** Click Close.

---

## Mail

Mail configuration depends on the software you use. The following steps are for use with Outlook Express. Installation on other clients just requires changing the SMTP server and/or POP mail server address(es). In either case, just change the addresses to the IP of the WinGate computer.

---

**TO CONFIGURE MAIL CLIENTS USING OUTLOOK EXPRESS, FOLLOW THESE STEPS:**

**1.** Open Outlook Express.

2. Click Tools⇒Accounts. You will be presented with a list of all current accounts. This should look similar to the one in Figure 9-82.

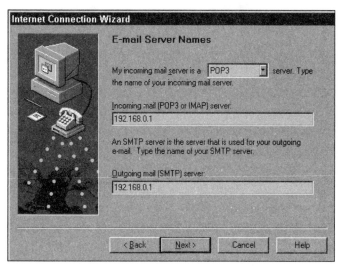

**FIGURE 9-82   E-mail server names**

3. Click the Mail tab.

4. Click Add, and then Mail.

5. In the Display name field, enter the name you want others to see when you send an e-mail.

6. Click Next.

7. Next, you will be prompted for your e-mail address so that others can reply to your messages. Enter this and click Next.

8. You will be prompted for the e-mail server names. This window is shown in Figure 9-82. For both the POP Mail and SMTP servers, enter the IP address of the computer running WinGate.

9. Click Next.

10. You will then see the window in Figure 9-83 requesting mail account information. Enter the information given to you by your Internet provider. Click Next.

11. Next, enter the friendly name for this account. This is used inside of Outlook Express only.

12. Click Next.

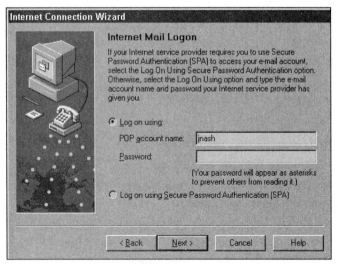

**FIGURE 9-83** Internet mail logon

**13.** Next, choose Connect using my local area network and click Next.

**14.** Click Finish.

**15.** Click Close.

## RealAudio

*RealAudio* is a new application that is quickly becoming popular on the Internet. It is used to send stereo sound over the Internet.

 web links   The RealAudio client can be obtained from `http://www.realaudio.com`.

RealAudio can support two different proxy servers. If the RealAudio site you are connecting to supports sending out the data over HTTP, you can use a normal HTTP, or Web, proxy. The problem is that many sites do not yet support this method and therefore you must use a RealAudio only proxy. Luckily, WinGate has supported RealAudio for a long time now.

**TO CONFIGURE REALAUDIO TO THE WINGATE PROXY, FOLLOW THESE STEPS:**

**1.** Load the RealAudio client.

**2.** Click View, then Preferences.

**3.** You will be shown the window in Figure 9-84.

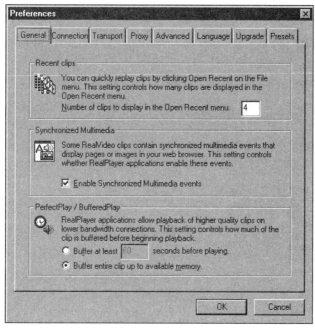

**FIGURE 9-84**   The Preferences window

**4.** Click the Proxy tab. Figure 9-85 shows the Proxy tab.

**5.** In the RealAudio proxy field, enter the IP address of the computer running WinGate.

**6.** Click OK.

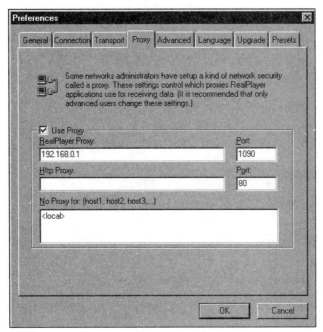

**FIGURE 9-85**   The Proxy tab

## IRC

*Internet Relay Chat*, or IRC, is a chat protocol commonly used on the Internet. There are many IRC clients out now, but only a few that support a proxy server. For the steps below, we will use the PiRCH client.

 web links   **You can obtain the latest version of PiRCH at** http://www.bcpl.lib.md.us/~frappa/pirch.html. **This is the client I use at home, and it has functioned very well with WinGate.**

You can support IRC users on your network two different ways with WinGate. One way uses what is known as a port mapping connection, while the other uses the SOCKS proxy built into WinGate. The following steps help you set up a port mapping connection. After that, we will cover using the SOCKS proxy.

**TO MAKE A PORT MAPPING CONNECTION, FOLLOW THESE STEPS:**

**1.** Open GateKeeper and log in.

**2.** Right-click on the Services selection in the right window pane, then select New, Service, TCP Mapping Service.

**3.** You will see the window shown in Figure 9-86.

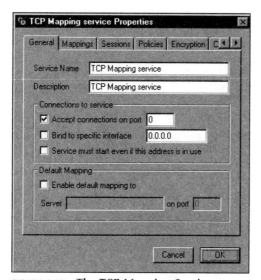

**FIGURE 9-86**    The TCP Mapping Service Properties window

**4.** If you want, you can change the Service Name and Description to something more descriptive. For the description you may want to put the name of the IRC server this mapping will connect to.

**5.** In the Accept connections on port field, enter **6667**. If you already have an IRC server mapping on Port 6667, choose another unused port.

**6.** Check the Enable default mapping box.

**7.** In the Server and Port field, put the IP address and port number of the IRC server you want to use.

**8.** Click OK.

Port mappings can be used for many different applications that do not directly support a proxy. A port mapping takes a connection made to WinGate and extends that connection to a predefined server. In the above example, you told WinGate to forward any connection it receives on Port 6667 to the server IP and port number you specified.

To use this mapping, enter the IP address of the WinGate server into your IRC client as the server to connect to.

If you use the PiRCH client, you can use the SOCKS proxy built into WinGate. The advantage of this setup is that the PiRCH client can connect to any IRC server, not just those that you set up as port mappings in WinGate.

---

**TO CONFIGURE PIRCH, FOLLOW THESE STEPS:**

**1.** Load PiRCH.

**2.** Select IRC, and then Proxy Setup.

**3.** You will see the window shown in Figure 9-87.

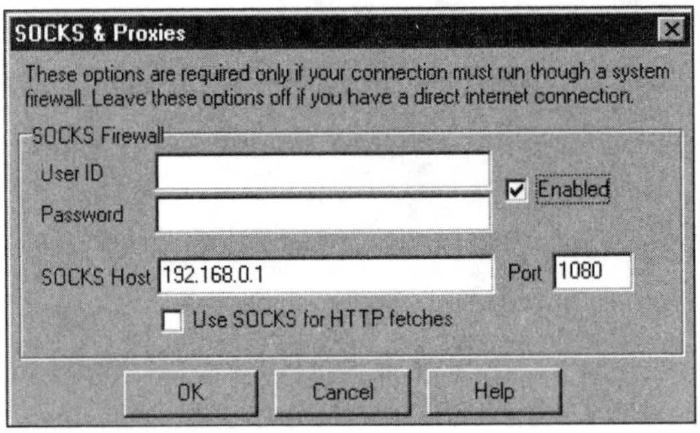

FIGURE 9-87    Proxy configuration

**4.** Check the Enabled box.

**5.** In the SOCKS Host field, enter the IP address of the computer running WinGate.

**6.** In the port field, enter **1080**.

**7.** Click OK.

---

## SOCKS client

As I said earlier, WinGate has an integrated SOCKS version 5 proxy server. This proxy allows any client that supports SOCKS to function through WinGate flawlessly. All connections to the WinGate server are handled behind the scenes away from the user. The application functions as though it was not working through a proxy and no extra configuration settings are needed.

When a SOCKS client application makes a request to a host outside of the local network, the request is redirected to the SOCKS server. The SOCKS server authenticates the user, if you have this enabled, and then authorizes the request and establishes a proxy connection, and then transparently passes data between the inside host and the outside host.

While SOCKS is a great thing, the problem is that most Internet applications do not support it. But do not despair! Luckily there is a free SOCKS client that replaces Winsock.dll in Windows 95 and Windows NT. This allows most non-SOCKS applications to support the SOCKS proxy. This all happens at the WINSOCK layer, without affecting the application.

caution

**A few warnings before we start: First, be careful when replacing** WINSOCK.DLL. **The instructions are simple, but if you mess up, particularly under Windows NT, you may crash your system. Second, not all applications function with the SOCKS client. Almost all that I have tested do, but it is not 100 percent.**

**Do not let the warnings scare you. The SOCKS client can be a great thing for WinGate users and is well worth trying out.**

First, you will need to get the SOCKS client, and then configure it.

web links

**The SOCKS client is available at http://**www.hummingbird.com/products/socks/index.html. **This client is free.**

To install the SOCKS client, simply run the Install.bat file that is included. Once you have installed the client, you need to configure it. SOCKS is configured by using a Socks.cnf file. This is a normal text file that can be edited with any text editor. Below is a sample file.

**LISTING 9-1:** **Sample SOCKS Configuration File**

```
# Sample Configuration File
#
# Each line is one of:
#
# DENY    [*=userlist] dst_addr dst_mask [op dst_port]
# DIRECT [*=userlist] dst_addr dst_mask [op dst_port]
# SOCKD [@=serverlist] [*=userlist] dst_addr dst_mask [op
 dst_port]
# SOCKD4 [@=serverlist] [*=userlist] dst_addr dst_mask [op
 dst_port]
# SOCKD5 [@=serverlist] [*=userlist] dst_addr dst_mask [op
 dst_port]
# GSS encryption_type
#
# Where:
# userlist      is a comma separated list of users (optional)
# dst_addr      is a dotted quad IP address
# dst_mask      is a dotted quad IP address
# op            is one of EQ NEQ LT GT LE GE
# dst_port      is the number or name of a destination port
# serverlist    is a comma separated list containing the name
 or IP addresses
# of SOCKS servers (use IP addresses for speed).       Each
 address
# or name may be optionally followed by an explicit port
 number
# as follows:
#    IPaddress:portNumber or name:portNumber
# Note that the default port number is 1080.
# encryption_type is:
#    0 - Authentication Only
#    1 - Integrity
#    2 - Confidentiality (Full Encryption)
# Note GSS is only available with the GSSAPI.DLL and KRB5.DLL
 from MIT
```

```
#
# On connect each line is processed in order and the first
  line that matches
# is used. If no line matches the address is assumed to be
  Direct.
#
# Matching is done by taking the destination address and
  ANDing it with the
# dst_mask. The result is then compared to the dst_addr. If
  they match, then
# if the userlist exists the current username is compared
  against this list.
# Also if the [op dst_port] exists, the destination port is
  compared to
# dst_port and if the "op" is true, the line is used.
#
# DENY           means to disallow the connect attemp.
# DIRECT means to attempt the connection as normal.
# SOCKD  means to go the specified SOCKD 4 server.
# SOCKD4 means to go the specified SOCKD 4 server.
# SOCKD5 means to go the specified SOCKD 5 server.
#
# If @=serverlist is not present the SOCKD server specified
  by the registry
# value:
#   LOCAL_MACHINE\SOFTWARE\HummingBird\SOCKS_SERVER
# is used. Note that the IP address or name of the server
  may be optionally
# followed by an explicit port number as follows:
#IPaddress:portNumber or name:portNumber
# Note that the default port number is 1080.
#
# Installation is best performed by the accompanying
  INSTALL.BAT file.
```

*(continued)*

```
#
# To manually install under Windows 95 WITHOUT the Winsock2
  API added:
#
# Restart Windows 95 in DOS mode. Rename the file
  \Windows\System\WSOCK32.DLL
# to WSOCK320.DLL and copy the new WSOCK32.DLL into
  \Windows\System. Place
# this file (socks.cnf) in the \Windows\System directory.
  Restart Windows 95.
#
# To manually install under Windows NT 3.51:
#
# Rename the file \Winnt\System32\WSOCK32.DLL to WSOCK320.DLL
  and copy the
# new WSOCK32.DLL into the \Winnt\System32 directory. Place
  this file
# (socks.cnf) in the \Winnt\System32 directory. It is now
  installed.
#
#SOCKD4 @=192.75.152.8 130.113.68.1 255.255.255.255
#
```

To get SOCKS to work with your WinGate server, you need to modify this file. By default, all lines in the file are commented out, and so they are not used. You just need to add one or two lines at the bottom to make it work. The first line to add should look like the following:

```
SOCKD5 @=IP_OF_WINGATE_COMPUTER:1080 0.0.0.0 255.255.255.255
```

This will cause all traffic to be routed through the SOCKS proxy.

If you need to send some data directly to a computer, and not through the proxy, you may need to use the DIRECT keyword. You can find more information on this in the SOCKS client documentation.

# TELECOMMUTING

Another popular service being added to almost every network is the ability for users to dial in and work from a remote location. Microsoft provides the ability to let users dial-in under Windows 95 (with the Plus! pack) and Windows NT.

 **Both Windows 95 and Windows NT Workstation only allow you to set up one modem for dial-in users. Windows NT Server allows you to handle up to 255 dial-in users.**

The first step in configuring this is to set up the dial-up server. You will do this separately for Windows 95 and Windows NT.

## Dial-up Server

The dial-up server is the connection between your network and the remote user. Usually the sever uses some sort of security mechanism to make sure only authorized users are allowed to use the service. If you want high security, the answer is clearly Windows NT. Windows 95's dial-in security is a simple password.

### *Setting up a dial-up server under Windows 95*

 **This section assumes you have installed the Plus! pack.**

The first step in setting up a dial-up server for Windows 95 is to install the *dial-up adapter*. The dial-up adapter is a piece of software that acts like a network card. The difference is, instead of being attached to a network, it enables you to dial into other networks.

**TO INSTALL THE DIAL-UP ADAPTER, FOLLOW THESE STEPS:**

**1.** Go to Control Panel.

**2.** Double-click the Network icon.

**3.** You will see the Network Components list.

**4.** Click the Add button.

**5.** Highlight Adapter and click Add.

**6.** In the Manufacturer list, choose Microsoft.

**7.** In the model list, choose Dial-Up Adapter.

**8.** Click OK.

**9.** Click OK again. (You will be required to reboot.)

Now for the easy part. Enabling and configuring the dial-up server is simple.

**TO ENABLE THE DIAL-UP SERVER, FOLLOW THESE STEPS:**

**1.** Open My Computer, and then the Dial-Up Networking folder.

**2.** Click Connections, then Dial-Up Server. You will see the window shown in Figure 9-88.

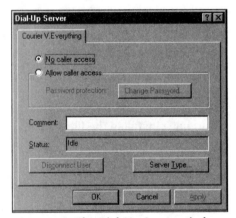

**FIGURE 9-88**    **The Dial-Up Server window**

**3.** To enable callers to dial in, change the first option to Allow caller access. It is a good idea to enable password security for your server. Pick a password that is easy to remember but hard to guess.

**The downside to this security on Windows 95 is that there is only one password. If you change the password, you must tell everyone that is dialing in.**

4. To set or change the password, click the Change Password button. Enter the old password (blank if this is the first time) and then enter the new password.

5. Finally, click OK.

6. Click the Server Type button to set the parameters for the server. In most cases you would leave the two boxes at the bottom checked. In the Type of Dial-Up Server drop-down box, you may want to change this to PPP. This will allow any PPP host to dial in.

7. Click OK, and then click OK again to finish setting the parameters. Windows 95 is now set up as a dial-up server.

## Setting up a dial-up server under Windows NT

Windows NT uses a piece of software called *Remote Access Service* to dial in and out to make network connections. Unlike Windows 95, Windows NT doesn't require you to install a fake network adapter, only a network service.

### TO INSTALL REMOTE ACCESS SERVICE, FOLLOW THESE STEPS:

1. Go to Control Panel.

2. Double-click the Network icon. You will see the Network window, as shown in Figure 9-89.

3. Click the Services tab.

4. Click the Add button.

5. Choose Remote Access Service and click OK.

6. You will see the window shown in Figure 9-90. Choose the modem you plan to use and then click OK.

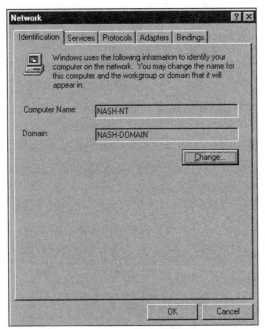

**FIGURE 9-89**    The Windows NT Network
properties window

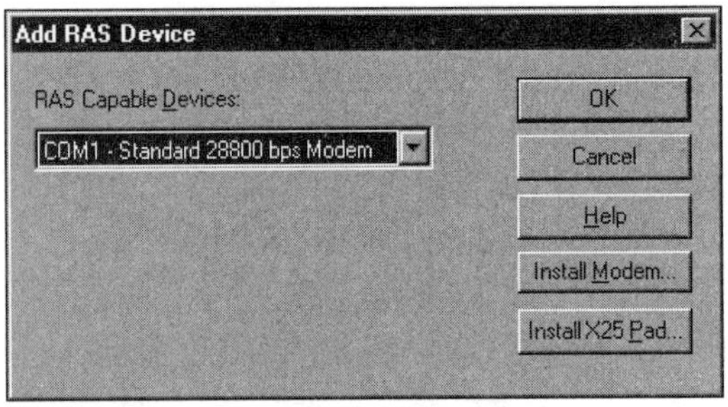

**FIGURE 9-90**    Adding an RAS device

**7.** At the window shown in Figure 9-91, click the Network button.

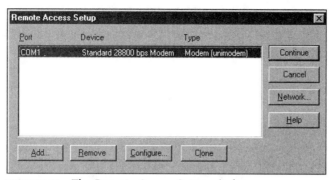

**FIGURE 9-91** The Remote Access Setup window

**8.** Choose the protocols you want to enable over the dial-up and click OK.

**9.** Click the configure button to display the window shown in Figure 9-92.

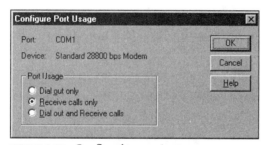

**FIGURE 9-92** Configuring port usage

**10.** Choose whether you will only dial in, dial out, or do both from this Windows NT computer.

**11.** Click OK.

**12.** Click Continue.

**13.** Click Close. (You will need to reboot your computer.)

The dial-in security for Windows NT is handled by the normal Windows NT security. A user must have an account on the computer or domain that they are dialing in to. You will also need to go into User Manager and enable the dial-in right for the users.

The nice thing about both of these dial-up servers is that they allow any PPP client to access them. All you need to do on either Windows 95 or Windows NT is to set up a new connection under Dial-Up Networking in My Computer.

# KEY POINT SUMMARY

This optional chapter was not required reading for the Network Essentials exam. In it, I covered how to add many useful services to your network, including:

- Network printing
- Network faxing
- Sharing CD-ROMs
- Internet access
- Telecommuting

Some of these services are built into your network operating system, while others require third-party products.

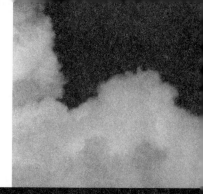

# Resources

# Microsoft Networking Essentials Exam Objectives

# EXAM 70-58: NETWORKING ESSENTIALS

This appendix consists of three parts:

- The first part contains a complete list of this exam's objectives.

- The second part lists the basic facts for this exam, including the number of questions, passing score, and time allowed to take the exam.

- The third part is a quick-reference chart listing the chapters and labs in this book that you should read and study to prepare for the exam.

 web links

**This exam information is current as of the date this book went to press but is subject to change by Microsoft at any time. You can ensure that you have the most current version of this exam's objectives by accessing the Microsoft Training and Certification Web site at** www.microsoft.com/train_cert.

# CREDIT TOWARD CERTIFICATION

A passing score on this exam counts as core credit toward certification.

# SKILLS BEING MEASURED

This certification exam measures your ability to implement, administer, and troubleshoot information systems that incorporate Microsoft Windows 95 and any products in the Microsoft BackOffice family. The exam covers only the networking knowledge and skills common to both Windows 95 and BackOffice products.

# EXAM OBJECTIVES

Before taking the exam, you should be proficient in the following job skills.

## Standards and Terminology

- Define common networking terms for local area network (LANs) and wide area networks (WANs).
- Compare a file and print server with an application server.
- Compare user-level security with access permission assigned to a shared directory on a server.

- Compare a client/server network with a peer-to-peer network.
- Compare the implications of using connection-oriented communications with connectionless communications.
- Distinguish whether SLIP or PPP is used as the communications protocol for various situations. Define the communication devices that communicate at each level of the OSI model.
- Describe the characteristics and purpose of the media used in IEEE 802.3 and IEEE 802.5 standards.
- Explain the purpose of NDIS and Novell ODI network standards.

# Planning

- Select the appropriate media for various situations. Media choices include:
  - Twisted-pair cable
  - Coaxial cable
  - Fiber-optic cable
  - Wireless

- Situational elements include:
  - Cost
  - Distance limitations
  - Number of nodes
- Select the appropriate topology for various Token Ring and Ethernet networks.
- Select the appropriate network and transport protocol or protocols for various Token Ring and Ethernet networks. Protocol choices include:
  - DLC
  - AppleTalk
  - IPX
  - TCP/IP
  - NFS
  - SMB

- Select the appropriate connectivity devices for various Token Ring and Ethernet networks. Connectivity devices include:
  - Repeaters
  - Bridges
  - Routers
  - Brouters
  - Gateways
- List the characteristics, requirements, and appropriate situations for WAN connection services. WAN connection services include:
  - X.25
  - ISDN
  - Frame relay
  - ATM

## Implementation

- Choose an administrative plan to meet specified needs, including performance management, account management, and security.
- Choose a disaster recovery plan for various situations.
- Given the manufacturer's documentation for the network adapter, install, configure, and resolve hardware conflicts for multiple network adapters in a Token Ring or Ethernet network.
- Implement a NetBIOS naming scheme for all computers on a given network.
- Select the appropriate hardware and software tools to monitor trends in the network.

## Troubleshooting

- Identify common errors associated with components required for communications.
- Diagnose and resolve common connectivity problems with cards, cables, and related hardware.

- Resolve broadcast storms.
- Identify and resolve network performance problems.

# EXAM FACTS

Number of questions on this exam:    58

Passing score:                  793

Time allowed to take exam:       75 minutes

# EXAM OBJECTIVES CROSS-REFERENCE CHART FOR STUDY PURPOSES

Table A-1 lists the stated objectives for Exam 70-58, Networking Essentials, in a cross-reference chart for study purposes. Use this table to help you determine the specific chapters in this book you should study, as well as the labs you should perform, to prepare for the exam.

| TABLE A-1   NETWORKING ESSENTIALS EXAM OBJECTIVES CROSS-REFERENCE CHART | | |
|---|---|---|
| **EXAM OBJECTIVE** | **CHAPTER(S)** | **LAB(S) (IF APPLICABLE)** |
| **Standards and Terminology** | | |
| Define common networking terms for LANs and WANs. | Chapter 1, pages 5-8 13-20 | |
| Compare a file-and-print server with an application server. | Chapter 1, pages 5-8, 13-20 | |
| Compare user-level security with access permission assigned to a shared directory on a server. | Chapter 7 | |

continued

| TABLE A-1 *(continued)* | | |
|---|---|---|
| EXAM OBJECTIVE | CHAPTER(S) | LAB(S) (IF APPLICABLE) |

**Standards and Terminology**

| | | |
|---|---|---|
| Compare a client/server network with a peer-to-peer network. | Chapter 1, pages 5-8 13-20 | |
| Compare the implications of using connection-oriented communications with connectionless communications. | Chapter 2, page 47 | |
| Distinguish whether SLIP or PPP is used as the communications protocol for various situations. | Chapter 5, pages 169-188 | Lab 5.15 |
| Define the communication devices that communicate at each level of the OSI model. | Chapter 6, pages 217-233 | |
| Describe the characteristics and purpose of the media used in IEEE 802.3 and IEEE 802.5 standards. | Chapter 2, pages 61-62; Chapter 4, pages 132-150 | |
| Explain the purpose of NDIS and Novell ODI network standards. | Chapter 3, pages 73-87 | Lab 3.4 |

**Planning**

| | | |
|---|---|---|
| Select the appropriate media for various situations. Media choices include the following items: | Chapter 3 | Lab 3.3, Lab 4.6 |
|    Twisted-pair cable | | |
|    Coaxial cable | | |
|    Fiber-optic cable | | |
|    Wireless | | |
| Select the appropriate media for various situations. Situational elements include the following items: | | |
|    Cost | | |
|    Distance limitations | | |
|    Number of nodes | | |
| Select the appropriate topology for various Token Ring and Ethernet networks. | Chapter 4, pages 121-126 | |

| EXAM OBJECTIVE | CHAPTER(S) | LAB(S) (IF APPLICABLE) |
|---|---|---|
| Select the appropriate network and transport protocol or protocols for various Token Ring and Ethernet networks. Protocol choices include the following items: | Chapter 5, pages 167–209 | Lab 5.11 |
| DLC | Chapter 5 | Lab 5.14 |
| AppleTalk | Chapter 5 | |
| IPX | Chapter 5 | Lab 5.13 |
| TCP/IP | Chapter 5 | Lab 5.12, Lab 5.15, Lab 8.31 |
| NFS | Chapter 5 | Lab 5.12 |
| SMB | Chapter 5 | |
| Select the appropriate connectivity devices for various Token Ring and Ethernet networks. Connectivity devices include the following items: | Chapter 6 | Lab 6.19 Lab 6.20 |
| Repeaters | Chapter 6, pages 217–219 | |
| Bridges | Chapter 6, pages 219–225 | |
| Routers | Chapter 6, pages 230–232 | |
| Brouters | Chapter 6, pages 231–232 | |
| Gateways | Chapter 6, pages 232–233 | |
| List the characteristics, requirements, and appropriate situations for WAN connection services. WAN connection services include the following items: | Chapter 5, pages 200–207 | |
| X.25 | Chapter 5, page 205 | |
| ISDN | Chapter 5, page 206 | |
| Frame relay | Chapter 5, pages 205–206 | |
| ATM | Chapter 5, pages 206–207 | |

*continued*

| TABLE A-1 *(continued)* | | |
|---|---|---|
| *EXAM OBJECTIVE* | *CHAPTER(S)* | *LAB(S) (IF APPLICABLE)* |
| **Implementation** | | |
| Choose an administrative plan to meet specified needs, including performance management, account management, and security. | Chapter 7 | Lab 7.21, Lab 7.22, Lab 7.23, Lab 7.24, Lab 7.26 |
| Choose a disaster recovery plan for various situations. | Chapter 7 | Lab 7.25 |
| Given the manufacturer's documentation for the network adapter, install, configure, and resolve hardware conflicts for multiple network adapters in a Token Ring or Ethernet network. | Chapter 3, pages 73–78 | Lab 3.2 |
| Implement a NetBIOS naming scheme for all computers on a given network. | Chapter 7, pages 245–248 267–268 | |
| Select the appropriate hardware and software tools to monitor trends in the network. | Chapter 8, pages 289–297 | Lab 8.29 |
| **Troubleshooting** | | |
| Identify common errors associated with components required for communications. | Chapter 8 | Lab 4.10, Lab 8.28, Lab 830 Lab 8.31 |
| Diagnose and resolve common connectivity problems with cards, cables, and related hardware. | Chapter 8 | Lab 6.17, Lab 8.29, Lab 4.7, Lab 4.8 |
| Resolve broadcast storms. | Chapter 8 | Lab 6.18 |
| Identify and resolve network performance problems. | Chapter 8 | Lab 3.1 |

# Mini-Lab Manual

Table B-1 lists all the lab exercises in this book, including the number and title of each lab, and the chapter in which the lab is presented.

**TABLE B-1** CRITICAL THINKING LABS IN THIS BOOK

| LAB NUMBER | LAB TITLE | CHAPTER |
|---|---|---|
| 3.1 | Overcoming network hardware bottlenecks | 3 |
| 3.2 | Managing network card resources | 3 |
| 3.3 | Deciding the correct cable type | 3 |
| 3.4 | Troubleshooting drivers | 3 |
| 3.5 | Crossing a highway | 3 |
| 4.6 | Planning network cabling | 4 |
| 4.7 | Troubleshooting connectivity | 4 |
| 4.8 | Troubleshooting Token Ring connectivity | 4 |
| 4.9 | Troubleshooting a Token Ring LAN | 4 |
| 4.10 | Finding a conflict | 4 |
| 5.11 | Expanding the network | 5 |
| 5.12 | Adding protocols | 5 |
| 5.13 | Adding NetWare protocols | 5 |
| 5.14 | New network printer | 5 |
| 5.15 | Remote connectivity | 5 |

*continued*

# CRITICAL THINKING LABS

Following are all the Critical Thinking labs that appear in this book. We've pulled them together for you in this Mini-Lab Manual to help you prepare for the certification exams.

*Critical Thinking labs* challenge you to apply your understanding of the material to solve a hypothetical problem. The questions are scenario based, requiring you to decide "why" or "how" or to devise a solution to a problem. You will need to be at a computer to work through some of these labs; for others, the goal is to make you analyse a problem and wxplain why a particular solution will or will not work and/or describe how best to solve the problem.

Some of the labs in this book have the potential to interfere with other computers on the same network. For this reason, it is recommended that you perform these labs on computers that are located on a network that is isolated form other network computers.

These labs are all extremely important to your exam preparation. Don't even think about skipping them! Refer to the "Hardware and Software You'll Need" section if you're sure you have the necessary equipment to do the Critical Thinking labs.

Answers to the labs can be found in Appendix C.

## Hardware and Software You'll Need

You will need access to various hardware and software to be able to do some of the Critical Thinking labs in this book. It is extremely important that you do these labs to acquire the skills tested by the Microsoft Certified Professional exams. There are only a few labs requiring the hardware and software listed below.

### Minimum hardware requirements

- Intel-based computer with 486/33 processor, 16MB RAM, and 500MB–1GB available hard disk space

- CD-ROM drive

- Mouse

- VGA monitor and graphics card

### Optional additional hardware

- Additional computer (with the same minimum specifications as the first one)

- Network adapter and cabling (if you have the addional computer listed above)

### Software requirements

- Microsoft Windows NT Workstation 4.0

- Microsoft Windows 95

## Lab 3.1 *Overcoming network hardware bottlenecks*

You have just added another fifty clients to your network, and now your server seems to be acting sluggish. You run some tests on the server and find that the CPU can handle the load fine, as can the hard drive subsystem. You pinpoint the bottleneck to be in the network card. Further investigation shows a normal 16-bit ISA network adapter. Which adapter type could you replace it with to improve performance? What factors might influence your decision?

## Lab 3.2 *Managing network card resources*

You are trying to install a network card into a computer with the following hardware: COM1, COM2, LPT1, PS/2 mouse, and an IDE hard drive controller. The NIC supports IRQs 3, 4, 5, 7, and 10. Which IRQ(s) could you use?

## Lab 3.3 *Deciding the correct cable type*

You are consulted to install new network cabling in a building. The building turns out to be a manufacturing center with a lot of heavy equipment in it. EMI could definitely become a problem. Another requirement is to be able to connect the new wiring to the existing administration office 400 yards away. Which cable should you use? Why would you not use the other cable types?

## Lab 3.4 *Troubleshooting drivers*

You are attempting to load a second protocol onto a computer on your network. For some reason the protocol will not bind to the network card. What might you surmise about the driver that the card is using?

## Lab 3.5 *Crossing a highway*

Your company has just purchased a new building. The new building is directly across a busy interstate from the existing building. An unbounded network media is required to cross the road. Security and speed are major factors to consider, and the company is not interested in acquiring special licenses. Which media would you choose and why?

## Lab 4.6 *Planning network cabling*

Your company is relocating to a new building that was prewired with Category 5 UTP cable by the previous occupants. There will initially be 150 clients and three servers on your network. The expected growth rate of the company will add twenty clients a year for the next four years. You have been asked to recommend a reliable, inexpensive network that can be easily expanded to accommodate future growth. What type of network do you recommend?

### Lab 4.7 *Troubleshooting connectivity*

Your network uses Windows 95 clients to connect to NetWare 3.12 servers. A new workstation is having problems connecting to the servers. However, the client can access other Windows 95 clients on the network. What is the most probable reason that this client cannot connect to the server?

### Lab 4.8 *Troubleshooting Token Ring connectivity*

You are installing a new 16/4 Token Ring adapter in a new workstation. The network is being slowly upgraded from a 4Mbps network to a 16Mbps network. The workstation is successfully configured and tested in your lab. When delivered to the customer's office, the system loses all network connectivity. The cable and port being used were working moments before on his old system. What is the most likely cause of the problem?

### Lab 4.9 *Troubleshooting a Token Ring LAN*

You notice your Token Ring LAN's speed has slowed considerably. Upon further examination, it is discovered that a system is beaconing the LAN. Where would you look to find the source of the problem?

### Lab 4.10 *Finding a conflict*

A workstation on your ARCNET network is having problems connecting to the network. The user is having trouble retrieving data from other systems on the network. This problem began when new workstations were added to the network. You also notice that the problem does not occur while the new part-time secretary is out of the office. What problem would cause these symptoms?

### Lab 5.11 *Expanding the network*

You administrate a network that currently has NetBEUI as its primary protocol. Your company is expanding and will soon be moving to a large office building with multiple floors. You have decided to split your network up with internetworking devices to handle the increased volume. Should you change your protocol choice? To what protocol(s) could you possibly change? Why?

### Lab 5.12 *Adding protocols*

Your company has just received a new UNIX server that uses TCP/IP as its only protocol. You need to let your clients easily access the data that is on the server. Which protocol might you use to handle this? Why?

### Lab 5.13 *Adding NetWare protocols*

The Microsoft clients currently on your network use NetBEUI, but a NetWare server was just added to work as a file server. What are your options for protocol choices?

### Lab 5.14 *New network printer*

A new Hewlett-Packard printer was just connected to your LAN. What changes must be made to the clients to allow them to print to it?

### Lab 5.15 *Remote connectivity*

Your company has recently decided to allow remote access for users that travel. There is a limited number of IP addresses available, so the company has decided to assign them dynamically to users when they are connected. Users will also need to use NetBEUI to access their printers remotely. Which protocol would users need to use to access the network?

### Lab 6.16 *Extending the network*

You are in charge of an Ethernet network that uses the bus topology. You are currently close to the maximum number of client workstations allowed on a single segment. Which network device would be the best choice to extend your network? What if your main protocol was TCP/IP?

### Lab 6.17 *Troubleshooting Ethernet*

A new hub was added to your 10Base-T network, but now the collision count per second is extremely high. Plugging in a new hub did not help. How could you begin to troubleshoot this problem?

## Lab 6.18  *Troubleshooting broadcast storms*

After installing a new router on your network, you have been hit with a number of broadcast storms. The protocol configuration in the router seems to be correct, but isolating that segment causes the storms to stop. What could be the problem?

## Lab 6.19  *Connecting distant LANs*

You have decided to connect the network used by the HR department in your company to the network used by Accounting. HR has a thinnet Ethernet network using coaxial cable, and Accounting is using a 10Base-T Ethernet network running over UTP cable. The signal is not currently strong enough to cover the distance effectively. What device would you use to connect the networks?

## Lab 6.20  *Ethernet bridging*

Would you want to use a source-route bridge on an Ethernet network? Why or why not?

## Lab 7.21  *Security planning*

You are the administrator of a small company network that is migrating to Microsoft networking products. Your users typically work on documents that they maintain, and control security. You also do not currently have a central file server. Would you choose to implement workgroups or domains? Why?

## Lab 7.22  *Windows NT administration*

Create a user account under Windows NT for yourself. Make sure that your password must be changed at next logon and that it never expires. Next, make yourself a member of the Administrators group so you can change the configuration of your computer.

## Lab 7.23  *Monitoring users*

You are suspicious that a user has gained access to the account files on your network. You need to find a way to catch the user and document them for your report to management. Which Windows NT feature could you use?

## Lab 7.24  *Sharing resources*

In Windows 95, share a directory with read permission and again with full permission using share-level security.

### Lab 7.25 *Backup strategies*

The data on your server undergoes many changes daily. You want to quickly back up the data several times a day. Which backup method would you choose?

### Lab 7.26 *Security considerations*

You have just installed a Microsoft network using workgroups. Which type of security will you use on the Windows NT Workstation computers in the workgroup? Why would you choose this type?

### Lab 8.27 *Planning the user environment*

A user on the network is complaining that his print jobs are going to the wrong printer. What is the quickest way to eliminate user error as the cause of the problem?

### Lab 8.28 *Detecting conflicts*

A user on your network is complaining that every time he uses his modem his serial mouse freezes. What is the likely cause of the problem?

### Lab 8.29 *Troubleshooting physical connections*

A user suddenly began having problems connecting to the network after redecorating his office. When his workstation is plugged into the Ethernet cable in his neighbor's office, it works properly. What would you suspect as the problem and what equipment could be used to verify the problem and locate the exact location of the problem?

### Lab 8.30 *Locating answers to problems*

A Windows NT computer is returning a specific error code when the messenger service fails to start. You can find no information about this specific error code in Windows NT Help or in your copy of the *Microsoft Windows NT Server Resource Kit*. Which resources would you use next to discover the meaning of the error code?

### Lab 8.31 *Configuring TCP/IP*

A user on the network is complaining about her new workstation. She can access resources on her floor but not those on the floor above her. The floors are separated by a router. TCP/IP is the only protocol installed on the network, and no other user is experiencing problems. What is the most likely cause of her problem?

# Answers to Instant Assessment Questions and Critical Thinking Labs

## Chapter 1: Basics of Networking

### *Answers to Instant Assessment Questions*

1. No. Implement server-based networking and setup permissions on the server to allow for the individual case needs.

2. Client; server

3. Security is handled differently between the network types. Peer-to-peer network security is much harder to maintain when the number of users exceeds ten.

4. File Services

5. Server

6. Protocols

7. Clients

8. Centralized computing

9. Distributed computing

10. Collaborative computing

11. Centralized computing

12. Server based

13. Server based

14. Yes. Win95 has peer-to-peer networking capabilities built-in.

15. Directory Services

16. T

17. T

18. F

19. F

20. T

21. T

22. F

23. F

24. T

25. F

26. B

27. A

28. C

29. D

30. C

31. B

32. A

33. D

34. D

35. C

# Chapter 2: The OSI Model

## Answers to Instant Assessment Questions

1. B

2. D

3. A

4. C

5. B

6. A

7. B

8. D

**9.** B

**10.** A

**11.** F

**12.** T

**13.** T

**14.** T

**15.** F

**16.** T

**17.** T

**18.** F

**19.** F

**20.** T

**21.** F

**22.** T

# Chapter 3: Network Media

## *Answers to Instant Assessment Questions*

**1.** B

**2.** C

**3.** D

**4.** B

**5.** D

**6.** A

**7.** D

**8.** C

**9.** D

**10.** A

**11.** T

**12.** T

**13.** F

**14.** F

**15.** F

**16.** T

**17.** T

**18.** T

**19.** F

**20.** T

## Answers to Critical Thinking Labs

### Lab 3.1  *Overcoming network hardware bottlenecks*
You could possibly use a MicroChannel, EISA, or PCI network adapter to increase performance. The deciding factors could be the manufacturer of your server, and when it was purchased. MicroChannel is proprietary to IBM, and PCI is a very new architecture.

### Lab 3.2  *Managing network card resources*
The only free IRQs would be 5 and 10.

### Lab 3.3  *Deciding the correct cable type*
The optimum solution would be fiber optic. It is immune to EMI interference and more than capable of being run 400 yards. UTP would not be a choice because of EMI, and coaxial cable has a shorter distance limit than needed.

### Lab 3.4  *Troubleshooting drivers*
The network driver may not be an ODI or NDIS driver, which would allow you to bind multiple protocols to the network card at once.

### Lab 3.5  *Crossing a highway*
Point-to-point infrared is an excellent choice because the buildings are directly across from one another. This method provides a high level of security with high speed. This method does not require an FCC license.

# Chapter 4: Network Designs

## *Answers to Instant Assessment Questions*

1. A
2. C
3. C
4. A
5. D
6. B
7. C
8. B
9. C
10. A
11. D
12. D
13. C
14. C
15. D
16. T
17. T
18. F
19. T
20. T
21. F
22. T
23. F
24. T
25. F

## Answers to Critical Thinking Labs

### Lab 4.6  *Planning network cabling*
10Base-T would be the best choice. This would provide an inexpensive option. Because the network cable is in place, the only expense would be adapters and hubs. This type of network allows for future growth.

### Lab 4.7  *Troubleshooting connectivity*
The Windows 95 workstation may be using an incorrect frame type. NetWare 3.12 defaults to Ethernet_802.2

### Lab 4.8  *Troubleshooting token ring connectivity*
The adapters setting for ring speed should be checked. Token Ring adapters that are set for 16Mbps do not work correctly on 4Mbps Token Ring. Because the network is being upgraded, the lab may possibly be operating at 16Mbps, and the users office is still 4Mbps.

### Lab 4.9  *Troubleshooting a token ring LAN*
The nearest active upstream neighbor of the beaconing system should be examined. A beaconing system is alerting the network to a problem with its neighbor.

### Lab 4.10  *Finding a conflict*
It is likely that the secretaries system is set for the same physical address as the system displaying the problem.

# Chapter 5: Network Protocols

## Answers to Instant Assessment Questions

1. A

2. D

3. B

4. C

5. B

6. A

7. B

**8.** B

**9.** A

**10.** D

**11.** F

**12.** T

**13.** T

**14.** F

**15.** T

**16.** T

**17.** F

**18.** T

**19.** F

**20.** T

## *Answers to Critical Thinking Labs*

### Lab 5.11 *Expanding the network*

You should change protocols since NetBEUI is nonroutable and will not function across the new internetworking devices. The possible choices for protocols are IPX/SPX and TCP/IP since they will both function in this environment.

### Lab 5.12 *Adding protocols*

The two ways to let them access files from UNIX would be FTP and NFS. NFS would be the better choice since you can connect to an NFS share and manage files easily. FTP requires a small client that normally works from the command line and is very cumbersome to use. FTP also does not allow you to open or manage files while they are on the server.

### Lab 5.13 *Adding NetWare protocols*

You either could add IPX/SPX as a secondary protocol to the clients or switch totally to IPX/SPX. If you kept NetBEUI and added IPX/SPX, you would benefit from the speed of NetBEUI, while Microsoft clients communicate with each other while still being able to connect to the NetWare server with IPX/SPX.

### Lab 5.14  *New network printer*

DLC must be added to the clients for them to use the new printer.

### Lab 5.15  *Remote connectivity*

PPP would need to be used. PPP allows for protocols other than TCP/IP and allows for dynamic addressing.

# Chapter 6: Connecting Networks

## *Answers to Instant Assessment Questions*

**1.** A

**2.** B

**3.** A

**4.** C

**5.** B

**6.** C

**7.** A

**8.** D

**9.** C

**10.** D

**11.** T

**12.** F

**13.** T

**14.** F

**15.** T

**16.** T

**17.** F

**18.** F

**19.** T

**20.** T

## Answers to Critical Thinking Labs

### Lab 6.16  *Extending the network*

A bridge would be the best solution to extend the network. It is cheap and easy to install. Your choice of protocol would not effect using a bridge. Even though TCP/IP is a routable protocol it can still be bridged since bridging uses MAC addresses. A router could also be used, but would cost more, be harder to configure, and might hurt performance.

### Lab 6.17  *Troubleshooting Ethernet*

Check for the 5-4-3 rule. You can not have more than four hubs between any two devices on a 10Base-T network.

### Lab 6.18  *Troubleshooting broadcast storms*

The new router may be a bridging router (brouter). Be sure that bridging is disabled.

### Lab 6.19  *Connecting distant LANs*

A repeater could be used. Repeaters can boost the signal, and they can be used to connect segments running the same network type over different cable types.

### Lab 6.20  *Ethernet bridging*

No. Source-route bridges use Token Ring frame information, instead of MAC addresses, to transmit packets.

# Chapter 7: Administration

## Answers to Instant Assessment Questions

1. D

2. D

3. C

4. D

5. B

6. B

**7.** C

**8.** D

**9.** B

**10.** F

**11.** T

**12.** T

**13.** T

**14.** T

**15.** F

**16.** T

**17.** F

**18.** T

**19.** F

## Answers to Critical Thinking Labs

### Lab 7.21  *Security planning*

Workgroup solution would be the best. With no central server, a domain is not possible. Also, users maintain their own documents and security.

### Lab 7.22  *Windows NT administration*

Using User Manager, select User and then New User. Fill out the information as needed. Next, double-click the Administrators group from the main User Manager window and add your new account as a member.

### Lab 7.23  *Monitoring users*

Auditing will allow you to see the user accessing the accounting files. From this you can print out copies from the Event Viewer's Security log to use as documentation.

### Lab 7.24  *Sharing resources*

First ensure that File and Print Sharing is installed. In Control Panel choose the Network icon. Examine your network configuration. You should have the Client for Microsoft Networks installed, a network adapter, a protocol such as NetBEUI, and File and Print Sharing Service. If one of these components is missing, click

Add and choose to add either a client, adapter, protocol, or service depending on which options are installed. You will then need to reboot. From the Start button, choose Programs, and then click Windows Explorer. From there, right-click the folder you wish to share and choose the sharing option.

### Lab 7.25  *Backup strategies*
Incremental backups can be used to back up all files that have changed since the last backup. They are then marked as archived, so they are not backed up again unless they change. This provides a quick method of backing up files.

### Lab 7.26  *Security considerations*
User-level security is used. Windows NT can not use share level security.

# Chapter 8: Troubleshooting

## *Answers to Instant Assessment Questions*

1. B
2. A
3. D
4. B
5. C
6. B
7. A
8. D
9. D
10. C
11. T
12. T
13. F
14. T
15. F
16. T

**17.** F

**18.** F

**19.** F

**20.** T

## Answers to Critical Thinking Labs

### Lab 8.27 *Planning the user environment*

Have the user show you exactly what steps he takes when trying to print. Although you can sometimes detect user error by simply talking with the user, this does not always work. Users may not understand the terms you are using and may be vague in their answers.

### Lab 8.28 *Detecting conflicts*

The serial mouse and modem are likely sharing IRQs by using either COM1 and COM3 or COM2 and COM4.

### Lab 8.29 *Troubleshooting physical connections*

The probable cause of the problem is damage to the Ethernet cable. Many diagnostic devices can detect if there is a break in the cable. Time-domain reflectors can be used to find the exact location of the problem.

### Lab 8.30 *Locating answers to problems*

The Microsoft Knowledge Base and TechNet contain information explaining the cause of many specific error codes as well as the resolution to the problem.

### Lab 8.31 *Configuring TCP/IP*

TCP/IP is probably configured incorrectly. A missing or incorrect gateway setting can cause this problem.

# Exam Preparation Tips

The Microsoft Certified Professional exams are *not* easy, and they require a great deal of preparation. The exam questions measure real-world skills. Your ability to answer these questions correctly will be greatly enhanced by as much hands-on experience with the product as you can get. Appendix D provides you some practical and innovative ways to prepare for the Microsoft Certified Professional exams for Networking Essentials.

concept link

**Read sections of Microsoft Roadmap to Education and Certification that apply to the exam you're taking. (This is found on the CD-ROM accompanying this book.) Pay particular attention to the exam objectives, and mentally note your relative strengths and weaknesses for study later.**

web links

**Although the Exam Objectives on the Microsoft Roadmap to Certification on the accompanying CD-ROM were current when this book was published, you may want to ensure that you have the most current version of the exam objectives by accessing the Microsoft Training and Certification Web site at** www.microsoft. com/train_cert.

# ABOUT THE EXAMS

An important aspect of passing the MCP Certification Exams is understanding the big picture. This includes understanding how the exams are developed and scored.

Every job function requires different levels of cognitive skills, from memorization of facts and definitions to the comprehensive ability to analyze scenarios, design solutions, and evaluate options. To make the exams relevant in the real world, Microsoft Certified Professional exams test the specific cognitive skills needed for the job functions being tested. These exams go beyond testing rote knowledge; you need to *apply* your knowledge, analyze technical solutions, solve problems, and make decisions — just like you would on the job.

## How the Certification Exams Are Developed

To help ensure the validity and reliability of the certification exams, Microsoft adheres to an eight-phase exam development process:

1. Job analysis

2. Objective domain definition

3. Blueprint survey

4. Item development

5. Alpha review and item revision

6. Beta exam

7. Item selection and cut score setting

8. Exam live

The following paragraphs describe each phase of exam development.

## Phase 1: Job analysis

Phase 1 is an analysis of all the tasks that make up the specific job function, based on tasks performed by people who are currently performing the job function. This phase also identifies the knowledge, skills, and abilities that relate specifically to the performance area to be certified.

## Phase 2: Objective domain definition

The results of the job analysis provide the framework used to develop objectives. The development of objectives involves translating the job function tasks into a comprehensive set of more specific and measurable knowledge, skills, and abilities. The resulting list of objectives, or the objective domain, is the basis for the development of both the certification exams and the training materials.

## Phase 3: Blueprint survey

The final objective domain is transformed into a blueprint survey in which contributors — technology professionals who are performing the applicable job function — are asked to rate each objective. Contributors may be selected from lists of past Certified Professional candidates, from appropriately skilled exam development volunteers, and from within Microsoft. Based on the contributors' input, the objectives are prioritized and weighted. The actual exam items are written according to these prioritized objectives. Contributors are queried about how they spend their time on the job, and if a contributor doesn't spend an adequate amount of time actually performing the specified job function, his or her data is eliminated from the analysis.

The blueprint survey phase helps determine which objectives to measure, as well as the appropriate number and types of items to include on the exam.

## Phase 4: Item development

A pool of items is developed to measure the blueprinted objective domain. The number and types of items to be written are based on the results of the blueprint survey. During this phase, items are reviewed and revised to ensure that they are:

- Technically accurate
- Clear, unambiguous, and plausible
- Not biased for any population subgroup or culture

- o Not misleading or tricky
- o Testing at the correct level of Bloom's Taxonomy
- o Testing for useful knowledge, not obscure or trivial facts

Items that meet these criteria are included in the initial item pool.

### Phase 5: Alpha review and item revision

During this phase, a panel of technical and job function experts reviews each item for technical accuracy and then answers each item, reaching consensus on all technical issues. Once the items have been verified as technically accurate, they are edited to ensure they are expressed in the clearest language possible.

### Phase 6: Beta exam

The reviewed and edited items are collected into a beta exam pool. During the beta exam, each participant has the opportunity to respond to all the items in this beta exam pool. Based on the responses of all beta participants, Microsoft performs a statistical analysis to verify the validity of the exam items and to determine which items will be used in the certification exam. Once the analysis has been completed, the items are distributed into multiple parallel forms, or versions, of the final certification exam.

### Phase 7: Item selection and cut score setting

The results of the beta exam are analyzed to determine which items should be included in the certification exam based on many factors, including item difficulty and relevance. Generally, the desired items are those that were answered correctly by anywhere from 25 to 90 percent of the beta exam candidates. This helps ensure that the exam consists of a variety of difficulty levels, from somewhat easy to extremely difficult.

Also during this phase, a panel of job function experts determines the cut score (minimum passing score) for the exam. The cut score differs from exam to exam because it is based on an item-by-item determination of the percentage of candidates who answered the item correctly and who would be expected to answer the item correctly. The cut score is determined in a group session to increase the reliability among the experts.

## Phase 8: Exam live

Microsoft Certified Professional exams are administered by Sylvan Prometric, an independent testing company. The exams are made available at Sylvan Prometric testing centers worldwide.

# Exam Items and Scoring

Microsoft certification exams consist of three types of items: multiple choice, multiple rating, and enhanced. The way you indicate your answer and the number of points you can receive differ depending on the type of item.

## Multiple-choice item

A traditional multiple-choice item presents a problem and asks you to select either the best answer (single response) or the best set of answers (multiple response) to the given item from a list of possible answers.

For a *multiple-choice* item, your response is scored as either correct or incorrect. A correct answer receives a score of 1 point and an incorrect answer receives a score of 0 points.

In the case of a multiple-choice, multiple-response item (for which the correct response consists of more than one answer), the item is scored as being correct only if all the correct answers are selected. No partial credit is given for a response that does not include all the correct answers for the item.

For consistency purposes, the question in a multiple-choice, multiple-response item is always presented in singular form, regardless of how many answers are correct. Always follow the instructions displayed at the bottom of the window.

## Multiple-rating item

A *multiple-rating* item presents a task similar to those presented in multiple-choice items. In a multiple-choice item, you are asked to select the best answer or answers from a selection of several potential answers. In contrast, a multiple-rating item presents a task, along with a proposed solution. Each time the task is presented, a different solution is proposed. In each multiple-rating item, you are asked to choose the answer that best describes the results produced by one proposed solution.

### Enhanced item

An *enhanced* item is similar to a multiple-choice item because it asks you to select your response from a number of possible responses. However, unlike the traditional multiple-choice item that presents you with a list of possible answers from which to choose, an enhanced item may ask you to indicate your answer in one of three ways:

o Type the correct response, such as a command name.

o Review an exhibit (such as a screen shot, a network configuration drawing, or a code sample), and then use the mouse to select the area of the exhibit that represents the correct response.

o Review an exhibit, and then select the correct response from the list of possible responses.

As with a multiple-choice item, your response to an enhanced item is scored as either correct or incorrect. A correct answer receives full credit of 1 point and an incorrect answer receives a score of 0 points.

# PREPARING FOR A MICROSOFT CERTIFIED PROFESSIONAL EXAM

The best way to prepare for an exam is to study, learn, and master the job function on which you'll be tested. For any certification exam, you should follow these important preparation steps:

1. Identify the objectives on which you'll be tested.

2. Assess your current mastery of those objectives.

3. Practice tasks and study the areas you haven't mastered.

This section describes tools and techniques that may be helpful as you perform these steps to prepare for the exam.

# Exam Preparation Guides

For each certification exam, an Exam Preparation Guide provides important, specific information about what you'll be tested on and how best to prepare. These guides are essential tools for preparing to take certification exams. You'll find the following types of valuable information in the Exam Preparation Guides:

- **Tasks you should master:** Outlines the overall job function tasks you should master

- **Exam objectives:** Lists the specific skills and abilities on which you should expect to be measured

- **Product resources:** Tells you what products and technologies with which you should be experienced

- **Suggested reading:** Points you to specific reference materials and other publications that discuss one or more of the exam objectives

- **Suggested curriculum:** Provides a specific list of instructor-led and self-paced courses relating to the job function tasks and topics in the exam

You'll also find pointers to additional information that may help you prepare for the exams, such as Microsoft TechNet, *Microsoft Developer Network* (MSDN), online forums, and other sources.

By paying attention to the verbs used in the "Exam Objectives" section of the Exam Preparation Guide, you can get an idea of the level at which you'll be tested on that objective. For more information about which verbs signal each level of the taxonomy, see "About the Exams" in this appendix. It's a good idea to be prepared to be tested at the analysis level or higher for each objective.

# Assessment Exams

When preparing for the exams, take lots of assessment exams. Assessment exams are self-paced exams that you take at your own computer. When you complete an assessment exam, you receive instant score feedback so you can determine areas in which additional study may be helpful before you take the certification exam. Although your score on an assessment exam doesn't necessarily indicate what your score will be on the certification exam, assessment exams give you the opportunity to answer items that are similar to those on the certification exams. And the assessment exams use the same computer-based testing tool as the certification exams, so you don't have to learn the tool on exam day.

An assessment exam exists for almost every certification exam. For a complete list of available assessment exams, see the Microsoft Roadmap to Education and Certification on the CD-ROM.

## Test–Taking Tips

Here are some tips that may be helpful as you prepare to take a certification exam:

- Be sure to read "What to Expect at the Testing Center" in this guide for important information about the sign-in and test-taking procedures you'll follow on the day of your exam.

- Arrive 10 to 15 minutes early, and don't forget your picture ID.

- Dress comfortably. The more comfortable you are, the more you'll be able to focus on the exam.

- If you have any questions about the rules for the exam, ask the exam administrator before the exam begins. The exams are timed, so avoid using valuable test time for questions you could have asked earlier.

- Answer the easy items first. The testing software enables you to move forward and backward through the exam. Go through all the items on the test once, answering those items you are sure of first; then go back and spend time on the harder items.

- Keep in mind that there are no trick items. The correct answer will always be among the list of choices.

- Eliminate the most obvious incorrect answers first. This will make it easier for you to select the answer that seems most right to you.

- Answer all the items before you quit the exam. An unanswered item is scored as an incorrect answer. So if you're unsure of an answer, it can't hurt to make an educated guess.

- Try to relax. People often make avoidable, careless mistakes when they rush.

- Remember, if you don't pass the first time, you can use your score report to determine the areas where you could use additional study and take the exam again later (for an additional fee).

- Do the Critical Thinking labs and review activities for each chapter in this book as you read it. Remember, the exams measure real-world skills that you can't obtain unless you use the product.

- Review the Key Point Summary sections *and* answer the Instant Assessment questions at the end of the chapters in this book just before taking an exam.

- Pay special attention to the exam preparation pointers scattered throughout this book — these pointers will help you focus on important exam-related topics.

- When you've finished reading all of the chapters (and have done all the labs) that pertain to a particular exam, take one or more practice tests to assess your readiness for the exam. Most practice tests will tell you what your weak areas are. Use this information to go back and study.

- Take as many practice exams as you can get your hands on before taking the exam. This will help you in two ways. First, some practice exam questions are quite similar to the real thing, and if you do enough practice exams, some of the questions you see on the exam might look familiar. Second, taking practice exams will make you more comfortable with the computer-based testing environment/process. This will reduce your stress when you take the actual exam. You can't take too many practice exams. It's virtually impossible to be *too* prepared for the exam.

- Take the exam preparation process seriously. Remember, these exams weren't designed to be easy — they were designed to recognize and certify professionals with specific skill sets.

- Consider joining (or becoming an associate member of) a professional organization or user group in your area that focuses on networking. Some user groups have a computer lab and/or lending library that can help you with your exam preparation. The meetings are a great place to meet people with similar interests, and potential employers, too.

- Consider subscribing to *Microsoft Certified Professional Magazine*. This magazine, which is an independent publication not associated with Microsoft, features an Exam Spotlight section where new Microsoft Certified Professional exams are critically reviewed as they are released. For more information about this magazine or to subscribe, visit the magazine's Web site at www.mcpmag.com.

o If possible, talk to friends or colleagues who have taken the exam for which you're preparing. Or check out the Internet for newsgroups or forums where people sometimes share their exam experiences. The experiences of others can shed some light on your potential weak areas that might benefit from further study. The MCSE list server at `saluki.com` is one example. Don't share (or ask friends to share with you) specific exam questions. However, it's fair game to share general topics that were strongly emphasized on the exam, and/or areas that had particularly detailed or tough questions.

o Consider forming a study group with friends or coworkers who are also preparing for the Networking Essentials exam. As a group you can share hardware and software resources, thus reducing your out-of-pocket costs for exam preparation.

o Check out the Internet.

o Do the labs. Do them again for practice.

o When taking the actual exam, pause every few minutes and take a couple of deep breaths — this will bring more oxygen into your body, and hopefully help you to think more clearly. More importantly, this should help you relax and relieve some of the tension of the testing environment.

o Don't drink a lot of coffee or other beverage before taking an exam. Remember, these tests last 90 minutes, and you don't want to be spending precious exam time running back and forth to the restroom.

o Don't study all night before the test. A good night's sleep is often better preparation than the extra studying.

o Don't get discouraged if you don't pass the test your first time — or second time. Many intelligent, seasoned professionals fail a test once, twice, or more times before eventually passing it. If at first you don't succeed, try, try again . . . perseverance pays.

o Try to schedule the exam during your own "peak" time of day. In other words, if you're a morning person, try not to schedule the exam for 3 p.m.

o Know your testing center. Call ahead. Ask about the hardware they use for their testing computers. If some computers are faster than others, ask for the seat numbers of the faster computers and request one of those seat numbers when scheduling your testing appointment with Sylvan

Prometric. Consider visiting a testing center before you schedule an exam there. This will give you an opportunity to see what the testing environment will be like.

o Do the labs!

# TAKING A MICROSOFT CERTIFIED PROFESSIONAL EXAM

This section contains information about registering for and taking a Microsoft Certified Professional exam, including what to expect when you arrive at the Sylvan Prometric testing center to take the exam.

## How to Find Out Which Exams Are Available

You can find a complete list of MCP exams and their registration costs on the online Microsoft Roadmap to Education and Certification on the CD accompanying this book. To get the latest schedule information for a specific exam, contact Sylvan Prometric at (800) 755-EXAM.

## How to Register for an Exam

Candidates may take exams at any of more than 700 Sylvan Prometric testing centers around the world. For the location of a Sylvan Prometric testing center near you, call (800) 755-EXAM. Outside the United States and Canada, contact your local Sylvan Prometric registration center.

To register for a Microsoft Certified Professional exam:

1. Determine which exam you want to take, and note the exam number.

2. Register with the Sylvan Prometric registration center nearest to you. A part of the registration process is advance payment for the exam.

3. After you receive the registration and payment confirmation letter from Sylvan Prometric, call a Sylvan Prometric testing center to schedule your exam.

When you schedule the exam, you'll be provided instructions regarding the appointment, cancellation procedures, and ID requirements, and information about the testing center location.

Exams must be taken within one year of payment. You can schedule exams up to six weeks in advance, or as late as one working day prior to the date of the exam. You can cancel or reschedule your exam if you contact Sylvan Prometric at least two working days prior to the exam.

Although subject to space availability, same-day registration is available in some locations. Where same-day registration is available, you must register a minimum of two hours before test time.

## What to Expect at the Testing Center

As you prepare for your certification exam, it may be helpful to know what to expect when you arrive at the testing center on the day of your exam. The following information gives you a preview of the general procedure you'll go through at the testing center:

- You will be asked to sign the log book upon arrival and departure.

- You will be required to show two forms of identification, including one photo ID (such as a driver's license or company security ID), before you may take the exam.

- The test administrator will give you a Testing Center Regulations form that explains the rules you will be expected to comply with during the test. You will be asked to sign the form, indicating that you understand the regulations and will comply.

- The test administrator will show you to your test computer and will handle any preparations necessary to start the testing tool and display the exam on the computer.

- You will be provided a set amount of scratch paper for use during the exam. All scratch paper will be collected from you at the end of the exam.

- The exams are all closed book. You may not use a laptop computer or have any notes or printed material with you during the exam session.

- Some exams may include additional materials, or *exhibits*. If any exhibits are required for your exam, the test administrator will provide you with them before you begin the exam and collect them from you at the end of the exam.

o Before you begin the exam, the test administrator will tell you what to do when you complete the exam. If the test administrator doesn't explain this to you, or if you are unclear about what you should do, ask the administrator before beginning the exam.

o The number of items on each exam varies, as does the amount of time allotted for each exam. Generally, certification exams consist of about fifty to one hundred items and have durations of 60 to 90 minutes. You can verify the number of items and time allotted for your exam when you register.

Because you'll be given a specific amount of time to complete the exam once you begin, if you have any questions or concerns, don't hesitate to ask the test administrator before the exam begins.

As an exam candidate, you are entitled to the best support and environment possible for your exam. In particular, you are entitled to following:

o A quiet, uncluttered test environment

o Scratch paper

o The tutorial for using the online testing tool, and time to take the tutorial

o A knowledgeable and professional test administrator

o The opportunity to submit comments about the testing center and staff or the test itself

For more information about how to submit feedback about any aspect of your exam experience, see the section "If You Have Exam Concerns or Feedback" in this appendix. The Certification Development Team will investigate any problems or issues you raise and make every effort to resolve them quickly.

## Your Exam Results

Once you have completed an exam, you will be given immediate, online notification of your pass or fail status. You will also receive a printed examination score report indicating your pass or fail status and your exam results by section. (The test administrator will give you the printed score report.) Test scores are automatically forwarded to Microsoft within five working days after you take the test. You do not need to send your score to Microsoft.

If you pass the exam, you will receive confirmation from Microsoft, typically within two to four weeks.

## If You Don't Receive a Passing Score

If you do not pass a certification exam, you may call Sylvan Prometric to schedule a time to retake the exam. Before retaking the exam, you should review the appropriate Exam Preparation Guide and focus additional study on the topic areas where your exam results could be improved. Please note that you must pay again for each exam retake.

One way to determine areas where additional study may be helpful is to carefully review your individual section scores. Generally, the section titles in your score report correlate to specific groups of exam objectives listed in the Exam Preparation Guide.

Here are some specific ways you can prepare to retake an exam:

o Go over the section-by-section scores on your exam results, noting objective areas where your score could be improved.

o Review the Exam Preparation Guide for the exam, with a special focus on the tasks and objective areas that correspond to the exam sections where your score could be improved.

o Increase your real-world, hands-on experience and practice performing the listed job tasks with the relevant products and technologies.

o Consider taking or retaking one or more of the suggested courses listed in the Exam Preparation Guide.

o Review the suggested readings listed in the Exam Preparation Guide.

o After you review the materials, retake the corresponding assessment exam.

# IF YOU HAVE EXAM CONCERNS OR FEEDBACK

To provide the best certification preparation and testing materials possible, we encourage feedback from candidates. If you have any suggestions for improving any of the Microsoft Certified Professional exams or preparation materials, please let us know.

The following sections describe what to do if you have specific concerns or feedback about the certification exams.

## If You Encounter a Problem with the Exam Software or Procedures

Although Microsoft and Sylvan Prometric make every effort to ensure that your exam experience is a positive one, if any problems should occur on the day of the exam, inform the Sylvan Prometric test administrator immediately. The Sylvan Prometric personnel are there to help make the logistics of your exam run smoothly.

## If You Have a Concern About the Exam Content

Microsoft Certified Professional exams are developed by technical and testing experts, with input and participation from job function and technology experts. Through an exhaustive process, Microsoft ensures that the exams adhere to recognized standards for validity and reliability and are considered by candidates to be relevant and fair. If you feel that an exam item is inappropriate or if you believe the answer shown is incorrect, write or send a fax to the Microsoft Certification Development Team, using the address or fax number listed in "For More Information."

Although we are unable to respond to individual questions and issues raised by candidates, all input from candidates is thoroughly researched and taken into consideration during development of subsequent versions of the exams. Microsoft is committed to ensuring the validity and reliability of our exams, and your input is a valuable resource.

# FOR MORE INFORMATION

To find out more about Microsoft Education and Certification materials and programs, to register with Sylvan Prometric, or to get other useful information, check the following resources. Outside the United States or Canada, contact your local Microsoft office or Sylvan Prometric testing center.

- **Microsoft Certified Professional program: (800) 636-7544.** Call for information about the Microsoft Certified Professional program and exams, and to order this Exam Study Guide or the Microsoft Roadmap to Education and Certification.

o Sylvan Prometric testing centers: (800) 755-EXAM. Call to register to take a Microsoft Certified Professional exam at any of more than 700 Sylvan Prometric testing centers around the world, or to order this Exam Study Guide.

o Microsoft sales fax service: (800) 727-3351. Call for Microsoft Certified Professional Exam Preparation Guides, Microsoft Official Curriculum course descriptions and schedules, or this Exam Study Guide.

o Education program and course information: (800) SOLPROV. Call for information about Microsoft Official Curriculum courses, Microsoft education products, and the Microsoft Solution Provider Authorized Technical Education Center (ATEC) program, where you can attend a Microsoft Official Curriculum course, or to order this Exam Study Guide.

o Microsoft Certification Development Team: Fax: (425) 936-1311. Call to volunteer for participation in one or more exam development phases or to report a problem with an exam. Address written correspondence to: Certification Development Team; Microsoft Education and Certification; One Microsoft Way; Redmond, WA 98052.

o Microsoft TechNet technical information network: (800) 344-2121. Call for support professionals and system administrators. Outside the United States and Canada, call your local Microsoft subsidiary for information.

o Microsoft Developer Network (MSDN): (800) 759-5474. MSDN is the official source for software development kits, device driver kits, operating systems, and information about developing applications for Microsoft Windows and Windows NT.

o Online services: (800) 936-3500. Call for information about Microsoft Connection on CompuServe, Microsoft Knowledge Base, Microsoft Software Library, Microsoft Download Service, and Internet.

o Microsoft Online Institute (MOLI): (800) 449-9333. Call for information about Microsoft's new online training program.

# Building Your Own Network

The best way to learn about networks is to set one up yourself and practice on it. This appendix covers the steps you go through in configuring a small network at home. You can use this network to review material covered previously.

 **This appendix assumes you have at least two fully working Windows 95 workstations. You also need two network adapter cards, as well as the appropriate cable and connectors to connect them. Depending on the brand and model of network card used, you may also need a software driver disk for it.**

# NETWORK CARD INSTALLATION

If you do not have your network adapter cards yet, you need to decide which brand and model to buy. When purchasing your cards, also consider the type of cable you want to use. If this is a small network you will only use for study purposes, you can buy some inexpensive Novell Eagle 2000 (NE 2000) clone cards, easily available for $20 to $30. An advantage to these cards is that almost all network operating systems come with NE2000 drivers. If you would like higher performance or higher quality cards, you may wish to go with a name brand. Popular brands are 3Com, Intel, and SMC.

Many higher quality cards come with lifetime warranties. A name brand PCI card can be had for $50 to $150.

After you have purchased your network cards, you also may need cable, connectors, and a hub. Many computer stores carry network cable. You can either buy the cable and connectors separately and build a network cable yourself to the length you want, or you can buy precut cable. Buying precut cable can be a good idea if you do not have the necessary tools to build one. Precut cable usually comes with molded-on connectors as well. Molded-on connectors can hold up to more stress than custom-made cable that is crimped. If the cable you choose is coaxial, don't forget the T connectors and terminators. It is a good idea to buy an extra of each, as they are cheap and can save you a trip back to the store.

The first step in building your new network is to install the network adapter cards properly into your computers. Depending on what type of card you have, you may need to set jumpers or DIP switches to configure them. Some new cards support software configuration through a utility provided by the manufacturer. New PCI bus cards are configured automatically by the computer itself.

concept link  **The settings you use to configure the card are extremely important. They must not conflict with any other device in the computer. Refer to Chapter 3, "Network Media," for information on the usual configuration parameters that you may need to set. Also consult the documentation that came with the cards to see how it should be configured.**

tip **When configuring your network adapter, pay very close attention to the cable type, or transceiver setting. This setting defines which type of media the card can use. Incorrectly setting this parameter keeps the computer from accessing resources over the network, even though the card may seem fine when looked at from within Windows 95.**

# WINDOWS 95 CONFIGURATION

Depending on the type of card you installed, Windows 95 may automatically detect it when you boot the computer. If not, you can manually add the network card driver to Windows. To manually add the network card, you can either let Windows 95 try to detect it or add it in the network properties. Both methods are described below. If you feel adventurous, you can do both methods on separate computers so that you are familiar with either approach.

 **If you are having trouble locating a driver for your network card, you can check** http://www.windows95.com.

## Autodetect Hardware

One of the best features of Windows 95 is the ability to automatically detect hardware and install the appropriate drivers. To force Windows 95 to try to detect hardware, go to Control Panel. Figure E-1 shows the Add New Hardware option in Control Panel.

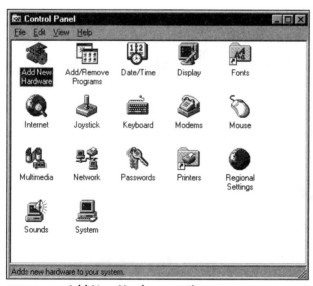

**FIGURE E-1**   Add New Hardware option

Double-click the Add New Hardware option to start the process. This opens the Add New Hardware Wizard. Click Next to continue. Figure E-2 shows the opening screen of the Add New Hardware Wizard.

**FIGURE E-2**   Add New Hardware Wizard opening screen

You are given the option to either let Windows try to detect the new hardware or manually specify the hardware to add. Figure E-3 shows these options.

**FIGURE E-3**   Detection options

Since you want to let Windows 95 try to detect the new hardware, click the Next button. Windows 95 shows a warning message, as seen in Figure E-4. Windows 95 then goes through all the devices it is aware of and tries to find the network adapter you added. Figure E-5 shows Windows searching for hardware.

**FIGURE E-4**    Warning

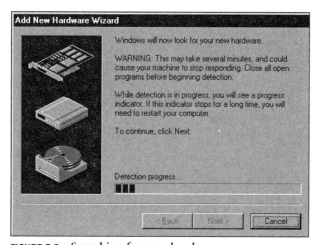

**FIGURE E-5**    Searching for new hardware

After you wait a minute or two for Windows 95 to go through its detection process, the final screen of the Add New Hardware Wizard appears. Click the Next button to list the devices that Windows 95 found in the process. If you did not receive a Next button on the dialog box, Windows 95 did not detect any new hardware. You may want to manually add it using the process described in the next section. Figure E-6 shows the hardware that Windows 95 found.

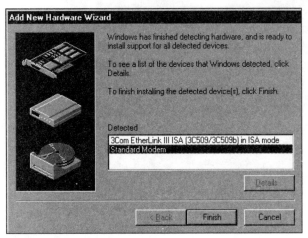

**FIGURE E-6**   **Detected hardware**

After Windows has added the appropriate driver, you need to finish adding components to the Windows networking. By default, the client for Microsoft networks, IPX/SPX-compatible protocol, and NetBEUI are installed automatically. You need to manually add TCP/IP. The instructions for that are in the next section.

## Manually Adding a Network Card

You may need to add the network card driver automatically if Windows 95 did not detect it. Windows 95 supports many different network cards. Most likely it already has a driver for the card you are installing. If it does not, then you need to get that driver and have it ready.

To start the process, go to Control Panel and double-click the Network option. You are presented with the main Network properties dialog box, shown in Figure E-7.

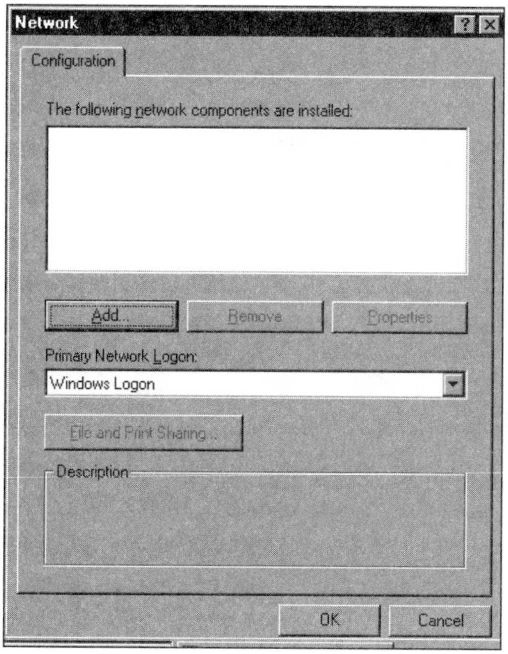

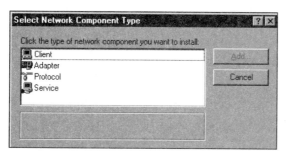

**FIGURE E-7**   Network properties dialog box

You may already have some components installed, especially if you use Windows 95 to dial up to the Internet. This does not affect the installation of the network card or protocols. To add your network card driver, click the Add button. You are then presented with a list of components to add. Figure E-8 shows the list.

**FIGURE E-8**   List of network components

From the component list, choose Adapter. A list of manufacturers and adapter models supported by Windows 95 appears. Figure E-9 shows this list.

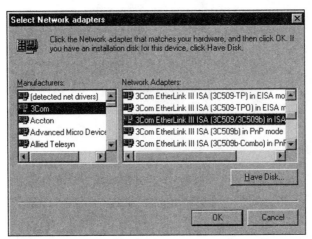

**FIGURE E-9**    **Adapter list**

Scroll down the list of manufacturers until you find the one that made your network cards. Remember, if your card is a clone of another, look under the manufacturer for the card it is compatible with. If you do not see your card listed, you can add a new driver to Windows 95 by clicking the Have Disk button. You then need to change to the directory or disk where you have stored the driver you wish to add.

After you have installed your network card driver, the Network properties dialog box appears again. By default, Windows 95 automatically adds the client for Microsoft networks, IPX/SPX-compatible protocol, and the NetBEUI protocol. Figure E-10 shows the newly installed components.

Now that the network card and client are installed, you can install the TCP/IP suite. Again, click the Add button and choose Protocol. From the listing of companies, choose Microsoft, and then TCP/IP. You then see the installed components again, and TCP/IP is now listed. Now that all the components are installed, you can move on to the client and protocol configuration. Figure E-11 shows the protocols list.

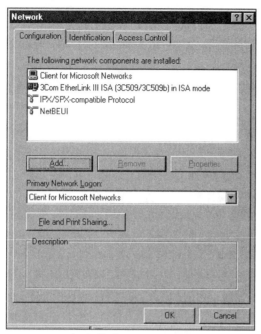

**FIGURE E-10**    Installed components

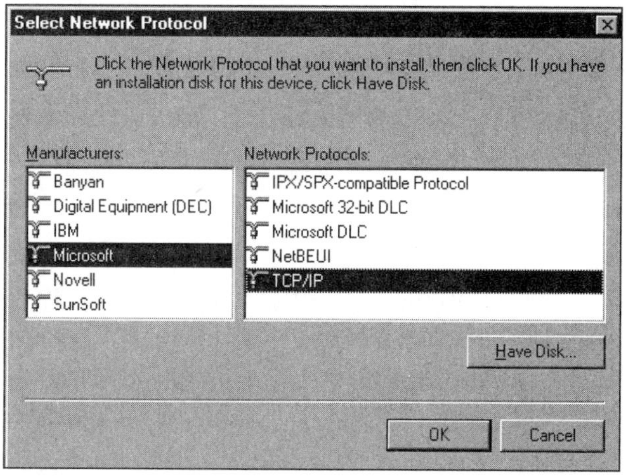

**FIGURE E-11**    Protocols list

# Client and Protocol Configuration

Configuring the Windows 95 networking components is very simple. You begin by giving your newly networked computer a name. From the Network properties dialog box, click the Identification tab. Figure E-12 shows the Identification options.

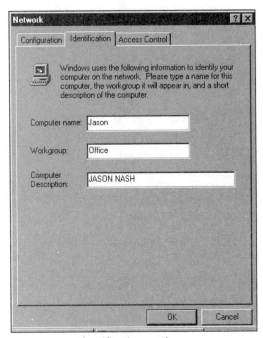

**FIGURE E-12    Identification options**

From the Identification dialog box, you can set your computer name, workgroup, and description. Choose a name that signifies the computer you are configuring. This name will be what others see on the network. On a large network you would want to use a descriptive name that possibly gives information on the computer's location. On a small network at home you can be more creative. Next, set the workgroup name to which your computer will belong. Workgroups make it easier to browse a network. When someone browses a network, they first get a list of all workgroups instead of a very large list of individual computers. The user can then look at the members of individual workgroups for a specific computer. Most likely all computers on your test network should belong to the same workgroup. The final setting on the Identification dialog box is the description. The description is just a bit of information that network users will see when browsing the network.

This can be the main user of the computer or information on how to locate the computer. When you are finished making changes to the Identification dialog box, click the Access Control tab. The Access Control tab is shown in Figure E-13.

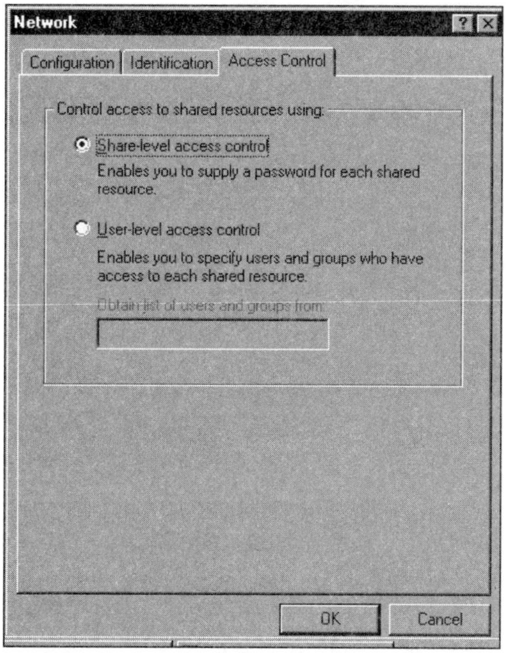

**FIGURE E-13** Access Control options

The Access Control dialog box lets you specify whether you want to use share-level security or user-level security. Share-level security is normally used in a workgroup environment, and user-level security is used when logging into a domain or a NetWare server. If this test network is a workgroup, make sure it is set for share-level security. When you are finished, click the Configuration tab to go back to the list of installed components.

The next step is to configure the individual protocols. NetBEUI has no settings that normally need to be changed. The only setting that may need to be changed in IPX/SPX is the frame type. If you do not have a NetWare server on the network with these workstations, you should be able to leave the type on AUTO. If you have a NetWare server, set the frame type to match the one on the server. Figure E-14 shows the IPX/SPX frame type setting.

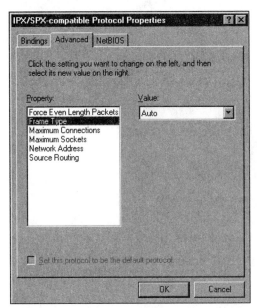

**FIGURE E-14**    Frame Type setting

TCP/IP can be the hardest protocol to configure. On a small home network, though, most configuration settings are not needed. The two required settings are IP address and subnet mask. To configure TCP/IP, double-click the TCP/IP protocol from the Network properties dialog box. Figure E-15 shows the TCP/IP configuration dialog box.

If your network is not connected to a larger network or the Internet, you can use any IP addresses you want. Just be sure to use the appropriate subnet mask. If you would like to use the official IP addresses for test networks, use the 192.168.0.0 range of addresses. The example in the figure uses an address of 192.168.0.1 with a subnet mask of 255.255.255.0. The other computers on your network can use 192.168.0.2, 192.168.0.3, and so on. The rest of the TCP/IP configuration settings are optional. If your network just has Windows 95 computers on it, they should most likely stay unconfigured. When you are finished configuring TCP/IP, click OK.

The final configuration task is enabling the sharing of files and printers. By default, a Windows 95 workstation cannot share out resources. To enable this, click the File and Print Sharing button from the main Network properties dialog box. A dialog box appears that allows you to enable or disable the file and print sharing capabilities. Figure E-16 shows this dialog box.

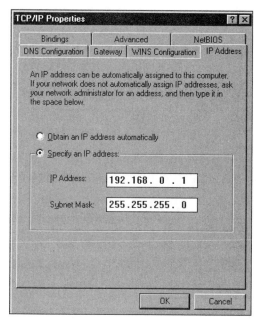

**FIGURE E-15**    TCP/IP configuration

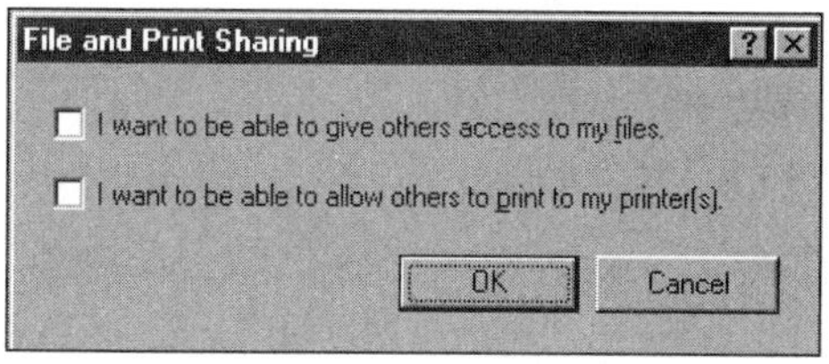

**FIGURE E-16**    File and Print Sharing dialog box

If you would like to enable these features, check the appropriate boxes and click OK. When you are brought back to the Network properties dialog box, click OK again. Your workstation will be rebooted.

# TESTING CONNECTIVITY

Once your workstation has rebooted, you need to test the network connectivity. There are a few simple tests you can quickly perform to check the different network components. If you receive any errors or unexpected results during these tests, double check the previous steps. (You may need to consult the troubleshooting section in Chapter 8.) First, double-click the Network Neighborhood icon on the desktop. You should see either the workgroups on your network, a list of computers, or a combination of both. If you want, you can double-click a computer in the list to view the resources it is sharing. Figure E-17 shows an example of a computer sharing resources.

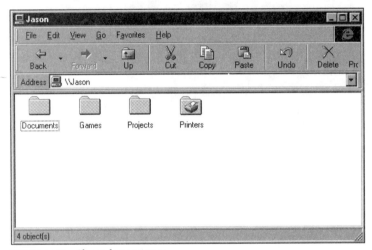

**FIGURE E-17** **Shared resources**

If you can see shared resources and access them, the network card, client, and at least one protocol is functioning. To test the TCP/IP protocol, you can use the Ping utility. Type **PING 192.168.0.2**, but replace 192.168.0.2 with the IP address of your workstation or another device on the network. Figure E-18 shows the Ping utility.

If the previous tests were successful, then congratulations! You can now use your network to test out ideas and study for the Networking Essentials exam.

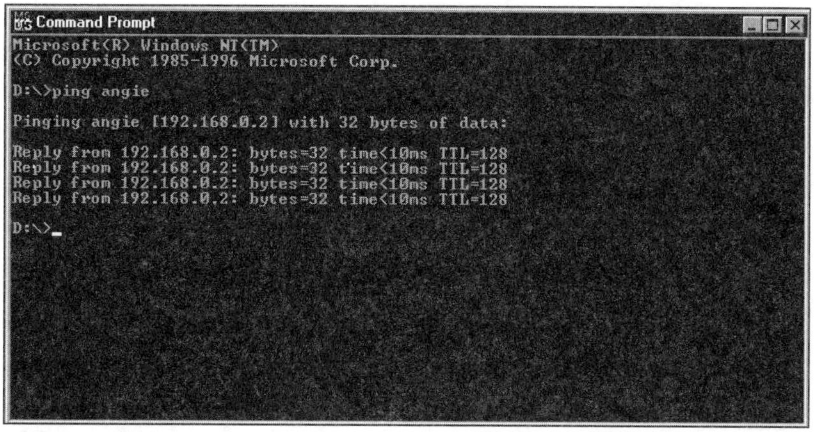

**FIGURE E-18** Ping

# What's on the CD-ROM

---

## CD-ROM CONTENTS

The CD-ROM included with this book contains the following materials:

- Adobe's Acrobat Reader

- An electronic version of this book, *Networking Essentials MCSE Study Guide,* in Adobe's Acrobat format

- An electronic version of three chapters of *MCSE Career Microsoft®!* (IDG Books Worldwide, 1997)

- An electronic version of three chapters of *Windows NT® 4.0 MCSE Study Guide* (IDG Books Worldwide, 1997)

- Microsoft Internet Explorer version 4.0

- MeasureUp test preparation tool and the MeasureUp Networking Essentials practice exams

- Microsoft Training and Certification Offline CD-ROM, including www.microsoft.com/train_cert (entire contents of Web site)

- *Micro House Technical Library* (evaluation copy)

# Installing and Using the CD-ROM

The following sections describe each product and include detailed instructions for installation and use.

## Adobe's Acrobat Reader and the Acrobat Version of Networking Essentials MCSE Study Guide

The Adobe's Acrobat Reader is a helpful program that will enable you to view the electronic version of this book in the same page format as the actual book.

## MCSE Career Microsoft! (Sample Chapters in Acrobat Format)

Most books covering the Microsoft Certified Professional program focus entirely on practice exams and their subject matter. *MCSE Career Microsoft!* focuses on the professional characteristics involved with obtaining a Microsoft Certification, as well as maintaining and advancing your career once you are certified. This book also provides many practical and essential references to information, training, and tools available to information technology professionals, including Microsoft Career Professionals (MCPs) and MCP candidates. Included here are excerpts from *MCSE Career Microsoft!*, including Chapters 1, 2, and 5. These chapters should give you a good impression of how useful and valuable this book can be. No other computer book on the market today provides a comprehensive approach to MCPs and their careers as does *MCSE Career Microsoft!*

**TO INSTALL AND RUN ADOBE'S ACROBAT READER AND VIEW THE ELECTRONIC VERSION OF THIS BOOK, FOLLOW THESE STEPS:**

**1.** Start Windows Explorer (if you're using Windows 95) or Windows NT Explorer (if you're using Windows NT), and then open the `Acrobat` folder on the CD-ROM.

**2.** In the `Acrobat` folder, double-click `Ar3230.exe` and follow the instructions presented onscreen for installing Adobe Acrobat Reader.

**3.** To view the electronic version of this book after you have installed Adobe Acrobat Reader, start Windows Explorer (if you're using Windows 95) or Windows NT Explorer (if you're using Windows NT), and then open the `Books\MCSE Net Essentials` folder on the CD-ROM.

**4.** In the `MCSE Net Essentials` folder, double-click the chapter or appendix file you want to view. All documents in this folder end with a `.pdf` extension.

**TO INSTALL AND RUN ADOBE'S ACROBAT READER TO VIEW *MCSE Career Microsoft!*, FOLLOW THESE STEPS:**

**1.** If you've already installed the Acrobat Reader to view the electronic version of this book, skip to step 3.

If you haven't installed Adobe's Acrobat Reader, start Windows Explorer (if you're using Windows 95) or Windows NT Explorer (if you're using Windows NT), and then open the `Acrobat` folder on the CD-ROM.

**2.** In the `Acrobat` folder, double-click `Setup.exe` and follow the instructions presented onscreen for installing Adobe's Acrobat Reader.

**3.** To view the *MCSE Career Microsoft!* sample chapters after you have installed Adobe's Acrobat Reader, start Windows Explorer (if you're using Windows 95) or Windows NT Explorer (if you're using Windows NT), and then open the `Books\Career Microsoft` folder on the CD-ROM.

**4.** In the `Career Microsoft` folder, double-click the chapter you want to view. All documents in this folder end with a `.pdf` extension.

## Windows NT 4.0 MCSE Study Guide (Sample Chapters in Acrobat Format)

This Microsoft-approved study guide prepares you for three MCSE exams that test implementing and supporting Windows NT products: No. 73 (Workstation 4.0), No. 70-67 (Server 4.0), and No. 70-68 (Server 4.0 in the Enterprise). You'll find three chapters in Adobe Acrobat format on the CD-ROM.

**TO VIEW *Windows NT 4.0 MCSE Study Guide* CHAPTERS, FOLLOW THESE STEPS:**

1. If you've already installed the Acrobat Reader to view the electronic version of this book, skip to step 3.

   If you haven't installed Adobe Acrobat Reader, start Windows Explorer (if you're using Windows 95) or Windows NT Explorer (if you're using Windows NT), and then open the `Acrobat` folder on the CD-ROM.

2. In the `Acrobat` folder, double-click `Ar32e30.exe` and follow the instructions presented onscreen for installing Adobe Acrobat Reader.

3. To view the **Windows NT 4.0 MCSE Study Guide** sample chapters after you have installed Adobe Acrobat Reader, start Windows Explorer (if you're using Windows 95) or Windows NT Explorer (if you're using Windows NT), and then open the `Books\MCSE Windows NT 4.0` folder on the CD-ROM.

4. In the `MCSE Windows NT 4.0` folder, double-click the chapter you want to view. All documents in this folder end with a `.pdf` extension.

## Microsoft Internet Explorer Version 4.0

This is a complete copy of Microsoft Internet Explorer. With Internet Explorer you'll be able to browse the Internet if you have an Internet connection, and view the contents of the Microsoft Training and Certification Offline CD-ROM (included on this CD-ROM).

**TO INSTALL AND RUN MICROSOFT INTERNET EXPLORER, FOLLOW THESE STEPS:**

**1.** Start Windows Explorer (if you're using Windows 95) or Windows NT Explorer (if you're using Windows NT), and then open the IE4 folder on the CD-ROM.

**2.** In the IE4 folder, double-click `Setup.exe` and follow the instructions presented onscreen for installing Internet Explorer.

**3.** To run Internet Explorer, double-click the Internet Explorer icon on the desktop.

## MeasureUp Test Preparation Tool and the MeasureUp Networking Essentials Practice Exams

These practice exams help you to assess your readiness for the actual Microsoft Certified Professional exams. They will also help you to determine the areas in which you need more preparation. USE THESE EXAMS — you'll be glad you did.

**TO INSTALL AND ACCESS THE MEASUREUP TEST PREPARATION TOOL AND THE MEASUREUP NETWORKING ESSENTIALS PRACTICE EXAMS, FOLLOW THESE STEPS:**

**1.** Start Windows Explorer (if you're using Windows 95) or Windows NT Explorer (if you're using Windows NT), and then open the MeasureUp folder on the CD-ROM.

**2.** In the MeasureUp folder, double-click `Setup.exe` file and follow the instructions presented onscreen for installing the MeasureUp Test Preparation Tool and the MeasureUp Networking Essentials practice exams.

**3.** After the installation is complete, you can access the practice exams by selecting Start ⇒ Programs ⇒ MeasureUp Certification Preparation ⇒ 70-058 Networking Essentials Exam Demo.

# Microsoft Training and Certification Offline CD-ROM

This offline CD-ROM includes the entire contents of a key Microsoft Web site where you can obtain MCSE certification requirements and view Microsoft Certified Professional exam objectives and Microsoft course information. In addition, you can view the most current version of this Web site by connecting to `www.microsoft.com/train_cert/` on the Internet.

---

**TO INSTALL AND ACCESS THE OFFLINE VERSION OF THE MICROSOFT TRAINING AND CERTIFICATION WEB SITE, FOLLOW THESE STEPS:**

**1.** Start Windows Explorer (if you're using Windows 95) or Windows NT Explorer (if you're using Windows NT), and then open the `Mscert` folder on the CD-ROM.

**2.** In the `Mscert` folder, double-click `Setup.exe` and follow the instructions presented onscreen for installing the Microsoft Train_Cert Offline Web site.

**3.** After the installation is complete, you can view the Web site by selecting Start ⇒ Programs ⇒ Microsoft Train_Cert Offline ⇒ Microsoft Train_Cert Offline.

---

 **You must have Microsoft Internet Explorer installed *before* you can view this Web site.**

# Microsoft Self-Administered Assessment Exam: Networking Essentials

This self-test is designed to measure your knowledge of network architecture, the OSI model, protocols, troubleshooting, and network devices. I recommend you take this self-administered assessment exam as part of your preparation just before you take the actual exam. It should give you a good indication of whether or not you're ready to tackle the real thing.

**TO INSTALL AND ACCESS THE NETWORKING ESSENTIALS SELF-ADMINISTERED ASSESSMENT EXAM, FOLLOW THESE STEPS:**

**1.** Start Windows Explorer (if you're using Windows 95) or Windows NT Explorer (if you're using Windows NT). Create a folder named `ExamPrep` on your computer's hard drive.

**2.** Use Explorer to copy the `Mscert\Download\Training\Asm1.exe`, `Asm2.exe and Asm3.exe` files from the CD-ROM to the `ExamPrep` folder you just created.

**3.** Run `Asm1.exe, Asm2.exe, and Asm3.exe` so that they expand files into the `ExamPrep` folder.

**4.** Double-click the `Setup.exe` file to start the installation.

**5.** Once Setup has finished you can access the tests by selecting Assessment Exams ⇒ Assessment Exams.

## Microsoft Certified Professional Program Exam Study Guide

This study guide presents interesting and valuable information about the Microsoft Certified Professional exams, including how the exams are developed, a description of the types of questions asked on exams, and some exam preparation tips.

**TO VIEW THE *Microsoft Certified Professional Program Exam Study Guide*, FOLLOW THESE STEPS:**

**1.** Start Windows Explorer (if you're using Windows 95) or Windows NT Explorer (if you're using Windows NT). Open the `Mscert\Download\Cert` folder.

**2.** In the `Cert` folder, double-click `Studgde4.doc`.

 note **You must have Microsoft Word, WordPad, or Word Viewer installed** *before* **you can view this study guide.**

## *Micro House Technical Library* (Evaluation Copy)

*Micro House Technical Library* is a useful CD-ROM-based set of encyclopedias that contains hardware configuration information. This evaluation copy of *Micro House Technical Library* includes only the Encyclopedia of I/O cards. Use this evaluation copy to determine whether or not you want to purchase the full version of the *Micro House Technical Library*.

**TO INSTALL AND ACCESS THE *Micro House Technical Library*, FOLLOW THESE STEPS:**

1. Start Windows Explorer (if you're using Windows 95) or Windows NT Explorer (if you're using Windows NT), and then open the Micro House folder on the CD-ROM.

2. In the Micro House folder, double-click Install.exe and follow the instructions presented onscreen for installing the **Micro House Technical Library**.

3. To run the **Micro House Technical Library**, select Start ⇒ Programs ⇒ MH Tech Library ⇒ MTL Demo Edition.

# Glossary

**100 VG-ANYLAN** A 100 VG-Anylan networks use voice-grade, fiber-optic cable, as well as Categories 3, 4, or 5 twisted-pair cable to provide a possible transmission rate of 100Mbps.

**10Base-2** 10Base-2 networks use RG-58 cable along with T connectors wired in a linear bus configuration to provide a transmission rate of 10Mbps.

**10Base-5** 10Base-5 networks use RG-8 cable with external transceivers and a vampire clamp. The clamp fastens directly into the cable, which is wired in a linear bus to provide a possible transmission rate of 10Mbps.

**10Base-FL** A network that operates over fiber-optic cable at 10Mbps using baseband signaling is a 10Base-FL network.

**10Base-T** 10Base-T is a network standard that utilizes 22-AWG UTP cable with RJ-45 jacks arranged in a star configuration to provide possible transmission rates of 10Mbps.

**Address Resolution Protocol (ARP)** ARP is used to dynamically discover the low-level physical network hardware address that corresponds to the high-level IP address for a given host.

**ADSP** *See* AppleTalk Data Stream Protocol.

**American National Standards Institute (ANSI)** ANSI is the primary organization for fostering the development of technology standards in the United States.

**amplitude shift keying (ASK)** ASK is a method of encoding that uses changes in amplitude to represent data.

**analog signal** An analog signal takes the form of a wave, which curves smoothly from one value to the next.

**ANSI** *See* American National Standards Institute.

**AppleShare** Appleshare is a group of client/server applications that provides access to network resources.

**AppleTalk** Appletalk is a set of communications protocols used to define networking on an AppleShare network.

**AppleTalk Data Stream Protocol (ADSP)** Part of the AppleTalk protocol suite, ADSP is a newer protocol that uses byte-streaming connections instead of transactions.

**AppleTalk Session Protocol (ASP)** Grouped with AppleTalk Transport Protocol, ASP allows for reliable data transfer.

**AppleTalk Transaction Protocol (ATP)** ATP provides a connectionless Transport layer protocol, but instead of being used strictly for data like others of this type, it is used for transactions.

**Application layer** The application layer is the top layer of the network protocol stack. The Application layer is concerned with the semantics of work.

**archiving** Archiving is the process of creating a redundant copy of computer file data. Used to protect the data if the original copy is damaged or otherwise irretrievable.

**ARCNET** ARCNET is a proprietary token-bus networking architecture that supports coaxial, twisted-pair, and fiber-optic cable-based implementations, and is capable of 2.5Mbps transmissions.

**ARP** *See* Address Resolution Protocol.

**ASK** *See* amplitude shift keying.

**ASN.1** ASN.1 is the language used by the OSI protocols for describing abstract syntax. This language is also used to encode SNMP packets.

**ASP** *See* AppleTalk Session Protocol.

**asynchronous** A data transmission method in which each character is sent one bit at a time. Each character has a start and stop bit to synchronize signals between the sending device and the receiving device.

**Asynchronous Transfer Mode (ATM)** ATM is a new type of network that uses fixed-size packets called cells and supports dynamic bandwidth allocation.

**ATM** *See* Asynchronous Transfer Mode.

**ATP** *See* AppleTalk Transaction Protocol.

**attachment unit interface (AUI)** An AUI is a 15-pin connector that allows for the use of an external transceiver.

**attenuation** Attenuation is the fading of the electrical signal over a distance.

**auditing** Auditing allows an administrator to track users' successful and failed attempts to log on to the network, access resources, shut the system down, and so on.

**AUI** *See* attachment unit interface.

**back up** Backing up is the process of copying data to another location. Important data is often backed up to a tape device, which allows for restoration if the original data is lost.

**baseband** Baseband is the transmission of a signal at its original frequencies, i.e., unmodulated.

**beaconing** The process used in Token Ring networks to report an error is beaconing. If a workstation detects a problem with its neighbor, the workstation sends its address, the address of its nearest active upstream neighbor, and the type of error known.

**bit synchronization** Bit synchronization is the process of coordinating timing between the sending device and the receiving device.

**BNC connector** A BNC connector is a bayonet-type coaxial cable connector of the kind commonly found on RF equipment.

**bridge** An internetwork device used to split a network segment to control traffic is called a bridge. Data is passed through or rejected depending on the destination device's MAC address.

**broadband** A communications channel with a bandwidth characterized by high data transmission speeds (10,000–500,000 bits per second). Often used when describing communications systems based on cable television technology.

**broadcast storm** A broadcast storm is an incorrect packet broadcast onto a network that causes multiple hosts to respond all at once, typically with equally incorrect packets which causes the storm to grow exponentially in severity.

**bus** Bus is the connection the adapter cards have to the rest of the computer. Bus also refers to the physical network topology where each device connects to the same cable.

**bus mastering**  This capability allows a card in a computer to communicate with other devices without the main CPU being involved.

**Carrier Sense Multiple Access/Collision Detection (CSMA/CD)**  A network access method for managing collisions of data packets is known as CSMA/CD. This method checks the media for other devices before transmitting.

**Carrier Sense Multiple Access/Collision Avoidance (CSMA/CA)**  CSMA/CA is a network access method that sends request before sending to control media access.

**CAU**  *See* Controlled Access Unit.

**centralized**  A computer network with a central processing node through which all data and communications flow is described as centralized.

**Channel Service Unit/Data Service Unit (CSU/DSU)**  A CSU/DSU connects a LAN to a Digital Data Service (DDS) line.

**checksum**  A checksum is a fixed-length block produced as a function of every bit in an encrypted message; a summation of a set of data items for error detection; a sum of digits or bits used to verify the integrity of data.

**circuit switching**  Circuit switching is a switching method in which a dedicated connection is made between the two communicating devices.

**client**  A client is one for whom services are provided.

**CLNS**  *See* Connectionless Network Services.

**coaxial**  Coaxial uses two conductors — a central, solid wire core, surrounded by insulation, which is then surrounded by a braided wire conductor sheath.

**collaborative**  A collaborative setup allows computers to share processing power across a network.

**collisions**  Collisions occur when two devices try to transmit at the same time and disrupt each other's signaling.

**Connectionless Network Services (CLNS)**  CLNS is a network layer protocol in the DNA protocol suite.

**Connection-Oriented Network Service (CONS)**  A CONS is a network layer protocol that provides reliable data delivery.

**CONS**  *See* Connection-Oriented Network Service.

**contention**  Contention is a media-access method that allows every device to transmit whenever it needs to. This freedom to transmit sometimes results in collisions on the network.

**Controlled Access Unit (CAU)** A CAU is an intelligent MAU used in Token Ring networks.

**CRC** *See* cyclic redundancy check.

**cross talk** Cross talk is the leaking of signals between two adjacent network wires.

**CSMA/CA** *See* Carrier Sense Multiple Access/Collision Avoidance.

**CSMA/CD** *See* Carrier Sense Multiple Access with Collision Detection.

**CSU/DSU** *See* Channel Service Unit/Data Service Unit.

**cyclic redundancy check (CRC)** A CRC is an algorithm designed to generate a check field used to guard against errors against which may occur in data transmission. The check field is often generated by taking the remainder after dividing all the serialized bits in a block of data by a predetermined binary number.

**DAP** *See* Digital Access Protocol.

**Data Link Control (DLC)** DLC is a nonroutable protocol used primarily for network printers.

**Data Link layer** The Data Link layer is the conceptual layer of control or processing logic existing in the hierarchical structure of a station that is responsible for maintaining control of the data link.

**datagram** A datagram is a finite-length packet with sufficient information to be independently routed from source to destination without reliance on previous transmissions; typically does not involve end-to-end session establishment and may or may not entail delivery confirmation acknowledgment.

**Datagram Delivery Protocol (DDP)** An organization of information processing such that both processing and data may be distributed over a number of different machines in one or more locations; a technique to enable multiple computers to cooperate in the completion of tasks, typically in a networked environment. Each computer that contributes to the completion of the total task does so by completing one or more individual subtasks independent of its peers, reporting the results from its subtasks as they are completed.

**DDCMP** *See* Digital Data Communications Message Protocol.

**DDP** *See* Datagram Delivery Protocol.

**DDS** *See* Digital Data Service.

**de facto** Latin for "existing in fact," this means the protocol is controlled by the entire industry. These are also known as *industry standards*.

**de jure** Latin for "according to law," means the protocol was designed by one company or organization. Normally, this organization maintains control of the protocol and is responsible for any additions or changes.

**DECnet** This is a set of networking protocols developed by Digital Equipment Corporation used in its VAX family of computers to exchange messages and other data.

**deterministic** A deterministic network has a system that determines transmitting order. For example, Token Ring is deterministic.

**differential backup** This is a method of file backup in which you backup selected files that have changed since the last backup. This method does not mark files as archived.

**Differential Manchester** This is an encoding scheme that uses mid-bit transitions for clocking. Data is represented by the presence of a transition at the beginning of the bit. Token Ring LANs utilize Differential Manchester.

**Digital Access Protocol (DAP)** DAP is a proprietary data transfer protocol that is used with FTAM. It allows for file management such as deletion, retrieval, and storage.

**Digital Data Communications Message Protocol (DDCMP)** DDCMP is a protocol from the original DNA specifications. It is proprietary to DEC and is included in Phase V as an option to retain compatibility with older versions of DNA. A frame in DDCMP is known as a *message*.

**Digital Data Service (DDS)** Similar to telephone lines, these digital lines are used to connect computers and LANs using special equipment.

**Digital Network Architecture (DNA)** The Digital Network Architecture was developed by Digital Equipment Corporation, Inc. in 1974. It has been revised many times over the years and is currently in its fifth revision, Phase V. Equipment by DEC (Digital Equipment Corporation) that operates within the specifications of DNA (Digital Network Architecture) is referred to as a *DECNet product*.

**digital signaling** Signals that can exist in only one of two values, so they go directly to the next value, typically changing between 0 and 1.

**digital volt meter (DVM)** DVMs allow checking for continuity on a network cable to see if there are any breaks in the physical media. By connecting the DVM to the ground mesh and to the central core, you can check for a short in the cable that will cause disturbances in the communications.

**direct memory access (DMA)** DMA allows your adapter cards to work directly with the computer's memory.

**distance vector routing** Distance vector routing is a routing method that simply calculates the shortest number of hops between two points. Distance vector can take a considerable amount of time to configure and change on a large network.

**distributed** In a distributed computing environment, data storage and processing can be done on the local workstation.

**DIX** A DIX 15-pin connector with two rows of pins created by Digital, Intel, and Xerox. This is the same as an AUI connector.

**DLC** *See* Data Link Control.

**DMA** *See* direct memory access.

**DNA** *See* Digital Network Architecture.

**DNS** *See* Domain Name System.

**DoD** DOD is the abbreviation of Department of Defense.

**domain** Domains are server-based networks that provide a higher level of security and central administration.

**Domain Name System (DNS)** DNS is the Internet naming scheme, which consists of a hierarchical sequence of names, from the most specific to the most general (left to right), separated by dots, for example nic.ddn.mil.

**driver** Drivers are software that allow the computer to access the hardware.

**EISA** *See* Extended Industry Standard Architecture.

**ELAP** This EtherTalk protocol lets you build AppleTalk networks on the popular Ethernet network protocols.

**electromagnetic interference (EMI)** EMI is commonly caused by fluorescent lights, transformers, a power company on a bad day, and almost anything else that creates an electrical field.

**EMI** *See* electromagnetic interference.

**end systems** The source and destination devices of data on the network are end systems.

**error control** Error control is the process of finding errors in transmitted data that is implemented by using checksums and CRCs (cyclic redundancy checks).

**Ethernet** A network cable and access protocol scheme originally developed by DEC, Intel, and Xerox but now marketed primarily by DEC and 3Com; a local area network and its associated protocol developed by (but not limited to) Xerox. Ethernet is a baseband system.

**Ethernet_802.2** Ethernet_802.2 is the IEEE frame type that contains three additional one-byte values. These values add flow control, error checking, and reliability to the previous 802.3 frame type. These packets also range from 64 to 1,518 bytes. This is the default frame type for NetWare 3.12 and 4.1.

**Ethernet_802.3** Ethernet_802.3 is the IEEE frame type that was developed and used by NetWare for its IPX/SPX protocol before the IEEE finished developing the standard. The frame size used in 802.3 is between 64 and 1,518 bytes and includes CRC (cyclic redundancy check) for error checking. This frame type, which doesn't fully comply to the standards developed by IEEE, is used primarily by NetWare 2.2 and 3.11.

**Ethernet_II** The Ethernet_II frame type can be used by both IPX/SPX and TCP/IP. This frame type doesn't identify the length of the packet but the type. This is used to specify whether the packet is IPX/SPX or TCP/IP.

**Extended Binary-Coded Decimal Interchange Code (EBCDIC)** EBCDIC is eight-bit code defined by IBM; includes values for control functions and graphics.

**Extended Industry Standard Architecture (EISA)** This bus was developed by a group of industry leaders and released as an open standard. The EISA bus ran at 8MHz and could transmit 32 bits at a time.

**Fast Ethernet** A Fast Ethernet network uses star topology with UTP cable. Fast Ethernet requires special adapter cards and hubs capable of 100Mbps transfers.

**FDDI** *See* Fiber Distributed Data Interface.

**FDM** *See* frequency-division multiplexing.

**Fiber Distributed Data Interface (FDDI)** An FDDI network uses fiber-optic cable in a ring topology with token passing. FDDI operates at 100Mbps and can support two counter-rotating rings.

**fiber optic** A fiber-optic cable uses glass and light to transmit data instead of copper and electrical signals.

**File Transfer Access Method (FTAM)** ISO 8571 is an OSI-compliant file-access protocol. FTAM is not a complete protocol itself but requires other protocol implementations to be complete. One such protocol is Digital Access Protocol. *See also* Digital Access Protocol.

**File Transfer Protocol (FTP)** FTP allows a user to transfer files electronically from remote computers back to the user's computer. FPT is part of the TCP/IP software suite.

**flow control** Flow control is the process of controlling the amount of data sent to a device so that it does not exceed the capabilities of the receiving system.

**frame** A frame is the sequence of contiguous bits bracketed by and including beginning and ending flag sequences. A typical frame might consist of a specified number of bits between flags and contain an address field, a control field, and a frame check sequence. A frame may or may not include an information field.

**frame relay** A new WAN connection technology, frame relay took the features of X.25 and stripped the error control and accounting from it to increase performance. *See also* X.25.

**frequency shift keying (FSK)** This method of encoding allows the frequency to represent a data value. For example, FSK uses one frequency to represent 1 and another frequency to represent 0.

**frequency-division multiplexing (FDM)** FDM is a method used in broadband transmissions to transmit analog signals. The channels are on different frequencies, with an area of unused frequency ranges separating them. These unused ranges are known as guardbands, and they prevent interference from other channels. This is the form of multiplexing used in cable TV systems.

**FSK** *See* frequency shift keying.

**FTAM** *See* File Transfer Access Method.

**FTP** *See* File Transfer Protocol.

**full backup** A full backup is a method of file backup used to back up all selected files. This process marks the files as archived.

**full-duplex** A full duplex conversation is one in which both sides can send data simultaneously.

**gateway** A gateway is the hardware and software necessary to make two technologically different networks communicate with each other. A gateway provides protocol conversion from one network architecture to another and may therefore use all seven layers of the OSI reference model.

Finally, a gateway is another term for a hardware/software package that runs on the OSI Application layer and allows incompatible protocols to communicate. Includes X.25 gateways.

**group accounts** Group accounts are special accounts that contain user accounts and are useful in combining users in the same department or with a similar function. When resources are shared, the group can be granted access instead of requiring that each user account be granted access.

**half-duplex** A half-duplex conversation is one in which only one side can send data at a time.

**High-level Data Link Control (HDLC)** HDLC is a communications protocol defined for high-level, synchronous connections to X.25 packet networks.

**Hub** Hubs are connection devices that receive a signal and then transmit the signal to the connected devices.

**I/O address** An I/O address is a way for devices to communicate with the main board. Each device has a different I/O address that is used to identify the device.

**ICMP** *See* Internet Control Message Protocol.

**impedance** In a circuit, impedance is the opposition that circuit elements present to the flow of alternating current.

**incremental backup** An incremental backup is a file back up method used to backup selected files that have been changed since the last backup. The files are then marked as archived.

**Industry Standard Architecture (ISA)** ISA is a bus designed by IBM and used in the IBM PC. This bus was originally designed to transfer 8 million bits per second (Mbps).

**infrared** Infrared light frequencies are just below the visible light spectrum and allow high data transmissions.

**Integrated Services Digital Network (ISDN)** ISDN allows you to send voice, data, and video over normal copper telephone lines by sending digital signals instead of analog.

**intermediate devices** Devices on the network through which data passes are intermediate devices.

**International Standards Organization (ISO)** Based in Paris, the ISO develops standards for international and national data communications.

**International Telecommunications Union, Telecommunications Standards Sector (ITU-T)** Formally known as Consultative Committee for International Telegraphy and Telephony, the ITU-T is an international organization in which governments and the private sector coordinate global telecom networks and services. ITU activities include the coordination, development, regulation, and standardization of telecommunications.

**Internet Control Message Protocol (ICMP)**  ICMP provides error reporting for TCP/IP.

**Internet Protocol (IP)**  IP is the Network layer protocol in the TCP/IP suite that provides connectionless data transmission.

**Internetwork Packet Exchange (IPX)**  Designed by Novell, IPX is a protocol that allows the exchange of message packets on an internetwork.

**internetworking device**  Internetworking devices are used to connect LANs to each other.

**IPX**  *See* Internetwork Packet Exchange.

**IRQ**  An interrupt request value is an assigned value that a device sends to the computer's processor to interrupt its processing when it needs to send some information.

**ISA**  *See* Industry Standard Architecture.

**ISDN**  *See* Integrated Services Digital Network.

**ISO 8327**  This generic OSI Session layer protocol handles half-duplex data transfer, connection establishment, and connection release.

**ITU-T**  *See* International Telecommunications Union, Telecommunications Standards Sector.

**jumpers**  Small pairs of metal pins that stick out of the adapter card. You change their configuration by putting small plastic covers with metal internal connectors over them. By doing this, you are actually completing the circuit between the two pins. A jumper with the plastic cover on it is considered closed, and one without is considered open.

**LAM**  *See* Lobe Access Module.

**LAN**  *See* local area network.

**link state routing**  A routing protocol that takes more into account than just hop count. It usually considers link speed, latency, and congestion.

**LLAP**  *See* LocalTalk Link Access Protocol.

**LLC**  *See* Logical Link Control.

**Lobe Access Module (LAM)**  A LAM (pronounced "lamb") allows intelligent expansion of CAUs. *See also* CAU.

**local area network (LAN)** A network in which communications are limited to a moderate-sized geographic area such as a single office building, warehouse, or campus, and that do not extend across public rights-of-way. A system that links computers together to form a network, usually with a wiring-based cabling scheme. LANs connect personal computers and electronic office equipment, enabling users to communicate, share resources such as data storage and printers, and access remote hosts or other networks.

**LocalTalk Link Access Protocol (LLAP)** A proprietary set of network protocols designed by Apple Computers. LocalTalk uses twisted-pair cable with a bandwidth of 230.4Kbps using the CSMA/CA contention system. With a maximum length of 300 meters and only thirty-two devices, it is well suited for a small workgroup network.

**Logical Link Control (LLC)** This sublayer of the Data Link Layer establishes and maintains data link connections between network devices. It is responsible for any flow control and error correction found in this layer.

**MAC address** The MAC Address is the physical address assigned to the network adapter usually during production.

**Manchester** Manchester is a means by which separate data and clock signals can be combined into a single, self-synchronizable data stream suitable for transmission on a serial channel.

**MAU** *See* Multistation Access Unit.

**media** Media is the means used to transmit data. Media can include cable, microwaves, radio waves, infrared rays, among other devices.

**Media Access Control (MAC)** The MAC portion of the IEEE 802 data station controls and mediates the access to the medium.

**mesh** A mesh network topology uses separate cables to connect each device to every other device on the network providing a straight communications path.

**message switching** Data is sent from device to device in whole across the network.

**metropolitan area network (MAN)** A MAN is a group of LANs located across city.

**MicroChannel Architecture (MCA)** A proprietary bus architecture developed by IBM. MCA operates at 32Mbps and uses software to configure the resource settings. MCA was not designed to be backward compatible with ISA, requiring people to buy new MCA adapters.

**microwaves** These waves travel at higher frequencies than radio waves and provide better throughput as a wireless network media.

**MLID** *See* Multiple Link Interface Driver.

**modem** MODulator/DEModulator. A modem is a device which modulates and demodulates signals transmitted over communication facilities.

**multimode** Multimode cable is fiber-optic cable with many light paths.

**Multiple Link Interface Driver (MLID)** Used in the IPX/SPX protocol suite, MLID is a network interface board driver specification. It is the software that makes the network card work inside a computer.

**multiplexer** A multiplexer is a hardware device that allows multiple signals to be sent across one transmission media.

**Multistation Access Unit (MAU)** A MAU (pronounced *mow*, as in "cow") is a Token Ring hub. This device is sometimes known as an IBM 8228 MAU and an MSAU. Devices connect to the hub in a physical star. The MAU internally links the workstations into a ring. MAUs have special ring in and ring out ports used to connect several MAUs to the ring. The ring out on one MAU is connected to a ring in on the next MAU. This continues until the ring out on the last MAU is connected to the ring in on the fist MAU, forming a ring.

**Name Binding Protocol (NBP)** NBP allows AppleTalk networks to use easily remembered names for devices, keep up with the dynamic changes in device addresses, and hide them from the user.

**NBP** *See* Name Binding Protocol.

**NCP** *See* NetWare Core Protocol.

**NDIS** *See* Network Device Interface Specification.

**NetBEUI (NetBIOS Extended User Interface)** NetBEUI is a local area network transport protocol provided with various Microsoft operating environments.

**NetBIOS** *See* Network Basic Input/Output System.

**NetWare Core Protocol (NCP)** NCP handles most network services including file services, printing, file locking, resource access, and synchronization.

**Network Basic Input/Output System (NetBIOS)** NetBIOS is a programmable entry into the network that allows systems to communicate over network hardware using a generic networking API that can run over multiple transports or media.

**network congestion** The amount of collisions and traffic on a network is known as network congestion.

**Network Device Interface Specification (NDIS)** Created by Microsoft and 3Com. These requirements are used by most companies in the PC networking community and allow multiple protocols to work with one NIC driver.

**network interface cards (NIC)** Adapters responsible for moving data from the computer to the transmission media. The network adapter transforms data into signals that are carried across the transmission media to its destination.

**Network layer** This layer of the OSI model is responsible for routing information from one network device to another.

**Network Link Services Protocol (NLSP)** NLSP is an advanced routing protocol using a link state routing mechanism to choose the best route.

**Network Services Protocol (NSP)** An original part of the DNA specification, and the only proprietary protocol in the middle layers. It is a full-duplex, connection-oriented protocol that is capable of prioritizing messages based on needs. It also implements flow control to handle the number of outstanding messages appropriately during times of congestion.

**Network Virtual Terminal Service (NVTS)** An NVTS provides terminal emulation over the network. It translates the data into a format that can be sent over the wire, and then handles the translating of the data back to its original form for the host or for display on a workstation.

**NIC** *See* network interface cards.

**NLSP** *See* Network Link Services Protocol.

**noise** Noise is interference on network cable caused by radio interference (RFI) or electromagnetic interference (EMI). *See also* RFI *and* EMI.

**Non-return-to-zero** A data-encoding scheme similar to Differential Manchester in that it uses a transition at the beginning of the bit to determine the value. A transition signifies one value while the lack of a transition signifies another value. This method does not use a mid-bit transition for clocking.

**NSP** *See* Network Services Protocol.

**NVTS** *See* Network Virtual Terminal Service.

**object** An object is an entity (for example, a record, page, program, printer, and so on) that contains or receives information.

**ODI** *See* Open Datalink Interface.

**Open Datalink Interface (ODI)** Novell's answer to the driver specification question. It allows for multiple protocols to use one NIC driver.

**Open Shortest Path First (OSPF)** A routing protocol that uses much more information than just the number of hops to make a decision. Usually OSPF is configured to figure in the hop count, the speed of the connection between the hops, as well as load-balancing to calculate the best way to route packets. OSPF is part of TCP/IP.

**oscilloscopes** An instrument used to show voltage over time. While used frequently in diagnosing problems with electrical equipment, they can also be used to test for faulty network cable.

**Open Systems Interconnect (OSI)** The OSI model is for network communications consisting of seven layers that describe what happens when computers communicate with one another.

**OSPF** *See* Open Shortest Path First.

**(OSI) model** *See* Open Systems Interconnect

**packet switching** A discipline for controlling and moving messages in a large data-communications network. Each message is handled as a complete unit containing the addresses of the recipient and the originator.

**PAP** *See* Printer Access Protocol.

**parity** Parity is a way to check for small errors in data that utilizes one bit to specify whether the byte has an even or odd value.

**passive hub** A passive hub uses no power and sends the signal to all workstations with no regeneration or amplification.

**patch cable** A patch cable is used to connect the workstation to a network jack in the office.

**patch panel** A patch panel is a set of jacks that allow the administrator to connect the individual wall jack cables to a network device such as a hub or router.

**PCI** *See* Peripheral Component Interface.

**PCMCIA** *See* Personal Computer Memory Card International Association.

**peer** Peers are computer/communication systems capable of performing equal or comparable tasks within defined limits or parameters.

**peer-to-peer** The communication between two network entities considered to be of equal stature; the designation for a local area network in which the resources of some or all the connected machines may be shared.

**Peripheral Component Interface (PCI)** The PCI bus type runs at up to 33MHz and can transfer 32 bits at a time.

**Personal Computer Memory Card International Association (PCMCIA)** An interface used primarily in notebook computers. It uses a 68-pin connector.

**phase shift keying (PSK)** A signaling method in which a change (or absence of change) can present a data value. For example, a phase change can represent 1, while the absence of a phase change can represent 0.

**Physical layer** The first layer of the OSI model is the Physical layer. The function of this layer is the transmission of bits over the network media. It provides a physical connection for the transmission of data among the network devices. The Physical layer is responsible for making sure that data is read the same way on the destination device as it was sent on the source device.

**Point-to-Point-Protocol (PPP)** The provides error checking to ensure the accurate delivery of the frames that it sends and receives. PPP also keeps a logical link control communication between the two connect devices by using the Link Control Protocol. PPP allows for dynamic host configuration and supports multiple protocols.

**polar** A data-encoding scheme that uses each level to represent a specific value. This scheme allows for a positive and a negative level to each represent a value.

**policies** Policies provide controls on user accounts. They can be used to manage passwords. Password length, duration, and uniqueness can be set. They can also control which computers a user can log in to and at what times.

**polling systems** A media access method in which a master device will go and check the other secondary devices on the network to see if they need to transmit. The order of the devices polled and their priority can be set by the administrator.

**PPP** *See* Point-to-Point Protocol.

**Presentation layer** The sixth layer of the OSI model, it negotiates and establishes the format that data is exchanged in.

**Printer Access Protocol (PAP)** A Session layer protocol that provides printing services to clients, but it can also do other services, as well. Printer Access Protocol is part of the AppleTalk suite.

**profiles** Profiles are used to set user variables such as defining a user's desktop settings.

**protocol**  A protocol is a specification for the format and relative timing of information exchanged between communicating parties.

**protocol analyzer**  You use a protocol analyzer to look at a network packet by packet and find out exactly what is being transmitted. You may even use it to debug network applications by using it to look at the "conversation" that is in progress.

**protocol stack**  A protocol stack is a collection of networking protocols that provides the communications and services needed to enable computers to exchange messages and other information, typically by managing physical connections, communications services and application support.

**PSK**  *See* phase shift keying.

**PSTN**  *See* Public Switched Telephone Network.

**Public Switched Telephone Network (PSTN)**  PTSN is the telephone system in place and used for many years all across the country.

**radio interference (RFI)**  RFI causes noise on network cable.

**radio waves**  Radio waves have frequencies between 10KHz and 1GHz.

**RAID 0**  Disk striping that separates the data into blocks and spreads the blocks across each drive or partition. All the devices combine to create one logical device.

**RAID 1**  Disk mirroring, duplicates all data and partitions to a separate physical disk. This provides two full copies of the system and all data.

**RAID 5**  Disk striping with parity. Data blocks are striped to several disks with a parity stripe written in varying locations. The data and parity are always written on different disks. The parity stripe contains information that can be used to reconstruct data.

**repeater**  A repeater is a device used to extend the length, topology, or interconnectivity of the physical medium beyond that imposed by a single segment, up to the maximum allowable end-to-end trunk transmission line length, by copying electrical signals from one network segment to another.

**resistance**  Resistance occurs when electricity moves through a medium. Resistance causes loss of electricity.

**resources**  A resource is any item on the network that can be shared or accessed.

**Return-to-Zero** This current-state encoding method translates a high voltage to one value while a low voltage represents another. Return-to-Zero includes a mid-bit transition to zero for clocking purposes.

**RFI** *See* radio interference.

**ring** A ring network topology looks like a circle, in which data travels from computer to computer in one direction.

**RIP** *See* Routing Information Protocol.

**RJ-45** Cable that looks very much like a normal telephone connector but larger. It uses twisted-pair cabling with four pairs of wires.

**router** A router is a software and hardware connection between two or more networks, usually of similar design, that permits traffic to be routed from one network to another on the basis of the intended destinations of that traffic.

**routing** Routing is the assignment of the path by which a message will reach its destination.

**Routing Information Protocol (RIP)** RIP is a routing protocol that uses the number of routers between you and the destination (hops) to decide the best way to route a packet.

**Routing Table Maintenance Protocol (RTMP)** RTMP is a routing protocol that uses a distance vector algorithm to decide the best path.

**RTMP** *See* Routing Table Maintenance Protocol.

**SAP** *See* Service Access Protocol.

**Sequenced Packet Exchange (SPX)** SPX is a protocol by which two workstations or applications communicate across the network. SPX uses NetWare IPX to deliver the messages, but SPX guarantees delivery of the messages and maintains the order of messages on the packet stream.

**Serial Line Internet Protocol (SLIP)** SLIP is a Physical layer protocol that provides no error checking and relies on the hardware (such as modem error checking) to handle this. It also only supports the transmission of one protocol, TCP/IP.

**server** A server is a computer in a network that is shared by multiple users, such as a file server, print server, or communications server; a computer in a network designated to provide a specific service as distinct from a general-purpose, centralized, multi-user computer system.

**Server Message Block (SMB)** SMB is a communications protocol used by Microsoft clients to share files.

**Service Access Protocol (SAP)** SAP is an IPX/SPX protocol which requires computers sharing a resource on the network to send out a SAP packet telling about the resource and where it is located.

**Session Control** The Session Control protocol acts as an intermediary between the Application and Transport layers of the OSI model. It is used in protocol stacks that are not OSI compliant.

**Session layer** The fifth layer of the OSI model, this layer lets users establish a connection between devices. This connection is called a *session*. Once the connection has been established, the Session layer can manage the dialogue.

**shared memory address** Shared memory address allows the network card and software driver to use a shared RAM memory address in the high memory range to communicate.

**share-level security** Share-level security is a security method that relies on assigning a password to resources that are shared on the network.

**shielded twisted-pair (STP)** STP cable has a mesh shielding that protects it from EMI, which allows for higher transmission rates and longer distances without errors.

**Simple Mail Transfer Protocol (SMTP)** SMPT is responsible for making sure that this e-mail is delivered. SMTP only handles the delivery of mail to servers, and between them. It does not handle the delivery to the final e-mail client application. SMTP is part of the TCP/IP suite.

**Simple Network Management Protocol (SNMP)** SNMP gets statistics from network devices on usage and errors.

**simplex** One-way communications are simplex.

**single mode** Single mode fiber-optic cable allows for one light path through the cable.

**sliding window** The sliding window method of flow control allows two communicating devices to negotiate the number of allowable outstanding frames.

**SLIP** *See* Serial Line Internet Protocol.

**SMDS** *See* Switched Multimegabit Data Service.

**SMTP** *See* Simple Mail Transfer Protocol.

**SNA**  *See* Systems Network Architecture.

**SNMP**  *See* Simple Network Management Protocol.

**SONET**  *See* Synchronous Optical Network.

**source-route bridge**  A source-route bridge is a Token Ring bridge that, instead of depending on MAC addresses, uses information in the token ring frame to determine whether to pass the data.

**SPX**  *See* Sequenced Packet Exchange.

**star**  Star topology uses a separate cable for each workstation. The cable connects the workstation to a central device, typically a hub.

**stop-and-wait flow control**  This is a green-light way of handling flow control. When the receiving device has no more memory left to store incoming data, it suspends transmission. When memory is free again, it sends a signal to the transmitting device to resume.

**STP**  *See* shielded twisted-pair.

**switched connections**  Switched connections allow multiple people to use a connection at once. They require special hardware to manage the connections but give you the benefit of lower cost for the connection to the service provider.

**Switched Multimegabit Data Service (SMDS)**  SMDS is a combination of X.25 and ATM. It was designed by Bell Communications Research and released in 1991. It uses cells like ATM, and creates virtual circuits like X.25. *See also* X.25 *and* ATM.

**switches**  Switches are multiport bridges that filter traffic between the ports on the switch by using the MAC address of computers transmitting through them.

**synchronous**  This is a data transmission mode in which synchronization is established for an entire block of data (message).

**Synchronous Optical Network (SONET)**  SONET specifies how to deliver voice, data, and video over WAN connections at speeds in excess of 2Gbps. It is a Physical layer standard that defines the transfer of data over fiber-optic media.

**Systems Network Architecture (SNA)**  SNA is the IBM network architecture, defined in terms of its functions, formats, and protocols.

**T-carrier system**  A T-carrier system is a wide area network connection technology provided by the phone company. Speeds can reach 45Mbps.

**TCP**  *See* Transmission Control Protocol.

**TDM** *See* time-division multiplexing.

**TDR** *See* time-domain reflectometer.

**Telnet** Telnet is the portion of the TCP/IP suite of software protocols that handles terminals. Among other functions, it allows a user to log in to a remote computer from the user's local computer.

**time-division multiplexing (TDM)** TDM multiplexing uses time slots to separate channels. Each device is given a time slot to transmit using the entire available bandwidth.

**time-domain reflectometer (TDR)** A TDR is used to determine exactly where a media break occurred. The TDR uses a sonar-like pulse that is sent down the cable. The signal bounces back from a break in the cable. The TDR calculates the time that the signal took to go down the cable and back and computes the distance.

**TLAP** *See* TokenTalk.

**Token passing** Token passing is a collision avoidance technique in which each station is polled and must pass the poll along.

**Token Ring** Token ring is a very reliable topology based on some of the best standards available. It uses token passing in a physical star configuration connected in a ring using hubs.

**TokenTalk** TokenTalk lets you build AppleTalk networks on the popular Token Ring network protocols.

**translational bridge** A translational bridge is a bridge that allows connection of dissimilar networks.

**Transmission Control Protocol (TCP)** A connection-oriented protocol from the Transport layer of the OSI model. TCP opens and maintains a connection between two communicating hosts on a network.

**transparent bridge** An internetworking device that uses hardware network card addresses to determine when to pass or filter data.

**Transport layer** The fourth layer of the OSI model is the Transport layer. It provides a transport service between the Session layer and the Network layer. This service takes information from the Session layer and splits it up if necessary. It then passes this information to the Network layer and checks to make sure that it arrived at the destination device successfully.

**twisted pair**  Twisted-pair cable consists of two wires of a signaling circuit that are twisted around each other to minimize the effects of inductance.

**UDP**  *See* User Datagram Protocol.

**uninterruptible power supply (UPS)**  A UPS is a backup power unit that provides continuous power even when the normal power supply is interrupted.

**unipolar**  A unipolor scheme of encoding data using a zero level to represent one value, while either a positive or a negative level represents the other value.

**unshielded twisted pair (UTP)**  Unshielded twisted-pair cable can be either voice grade or data grade depending on the application. UTP cable normally has an impedance of 100 ohms. *See also* twisted pair.

**UPS**  *See* uninterruptible power supply.

**user**  Users are human beings or computer processes that possess the right to log in to a particular computer system.

**User Datagram Protocol (UDP)**  UDP is a connectionless transport protocol that is used when the overhead of TCP is not needed. UDP is just responsible for transporting datagrams.

**user-level security**  User-level security requires the proper user name and password to access a resource.

**virtual circuit**  A virtual circuit is a communication arrangement in which data from a source user may be passed to a destination user over various real circuit configurations during a single period of communication (during a single session).

**WAN**  *See* wide area network.

**wide area network (WAN)**  A WAN consists of two or more LANs (local area networks) in separate geographic locations connected by a remote link.

**workgroup**  A workgroup is a group of users on a network who have information or resources that they wish to share among themselves.

**X.25**  Developed in 1974 by the CCITT as a Network layer packet-switching protocol (now the ITU-T), it specifies how internetwork devices connect over a packet-switched network.

**X.400**  X.400 is a messaging standard that allows different e-mail systems to communicate seamlessly.

**X.500**  X.500 is an international address-to-name resolution and directory services standard.

# Index

*(continued)*

# D

*(continued)*

*(continued)*

*(continued)*

## X

## Z

# MEASUREUP LICENSE AGREEMENT

**Important: Read this carefully before installing.** You may only use the software contained in this package ("Software") according to the terms of this License Agreement ("License"). Installing this Software will acknowledge your acceptance of the terms of this License. If you do not agree to the terms of this License, then do not open this Software, and return the Software within thirty (30) days of your receipt of the Software to obtain a refund of the License fee you paid for the Software.

You may use the Software according to the following type of license on a nonexclusive, nontransferable, limited right to use basis:

Single User License — Entitles you to install the Software on the permanent memory of a computer for loading into the RAM memory of the same computer for use by a single user.

By installing this Software, you agree that:

You may not make any copies of the Software. The Software is protected under U.S. copyright law. You own the CD-ROM containing the Software, but MeasureUp owns the Software. You only have the right to use the Software as expressed in this License, and you have no other right to use the Software. You may not modify, disas⌐ mble, or reverse-engineer the Software. You may be held liable for copyright infringement if you violate any terms of this License.

This License shall automatically terminate upon failure by you to comply with its terms.

Disclaimer of Warranty. THE SOFTWARE IS LICENSED TO YOU ON AN "AS IS" BASIS, AND MEASUREUP DISCLAIMS ANY AND ALL WARRANTIES, WHETHER EXPRESS OR IMPLIED, INCLUDING, WITHOUT LIMITATION ANY WARRANTIES OF MERCHANTIBILITY, FITNESS FOR A PARTICULAR PURPOSE, OR NONINFRINGEMENT.

Limitation of Liability. IN NO EVENT SHALL MEASUREUP BE LIABLE FOR ANY INDIRECT, INCIDENTAL, CONSEQUENTIAL, SPECIAL, OR EXEMPLARY DAMAGES, INCLUDING ANY LOST PROFITS OR LOST SAVINGS, EVEN IF A MEASUREUP REPRESENTATIVE HAS BEEN ADVISED OF THE POSSIBILITY OF SUCH DAMAGES, OR FOR ANY CLAIM BY ANY THIRD PARTY. MEASUREUP'S TOTAL LIABILITY FOR ANY DAMAGES WHATSOEVER SHALL NOT EXCEED THE ACTUAL FEES RECEIVED BY MEASUREUP FOR THIS LICENSE. Some states do not allow the limitation or exclusion of liability for incidental or consequential damages, so this paragraph may not apply to you.

This License shall be construed and governed in accordance with the laws of the State of Georgia. If any provision of this License is for any reason held unenforceable or invalid, then this License shall be construed as if such provision were not contained herein. Should you have any questions concerning this License, please contact MeasureUp at: (770) 521-9039.